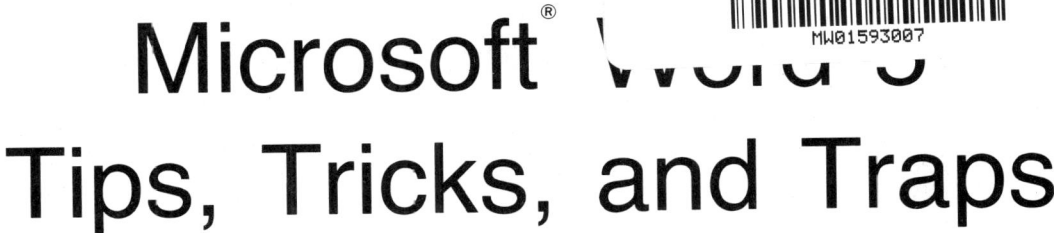

Microsoft® Word 3
Tips, Tricks, and Traps

IBM® Version

Bryan Pfaffenberger

CORPORATION

LEADING COMPUTER KNOWLEDGE

Microsoft® Word 5 Tips, Tricks, and Traps

IBM® Version

Copyright © 1989 by Que® Corporation

Library of Congress Catalog No.: 89-60533

ISBN 0-88022-452-5

93 92 91 90 89   8 7 6 5 4 3 2 1

Interpretation of the printing code: the rightmost double-digit number is the year of the book's printing; the rightmost single-digit number, the number of the book's printing. For example, a printing code of 89-1 shows that the first printing of the book occurred in 1989.

Microsoft Word 5 Tips, Tricks, and Traps: IBM Version is based on Microsoft Word Versions 4 and 5.

DEDICATION

For Michael and Julia

Publishing Manager

Lloyd J. Short

Production Editor

Jeannine Freudenberger

Editors

Kelly Currie
Alice Martina Smith

Technical Editor

Franklyn Jones

Editorial Assistant

Fran Blauw

Indexed by

Sherry Massey

Book Design and Production

Dan Armstrong
Brad Chinn
Cheryl English
David Kline
Lori A. Lyons
Jon Ogle
Jennifer Matthews
Dennis Sheehan
Peter Tocco

Composed in Helvetica and Excellent No. 47
by Que Corporation

ABOUT THE AUTHOR

Bryan Pfaffenberger

A nationally known writer on computer-related topics, Bryan Pfaffenberger, Ph.D., teaches in the School of Engineering and Applied Science at the University of Virginia, where he is the Assistant Professor of Humanities. He is contributing editor of the *Research in Word Processing Newsletter* and the author of more than a dozen books, including *Using Microsoft Word 5: IBM Version*, *Microsoft Word Techniques and Applications*, and *Using Sprint*, all published by Que Corporation. Dr. Pfaffenberger's interests include the social history and sociology of technology, international studies (he is the associate director of the University of Virginia's Center of South Asian Studies), and the anthropology of science and engineering. Dr. Pfaffenberger also enjoys spending time with his children. He lives in Charlottesville, Virginia.

TABLE OF CONTENTS

ix

ACKNOWLEDGMENTS

A project like this one necessarily involves the work of many people. I'd like to thank Lloyd Short, Publishing Manager, and Jeannine Freudenberger, Production Editor.

And very special thanks are due to an unusually thorough and Word-knowledgeable editor, Alice Martina Smith, who unfailingly flagged errors, lacunae, and various sins of omission (and commission).

TRADEMARK
ACKNOWLEDGMENTS

Que Corporation has made every effort to supply trademark information about company names, products, and services mentioned in this
book. Trademarks indicated below were derived from various sources. Que
Corporation cannot attest to the accuracy of this information.

IBM is a registered trademark of International Business Machines Corporation.

InSet is a registered trademark of INSET Systems Inc.

LaserJet and DeskJet are trademarks of Hewlett-Packard Co.

Lotus is a registered trademark of Lotus Development Corporation.

Macintosh and LaserWriter are registered trademarks of Apple Computer, Inc.

Microsoft is a registered trademark of Microsoft Corporation.

PC Tools is a trademark of Central Point Software.

PostScript is a registered trademark of Adobe Systems Incorporated.

SideKick is a registered trademark of Borland International, Inc.

WordPerfect is a registered trademark of WordPerfect Corporation.

WordStar is a registered trademark of MicroPro International Corporation.

Word Finder is a trademark of Mycrolytics, Inc.

CONVENTIONS USED IN THIS BOOK

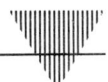

The conventions used in this book have been established to help you learn to use the program quickly and easily. As much as possible, the conventions correspond with those used in the Microsoft Word 5 documentation.

In instructions to the reader, letters typed to select a command are printed in boldface: the **F**ormat **T**ab **S**et command. Fields and options from the menus and on-screen messages are printed in a special typeface: the alignment field, the Yes option. Material that the user types is set off on a line by itself or printed in italic: Type the word *Corporation*.

Introduction

Microsoft® Word brings to IBM®-standard personal computers an impressive storehouse of word processing power. Few programs can rival Word's armada of high-productivity word processing features. And, bucking the trend toward added complexity at the cost of making a program more difficult to use, Word incorporates friendly Macintosh®-like features, such as pop-up menus, a graphics interface, full use of the mouse for editing text and giving commands, and a "what you see is what you get" display philosophy. Thousands of writers find the combination irresistible.

From this program's humble beginnings in Version 1, Word has steadily evolved into a powerhouse package, including such features as a 120,000-word spelling dictionary, a 220,000-word thesaurus, an outlining mode that's dynamically tied to your document's structure, multiple windows, automatic index and table of contents generation, fully programmable keyboard commands for text formatting (created with style sheets), and command automation with keyboard macros. Along the way, however, Word also earned an unenviable reputation as a big, difficult program that forced users to adapt to its demands (instead of adapting itself to user needs).

If that's what you have heard about Word, here's some excellent news. Powerful new graphics features aren't the only thing new with Version 5. Microsoft's ace programmers, chastened by user gripes and suggestions, combed through the entire program, simplifying procedures and vastly expanding the program's responsiveness and flexibility. For anyone who has used previous versions of Word, Version 5 is like a dream come true. Substantially less fussing and keystroking are involved, and what's more, several roundabout, clunky procedures have been eliminated. The changes add up to enhanced power and, at the same time, a significant improvement in the program's ease of use. Bravo, Microsoft!

The new text-and-graphics integration features fully realize the program's commitment to the what-you-see-is-what-you-get display philosophy:

❑ The Show Layout mode displays multiple columns on-screen even while you're editing.

❑ Print preView, a new option in the Print menu, displays all document formats—including running heads, graphics, page numbers, margins, footnotes, and proportional line spacing—just the way these formats will print.

❑ You can incorporate graphics into Word documents and, within Word, size, box, position, and anchor graphics so that text "floats" around the pictures.

❑ The Show Line Breaks mode displays accurately how many letters of a certain font can fit into a printed inch, which greatly simplifies the task of aligning proportionally spaced text. The tab ruler adjusts to different font sizes, too.

❑ Page breaks appear automatically as you type, showing you precisely where Word intends to start printing a new page. And the page breaks are active—if you insert or delete text, Word automatically repositions the breaks.

For (long-suffering) users of previous versions of Word, here's a quick overview of what's in store for you as you explore Version 5:

❑ Version 5 is even faster than Version 4, which trounces WordPerfect® in everyday functions like loading files and replacing text. Gone are the days of sluggish performance. Even though Word is a huge and complex program, it performs snappily even on an old 8088-based system. On an 80386 system, screens pop and flash so fast that you have to keep your eyes open to keep track of what you're doing.

❑ Setting tabs with previous versions was a chore bordering on hard labor. You couldn't see the effects of your tab choices until you carried out the Format Tab Set command, and if the choices weren't good ones, you had to go through all the required keystrokes to use the command again. With Version 5, you see the impact of your choices right on-screen, even before you carry out the command. And if you're using the mouse, you simply click tabs right on the ruler—without even using the Tab command.

❏ The new autosave feature protects your work if the power is interrupted before you save your data. When the power returns, you see a message informing you that you had some unsaved work and asking whether you want Word to reconstruct it. In just a moment, all that "lost" work reappears on-screen! This new feature is a blessing for professional writers, who know all too well that computer crashes can result in missed deadlines and increased job stress.

The list of Version 5 improvements goes on and on. With the program's new graphics features and the dozens of improvements, Word has become more visual, more intuitive, and easier to use. You need fewer keystrokes to accomplish most tasks.

Version 5 is, by any standard, a *major* revision—perhaps the most significant revision in the program's history. And that's why *Microsoft Word 5 Tips, Tricks, and Traps: IBM Version* has been thoroughly rewritten for this exciting new version of Word. Version 5's new features call for major changes in the way most users should approach common Word tasks—and that statement is especially true for anyone contemplating a sojourn into the intermediate and advanced levels of the program. This book, therefore, is not just a rehash of an existing text with a few new passages noting Word 5's new features. Every page of this book has been written with Word 5 and with Word 5's enormous potential in mind.

Who Should Use This Book?

Microsoft Word 5 Tips, Tricks, and Traps: IBM Version presents the approaches developed by professional writers to help them write faster, produce better-looking documents, and even improve the quality of their work. This book is intended for readers who have some previous experience with Word.

If you're a beginner with Word 5 and with personal computing, Que Corporation's *Using Microsoft Word 5: IBM Version*, by Bryan Pfaffenberger, may be a better choice for you. *Using Microsoft Word 5* covers much of the same material you find here, but in a tutorial, keystroke-by-keystroke fashion, beginning with the basics. But don't take *Microsoft Word 5 Tips, Tricks, and Traps* back to the store just yet! This book will prove useful as a supplementary volume. And as your knowledge of personal computing and of Word increases, you will find the information contained in this text increasingly helpful. If you're running into problems with Word or suspect that another (and possibly better) way of accomplishing a task exists, chances are that you will find those traps—and tricks—discussed in this book. (If not, let us know by filling out the registration card at the end of this book.)

If you are new to Word but you're a "power user," you may find this book's organization more suited to your needs than *Using Microsoft Word 5*'s keystroke-by-keystroke approach. You undoubtedly already know the fundamentals of using your computer and software, such as choosing commands from menus, using the Ctrl and Alt keys to give commands, and saving your work to disk. As you learn Word 5, you will want to move quickly to the high-productivity, quality-enhancing techniques used by Word pros, but you don't need your hand held at every step of the way. The tips, tricks, and traps format of this book highlights the special techniques—as well as the pitfalls—that Word users have discovered as they have put Word to work.

If you have some experience with Word, either with Word 5 or with previous versions of the program, this book should prove especially useful to you. As you already know, Word 5 contains new, glitzy graphics features, which are designed to go head-to-head with WordPerfect's text-and-graphics integration capabilities. These new features are welcome indeed, but what's even more welcome is the fact that Word suddenly is significantly easier to use. For new users, this improvement is great. For old users, however, it means unlearning old ways of doing things and learning new, simpler ways—old-dog-and-new-tricks time.

To make full use of these new ways of using Word, you need help—and you get it in these pages. Any tip, trick, or trap that highlights a new Word 5 technique is highlighted with a Word 5 icon in the margin. Often, these icons point not just to new features but also to major improvements in old ways of doing things with Word. In some cases, you need to learn completely new ways of accomplishing tasks with Word.

Experience aside, this book is aimed at a wide range of users, including business, professional, academic, creative, and technical writers. You probably write plenty of memos and letters, but beyond these one- or two-page documents, you also may write longer reports, proposals, journal articles, short stories—and yes, some of you will write novels, screenplays, best-selling nonfiction books, and Ph.D. dissertations. You want to know how you can produce handsome, well-organized, high-quality work. If so, Word 5 and this book are ideally suited for you.

What This Book Covers

A big, power-packed program like Word 5 is in some respects its own worst enemy. The program may very well be loaded with features, but some of them are so new and differ so radically from the way you're used to accomplishing writing tasks that the feature's value just isn't understood. For instance, you can restructure a huge Word document with just a few keystrokes by rearranging headings in an outline. For anyone who writes long complex documents, such as proposals or business reports, this feature is reason enough to prefer Word over every other program on the market.

Yet few Word users realize what you can do with a Word outline or with many other "advanced" features of Word. Most books about Word (as well as Word's own documentation) aren't much help in clarifying the meaning of such features: the material tells you which key to press but often fails to explain why you're pressing it. What's more, most books on Word (and Word's own documentation) draw a rigid distinction between beginning, intermediate, and advanced features. That separation is just fine for true beginners, who need to minimize the "information shock" encountered when learning new software. But more experienced users want to know how they can realize the full potential of a program like Word, and that means putting intermediate or advanced features to work immediately, even on basic tasks like saving or printing.

That need is why this book is different. As you will see, some Word features normally treated as intermediate or advanced, such as multiple windows, macros, style sheets, and outlining, are treated as fundamental—and for one simple reason. Professional writers who use Word in demanding high-productivity settings have learned how to employ these features to reduce, often dramatically, the time and effort expended on the writing process. In this book, you learn the techniques the pros use to write faster, to produce better-organized and better-written documents, and to print them in a way that makes people notice your commitment to professionalism and quality.

Following this philosophy, this book covers the fundamental aspects of the writing process: composing text, organizing complex documents, formatting, editing, checking spelling, saving, and printing. The agenda sounds elementary, at least on the surface. But as you will quickly discover, this book's goal is to show you how to put some of Word's most advanced high-productivity features to work during every phase of the daily writing process. You find dozens of suggestions, for instance, for ways to put macros and style sheets to work on everyday tasks.

In this book, you discover that advanced techniques are not just for rarefied, sophisticated applications but are useful every time you turn on your computer. These techniques are useful at every stage of the writing process—planning, creating text, editing, formatting, proofing, and printing.

Personal computing promises much: improved productivity, better writing, better-looking documents. But too often this promise remains just a potential. This book unlocks the potential.

What This Book Doesn't Cover

Microsoft Word 5 Tips, Tricks, and Traps: IBM Version doesn't try to be encyclopedic, covering every feature in comprehensive detail. The book doesn't present tutorials, and it assumes that the reader has some familiarity with Word. Moreover, the book doesn't cover specific Word applications, such as creating tables, indexes, form letters, newsletters, business forms, and illustrated manuals. This book's focus is on the everyday writing process, from creating a document through formatting, editing, and printing. Because the goal is to show you techniques for significantly cutting document-preparation time, the text selectively presents just the right techniques.

While you're using this book, you may want to keep Que Corporation's *Microsoft Word 5 Quick Reference* by your computer. Organized alphabetically, this compact guide lists Word 5 commands and keyboard shortcuts in a handy, quick-reference format.

An Overview of This Book's Contents

Chapter 1, "Configuring Your System for Word 5," surveys the minimum and optimum systems for Word 5, considering its many new features. This chapter also shows you how to configure your hard disk for maximum productivity—an extremely important step on your way to Word 5 mastery.

Chapter 2, "Getting Started with Word 5: Starting, Saving, and Quitting," presents the pro's tricks and techniques for these basic Word 5 operations. You learn how to take advantage of many important new Version 5 features—especially for saving your work. If protecting your work is important to you as a business or professional writer, you don't want to miss the macros at the end of this chapter.

Chapter 3, "Getting Oriented: Finding Your Way in Word 5," provides numerous tips and suggestions for the essentials of navigating Word: getting around in command menus, moving the cursor and scrolling, and using commands.

Chapter 4, "Customizing Word 5: The Display Screen and Operating Characteristics," shows you more about how to have your way with Word by changing program defaults and customizing Word's screen. You learn, too, how professional writers set up Word for daily operation.

Chapter 5, "Writing Strategies: Word and the Composing Process," covers the fundamentals of writing with Word, including entering text; joining and splitting paragraphs; starting new lines; using hyphens; creating footnotes; creating page breaks; using foreign language and mathematical characters; controlling the cursor and scrolling; copying, deleting, and moving text; and formatting text while you write.

In Chapter 6, "More Writing Strategies: Using Outlines and Windows," you explore the many ways these sophisticated and powerful features can help you compose text. You learn how to create and manipulate outlines and link them dynamically to the structure of your document, and how to display up to eight windows on-screen at a time.

Chapter 7, "Formatting Your Document: Character and Paragraph Styles," opens a two-chapter, in-depth discussion of Word's formatting tools. Among the subjects surveyed are character emphasis, fonts and font sizes, paragraph alignment, line spacing, hanging indents, blank lines, side-by-side paragraphs, and techniques for searching for and replacing character and paragraph formats. You learn how to solve all the shortcomings of Word's default formatting settings, using one of Word's most powerful features: style sheets.

Chapter 8, "Formatting Pages and Page Styles," covers the Word commands that govern page design throughout your document. You learn how to position page numbers, set up complex patterns of running heads, print documents with line numbers, and split your document into divisions, each with its own page-numbering and running-head formats. You learn more, too, about how to use style sheets to modify Word's default formatting settings.

In Chapter 9, "Strategies for Effective Editing," you discover Word's extraordinary power as a tool for revising the text you have created.

You learn how to use printed copy as a pinpoint guide for on-screen revision, move quickly in a large document, search for text, use multiple windows for editing, cut text to glossaries for editing purposes, restructure huge amounts of text in a few keystrokes by using outlines, and replace text automatically throughout your document. You learn also how to use Word 5's wonderful redlining and annotation tools for collaborative writing.

Chapter 10, "Using the Thesaurus and Checking Spelling," surveys Word's tools for helping you choose the correct word—and making sure that it's spelled correctly. You learn how to take full advantage of the new (and much better) Spell program supplied with Version 5.

Chapter 11, "Printing Your Work," discusses printing in depth, with special emphasis on taking full advantage of today's multiple-font printers. You learn how to use new Word 5 features that enable you to predict—and preview—font and other formatting choices before you waste expensive laser toner and paper on an improperly formatted draft. You learn, too, how to add new fonts to your printer driver so that all your printer's capabilities are at your fingertips and how to download disk-based fonts automatically within Word.

Chapter 12, "Style Sheets," shows you how to take full advantage of the style sheet entries suggested throughout this book. You learn also about significant new features of style sheets that make them almost essential for every Word user, even if you're just getting started with the program. Using this chapter in tandem with the hard disk organization strategy suggested in Chapter 1, you learn how you can set up your system to format a variety of documents automatically, each with its own set of fonts, page styles, and custom keyboard commands. This chapter fully discloses the path to high-productivity formatting with Word 5.

Chapter 13, "Macros," introduces Word 5's powerful macro programming language, which provides tools for automating Word. You learn how to create and use the many macros suggested throughout this book.

Chapter 14, "Creating and Printing Form Documents," shows you how to take full advantage of Word's Print Merge feature, which prints personalized form letters and mailing labels.

About the Macros in This Book

A highlight of this book is its extensive coverage of Word 5 macros. You will find macros in almost every chapter. And in most cases, you will find that the macros are close to indispensable—they're specifically designed to overcome Word 5 shortcomings, to bypass complexities, and to make this big, powerful program more manageable—and your work more productive. You will find full instructions on how to use these macros on your system in Chapter 13, "Macros." Taken together, the macros amount to a major improvement in Word's functionality and viability, an improvement that you're sure to find valuable.

You're about to make Word 5 jump through hoops. And the high-productivity techniques begin right away, in Chapter 1, which shows you how to configure your system to take full advantage of new Word 5 features and capabilities. Even if you're familiar with previous versions of the program, and even if you have already installed Word, you should at least skim this chapter. If you're using a hard disk, pay particular attention to the section on configuring your hard disk for maximum productivity with Word 5; the configuration is vital to the macro and style sheet approaches presented throughout this book.

1

Configuring Your System
for Word 5

Word 5 is a big, powerful program, but—amazingly enough—it runs on nearly any IBM PC or compatible computer, including even two-floppy 8088 systems. To be sure, you can enhance Word's performance considerably by upgrading your system and, in particular, adding a hard disk. Although Word 5 doesn't require a hard disk, it's almost a necessity for business and professional writing applications. This chapter serves as a complete guide to this and other system configuration options.

Also included is a strategy for configuring your hard disk for Word 5. New Version 5 features, especially some small but intelligent changes to the way Word handles style-sheet and glossary files, suggest an optimum configuration, which is explained in detail in this chapter. Even if you have already installed Word, you should read this section; it's not too late to configure your disk in the best way.

Finally, this chapter covers the installation process, focusing on the SETUP program supplied with Word.

Optimizing Your Hardware for Word 5

Any of you who are still using an entry-level PC or compatible based on the 8088 chip are probably paging enviously through computer magazines and thinking about forking over big bucks for a system based on the 80286 or 80386 chip. But here's some good news: Word 5 is *fast*, significantly faster than Word 4. You can use Word 5 on an

8088- or 8086-based system without unacceptable processing delays. Of course, the program runs even faster on 80286 and 80386 systems. But the Word 5 design team wanted to create a program that would take full advantage of the newer machines while still running acceptably on older ones. Remarkably enough, the design team succeeded.

One of the real advantages of Word 5, therefore, is that you can use it on just about any IBM-compatible computer, as long as it has two 360K floppy drives and DOS 2.0 or later. You can create a document at work on your boss's super-fast 80386, and then, with your copy of Word in your briefcase, take the disk home and polish it up on your kid's Radio Shack T-1000! You should, however, note one small flaw in this appealing picture, as the first trap suggests.

Trap   **Version 5 requires at least 384K of free memory.**

Previous versions of Word could run on computers with 256K of main memory, but those days are gone. You need at least 384K of *free* memory to run Word. This requirement means that you must have 384K of memory available after loading DOS and any memory-resident programs, such as SideKick®. If not enough memory is available, you see the message Insufficient memory to run Word.

To find out how much memory is free on an IBM-format computer, run the DOS program called CHKDSK before you run Word.

Tip   **To avoid** Insufficient memory **messages when performing searches and sorts, you need 640K of RAM.**

Although Word runs on a system with only 384K of free memory, the program cannot perform some memory-intensive operations, such as searching and replacing throughout a document. If you try these types of tasks, you may receive the message Insufficient memory. If you do receive this message, your only option is to divide your document into separate small files and try the operation again. Obviously, this solution is unsatisfactory, so if you're planning to create documents longer than a few pages, you need 640K of RAM.

The commands that eat up memory include Replace, Library Autosort, Library Table, Library Index, the math commands, and long macros.

Even if you manage to use these commands successfully on a system with limited memory, you still may pay a price. After using one of these commands, you may find that the SAVE indicator—a warning message on the status line—comes on and starts blinking. This indicator warns you that Word is almost out of free memory. If you continue without saving, Word may prohibit any further text entry or editing until you save your document. And sometimes the SAVE indicator stays on even after you save, leaving you no option but to use the Transfer Clear All command, which clears the screen. To continue working, you have to reload your document.

You can avoid this hassle, for the most part, by upgrading your system to the maximum 640K. You still may see the SAVE indicator, however, if you try to perform these operations on long documents or use Word in all-day editing sessions.

Tip   **Word 5 can use expanded memory.**

Word 5 automatically supports expanded memory, as long as it conforms to the Lotus-Intel-Microsoft (LIM) expanded memory specification, 3.2 or higher. If you have a free slot in your computer, you can purchase an expanded memory board containing additional RAM, above the 640K limit. This fact is wonderful news for any of you who write long documents and want to make full use of Word 5's indexing, table-of-contents generation, sorting, and math features, which gobble up copious amounts of memory.

Tip   **If you run Word with OS/2, the program automatically uses all available system memory.**

The 640K RAM limit of DOS disappears when you're running OS/2. Word, which is entirely OS/2-compatible, automatically uses all system memory. If you're planning to use Word for professional document production activities, by all means consider an 80286 or 80386 system running OS/2 and 2M or 3M of RAM. With such systems, Word's potential as a serious document production system becomes a reality.

Trap   **If you try to place Word 5 in a RAM drive on 640K systems, you experience memory problems.**

For some years, Word cognoscenti have been placing Word in RAM drives, special sections of memory set up to behave as if they were super-fast disk drives. (You need special software to set up your memory this way.) This method is no longer advisable, however, although it's still possible. Word 5 is just too big, and too little memory is left for memory-intensive operations. You would have to love the SAVE indicator inordinately to run Word in a RAM disk with a 640K system.

Tip   **The most economical way to improve a basic system for Word is to add a hard disk.**

Word goes to disk frequently to retrieve program instructions and to page text in and out of memory. For this reason, even with the speed improvements in Version 5, Word's performance drops when disk operations begin. Adding a hard disk brings big performance gains—and not only in speed. If you're using a hard disk, you avoid a major hassle: the need to clear Word periodically and reload your document so that you can continue working.

Here's why you must routinely perform that tedious operation on a floppy system. As you work with Word, the program records all your keystrokes, as well as additional information, in a variety of temporary files. The longer you work, the bigger the files get. Sooner or later, depending on how much free disk space you have, you see the SAVE indicator. Even if you save your work, the indicator probably will stay on. And then Word displays the message Scratch file full, and you cannot enter another keystroke of text. Your only option at this point is to save your work and use the **T**ransfer **C**lear **A**ll command—which clears Word's memory completely. To continue working, you then have to reload your document, scroll to the point at which you stopped, and try to remember what you were doing.

Another reason why using a dual-floppy system is so tedious is that you must swap disks in and out to use Spell and Thesaurus.

Tip **Try using Word with a mouse.**

You can use Word without the mouse if you prefer. Most—but not all—of Word's features are available from the keyboard. And many users do choose, at least initially, to skip the mouse. Accomplished typists, in particular, often believe that they don't want to take their fingers off the keyboard. But many of these users change their minds after trying the mouse, which greatly speeds text editing operations. One user says, "One day I edited a report on a system that didn't have the mouse, and I had to use the keyboard commands. I felt constrained and frustrated, as if someone had tied one of my arms behind my back."

Tip **Word is at its best with graphics monitors.**

Word operates in two basic modes, the *text mode* and the *graphics mode*. In text mode, scrolling is fast, but the only character emphases you can see are underlining and boldface. In graphics mode, scrolling is somewhat slower, but you can see italic, superscript, subscript, and other character emphases. You can display the graphics mode only if you have equipped your system with a graphics video card and a graphics monitor. Graphics video cards are standard features of most systems these days; but if you're using Word on an old system equipped with the IBM Monochrome Adapter, which isn't capable of graphics, you may want to upgrade.

Tip **Consider a high-resolution color system for Word 5.**

Back when the only color systems available used the Color Graphics Adapter (CGA) and compatible monitors, color wasn't an attractive choice for word processing applications. The definition of individual characters is poor on CGA systems. Then the Enhanced Graphics Adapter (EGA) and later the Video Graphics Array (VGA) adapter came along, offering improved character definition. Beyond the price of EGA or VGA adapters and monitors, you have nothing to lose by going for color—and with Word 5, you have much to be gained. Here's why.

Despite major improvements in Word 5's capability to deliver on the "what you see is what you get" promise, Word still does not display fonts (type styles) or font sizes. You can format your text with any font or font size your printer can handle, but everything you type appears on-screen as 12-point, fixed-width Pica. In a document in which you have used more than one font or font size, this uniform text display makes distinguishing fonts and font sizes difficult.

With Word 5's greatly improved color customization features, however, you can display font sizes in distinctive colors. To distinguish 14-point headings, for instance, you can display 14-point type in red. The new show colors field in the Options menu enables you to assign colors to font sizes.

You learn more about color-coding font sizes in Chapter 4. For now, note that an EGA or VGA color adapter and display are excellent choices for writing with Word 5.

Tip **With the EGA and Hercules adapters, you can toggle between 25- and 43-line text displays.**

Here's another good reason to equip your system with an EGA adapter and monitor: you can see up to 43 lines of text in an optional high-resolution display. That number is not new. Previous versions permitted you to *start* Word in a 43-line mode, but you were then stuck with it. You had to quit Word and restart the program to change back to the normal 25-line display. With Word 5, however, you can toggle among available display modes by using the display mode field in the Options menu. Switch to the 43-line display to see what you're writing in a wider context; switch back to the 25-line display for normal writing and editing.

If you prefer a monochrome monitor, the 43-line display is also available with Hercules and Hercules-compatible graphics adapters and TTL monochrome displays.

Tip **With a VGA adapter, you can display 50 or 60 lines at a time.**

The VGA display standard is rapidly supplanting its predecessor, EGA, and for good reason. VGA is fast, its resolution (capability to show fine detail) is excellent, and with many applications it offers more colors. With a VGA adapter and monitor, either monochrome (such as a "paper-white" monochrome monitor) or color, Word is at its best: the display is beautifully crisp and detailed, and scrolling is fast. What's more, you can display almost a whole page of text in special 50- and 60-line display modes.

Tip **Word 5 fully supports the Genius full-page display adapter and monitor.**

If you're planning to set up a professional document-production system with Word 5, consider adding a Genius full-page adapter and display to your system. With Word 5 in graphics mode, you see a full page of text displayed with stunningly high resolution (1,024 dots horizontally by 768 dots vertically).

Configuring Your Hard Disk for Word 5

Word does run on dual-floppy systems, but, as noted in the preceding section, a hard disk is necessary for doing serious work with Word 5. And although Word's documentation doesn't contain a word about this topic, certain program features imply an ideal way to organize your hard disk for maximum performance with Word. Professional writers have already discovered this configuration. With a few preliminaries here, this configuration follows.

Tip **You must understand the concept of directories to use Word efficiently on a hard disk.**

Compared to a 360K floppy disk, a 20M or 40M hard disk seems to have all the wide open space of Montana. You will be amazed, however, at how quickly you can fill your hard disk with files. And the minute you get more than two or three dozen files, you run into a problem: reading the disk directory becomes difficult when you use the DOS DIR command. You see a long list of incomprehensible file names scrolling by at high speed.

If you divide your hard disk into directories, however, you don't experience this problem. Directories divide your disk into sections, each containing a manageable number of files. Using directories is practically a prerequisite for high-productivity work with a hard disk. With Word 5, directories are indispensable.

A directory is a special named section of your hard disk in which you can store files so that they're kept apart from others. In this sense, a directory is like a file folder. Directories provide an ideal way to organize your files so that you can keep track of them.

Unlike file folders, however, directories are organized hierarchically—probably like the organization you work for, with the boss at the top, mini-bosses in each department, and the rest of us slaves beneath. In a hard disk, the "boss"—the top level of the hierarchy—is called the *root directory*. Under the root directory you can place subdirectories. And subdirectories can have their own subdirectories, as figure 1.1 shows.

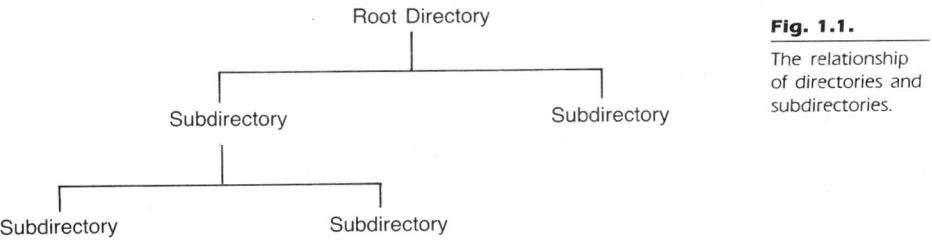

Fig. 1.1.

The relationship of directories and subdirectories.

When you use the DOS DIR command in a directory, you see only the files stored in that directory. Subdirectories of that directory are listed by name, but you see the code <DIR> rather than an extension.

Directory names are like DOS file names: you can use a maximum of eight characters (but extensions aren't allowed).

Note: The DOS nomenclature for directories is confusing because all directories, no matter what their positions, are referred to generically with the term *directories*. To distinguish one from the other, this book uses the following terms:

❏ *Root directory* refers to the top-level directory on your hard disk.

❏ *Current directory* refers to the current default directory, the one DOS uses for file operations unless you specifically instruct it otherwise.

❑ *Parent directory* refers to the directory immediately above the current directory.

❑ *Subdirectory* refers to the directory immediately below the current directory.

Tip   To get maximum performance from your hard disk, keep the number of files in your root directory to a minimum.

The root directory must contain all the files you need to start your computer, such as the hidden DOS files, COMMAND.COM, and other start-up files (such as AUTOEXEC.BAT and CONFIG.SYS, which are discussed in subsequent tips in this chapter).

Your hard disk's performance deteriorates, however, if you pack your root directory full of additional files. And whenever you try to view the list of these files by using the DOS DIR command, you see too many files. The solution is to keep the number of files in your root directory to a minimum. In particular, place all your application program files—including Word 5—in subdirectories (see fig. 1.2). With the exception of the files DOS needs to start your computer, put all the transient (disk-based) DOS files in a subdirectory called SYSTEM.

Fig. 1.2.

Organizing directories for application software.

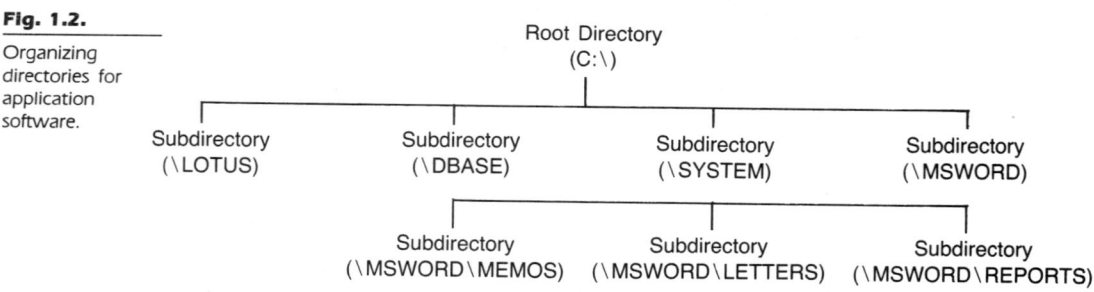

Before you begin creating directories, you need to understand a couple of key concepts, which are discussed in the next two tips.

Tip   To use directories, you must understand the concept of the default drive or directory.

The *default* drive or directory is the one DOS searches when you give a command. You can tell which drive is the default by looking at the DOS prompt. If the prompt says A>, drive A is the default drive. If a program you want is on drive C and you try to start the program while you're in drive A, you see the message Bad command or file name. To start the program, you must switch to drive C (by typing *C:* and pressing Enter), making drive C the default.

You also can make a directory the default. When you use the DOS command that switches directories (CHDIR), the directory to which you have switched becomes the default. And if you try to load a program that isn't in that directory, you see that familiar message, Bad command or file name.

Tip **You also must understand the concept of a path name in order to use directories.**

A *path name* tells DOS where to find a file if it isn't in the default directory. Although path names are tedious to type, you probably will have to use them occasionally. (The hard disk configuration you're developing for Word 5 in this chapter, however, ensures that you will need to use path names only rarely with Word.) Here's an example of a path statement:

\MSWORD\REPORTS\1988\REPORT1.DOC

This path name tells DOS, in effect, "The file called REPORT1.DOC can be found in the directory called 1988, which is a subdirectory of the REPORTS directory, which is a subdirectory of the MSWORD directory, which is a subdirectory of the root directory." Note the beginning backslash character that indicates the root directory, and the backslashes that separate the directory names.

After these preliminaries, you're ready to learn the DOS commands for creating directories—and moving around from directory to directory.

Tip **Learn the DOS commands for creating and deleting directories.**

Table 1.1 summarizes the DOS commands you need.

Table 1.1
DOS Commands for Creating and Managing Directories

Command	Example	Effect
CHDIR or CD	CD C:\MSWORD	Changes to the named directory and makes it the new default directory
CD \		Returns to root directory

Table 1.1—Continued

Command	Example	Effect
CD..		Changes to parent directory

(For example, if the current directory is REPORTS, a subdirectory of MSWORD, this command changes to the MSWORD directory.)

Command	Example	Effect
CD directory name	CD REPORTS	Changes to subdirectory under current directory

(You don't need to type the full path name.)

Command	Example	Effect
CD MKDIR or MD	MD C:\MSWORD	Creates a directory with the given name
PATH	PATH C:\MSWORD	Tells DOS where to look for a program if it is not in the default directory
RMDIR or RD	RD C:\JUNK	Removes a directory, if all the files in it have first been removed

Tip **Prepare your hard disk for Word by creating directories and subdirectories.**

With Version 5, the optimum way to use Word is to start the program from document subdirectories. The reason is a little technical, and you will understand it better as your knowledge of Word grows. When you start Word from a document subdirectory, Word automatically loads the style sheet and glossary files found in that document subdirectory. Therefore, you can create separate style sheets and glossary files (which contain macros) for each kind of document you create.

For instance, when you start Word from the directory called LETTERS, you can have Word automatically load the style sheet that prints your document in Courier typeface and with ragged right margins (so that it looks as if it were typed). You also can have Word load macros that automate envelope addressing. In contrast, when you start Word from the directory called REPORTS, you can have Word automatically load the style sheet that prints your document in Helvetica type and with right-margin justification, so that the document looks as though it were printed.

If you set up your hard disk this way, you get the same benefits without leaving Word. When you use the **T**ransfer **O**ptions command to name a new default directory, for instance, the style sheet in that directory becomes the new default style sheet.

You learn more about all these matters in subsequent chapters, so don't worry if you're mystified now. But if you're looking for avenues to high-productivity Word techniques, this method is an interstate freeway.

Here's how to create a hard disk directory called MSWORD:

1. Display the DOS prompt for drive C by typing *C:* and pressing Enter.

2. Type *MD \MSWORD* and press Enter.

3. Switch to the directory by typing *CD \MSWORD* and pressing Enter.

Once you have created a directory, you can create all the subdirectories you need. Follow these instructions to set up your hard disk for Word:

1. Think about the documents you want to create. Divide them into distinct categories, such as LETTERS, REPORTS, MEMOS, ARTICLES, NOTES, and so on.

2. If the MSWORD directory isn't the default, change to it by using the CHDIR (change directory) command (type *CD \MSWORD* and press Enter).

3. Create a subdirectory (in the MSWORD directory) for each type of document. To create the subdirectory called REPORTS, for example, type

    MD \MSWORD\REPORTS

4. Repeat step 3 until you have created subdirectories for all the types of documents you want to create.

Don't worry if you omit some document types. You can create new subdirectories at any time.

Tip **Create an AUTOEXEC.BAT file.**

When you start your computer, DOS looks for a file called AUTOEXEC.BAT on your start-up disk. If DOS finds a file by this name, the operating system begins executing the DOS instructions contained in the file, just as if you were typing them at the keyboard.

When you install Word, SETUP creates an AUTOEXEC.BAT file (or modifies the existing one). There's a good reason for creating your own file, however, before using SETUP. As you already know, the DOS prompt shows you the current default disk drive (such as A> or C>). But the prompt doesn't show you the current default directory. If the current subdirectory is the one called REPORTS, the prompt is still just C>, which can be confusing. Showing the default directory would be helpful. And you can.

A DOS command that modifies the DOS prompt is available. It's called PROMPT. If you use the PROMPT command with the right instructions, the DOS prompt always shows the current directory as well as the current drive. The trouble with PROMPT is that you must enter it manually every time you start your system—unless, that is, you include the command in an AUTOEXEC.BAT file.

Another reason for creating an AUTOEXEC.BAT file is to tell DOS where to find Word. SETUP adds this instruction to the AUTOEXEC.BAT file automatically, but learning how to do it yourself is a good idea. As you will probably discover, the installation utilities of some programs wipe out your AUTOEXEC.BAT file and substitute their own—without even having the courtesy to ask you. If your AUTOEXEC.BAT file is erased, you cannot start Word from document subdirectories, so you should take some time to learn how to create an AUTOEXEC.BAT file. You can create the file with Word or with DOS.

To create an AUTOEXEC.BAT file with DOS, follow these steps:

1. Type *CD C:* and press Enter to return to the root directory.

2. Type *COPY CON AUTOEXEC.BAT* and press Enter.

   This instruction tells DOS to copy the lines you type to a file called AUTOEXEC.BAT.

3. Type *PROMPT=$P $G* and press Enter.

4. Type *PATH C:\MSWORD* and press Enter.

5. Type *CD C:\MSWORD* and press Enter.

6. Press Ctrl-Z.

To create the file with Word, just include the information in steps 3, 4, and 5, and save the file, using the file name AUTOEXEC.BAT and the Text-only option in the Transfer Save menu.

Beyond this overview, you can learn much more about subdirectories in particular and hard disk management in general. See *Managing*

Your Hard Disk, 2nd Edition, by Don Berliner (Que Corporation, 1988) for a practical guide to these matters. For more on DOS, see *Using PC DOS*, 2nd Edition, by Chris DeVoney (Que Corporation, 1987).

Installing Word 5 with SETUP

SETUP, Word's installation program, is by far the best way to install Word 5. With previous versions of Word, you could use DOS to install the program if you preferred. But using DOS is not recommended with Version 5. Word 5's version of SETUP constructs a screen driver, a file called SCREEN.VID, which contains information about the video adapter you're using. You need SCREEN.VID to take full advantage of your video adapter's capabilities. Without SCREEN.VID, you can use only the text mode.

SETUP can install Word on almost any system you can imagine—and in the optimum way. The SETUP program is on Utilities Disk #1. Here's a brief overview of what the program does:

❑ Copies the Word program files to your program disks or Word directory

❑ Constructs the screen driver you need

❑ Copies the printer driver you need from the Printers disk (A *printer driver* is a file containing information about your printer. Without the driver, Word cannot print your documents.)

❑ Modifies or creates two DOS system files, called AUTOEXEC.BAT and CONFIG.SYS, on your DOS start-up disk or root directory (Word may not run if these modifications are not made.)

If you're installing Word on a hard disk, SETUP also gives you the option of copying Help, the hyphenation file, the Learning Word tutorial, Spell, Thesaurus, and certain utilities to Word's directory.

Tip **The first time you use SETUP, go through each operation in order.**

The SETUP program contains several options in its initial display screen (see fig. 1.3). Be sure to complete all of them (except the mouse option, if you don't have one).

Fig. 1.3.

SETUP's main
menu.

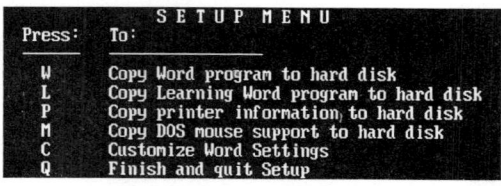

```
W O R D   5 . 0   S E T U P


    If you are setting up Word 5.0 for the first time, Setup
suggests you perform the steps below in the following order.

    If you're changing or adding something, you can choose
only the steps that apply.

           S E T U P   M E N U
    Press:   To:

      W     Copy Word program to hard disk
      L     Copy Learning Word program to hard disk
      P     Copy printer information to hard disk
      M     Copy DOS mouse support to hard disk
      C     Customize Word Settings
      Q     Finish and quit Setup
```

Tip **Don't worry about losing your AUTOEXEC.BAT and CONFIG.SYS files if you run SETUP.**

Many experienced personal computer users have learned (the hard way) to avoid installation programs. The more cavalier of them wipe out the AUTOEXEC.BAT and CONFIG.SYS files on your hard disk—files you may have created to customize your system's performance—without even asking for confirmation. If you're worried about SETUP for this reason, rest assured: the program is well mannered. SETUP either appends instructions to these files, or creates the files if they don't exist, but you don't have to worry about losing them.

Tip **Make sure that you are prepared before you run SETUP.**

Before running SETUP, you should have the following items and information at hand:

❑ All disks that came with your version of the program

❑ The make and model of all printers you may use

❑ The make and model of your video adapter

❑ Blank disks (if you are installing the program on a two-floppy disk system)

❏ A name for the directory in which you want to store the program files (if you have a hard disk system)

If you followed the suggestions elsewhere in this chapter, you have already created a Word directory called MSWORD. Type this name when SETUP asks for the directory for program files

Tip **If you're installing Word on a hard disk system, install all the files SETUP suggests unless you're low on disk space.**

These files, such as Thesaurus and Spell, greatly enhance Word's capabilities. If you fill your hard disk, chances are that you don't use many of the files on your disk. Consider backing up some of them on floppies to clear the space you need for Word.

Tip **After you install the Word program files, specifying the name of your video adapter is a vital step.**

Choose your video adapter carefully from the menu, which is shown in figure 1.4. This step is essential. After you choose your video adapter, SETUP constructs the file called SCREEN.VID and places it in your Word program directory.

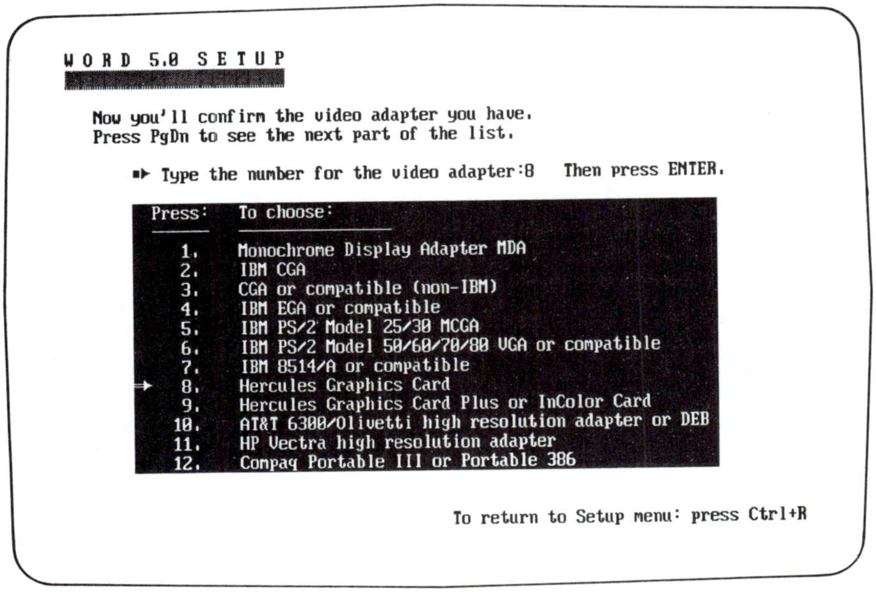

Fig. 1.4.

Installing a screen driver.

```
W O R D  5.0  S E T U P

  Now you'll confirm the video adapter you have.
  Press PgDn to see the next part of the list.

    ▪▶ Type the number for the video adapter:8   Then press ENTER.

       Press:   To choose:

         1.     Monochrome Display Adapter MDA
         2.     IBM CGA
         3.     CGA or compatible (non-IBM)
         4.     IBM EGA or compatible
         5.     IBM PS/2 Model 25/30 MCGA
         6.     IBM PS/2 Model 50/60/70/80 VGA or compatible
         7.     IBM 8514/A or compatible
    ▶    8.     Hercules Graphics Card
         9.     Hercules Graphics Card Plus or InColor Card
        10.     AT&T 6300/Olivetti high resolution adapter or DEB
        11.     HP Vectra high resolution adapter
        12.     Compaq Portable III or Portable 386

                         To return to Setup menu: press Ctrl+R
```

Trap **If you find that you cannot use the graphics mode in Word, you must run SETUP and install Word again.**

If you install Word without SETUP and then see the message `Cannot switch display modes` when you try to change to the graphics mode, you must run SETUP. Unfortunately, you have to go through the time-consuming process of recopying the entire Word program before you get to the screen driver installation menu. You should do it right the first time: use SETUP to install Word.

If you did use SETUP to install Word, but you still have trouble switching to graphics mode, you may have accidentally deleted or renamed SCREEN.VID. Run SETUP again.

Trap **You can select only one screen driver.**

You cannot select more than one video adapter, and SETUP creates only one file called SCREEN.VID. If your system has two video adapters, and you want to use both of them with Word, you have to get tricky. One suggestion, if you have plenty of disk space, is to create two different Word directories by running SETUP twice. Give each its own SCREEN.VID.

Tip **You can copy more than one printer description file to your Program disk or hard disk.**

The SETUP program guides you through the process of choosing printer description files (see fig. 1.5). You may install more than one printer description file from the list of files available. Each printer description file contains information about a printer's capabilities, including the fonts, font sizes, and print colors the printer can produce. When you choose a printer description file, SETUP copies it from one of the Printers disks to your Program disk or hard disk.

Why should you bother installing more than one printer description file? One reason is that even if a printer isn't connected to your computer, you can create, format, and save documents with formatting information specific to that printer. By choosing **P**rint **O**ptions, you can select any printer whose printer description file is available either on the Word Program disk or on your hard disk. When you select a printer, Word makes available the fonts, sizes, and colors the new printer can produce, even if that printer isn't connected to the computer. And when you save your document, Word stores this information and other formatting commands you have used.

You can use this feature to take full advantage of a printer located elsewhere. For example, if you work at home on a system equipped

```
W O R D   5.0   S E T U P


    Choose a printer from this list.
    Press PgDn to see the next part of the list.
    If your printer is not on this list, choose Other.

       ► Type the number for the printer:5    Then press ENTER.

          Press:   To choose:

             1.    ALPS ALQ 200
             2.    ALPS ALQ 200 with support for 3 Bins
             3.    ALPS ALQ 300
             4.    ALPS ALQ 300 with support for 3 Bins
             5.    Apple LaserWriter, LaserWriter Plus, NT, NTX
             6.    Adobe Download Font Support - Single Bin
             7.    Adobe Download Font Support - Dual Bin
             8.    AST TurboLaser (portrait mode)
             9.    AST TurboLaser (landscape mode)
            10.    AST TurboLaser PS
            11.    AST TurboLaser PS with Adobe Download Fonts
            12.    Businessland 45LQ

                        To return to Setup menu: press Ctrl+R
```

Fig. 1.5.

Installing a printer driver.

with an inexpensive dot-matrix printer, you can prepare documents to print at work on your office LaserJet™.

Tip   **Use a general printer description file if you cannot find one that is specific to your printer.**

If your printer's name does not appear on the list displayed by the SETUP program, you can use one of the general printer description files. The most general one, TTY.PRD, is already on the Word Program disk; you do not have to copy TTY.PRD from one of the Printers disks to use this file. TTY.PRD enables the use of boldface, underlined, and strike-through characters, but it may not support other printer characteristics. If you have an unsupported daisy-wheel printer, try TTYWHEEL.PRD.

Tip   **If the SETUP list doesn't include your printer, you may be able to use one of the other named printer description files.**

If your printer does not appear on the list of supported printers in SETUP, check to find out whether your printer is compatible with the Epson dot-matrix printer, Diablo letter-quality impact printer, or one of the Hewlett-Packard LaserJet laser printers. Many unsupported dot-matrix printers conform to the Epson standard, just as many unsupported daisy-wheel printers conform to the Diablo standard. And many laser printers recognize Hewlett-Packard printer instructions.

Read your printer's manual to discover whether the printer is code-compatible with one of these more widely known brands.

Trap   **If you have used SETUP but cannot use your printer, you may have deleted the printer description file.**

If you see the message File or directory does not exist when you name your printer with the **Print O**ptions command, you probably have deleted the printer description file accidentally. Run SETUP again, or just use DOS to copy the printer description file from the Printers disk.

Tip   **To use the mouse, you must start your computer with a disk containing the correct instructions in the CONFIG.SYS file.**

When you start your computer, DOS looks on your start-up disk for a file called CONFIG.SYS. If you want to use the mouse, CONFIG.SYS must contain a line with the following information:

DEVICE = MOUSE.SYS

The disk with which you start your system also must contain the file MOUSE.SYS. If you're using a two-floppy system, you need these files on your DOS start-up disk. If you're using a hard disk, you need these files in your hard disk's root directory.

SETUP copies the needed information to your disk automatically.

Trap   **If your mouse does not work, you may be using the wrong CONFIG.SYS file.**

If you use a two-floppy system, you probably have more than one copy of the DOS system disk. If you start your computer with a disk other than the one SETUP modified, however, you may find that your mouse doesn't work. The reason is that the disk doesn't contain the correct instruction in the CONFIG.SYS file—and may not contain CONFIG.SYS at all. Restart your system with the correct start-up disk.

If you're using the disk that SETUP modified, you may have erased or modified the CONFIG.SYS file that SETUP copied to your DOS start-up disk or your hard disk. You can solve the problem by running SETUP again, but that method is tedious. Here's a quicker way: just create a new CONFIG.SYS file with Word. Add the following instructions to the file:

DEVICE = MOUSE.SYS

Tip   **Be sure to read the information files.**

New documentation accompanies each new version of Word. Unfortunately, this documentation contains occasional omissions or errors. Microsoft plugs holes and corrects errors by providing supplementary information about the program in text files stored on the Utilities disk. In recent versions of Word, a file called README.DOC provides general updates and corrections and lists other more specific information files.

Use the DOS TYPE command to read these information files. Or load the information files into Word so that you can read them on-screen or print them. You can solve many mysteries by reading these files.

Trap   **You must restart your computer to use Word with the mouse after running SETUP.**

The mouse doesn't work—and neither does the PATH instruction in AUTOEXEC.BAT—unless you restart your computer after running SETUP. To restart your computer, hold down the Ctrl and Alt keys and press Delete.

Using Word 5 on a Two-Floppy System

Word 5 is severely constrained on systems with two 360K drives. Laptops with 720K or 1.4K drives, however, provide a much more hospitable home for Word. With these higher-density drives, the Word Program disk has more room for all the files Word needs. On 360K systems, you have to take special steps to use the program conveniently.

Trap   **If you're installing Word on a 360K system, you cannot take full advantage of your printer unless you use the document disk that SETUP creates (or a copy of the document disk).**

At the conclusion of the installation process, SETUP will have created a 360K *document disk* containing the printer driver you need. If you use a document disk that doesn't contain this file, you cannot print your work. As a safeguard make several copies of the document disk that SETUP creates and put the document disk that SETUP created in a safe place. Then you can always make new copies of the document disk, as needed.

Trap   **You frequently will run out of space on a 360K Program disk.**

When you use SETUP to create a copy of the Word Program disk, SETUP copies the files that Word must have in order to function. Then

SETUP copies the printer description files you need. After SETUP is finished, however, little room is left on the disk. As you will quickly discover, this situation causes problems. Here's why.

As mentioned previously in this chapter, as you work, Word stores all your keystrokes in a temporary file called the *scratch file* and creates other temporary disk files as needed. When no room is left, Word displays the message Word disk full, and you cannot continue to work. In most cases, you have to save your document, use the **T**ransfer **C**lear **A**ll command, and reload your document before you can continue. To avoid this tedious and often frustrating interruption, however, you can use the following strategies to clear space on your Program disk.

Trick **To avoid filling up your disk frequently, add a SET instruction to an AUTOEXEC.BAT file on your DOS start-up disk.**

Here's the instruction:

SET TMP = b:\

This instruction tells DOS to set up a variable called *TMP* and give it the value *b:*. When you start Word, the program detects the existence of this variable and alters the storage location of the TMP files (the temporary files Word creates) accordingly. If you add this instruction to an AUTOEXEC.BAT file and always start your computer with the disk containing this file, Word always stores the temporary files on drive B.

Tip **Remove BAK files from your document disks to free space.**

Word automatically makes a backup file whenever you load an existing document, make changes to it, and save it to disk. The backup file, stored with the extension BAK, contains the old version of your work—the version that existed before you made changes. If you do not want to save the old versions, you can erase them by using the DOS ERASE or DEL command.

Trap **When you see the** Document disk full **message, you must save your work on another disk.**

If you're using a 360K system, you had better get used to seeing this message, because you're going to run out of disk space frequently. But don't worry about losing your work. Word handles such situations gracefully. To save your document, simply insert a blank, formatted disk in the drive (or any other formatted disk with some free space on it) and use the **T**ransfer **S**ave command again. If you don't have a formatted disk handy, use the **L**ibrary **R**un command to format one. (This command gives you access to DOS.) Use the command, place your DOS disk in drive A and a new, unformatted disk in drive B, and then type

FORMAT B:

If you don't have any disks at all, don't panic and shut off your computer. Leave it on and go get some disks.

Chapter Summary

Word is at its best with high-resolution graphics monitors, and unless you're strapped for cash, you surely will want to add a hard disk to your system. Put Word in a directory called MSWORD and create subdirectories within this directory for your documents. Make sure that your AUTOEXEC.BAT file contains the PATH instruction which lets you start Word from any directory. Even if you're a super DOS whiz, install Word with SETUP—you will disable the graphics mode if you don't.

Now that you have configured your system for Word and installed the program correctly, you are ready to make a foray into the program itself. Chapter 2 covers the basics of starting, saving, and quitting Word 5.

2

Getting Started with Word 5: Starting, Saving, and Quitting

Word 5's new features add power to the program while simplifying it considerably. If you have used previous versions of Word, you will notice this point right away when you review Word's start-up options. You no longer need to set screen modes from the DOS prompt, for example, because you can toggle screen modes to your heart's content, using the new (and much improved) Options command. Seemingly small improvements in Word 5's macro capabilities have created vast new possibilities for automating basic operations, such as backing up your work and archiving it in day-to-day writing sessions. You should therefore review the basics of starting Word, saving your work, and quitting—even if you have already installed the program and created and saved documents. In particular, you will not want to miss the backup and document-archiving macros presented in this chapter.

Starting Word

Previous versions of Word offered many start-up options in the form of *switches*, or characters you could add to the Word start-up command when you issued it at the DOS prompt. Now that so many Word options are available with the Options menu, however, most of these switches have been disabled. Table 2.1 lists the start-up options for Word 5.

Table 2.1
Start-Up Options for Word 5

Command	Explanation
WORD	Starts Word and displays a new, blank document
WORD *filename*	Starts Word and opens the named document
WORD /L	Starts Word and opens the last document used
WORD /K	Starts Word in a special mode appropriate for use with memory-resident programs, such as SideKick

Tip **You can open a document at the same time you start Word.**

If you have already created a Word document and want to work with it again, type *word* followed by a space and the document's file name. If the document is not in the default directory or drive, you have to include the document's path name. For example, if you want to update a document called REPORT1.DOC in the REPORTS directory, type

WORD C:\MSWORD\REPORTS\REPORT1

and press Enter. If you have used the standard Word extension for document files (DOC), you need not type the period or extension after the file name.

Tip **You can start Word from your document directory to avoid having to type lengthy path names in the start-up command.**

Typing long path names can be quite a hassle, and you can easily make a typing mistake. If you do, you get the message File does not exist, which can be terrifying—especially if the file you're trying to load contains something precious and you have no backup copy. But don't panic. Almost certainly you have merely misspelled the file name. Use the **T**ransfer **L**oad command and try again. (For information on using commands, see the section on "Using Commands" in Chapter 3.)

A much better method, however, is to set up your hard disk as suggested in Chapter 1 (see the section titled "Configuring Your Hard Disk for Word 5"). With the correct PATH statement in your AUTOEXEC.BAT file, the statement that tells DOS where to find Word, you can start Word from your document subdirectory and so avoid all the backslashing, directory-name typing, and general aggravation.

Here's how to start Word and load the file REPORT1.DOC, using this technique:

1. If you haven't already done so, add the line *CD \MSWORD* to the end of your AUTOEXEC.BAT file.

   When you include this instruction, DOS automatically makes Word's directory the default at the beginning of the session.

2. At the DOS prompt, type *CD REPORTS* and press Enter. (When you're moving to the next subdirectory down, you can simply type the directory's name without the backslash. You don't have to type the full path name.)

3. Type *WORD REPORT1* and press Enter. Word starts and loads the document titled REPORT1.DOC.

Tip **You can open a document with an extension other than the standard DOC, at the same time you start Word.**

For documents with extensions other than DOC, you must type the period and the extension after the document's file name. For example, to load a table of data saved as REPORT1.TBL, start Word by typing

   WORD REPORT1.TBL

and pressing Enter.

Trap **If you do not type a period and an extension when naming a file, Word automatically supplies the period and the default extension DOC.**

Word assumes that you want the DOC extension unless you deliberately supply another one. Saving documents with the default extension (DOC) is almost always better than using another extension. If you forget that you used a different extension for a document, Word cannot find it. For example, if you try to load REPORT1.TBL by typing *REPORT1*, you get the dreaded (and usually misleading) message File does not exist.

Trick **To start Word and open a document that has no extension, type a period after the file name.**

Typing the period after the file name overrides Word's default extension. For example, here's how to open the document SUMMARY and start Word at the same time:

   WORD SUMMARY.

Tip **You can start Word and automatically return to the same place in the document you were when you last quit Word.**

Just use the /L switch at the DOS prompt when starting Word. Type

   WORD /L

and press Enter. You don't need to type the file name; Word stores the name of the file on which you last worked. You can type the *L* in upper- or lowercase, and you can include or omit the space before the slash.

Saving Your Work

The work you create with a computer isn't saved to disk unless you deliberately instruct the computer to do so. With Word, the commands you need are found in the Transfer menu. You also can use function key shortcuts and, as you will discover in this section, a particularly useful macro.

You learn more about choosing and using commands in the next chapter, but surveying your saving options is appropriate at this point. You have undoubtedly already started to experiment with Word 5. And perhaps you have already come up with a world-class poem that you don't want to lose!

Tip **The first time you save, use the Transfer Save command to name the file.**

To save your work, follow these steps:

1. Press Esc to activate the command menu, and then type the Transfer Save command's first letters: *TS*.

2. When the Transfer Save menu appears (see fig. 2.1), type a name for your document at the filename prompt. You can use up to eight alphanumeric characters, including underscores, hyphens, and these punctuation marks:

   ! @ # $ % & ( ) ' { } ˜ ˆ '

   Omit the period and extension so that Word automatically supplies its default extension, DOC.

3. Press Enter.

```
TRANSFER SAVE filename: █
                format:(Word)Text-only Text-only-with-line-breaks RTF
Enter filename
Pg1 Col         {}              ?              2M        Microsoft Word
```

Fig. 2.1.

The Transfer Save menu.

Tip ***Saving your document as an ASCII text file is easy with Word 5.***

You sometimes may need to save your work as an ASCII text file, with a hard carriage return at the end of every line and no formatting codes. Such files are required, for instance, for most telecommunications applications.

In previous versions of Word, saving your file this way required a tedious roundabout process that involved printing your work to a file with a special plain printer driver, removing top and bottom margins from your document, and other not-very-user-friendly hassles. With Word 5, however, the procedure is easy. To save your document as an ASCII text file, simply choose the Text-only-with-line-breaks option in the format field of the Transfer Save menu. (Press T, press S, highlight the format field with the arrow keys, and press T.)

Trap **You may see the message** Not a valid filename **when you try to save your work.**

If Word displays this message, you have used illegal characters or more than eight characters in your file name. Retype the name and try again.

Trap **You may see the message** Document disk full.

If Word displays this message, you are using a two-floppy system and have filled up your disk. Here are your options:

❑ Use the Transfer Delete command. When the command menu appears, press F1 to see a list of files. Use the arrow keys to highlight the name of a file you do not want to keep, and press Enter. (If you have saved many documents to this disk, try deleting some old BAK files.) Then try saving your document again. *Note:* You cannot delete any file that Word has consulted during the current editing session.

❑ Remove the full disk and insert a formatted disk that has some room on it. You will have to swap disks in and out, unfortunately, but that's better than losing your work.

❑ If you don't have a formatted disk, use the **Library Run** command to format one. Remove your document disk and insert the unformatted disk into drive B. When the Library Run menu appears, press Enter to accept the proposed response, command, which gives you the DOS system prompt. Then press Enter to carry out the command. When you see the message prompting you to switch disks, insert your DOS disk into drive A. Then format your disk, using the FORMAT B: command. After the formatting is complete, put your Word Program disk back into drive A, press any key to return to Word, and save your work. You will have to swap disks in and out of drive B.

Trap   **You may see the message** File already exists. Enter Y to replace or Esc to cancel.

If Word displays this message, the disk already contains a file with the name you have chosen. Press Y to overwrite that file. If you don't want to erase the file, however, press Esc and choose another file name.

Tip   **Understand what Word is doing when it creates a backup file (BAK).**

When you create a new document and save it for the first time, Word saves it with the default extension DOC (unless you have used another extension). When you reload this document for further editing, however, Word doesn't make any changes to the file on disk. (All the changes are kept in temporary files until you use the **Transfer Save** command.) When you resave your work by using **Transfer Save** (or by pressing Ctrl-F10), Word renames the existing disk file with the extension BAK, and creates a new DOC file containing your changes.

A BAK file, in other words, always contains the next-to-last version of your document that you saved to disk. If you're the type of writer who wants to keep all previous versions of a document intact, however, don't look to this feature for a way of preserving previous drafts. If you're saving your work frequently, as you should, your BAK file will probably closely resemble the final version of your document.

Tip   **If you accidentally erase your document, rename the BAK file with the extension DOC.**

Most personal computer users know firsthand how it feels to erase a file accidentally. To protect against such catastrophes, you're wise to equip your system with a file-undelete utility. (Most shareware distribution firms offer utility disks with these utilities, or you can purchase a commercial utilities program, such as PC Tools™.)

Sometimes, however, even these utilities cannot recover your files. If so, you will find that the BAK file contains almost all your work, right up to the next-to-last time you saved it.

Tip **To get maximum benefit from Word's document-retrieval capabilities, always complete the document summary sheets.**

After you save your document for the first time, Word presents you with a blank document summary sheet (see fig. 2.2). At the minimum, complete the `title` and `keywords` fields. If you do, you can use **L**ibrary **D**ocument-retrieval to find files in seconds, even if they're tucked away in obscure directories on a giant hard disk.

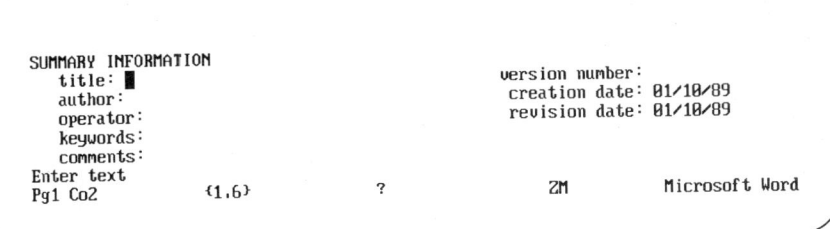

Fig. 2.2.

The document summary sheet.

```
SUMMARY INFORMATION
   title: █                        version number:
  author:                            creation date: 01/10/89
operator:                            revision date: 01/10/89
keywords:
comments:
Enter text
Pg1 Co2        {1,6}        ?          2M        Microsoft Word
```

If more than one person uses the computer, be sure to fill in the `author` field as well. Complete it exactly the same way each time. Don't use your first name on one sheet and your last name on another. If you always type your name exactly the same way, you can use **L**ibrary **D**ocument-retrieval to find all the documents you have created.

The Library Document-retrieval command is discussed in detail in Chapter 9, "Strategies for Effective Editing."

Tip **Word always saves your work to the default drive or directory unless you specifically instruct otherwise.**

With Word, the default drive or directory is the one from which you started Word. Now here's an important point: the default drive or directory isn't necessarily the one in which you have stored Word. SETUP inserts in your AUTOEXEC.BAT file a PATH statement that tells DOS where to find Word. As long as you start your computer with AUTOEXEC.BAT in your root directory or start-up disk, you can start Word from any drive or directory, and that drive or directory becomes the default.

Word always saves your work to the default drive or directory, unless you specifically instruct otherwise by supplying path information in the `filename` field of the Transfer Save command menu. For instance, when the default directory is C:\MSWORD\REPORTS, typing *A:\REPORT1* saves the document to drive A. If you just type *REPORT1*, though, Word saves the file to C:\MSWORD\REPORTS.

Now you know one good reason to start Word from a document directory. When you do, the document directory (such as LETTERS) becomes the default. You thus don't have to provide any path information to save the file to the document directory. You just type the file name, and Word does the rest automatically.

Trick **You can change the default directory by using the Transfer Options command.**

The Transfer Options command is extremely important: it gives you a way to change the default directory without restarting Word from a different directory. If you start Word from the directory called REPORTS, for instance, that directory is the default. But suppose that you finish writing your report and want to write a letter. Before you do, use the **T**ransfer **O**ptions command (see fig. 2.3). Make the LETTERS directory the new default by typing the directory's complete path name in the `setup` field of the Transfer Options menu. That way, when you save your letter, you don't have to type additional path information to get Word to save your letter in the appropriate directory.

Fig. 2.3.

The Transfer
Options menu.

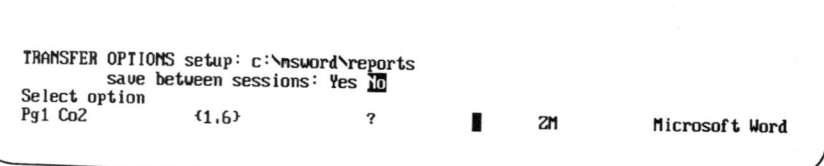

```
TRANSFER OPTIONS setup: c:\msword\reports
            save between sessions: Yes No
   Select option
   Pg1 Co2         {1.6}           ?          █     2M        Microsoft Word
```

Of course, adding path information when you're using Transfer Save isn't all that hard. Some of you may conclude that using Transfer Options to switch default directories is too much trouble. But you should get in the habit of doing so right now. The reason requires a little explanation and may not be completely comprehensible if you're not familiar with style sheets yet. But here's a quick overview.

As you learn in Chapter 12, "Style Sheets," Word automatically uses the default style sheet, called NORMAL.STY, that is found in the default directory. The whole process is completely automatic. You can set up one default style sheet for memos, another for letters, and a third for reports, each with its own appropriate formats, including printer fonts. When you place the version of NORMAL.STY you have created for letters in the directory called LETTERS, Word uses that style sheet automatically whenever you make this directory the default. In short, if you customize your system the way this book suggests, you automatically attach exactly the right style sheet just by changing default directories with Transfer Options.

Trap   **If you choose** Yes **in the** save between sessions **field of the Transfer Options menu, you cannot set the default by starting Word from a document directory.**

The save between sessions field, new to Word 5, lets you set up a permanent default directory, one that Word uses no matter which directory or drive you use to start Word. If you follow this book's suggestion to start Word from document directories, however, you should always choose the No option in this field.

Tip   **After you have named the file, resave your work with Ctrl-F10, and reuse Ctrl-F10 every 10 or 15 minutes.**

Ctrl-F10 is one of Word's handy keyboard shortcuts. It does exactly the same thing that the Transfer Save command does, except Ctrl-F10 uses the current file name. This keyboard shortcut saves several keystrokes when you want to save your file.

Saving your work frequently is a good practice for two reasons. First, you protect yourself from losing your work if the power fails momentarily. Even if you're using Word's new autosave feature, which is described later in this section, you should save your work every 10 or 15 minutes. Autosave doesn't actually save your document but just creates a special backup file, which in the event of a power interruption, Word can use to reconstruct your work.

Second, when you save to disk, you clear part of your computer's memory and thus decrease the amount of memory Word requires. You leave more room available for operations like searches, sorts, math, and macros, and you reduce the chance that you will see an Insufficient memory message. Saving frequently improves Word's performance.

Tip   **Use the autosave feature at all times.**

Word's new autosave field is a wonderful, welcome, and "intelligent" feature. Autosave automatically constructs backup files so that if your computer crashes or the power fails, Word can reconstruct your work. And autosave doesn't just back up your document. Autosave also backs up glossary files, style sheets, and any other documents that may be open at the time. As your Word expertise grows, you will probably always have at least one style sheet and one glossary open (glossaries contain the macros you create).

Unexpected power failures, as you're doubtless already aware, occur frequently, although some areas are more susceptible than others. (In our neighborhood, the power company likes to go on one-minute vacations about twice a week—especially on Saturday and Sunday mornings, when the maintenance people are all tucked into their nice, warm beds.) And sooner or later, the power will go off when you have been on a hot writing streak—too hot to pause briefly to save. Few computer catastrophes are more aggravating—or more professionally dangerous. Many people have suffered the embarrassment of missing critical deadlines because a power failure wiped out hours of work.

Don't let this disaster happen to you. Use autosave regularly. To be sure, this feature isn't without its penalties. It periodically updates the special files it creates, and this updating causes delays, particularly the first time autosave goes to work. Unless you're using a super-fast system, you may have to pause for a few seconds to let autosave do its thing. But that's a small price to pay for the protection autosave gives you.

To turn on the autosave feature,

1. Press Esc to highlight the command menu, and press O to open the Options menu (see fig. 2.4).

2. Use the arrow keys to highlight the `autosave` field.

3. Press 5. Autosave will then back up your work every 5 minutes.

4. Press Enter to carry out the command.

Word saves the choices you make in the Options menu, so they become the new program defaults. If you want to turn off autosave, just press 0 in the `autosave` field and then press Enter.

If the power fails while you're using autosave, when you restart Word, you see a message asking whether you want to reconstruct the files that weren't saved. Just press Y, and Word does the job.

Trap **Don't confuse the autosave process with saving your work.**

Do remember that using autosave isn't the same thing as using Transfer Save. Even if you're using autosave, you don't save your work to disk unless you do so deliberately with **Transfer Save** or Ctrl-F10—or with Word 5's new **Transfer Allsave** command, the subject of

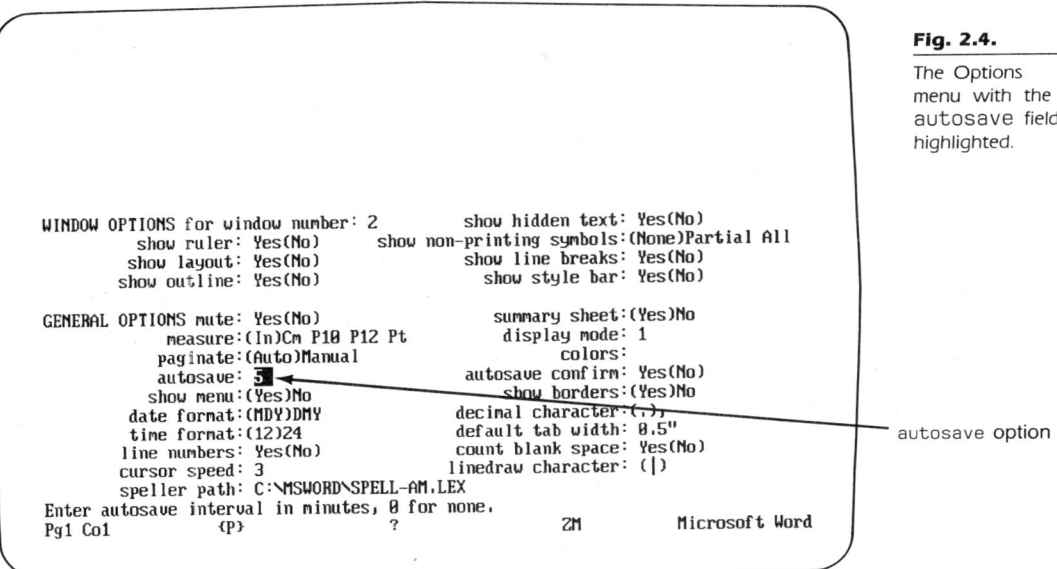

Fig. 2.4.

The Options
menu with the
autosave field
highlighted.

the next tip. And remember, saving your work reduces the amount of
memory Word is using and improves the program's performance.

Tip **Use Transfer Allsave to save all open documents, style
sheets, and glossaries.**

As you learn in subsequent chapters, you can open as many as eight
documents simultaneously, switching among them at a keystroke. You
also can use style sheets and glossaries, which contain macros. In a
session in which you have opened and modified several files, saving
them one-by-one with Transfer Save (and the special save commands
for style sheets and glossaries) is tedious. In response to user
suggestions, Microsoft has created a new command, Transfer Allsave.
This command saves all open documents, style sheets, and glossaries
in one automatic operation. Use Transfer Allsave rather than Ctrl-F10 if
you're working with more than one file at a time.

Tip **Use a macro to save your work and to copy the file to a
floppy in just two keystrokes.**

As you're doubtless aware, hard disks sometimes fail. This problem
isn't much fun to think about, but it happens. A wise user committed to
high-productivity word processing regularly backs up critical documents
to floppy disks. The trouble is that backing up is a time-consuming,
monotonous job, and you must remember to do it. You easily can be

lulled into a sense of security when your system seems to work perfectly day after day. But the day your system doesn't work is what causes the anguish.

The following macro, one of the most important in this book, kills two birds with one stone. The macro not only saves your work to your hard disk but also automatically copies the file (including its backup BAK file) to a floppy disk. You just sit back and watch the show. All you have to do is put a floppy into drive A when instructed to do so. When the macro finishes running, your document reappears, with the cursor in precisely the position it was in when you gave this macro command.

Here's the macro:

```
«SET echo = "off"»
«SET promptmode = "ignore"»
<esc>o<down 4>y<enter>
<ctrl esc>ts
«SET filename = field»<enter>
<esc>ldq«filename»<f10><backspace 3>*<enter><ctrl space>
«PAUSE Insert backup disk in drive A and press Enter»
ca:\<tab>n<enter>
q<del><enter>e
<esc>o<down 4>n<enter>
```

To create and use this macro, follow the instructions in Chapter 13, "Macros." Save the macro, using the name

```
quick_backup.mac^<ctrl q>b
```

Because this macro is the first one presented in this book, please note that you don't have to understand how it works to make it work for you. You learn more about creating your own macros in Chapter 13. For now, follow the instructions in that chapter to add this macro to your system, and then give it a try. As your knowledge of macros develops, you will begin to understand how a macro like this one operates. Before long, you will be writing your own macros—and maybe even improving the ones in this book!

Tip   **Use a macro to delete a document from your hard disk and to archive the document to a floppy in just two keystrokes.**

You have no reason to keep a file on your hard disk when you're completely finished with the file. It just takes up room and slows DOS. Therefore, after printing that final draft, use this macro. It saves the document one last time, clears the screen, and uses Library Document-retrieval to archive the document (and its BAK file) to a floppy, deleting the document from your hard disk in the process.

```
«SET echo = "off"»
«SET promptmode = "ignore"»
<esc>o<down 4>y<enter>
<ctrl esc>ts
«SET filename = field»<enter>
<esc>tcw
<esc>ldq«filename»<f10><backspace 3>*<enter><ctrl space>
«PAUSE Insert backup disk in drive A and press Enter»
ca:\<tab>y<enter>
q<del><enter>e
<esc>o<down 4>n<enter>
```

To create and use this macro, follow the instructions in Chapter 13, "Macros." Save the macro, using the name

```
quick_archive.macˆ<ctrl q>a
```

Trick **If more than one person uses your computer, use a macro to archive all of each user's files to a floppy.**

Macro

In many offices, more than one person uses a single computer, resulting in what ecologists call the "tragedy of the commons": all users regard the common resources as infinite and so never bother to erase their files. As a result, the hard disk fills up quickly, and someone has to lean on all the users to clean up their files. (You don't dare erase others' files. They're sure to decide that the files were immeasurably valuable, even if they had been long forgotten.)

The following macro provides a solution to this computer-management human dilemma. At the end of a working session, the macro clears all the files created by a specific user from the hard disk and archives them to a floppy backup. Here's the macro:

```
«SET echo = "off"»
<esc>o<down 4>y<enter>
«SET promptmode = "ignore"»
«ASK name = ?Type author's name and press Enter»
<ctrl esc>ta<enter>
<esc>tcw
<esc>ldq<tab>«name»<enter>
<ctrl space>
«PAUSE Insert backup disk in drive A and press Enter»
«SET echo = "off"»
ca:\<tab>y<enter>
q<del><down><del><enter>
<esc>o<down 4>n<enter>e
```

To create and use this macro, follow the instructions in Chapter 13, "Macros." Save the macro, using the name

    quick_userarchive.mac^<ctrl q>u

Quitting Word

Exiting Word is a simple matter. First choose **Q**uit from the command menu by pressing Esc and then pressing Q. If you have modified the document, Word highlights the document name and asks whether you want to save it. Press Y if you want to save the document, N if you want to abandon the changes you have made, or Esc if you want to retreat from the Quit command.

Trap **Simply switching off the power when you're finished with Word can be dangerous.**

The Quit command provides an orderly exit from Word. The command clears temporary files from the disk, saves the choices you have made in the Options menu, and warns you if you have failed to save your work. Always use **Q**uit to leave Word so that you can protect yourself and your files.

Tip **Use a macro to save all documents and to quit the program with two keystrokes.**

When you're done with an editing session, use this macro to save all open documents (including style sheets and glossaries) and to quit Word:

    <ctrl esc>ta
    <esc>q<enter>

To create and use this macro, follow the instructions in Chapter 13, "Macros." Save the macro, using the name

    quick_quit.mac^<ctrl q>q

Chapter Summary

As you have discovered in this chapter, Version 5 is truly a significant revision of this power-packed program. The new Word 5 features suggest a completely new approach to configuring your system, especially your hard disk. In the chapters to come, you learn many ways to take advantage of document directories as you develop high-productivity techniques with Word 5. And as the macros presented in the last section of this chapter clearly show, learning to create and use macros is one of the royal roads to Word 5 mastery.

3

Getting Oriented: Finding Your Way in Word 5

Many users, eager to take a powerful program like Word to the limit, skip such preliminaries as fully understanding the display screen and trying out all the various cursor-control and command-entry options. But you should pay some attention to such matters. Power users know that program mastery means choosing, from all the possible control options, a repertoire that best suits your working style. In this chapter, you learn which techniques and options are preferred by professional writers.

This chapter covers the following topics:

- ❏ Understanding the display screen
- ❏ Controlling the cursor and scrolling
- ❏ Using commands
- ❏ Getting help

Understanding the Display Screen

The first time you start Word 5 after installing it, the program displays the screen shown in figure 3.1. (The screen displays of previous versions are slightly different.) Word initially divides the screen into two areas:

- ❏ The *document area*, enclosed by the rectangle, shows the text with which you're working.

❑ The *command area* consists of the last four lines on the screen. This area contains a menu of commands, a message line, and a status line.

Fig. 3.1.

The document area and the command area.

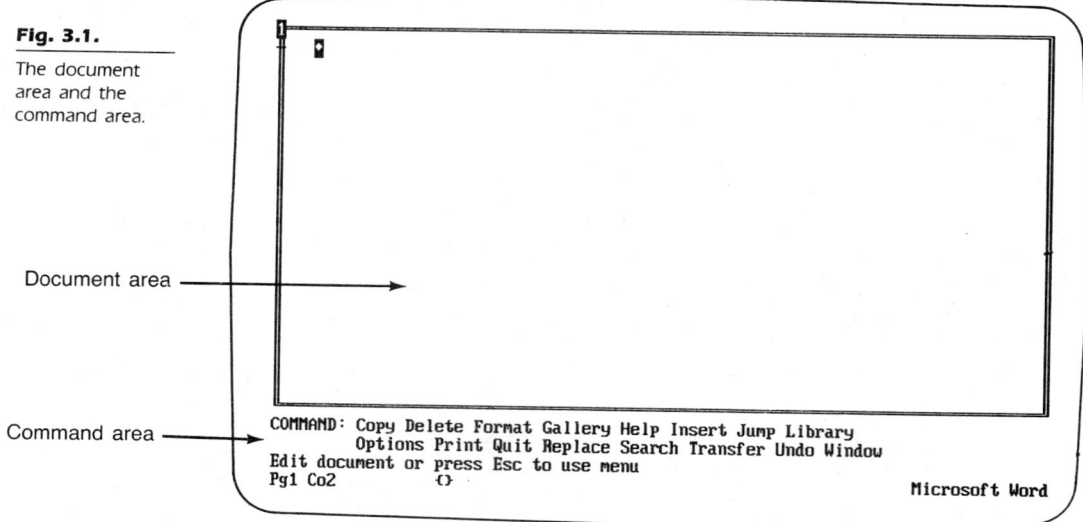

Document area ⎯⎯⎯⎯⎯⎯

Command area ⎯⎯⎯⎯⎯⎯

```
COMMAND: Copy Delete Format Gallery Help Insert Jump Library
         Options Print Quit Replace Search Transfer Undo Window
Edit document or press Esc to use menu
Pg1 Co2              {}                              Microsoft Word
```

Word has two basic modes, which correspond to these areas. When Word is in the *edit mode*, you can work in the document area. In edit mode, the message line displays Edit document or press Esc to use menu. When Word is in the *command mode*, you can select commands; the message line displays a description of the highlighted command. The Esc key moves the highlight from one mode to the other.

In the document area, you find the following features (see fig. 3.2):

❑ The *window number* helps you keep track of up to eight windows simultaneously. Only one window at a time can be active, and that window's number is highlighted.

❑ The *end mark*, a diamond-shaped mark, shows the end of the file. If you try to delete this character, you see the message End mark cannot be edited. When you start Word without loading a document, the highlight (a rectangle highlighted in reverse video) is superimposed on the end mark, as shown in figure 3.2. The highlight shows where text appears when you press letter and number keys on the keyboard.

Window number

End mark

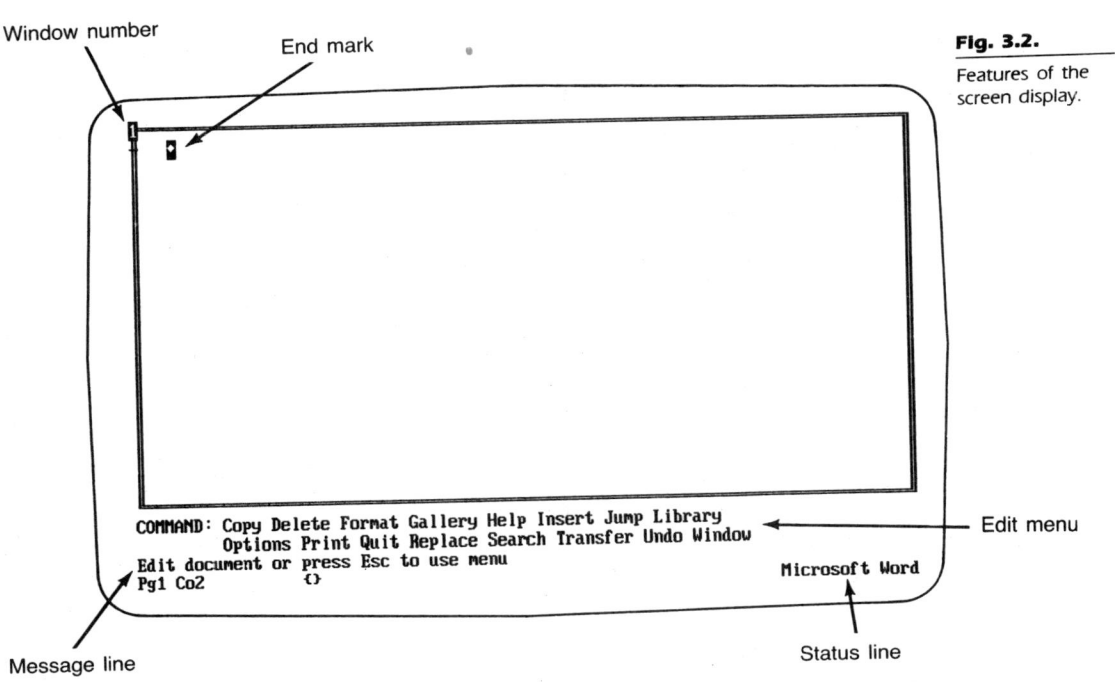

Fig. 3.2.

Features of the screen display.

COMMAND: Copy Delete Format Gallery Help Insert Jump Library
        Options Print Quit Replace Search Transfer Undo Window
Edit document or press Esc to use menu
Pg1 Co2   {}

Microsoft Word

Edit menu

Message line

Status line

The command area displays the following features:

❑ The *edit menu*, the first two lines of the command area, shows the names of Word's commands.

❑ The *message line*, the next-to-last line on the screen, displays Word's messages.

❑ The *status line*, the last line on the screen, includes the current page number and the scrap (a temporary parking place for deleted text).

Figure 3.3 shows the status line in more detail. The status line includes these features:

❑ The *page number indicator* shows your position in the document. In previous versions of Word, the page number displayed Page 1 until you paginated your document by printing it or using the Print Repaginate command. With Version 5's default setting of Yes in the paginate field of the Options menu, however, the program inserts page breaks automatically. The page number indicator thus always shows an accurate count of pages.

Fig. 3.3.

The status line.

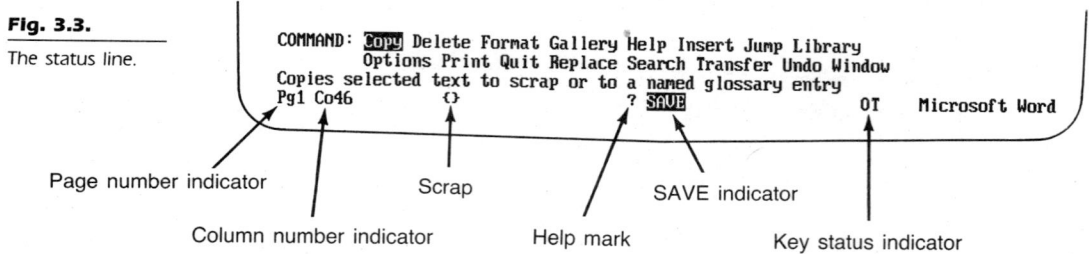

```
COMMAND: Copy Delete Format Gallery Help Insert Jump Library
         Options Print Quit Replace Search Transfer Undo Window
Copies selected text to scrap or to a named glossary entry
Pg1 Co46              {}              ? SAVE              OT   Microsoft Word
```

Page number indicator

Column number indicator

Scrap

Help mark

SAVE indicator

Key status indicator

❏ The *column number indicator* shows where the cursor is positioned horizontally on the screen. This indicator is useful for aligning columns when you don't trust your eyes.

❏ The *scrap* is a temporary storage area for text you copy or delete from the screen. You can use the scrap to store text you have cut from your document, and then you can insert this text later at another location. The scrap holds only one unit of text at a time. When you copy or cut any text to the scrap, the scrap's previous contents are wiped out. When the scrap is empty, you see two curly braces, as shown in figure 3.3. When you have copied or cut something to the scrap, however, that text is displayed within the braces. If the text in the scrap is longer than 15 characters, only the first and last sections are shown, with an ellipsis in the middle.

❏ The *help mark* appears as a question mark in the middle of the status line. You see this mark only if you have installed a mouse. Clicking the help mark with either button brings up the help menu.

❏ The SAVE *indicator* lets you know when you should save your work. If you see this indicator, save your work immediately with the **T**ransfer **S**ave or **T**ransfer **A**llsave command.

❏ The *key status indicator* informs you when you have toggled on one of Word's special program modes, such as the overtype mode.

If you're using a mouse, note these additional features of the initial display screen, as shown in figure 3.4:

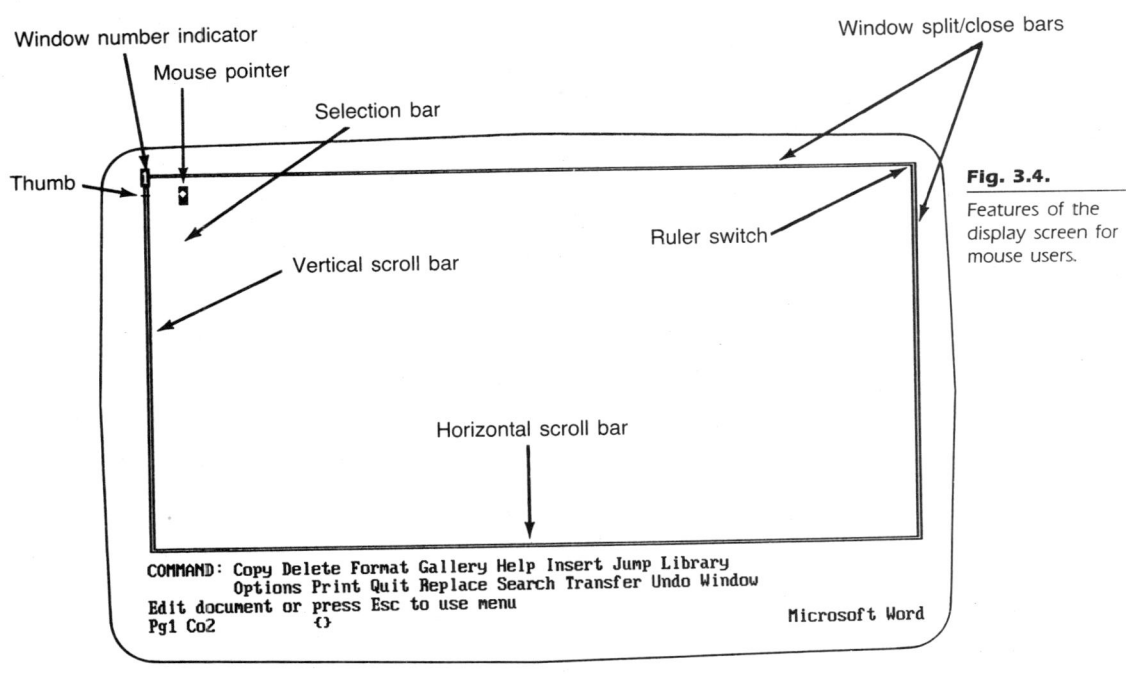

Window number indicator

Mouse pointer

Selection bar

Window split/close bars

Thumb —

Vertical scroll bar

Ruler switch

Fig. 3.4.

Features of the display screen for mouse users.

Horizontal scroll bar

```
COMMAND: Copy Delete Format Gallery Help Insert Jump Library
         Options Print Quit Replace Search Transfer Undo Window
Edit document or press Esc to use menu
Pg1 Co2          {}                                Microsoft Word
```

☐ The *mouse pointer* (an arrow in graphics mode and a blinking square in edit mode) moves around the screen as you move the mouse on your desk. In the document area, clicking the left mouse button instantly moves the cursor to the pointer's location. In the command mode, clicking a command's name or field selects it.

☐ The *window split/close bars* are the top and right window borders. When you move the mouse pointer to these areas, the pointer changes shape. In edit mode, the pointer becomes a rectangle, like the cursor. In graphics mode, the pointer becomes a box. When you see this shape change, you can press the left mouse button to split the screen into two windows that both display the same document. Windows and more mouse techniques to control them are covered in Chapter 6.

☐ The *ruler switch* area is at the upper right corner of the screen. If you move the mouse pointer to this area and click, you turn on the ruler in the upper window border.

☐ The *horizontal* and *vertical scroll bars* (the bottom and left window borders) give mouse users a way to scroll left and right or up and down without using the keyboard. For more information on scrolling with the mouse, see this chapter's section on "Controlling the Cursor and Scrolling."

❏ The *selection bar*, a blank column running down the screen between the text and the left window border, is used for selecting text with the mouse. In edit mode, when you move the pointer to the selection bar, the pointer shape changes from a square to a slightly larger rectangle. In graphics mode, the left-leaning arrow changes so that it points to the upper right. You find more information on text selection in Chapter 5.

❏ The *thumb* shows your relative position in a document. If the thumb is positioned near the top of the left window border, you're at the beginning; if the thumb is in the middle, you're near your document's middle; and so on.

Trick   **You can press A to return to edit mode.**

If you're accustomed to using the Alpha command (dropped in Version 4) to return to your document, you may want to continue pressing A whenever you want to return to edit mode. Word 5 allows you to do so. This undocumented feature probably interests only users of previous versions. The feature may be dropped in future versions of Word.

Trap   **If Word is in command mode, but you think it's in edit mode, typing characters can set off a command you don't want to give.**

You can choose commands in several ways. One method is using the arrow keys to highlight a command name and then pressing Enter. But Word also responds to the command's first letter. This feature is convenient for good typists; however, if you inadvertently type text while you are in command mode, you may set in motion an unwanted command. The results can damage your work. If you experience this type of problem, try using the **U**ndo command, which undoes some—but not all—effects of Word commands.

Most of the time, if you accidentally type while in command mode, you type letters Word doesn't recognize as command names. If so, you hear a beep and see this message:

    Not a valid option

Just press Esc to return to the edit mode.

Tip **Learn how to toggle the special modes on and off.**

Word has several special operating modes in which the program's characteristics change. In the overtype mode, for instance, typed characters rub out existing characters. (In Word's default mode, the insert mode, typed characters push existing characters right and down.) All these modes are controlled by toggle switches. A *toggle switch* is a command key that turns a mode on if it's off, and off if it's on. Pressing F5, for instance, turns on the overtype mode if Word is in the default mode; pressing F5 again turns off the overtype mode.

If you're not familiar with these features, you can get confused and frustrated if you have accidentally given one of the commands that toggles on a mode. The mouse, for example, doesn't work in the record macro mode; the highlight stays where it is. If you accidentally switch to this mode, you may wrongly conclude that the program has crashed and that you must reboot your computer to continue working. If you do reboot your computer, however, you lose your work. All you really have to do is press Shift-F3 to switch off the record macro mode, press Esc when the Copy command appears, and continue working.

You would be wise, therefore, to learn to recognize the key indicator codes that display in the status line, telling you when a mode has been switched on. Table 3.1 lists these key indicator codes, along with the toggle switches that turn them off and on and brief descriptions of the modes. In subsequent chapters, you learn more about the functions of these toggle switches. For now, learn to recognize the codes displayed on-screen so that you know which key to press if you accidentally turn on one of the modes.

Trap **Word cannot display all your operating mode choices at the same time.**

Word Versions 4 and 5 can display in the key indicator up to six different codes at the same time. EX (extend select) and CS (column select) are mutually exclusive and overwrite each other—but that's no problem because you don't need both modes at the same time.

Three positions on the status line are shared by the code pairs LD and NL, MR and OT, and ZM and SL. The codes taking precedence over others are LD, MR, and ZM. When you're in line drawing mode (LD), Num Lock has no effect, so you don't need to see the NL code. And in the revision marking mode (MR), overtyping is canceled even if you have toggled it on. When you're in the zoom mode (ZM), however, you could very well have pressed the Scroll Lock key without realizing it,

Table 3.1
Key Indicator Codes and Mode Toggle Switches

Code	Key/Command	Description
CL	Caps Lock	Letters entered as capitals
CS	Shift-F6	Column select mode (used for selecting columns of text on-screen, especially in tables or math operations)
EX	F6	Extend select mode (used for selecting text with the keyboard)
LD	Ctrl-F5	Line drawing mode
MR	**F**ormat revision-**M**arks **O**ptions	Marks revisions without deleting them
NL	Num Lock	Numbers from numeric keypad entered as numbers (arrow keys disabled)
OT	F5	Overtype mode (characters typed at keyboard rub out existing text)
RM	Shift-F3	Record macro mode (keystrokes recorded as macro)
SL	Scroll Lock	Direction keys can be used to scroll (arrow keys disabled)
ST	Ctrl-F3	Step mode (used for editing macros)
ZM	Ctrl-F1, or click window number with right mouse button	Window has been zoomed to full size; another window (or windows) may be hidden underneath

causing the arrow keys to scroll the screen rather than just move the cursor. That's no disaster. If it happens, just press the Scroll Lock key to restore normal functions.

Controlling the Cursor and Scrolling

Because Word is designed for full use both with and without the mouse, you have many options for moving the cursor and scrolling. You can rely exclusively on keyboard commands if you prefer. Word's keyboard cursor-control configuration is a model of intelligent use of the IBM PC keyboard. For added convenience and speed, you can reposition the cursor and scroll with the mouse.

Tip **Most Word cursor-movement keys are also scrolling keys.**

Many programs distinguish clearly between moving the cursor and scrolling so that cursor-movement keys move only the cursor's position on the screen. Scrolling keys, in contrast, move the text up or down in the document window without moving the cursor. In Word, the two are not clearly differentiated with most commands. Almost all Word cursor-movement keys result in scrolling if you hold them down. For instance, holding down the down-arrow key scrolls the screen after the cursor reaches the bottom window border. Table 3.2 lists Word's cursor-movement keys and indicates which ones repeat if you hold them down.

Table 3.2
Moving the Cursor with the Keyboard
(Scroll Lock Off)

Key	Moves Cursor to	Repeats
Up arrow	Next character up	Yes
Down arrow	Next character down	Yes
Left arrow	Next character left	Yes
Right arrow	Next character right	Yes
Home	Beginning of line	No
End	End of line	No
PgUp	Next window up	Yes
PgDn	Next window down	Yes
Ctrl-up arrow	First character of preceding paragraph	No
Ctrl-down arrow	First character of next paragraph	No
Ctrl-left arrow	First character of word left	Yes

Table 3.2—Continued

Key	Moves Cursor to	Repeats
Ctrl-right arrow	First character of word right	Yes
Ctrl-Home	First character in window	No
Ctrl-End	First character in last line of window	No
Ctrl-PgUp	First character in document	No
Ctrl-PgDn	Last character in document	No

Trap **Sometimes when you try horizontal scrolling, your commands have no effect.**

You cannot scroll left or right unless at least one line is longer than the window display space available. If your horizontal scrolling doesn't work, evidently all the lines of your document fit within the display window. To see how horizontal scrolling works, choose the **F**ormat **D**ivision **M**argins command and change the right and left settings to 0.2 inch each. Type some text, and note that the screen scrolls right to accommodate your typing and jumps back left when word wrapping occurs.

Trap **Pressing Scroll Lock disables the right- and left-arrow keys for cursor movement.**

When you press the Scroll Lock key, the code SL appears in the key status indicator, and the functions of many cursor-movement keys change. These keys now scroll the screen before reaching the borders. If you like to use the arrow keys to move the cursor, you may not like the scroll lock mode, which restricts the functions of the left- and right-arrow keys to lateral scrolling. Table 3.3 lists the effects of Scroll Lock on Word's cursor-movement keys.

Tip **By far the easiest way to reposition the cursor is to use the mouse.**

To use the mouse to reposition the cursor on the screen, you simply point to the cursor's new location and click the left button. The process is fast and effortless. With the keyboard, you would probably have to use two or more keys to accomplish the same end, and peck away at them several times.

Table 3.3
Moving the Cursor with the Keyboard
(Scroll Lock On)

Key	Scrolls	Repeats
Up arrow	Up one line (moves cursor)	Yes
Down arrow	Down one line (moves cursor)	Yes
Left arrow	Left one-third windowful (without moving cursor)	Yes
Right arrow	Right one-third windowful (without moving cursor)	Yes

Note: Left and right scrolling works only when line lengths exceed available window display space.

Tip **The mouse scrolling techniques fully distinguish between moving the cursor and scrolling.**

When you use the mouse scrolling techniques, listed in table 3.4, notice that the cursor stays put—in fact, it may even scroll off the screen, out of view. You have to click a new cursor location after scrolling with the mouse.

Table 3.4
Mouse Scrolling Techniques

Pointer location	Button	Effect
Left scroll bar	Left	Scrolls screen up
Left scroll bar	Right	Scrolls screen down
Bottom scroll bar	Left	Scrolls screen left
Bottom scroll bar	Right	Scrolls screen right

Note: All mouse scrolling techniques involving window borders do not work when the screen borders field in the Options menu is set to No. Left and right techniques work only when line lengths exceed available window display space.

To use the mouse scrolling techniques, move the pointer to the left (vertical) or bottom (horizontal) scroll bar (again see fig. 3.4), and wait for the mouse to change to a shape showing two arrows. Then click the left or right button.

The mouse scrolling techniques allow you to control the amount of the screen that scrolls. If you position the pointer near the top of the scroll bar, for instance, Word scrolls only part of the screen. If you position the pointer farther down the scroll bar, Word scrolls farther.

Trap **If you turn off the screen border, you cannot use the mouse to scroll.**

If you have only one window on the screen and have selected the No option for screen borders in the Options menu, you have disabled the mouse scrolling techniques. To recover them, select the Yes option.

Trap **The cursor disappears when you scroll with the mouse.**

Unlike the keyboard scrolling commands, the mouse scrolling techniques do not move the cursor, and it may scroll out of view. To reposition the cursor in the text you see, just click the mouse pointer anywhere in the document area.

Trap **After scrolling, you start typing, but the screen display jumps back to your preceding location in the document.**

You have scrolled with the mouse and left the cursor behind. After scrolling with the mouse, be sure to click a new cursor position somewhere in the text you see. Otherwise, what you type appears in the midst of text you have already created.

Trick **Use the mouse to scroll to text elsewhere in the document, but return to the place you're editing in one keystroke.**

Here's a trick that turns the preceding trap into an asset. Sometimes you want to scroll from where you're working in order to check some material elsewhere in your document. Use the mouse to scroll, leaving the cursor where it is. When you're ready to return to where you were, press the right- or left-arrow key. Word jumps back to your point of departure, no matter how far you have scrolled.

Trick **"Thumb" to a new position by moving to the vertical scroll bar (left window border) and clicking both buttons.**

The vertical scroll bar displays a small horizontal mark about the size of a hyphen. This mark, the *thumb*, shows the window's present position relative to the beginning and end of the document. If the window shows text near the beginning of the document, the thumb is near the top of the scroll bar; if the window is near the end, the thumb is near the bottom. You can reposition the thumb—and in so doing, reposition the window relative to the beginning and end of the document—by clicking the vertical scroll bar with both buttons.

The term *thumb* comes from the way you open a big dictionary—you stick your thumb within the pages at the approximate position you want and open the book. Similarly, thumbing with the mouse isn't too accurate (you rarely see exactly the window you want), but it's a fast way to move to a general area of a document. Once you're there, you can page up or down to find the specific text you need.

Trick **If you don't have a mouse, create macros to emulate WordStar cursor-movement commands.**

If you're a good typist, and you don't have a mouse, you may think that using the arrow and function keys to move the cursor is a cumbersome method—you must take your fingers off their positions and your eyes off the screen. If you feel this way, try the macros listed in table 3.5. They emulate the good old tried-and-true WordStar keyboard commands for cursor movement. Arranged like a diamond within reach of the fingers of your left hand as it presses the Ctrl key, these commands let you move the cursor without repositioning your hands on the keyboard (or taking your eyes off your work). Because so many programs emulate the WordStar keyboard, chances are you're already familiar with some or all of these commands. For information on creating these macros, see Chapter 13.

Table 3.5
Macros To Emulate WordStar Cursor and Scrolling Commands

Macro name	Macro code
character_left.mac (Ctrl-S)	\<left\>
character_right.mac (Ctrl-D)	\<right\>
word_left.mac (Ctrl-A)	\<f7\>
word_right.mac (Ctrl-F)	\<f8\>
line_up.mac (Ctrl-E)	\<up\>
line_down.mac (Ctrl-X)	\<down\>
scroll_up.mac (Ctrl-Z)	\<scrolllock\>\<up\>\<scrolllock\>
scroll_down.mac (Ctrl-W)	\<scrolllock\>\<down\>\<scrolllock\>
screen_up.mac (Ctrl-C)	\<pgup\>
screen_down.mac (Ctrl-R)	\<pgdn\>

Tip **The Jump Page command is much more useful in Version 5.**

Now that Word paginates your document actively as you write and edit, the page number indicator always shows the correct page number. For this reason, you can use the **J**ump **P**age command to move quickly in your document. To use this command, press Esc to bring up the edit menu. Then type *jp* and type in the number field the page number you want. Alternatively, use the Alt-F5 keyboard shortcut to bring up the number field directly.

Using Commands

Word's command menus provide an easy way to give commands without memorizing dozens of keyboard commands or function key combinations. That's why Word is much easier to learn than the many programs that rely heavily on keyboard commands rather than menus. Once you have learned the program, however, using keyboard commands is more convenient than using menus—keyboard commands are significantly faster. For that reason, Word comes equipped with many keyboard shortcuts for popular commands. And with Word's macro capabilities, you can reconfigure the keyboard to your heart's content, placing the commands you use most often in keyboard shortcuts of your own devising.

Learning how to take advantage of this command system is the route to high productivity with Word. And because your goal is to expand Word's keyboard flexibility by writing macros for common commands, you would be wise to choose one command technique above others. In this technique, you give commands by typing the capitalized letters in a command's name, such as typing *fc* for **F**ormat **C**haracter or *ld* for **L**ibrary **D**ocument-retrieval. (Throughout this book, when you are told to carry out a command, these letters have been not only capitalized but also boldfaced so that you can see them plainly.) This technique is discussed in the section on "Choosing Commands." And as you learn in Chapter 13, you use this method when you include commands in macros. If you begin learning to give commands this way now, you will develop skills and knowledge that you can incorporate directly into your macros.

The only exception to this advice involves the mouse. Several mouse techniques involve speedy ways to choose and carry out commands. Unfortunately, you cannot include mouse actions in macros, so exploring all the keyboard techniques in detail is a good idea even if you're a mouse user. But if you're using a mouse, be sure to investigate the mouse techniques too.

Tip **Explore and master the pathways of Word's commands.**

As command menus go, Word's edit menu—the one you see on Word's initial display screen—isn't as awe-inspiring as those found in many programs, in which you encounter literally hundreds of commands hidden here and there on circuitous, confusing pathways. You need to understand, though, that Word's commands fall into four different categories.

❏ Some commands present no submenus after you choose the command. Instead, the program presents you immediately with a command field requiring your response (as in the Copy, Delete, and Insert commands) or carries out the command's function immediately (as in the Quit and Undo commands).

❏ Other commands produce a submenu of options that refine the initial command. For example, the Window command's submenu, shown in figure 3.5, allows you to specify what you want to do with a window. To choose one of these options, either highlight it with the arrow key, press the capitalized letter (such as *S* in Split), or click the option with the left mouse button.

```
WINDOW: Split Close Move

Press capital letter of the menu item you want
Pg1 Co1              {}              ?              Microsoft Word
```

Fig. 3.5.

The Window menu.

❏ Still other commands produce a command menu (see fig. 3.6), which contains one or more *command fields*, or areas where you make choices about specific aspects of the command. Command fields fall into two categories: multiple-choice fields, in which you choose from a list of options; and text fields, in which you type a response.

```
FORMAT CHARACTER bold: Yes No      italic: Yes(No)      underline: Yes(No)
        strikethrough: Yes(No)     uppercase: Yes(No)   small caps: Yes(No)
        double underline: Yes(No)  position:(Normal)Superscript Subscript
        font name: Courier         font size: 12        font color: Black
        hidden: Yes(No)
Select option
Pg1 Co1              {}              ?              Microsoft Word
```

Fig. 3.6.

The Format Character menu.

❑ Choosing the fourth type of command replaces both the document area and the menu with a new window and menu (see fig. 3.7). This event can be disconcerting to first-time Word users. If you accidentally choose one of these commands—**G**allery, **H**elp, **L**ibrary **S**pell, **L**ibrary **T**hesaurus, **L**ibrary **D**ocument-retrieval, or **P**rint pre**V**iew—don't worry. Your document isn't lost. Just press Esc to exit the Thesaurus, or choose the **E**xit command from the command menu to exit the other commands.

Fig. 3.7.

The new screen displayed by the Gallery command.

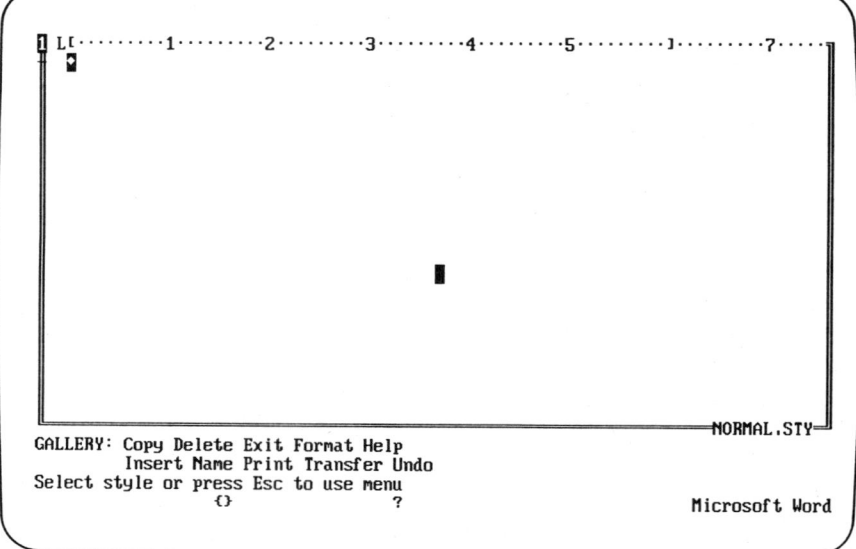

```
NORMAL.STY

GALLERY: Copy Delete Exit Format Help
         Insert Name Print Transfer Undo
Select style or press Esc to use menu
              {}              ?                    Microsoft Word
```

Tip   To find out what a command does, highlight it with the arrow keys and look at the message line.

If you highlight the **W**indow command, for instance, the message line reads Opens, closes, resizes, and moves windows. If you choose **W**indow and then highlight **M**ove on the submenu, the message line reads Resizes specified window. If you choose **M**ove, the message line prompts you to Enter number as you activate each of the command's three options.

Tip   You should note an important difference between choosing a command and carrying it out.

To *choose* a command means to select an option from a command menu or submenu so that you can make further choices. To *carry out* a command means to confirm the choices you have made and then return to your work. You can choose commands in several ways, as described in the next section. To carry out a command after choosing options, just press Enter or click the command name. To cancel the options you have chosen without carrying them out, just press Esc or click both mouse buttons.

Trick **Press Ctrl-Esc to return to the top level of the command menu.**

If you choose the wrong command and need to try again, press Ctrl-Esc instead of returning to the edit mode (by pressing Esc) and then again entering the command mode. Ctrl-Esc always moves the highlight to the first level of the edit menu.

Choosing Commands

Trick **Quickly select options in a command menu or submenu by typing the code letter of the command.**

If you prefer, you can fuss with the arrow keys, the Tab key, the space bar, and the Backspace key to choose options from menus and submenus, and you can press Enter to move to the next command level. But by far the fastest way to choose commands is to press the command's capitalized letter or letters, as in **Q**uit or **F**ormat. Word selects the option from the menu and executes it without your having to press Enter or click the mouse, thus saving you keystrokes. You see the submenu (or get results) immediately.

For added speed, enter all the codes for subcommands at the same time so that you don't have to wait for submenus to be displayed. For example, to choose **F**ormat **D**ivision **M**argins, press Esc and then type *fdm*. Word immediately displays the Format Division Margins menu.

On some menus, more than one option may begin with the same letter. For this reason, sometimes the capitalized letter isn't the first letter. For instance, you must type *fe* to use the **F**ormat s**E**arch command.

Trap **You cannot select the names of most command fields by typing the field's first letter.**

In most command menus, the names of command fields aren't capitalized—which means that you cannot select them by typing the first letter. For example, the font field of the **F**ormat **C**haracter command isn't capitalized. To choose the font field, you can type *fc* to bring up the Format Character menu, but you must then use the mouse, the Tab key, or the arrow keys to highlight the font field. You must do the same when you're writing macros.

Microsoft didn't set up Word this way just to be cruel. Most command menus include so many options that two, three, or more begin with the same letter. In the Options menu, 11 options begin with the letter s. In such situations, the first letter doesn't distinguish among options, and using other letters would produce a welter of un-mnemonic codes.

Tip   **Many mouse users like to use the capital-letter technique to choose a command and then click the appropriate option with the mouse.**

This combination technique gets around the limitation just mentioned and eliminates fussing with the arrow keys.

Trick   **Learn the function keys that provide shortcut routes to command fields embedded in lengthy command menus.**

Some commands present menus with many options. And once you get to the command menu, you may have many fields from which to choose. If you don't have a mouse, you have to use the arrow keys, the Tab key, or Shift-Tab to select the command field you want. (These options are discussed in detail in this chapter's section titled "Working with Command Menus and Submenus.") If you're using the keyboard, then, you should explore the function keys that provide shortcut routes to command fields.

Because selecting options from lengthy menus can be a tedious job, Word's function-key assignments include several that take you directly to an oft-used but deeply buried command field. Table 3.6 lists these function keys.

Table 3.6
Function-Key Shortcuts to Frequently Used Command Fields

Shortcut	Task
Alt-F1	Set tab (displays position field in Format Tab Set menu)
Shift-F2	Toggle outline edit mode on/off (toggles setting in show outline field of Options menu)
Alt-F4	Show layout (toggles setting in show layout field of Options menu)

Table 3.6—Continued

Shortcut	Task
Alt-F5	Go to page (displays number field in Jump Page menu)
Ctrl-F7	Load file (displays filename field of Transfer Load menu)
Alt-F7	Show line breaks (toggles setting in show line breaks field of Options menu)
Alt-F8	Name font (displays font field of Format Character menu)
Alt-F9	Toggle display mode (toggles between last two options chosen in the display mode field of the Options menu)
Alt-F10	Record style (displays Format Style Record menu)

Tip **Learn the function keys that execute commands immediately.**

Some function keys carry out commands immediately, bypassing submenus and command fields. Table 3.7 lists these keys. Be sure to explore them. Although memorizing all of them wouldn't pay, some—especially the commands for Spell, Thesaurus, saving, and printing—are handy.

Tip **Some function key commands are not duplicated by commands you choose from command menus.**

Word's documentation creates the impression that the program's commands are all contained in command menus, but that impression is not accurate. Many function-key commands simply offer keyboard shortcuts for menu commands. But other function keys, such as F2, perform functions not found in the command menus. (F2 performs calculations on selected numbers.) And some of these commands, such as the function keys for manipulating windows and selecting text, are essential for users who do not have a mouse. See table 3.8, later in this section, for a list of the function-key assignments for Word 5.

Trick **Repeat a command by pressing F4.**

Few Word users take advantage of this trick, probably because its effects are difficult to predict unless you have explored what it does. F4 simply repeats whatever you just did. If you just finished typing a unit of text, pressing F4 repeats what you have just typed, starting

Table 3.7
Function Keys That Carry Out Commands Directly

Key	Task
Shift-F1	Same as choosing Undo
Ctrl-F2	Format selected paragraph as header
Alt-F2	Format selected paragraph as footer
Alt-F3	Copy selection to the scrap
Shift-F4	Repeat last Search or Replace command, using the same settings
Ctrl-F6	Same as choosing Library Spell
Alt-F6	Same as choosing Library Thesaurus
Ctrl-F8	Print, using current options in the Print Options menu
Ctrl-F9	Preview document formatting in print preview mode
Ctrl-F10	Save document, using the current file name
Ctrl-F10	Same as choosing Transfer Save

from the last command you issued or the last place you moved the cursor. If the last thing you did was to give a command (a formatting command, for instance), Word repeats the command, just the way you gave it.

Not every command is repeated this way. The repeatable commands are Copy, Delete, Format, Insert, Library Autosort, Library Hyphenate, Library Index, Library Table, Gallery Name, Transfer Merge, and Undo. If you want to insert some text from the scrap throughout a document, for instance, use the Insert command the first time, and then press F4 repeatedly.

Note: You can move the cursor between presses of F4, but if you stop and enter some text, you get text the next time you press F4.

Trap **Word 5's function-key assignments are slightly different from those of Word 4.**

Word 4 users take note. Three function-key assignments have changed in Word 5:

❑ Ctrl-F4, which formerly updated the list in the library document-retrieval mode, now toggles a selection between upper- and lowercase letters.

❑ Alt-F4, which used to display the Format Division Margins menu, now toggles the show layout mode on and off.

❑ Ctrl-F9, which used to choose the Print Repaginate command, now sets the print preview mode in motion.

You learn more about these new function-key assignments in subsequent chapters. For now, just note that the assignments have changed. Table 3.8 lists Word 5's function-key assignments, with the new assignments shown in boldface type.

Table 3.8
Function-Key Assignments for Word 5

	Key Alone	*With Shift*	*With Ctrl*	*With Alt*
F1	Next window	Undo	Zoom window	Set tabs
F2	Calculate	Outline edit	Header	Footer
F3	Glossary	Record macro	Step macro	Copy to scrap
F4	Repeat edit	Repeat search	Toggle case	Show layout
F5	Overtype	Outline organize	Line draw	Go to page
F6	Ext. select	Column select	Thesaurus	Spell
F7	Word left	Sentence left	Load	Show line breaks
F8	Word right	Sentence right	Print	Select font
F9	Prev. para.	Current line	Print preView	Toggle display
F10	Next para.	Whole document	Save	Record style

Tip **Choose commands quickly with the mouse.**

When you choose a command with the mouse, you simply point to the command name you want and click the left button. You don't need to press Esc.

Trick **The right mouse button chooses an option and carries it out at the same time.**

If you point to an option and click the left mouse button, you select the option and move to the next level of the command. If you press the right mouse button when pointing to an option, however, you not only select it and move to the next level, but you also carry out the command. For example, if you have already saved a file and given it a file name, just right-click the Save option in the Transfer submenu to save the document immediately.

Many command submenus are designed with this technique in mind: the first option is the one you carry out when you right-click the command. See table 3.9 for a survey of the effects of right-clicking command names in submenus.

Table 3.9
Effect of Clicking the Right Mouse Button
on Command Names

Command	Effect
Copy	Copies selected text to scrap
Delete	Deletes selected text to scrap
Format	Opens the Format Character menu
Insert	Inserts any text stored in scrap
Jump	Selects Jump Page and prompts for number of destination page
Library	Selects Library Autosort
Print	Selects Print Printer and starts printing immediately
Transfer	Selects Transfer Load and prompts for name of file to load
Window	Selects Window Split Horizontal and prompts for line number at which to split window

Working with Command Menus and Submenus

When a command (such as Format or Window) produces a submenu or a command menu, you may choose submenu options in several ways:

- [ ] To choose an item from a submenu, left-click the item or type the item's capitalized letter.

- [ ] In a command menu, press the arrow keys to select the field, or move to the field you want and then click the left mouse button. You also can press the Tab key to move forward and down from field to field; press Shift-Tab to move backward and up.

- [ ] In a list of options, *parentheses* show the option currently selected. You can change the selected option by highlighting the field and typing another option's capitalized letter. You also can toggle among the options by pressing the space bar to toggle right or Backspace to toggle left.

- [ ] In some text fields, Word enters a highlighted *proposed response*; the program assumes that you're most likely to make this response. For instance, when you're saving a document you have already named, Word presents as the proposed response the file name you used. To accept the proposed response, just execute the command. If you want to change the response, just select the field and start typing. The proposed response disappears automatically.

- [ ] When you finish choosing options in a command menu, press Enter or click the command name with the left button to carry out the command. To abandon your choices, just press Esc or click both buttons.

Tip **Press F1 to enter in text fields information from a list of choices.**

Most of Word's command menu options are multiple choice. But you're not on your own when completing text fields. If the message Press F1 to select from list is displayed on-screen, you can press F1 for a list of currently available options.

Using this feature is usually a good idea, for several reasons. First, you don't have to type the text yourself. Once the list appears, you use the arrow keys or the mouse to select the option you want. And after you right-click your choice or press Enter, Word places your selection in the text field. Second, the F1 list shows you the current legal options for this field. You don't have to remember what these options are or how to spell them correctly. If you let Word insert the options from the list, you remove the chance of choosing the wrong option or misspelling the option's name.

For example, to select a font from a list of available choices, choose **F**ormat **C**haracter, highlight the font name field, and press F1. Word clears the screen and displays a list similar to the one in figure 3.8. (The list varies, depending on the printer you selected with the **P**rint **O**ptions command, which is discussed in the section called "Choosing Printing Options," in Chapter 11.) The list shown is the one you see if you choose the PostScript® printer driver. You then use the direction keys to highlight the font you want, and press Tab or Enter to enter the selected font into the font name field.

Fig. 3.8.

List produced by pressing F1 in font name field of Format Character menu (PostScript printer driver).

```
┌─────────────────────────────────────────────────────────────────┐
│                                                                   │
│   Courier (modern a)            Helvetica (modern i)              │
│   AvantGarde (modern j)         HelveticaNarrow (modern k)        │
│   Bookman (roman a)             Times-Roman (roman i)             │
│   NewCentSchlbk (roman j)       Palatino (roman k)                │
│   ZapfChancery (decor c)        Symbol (symbol a)                 │
│   LineDraw (symbol b)           ZapfDingbats (symbol e)           │
│                                                                   │
│                                                                   │
│                                                                   │
│                                                                   │
│                                                                   │
│                                                                   │
│   FORMAT CHARACTER bold: Yes(No)      italic: Yes(No)      underline: Yes(No) │
│      strikethrough: Yes(No)      uppercase: Yes(No)     small caps: Yes(No)   │
│      double underline: Yes(No)   position:(Normal)Superscript Subscript       │
│      font name: Courier          font size: 12         font color: Black      │
│      hidden: Yes(No)                                                          │
│   Enter font name or press F1 to select from list                            │
│   Pg1 Li1 Co1        {Use·th...ormats} ?                                      │
│                                                      Microsoft Word           │
└─────────────────────────────────────────────────────────────────┘
```

Trick **Press the right mouse button in a text field to see the list.**

Normally, pressing the right button executes an option. If you see the message Press F1 to see a list of options, however, clicking the right button is the same as pressing F1.

Trap **If you see the message** List is empty, **you are probably in the wrong drive or directory.**

This message doesn't mean that the file or option you want is missing. Word may not be able to find the file because the program is looking in the wrong drive or directory. Word always searches the default directory first—the directory from which you started Word (or if you used the Transfer Options command, the directory you typed in the setup field).

Trick **To tell Word to search other drives or directories after you press F1, highlight the drive or directory name and press F1 again.**

This feature is one of those wonderful—seemingly minor—new characteristics of Word 5 that make the program so much easier to use. With previous versions, if you got the message List is empty after you pressed F1, you had to remember the names of other directories, use the command all over again, type the directory name in the text field, and press F1 again.

Now Word displays directory and drive names in addition to file names (see fig. 3.9). The drive and directory names are enclosed in brackets in order to distinguish these names from options you enter directly. To explore the contents of these drives or directories, you simply highlight the drive or directory name and press F1 again—and again, if necessary. By repeating this process, you can explore an entire hard disk without exiting the command or having to remember a single directory name.

Trick **To move to the parent directory, choose the** [..] **symbol from the F1 file list.**

In DOS, the symbol .. (two periods) represents the parent directory. If your directory path is C:\MSWORD\REPORTS, for example, and the current directory is REPORTS, the parent directory is MSWORD. To explore a hard disk by using an F1 list, choose the [..] symbol to exit a subdirectory, and keep choosing that symbol until you reach the root directory. Then you see all the subdirectory names immediately beneath the root directory's level.

Trick **Edit the response you have made in a text field (or Word's proposed response) by pressing F9 or F10.**

Sometimes you don't realize that you have made a mistake typing something in a text field until you have carried out the command. You hear a beep and see an error message, and the command menu stays

Fig. 3.9.

Choosing drives
and directories
from an F1 list.

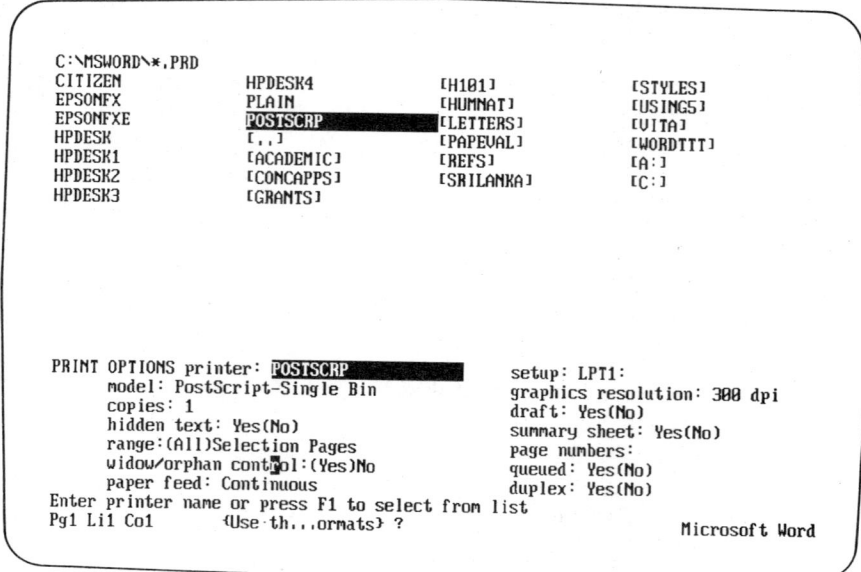

```
C:\MSWORD\*.PRD
CITIZEN          HPDESK4        [H101]          [STYLES]
EPSONFX          PLAIN          [HUMNAT]        [USINGS]
EPSONFXE         POSTSCRP       [LETTERS]       [VITA]
HPDESK           [..]           [PAPEVAL]       [WORDTTT]
HPDESK1          [ACADEMIC]     [REFS]          [A:]
HPDESK2          [CONCAPPS]     [SRILANKA]      [C:]
HPDESK3          [GRANTS]




PRINT OPTIONS printer: POSTSCRP            setup: LPT1:
          model: PostScript-Single Bin     graphics resolution: 300 dpi
          copies: 1                        draft: Yes(No)
          hidden text: Yes(No)             summary sheet: Yes(No)
          range:(All)Selection Pages       page numbers:
          widow/orphan control:(Yes)No     queued: Yes(No)
          paper feed: Continuous           duplex: Yes(No)
Enter printer name or press F1 to select from list
Pg1 Li1 Co1        {Use th...ormats} ?                Microsoft Word
```

on-screen—but your entry is highlighted. The problem is that if you try
to correct the entry by pressing the arrow keys, the cursor goes
hopping off to some other field. And if you type just one letter, the
whole selection disappears—which can be irritating if you have just
typed a long directory name.

Fortunately, Word offers a way to correct an error after the program
highlights it. Just press F9 or F10, whose functions change in
command menus. Pressing F9 moves the cursor to the first character
of the field; then each press of F10 moves the cursor one character to
the right. Similarly, when the contents of the entire text field are
highlighted, pressing F10 moves the cursor to the last character; then
each press of F9 moves the cursor one character to the left. After
pressing one of these keys, you can edit the text by using the
Backspace and Del keys, without making the entry disappear.

Trick   Use F7 and F8 to select words in a text field.

You can use the F7 and F8 keys to select a word in an option's text
field, just as in a document. When used in a command field, these
keys, like F9 and F10, enable you to edit a highlighted response
without making it disappear. The F7 key selects the word to the left of
the highlight, and the F8 key selects the word to the right.

Tip **Word tells you what kind of response you should make in a field.**

When you select a command field from a command menu, Word displays a message that tells you what kind of response you should make. In a multiple-choice command field, for instance, Word displays the message Select option on the message line. In a field that requires you to type a measurement, you see the message Enter measurement.

The messages are often less cryptic than these and merit your attention. For example, in the cursor speed command field from the Options menu, you're instructed to Enter a number from 0 to 9.

Here are some other messages you may see:

    Enter drive or directory
    Enter filename or press F1 to select from list
    Enter font name or select from list

If you see the message Command field requires response, you cannot carry out the command until you type something in the text field.

Getting Help

Word 5 comes equipped with what is probably the best on-screen help utility available for any word processing program. Like the best of its peers, the help program is context-sensitive, meaning that you see information relevant to what you're doing when you ask for help. What's even more impressive, however, is the Tutorial program, which draws a link between context-sensitive help and the lessons on the Learning Word disks. If you're having trouble with a Word command, operation, or feature, you can pause and take a lesson; then you can resume writing or editing. You don't even have to leave your document. You can ask for help in either the edit or the command mode.

Trick **To get "Quick Help" on any command or command field, highlight the command or field and press Alt-H.**

If you press Alt-H while the cursor is positioned in the font name field of the Format Character menu, for instance, Word displays the help screen shown in figure 3.10.

Fig. 3.10.

Help for the
Format Character
command.

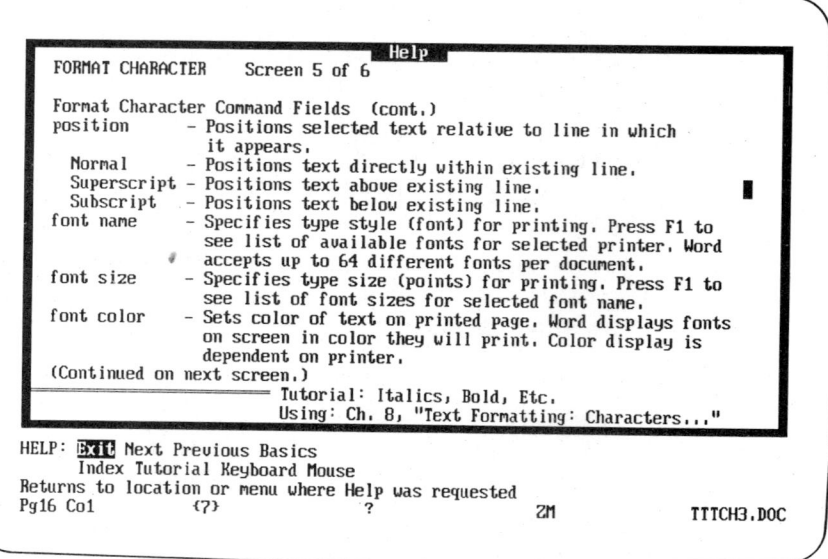

```
┌─────────────────────────────────────────────────────────────┐
│                              ┌─────┐                          │
│                              │Help │                          │
│  FORMAT CHARACTER      Screen 5 of 6                          │
│                                                               │
│  Format Character Command Fields  (cont.)                     │
│  position         - Positions selected text relative to line in which │
│                     it appears.                               │
│    Normal         - Positions text directly within existing line. │
│  Superscript  - Positions text above existing line.           │
│    Subscript      - Positions text below existing line.       │
│  font name        - Specifies type style (font) for printing. Press F1 to │
│                     see list of available fonts for selected printer. Word │
│                     accepts up to 64 different fonts per document. │
│  font size        - Specifies type size (points) for printing. Press F1 to │
│                     see list of font sizes for selected font name. │
│  font color       - Sets color of text on printed page. Word displays fonts │
│                     on screen in color they will print. Color display is │
│                     dependent on printer.                     │
│  (Continued on next screen.)                                  │
│  ═══════════════════════════ Tutorial: Italics, Bold, Etc.   │
│                              Using: Ch. 8, "Text Formatting: Characters..." │
└─────────────────────────────────────────────────────────────┘
  HELP: Exit Next Previous Basics
        Index Tutorial Keyboard Mouse
  Returns to location or menu where Help was requested
  Pg16 Co1          {?}              ?            2M        TTTCH3.DOC
```

Trick **Access help directly for quick assistance with keyboard commands.**

If you don't have your keyboard reference chart handy, use the **H**elp command in the edit menu and then choose the **K**eyboard option. The first screen shows Word's function-key assignments. Subsequent screens show all preset keyboard commands, including character and paragraph formatting key codes.

Tip **The help index is extremely comprehensive—just about every aspect of the program is mentioned.**

You can use this index to locate information you need rapidly. To use the help index, choose the **H**elp command from the edit menu and then choose **I**ndex from the submenu (see fig. 3.11).

Trick **Access help quickly by clicking the question mark on the status line.**

If you have a mouse, Word displays a question mark on the status line. If you need help with a command or command option, highlight the command name or option and left-click the question mark.

Align Left	Glossaries	Repaginate
Align Right	Graphics	Repeat
Annotations	Headers	Replace
ASCII file	Hidden text	Revision marks
Autosave	Hyphens	Ruler
Backup	Indent	Running heads
Block	Index	Save
Bold	Italics	Screen borders
Bookmarks	Jump	Search
Bulleted list	Justify	Select text
Calculate	Keyboard	Show layout
Center	Leader character	Side by side
Colors	Line break	Small caps
Columns	Line drawing	Sort
Commands	Line spacing	Speed keys
Copy	Load document	Spell
Cross referencing	Macros	Spreadsheet link
Delete	Mailing labels	Strikethrough
Division break	Margins	Style sheets

HELP INDEX: Align Left

Select Help topic; press PgDn for more topics
Pg26 Co37   {ip}   ?   2M   TTTCH3.DOC

Fig. 3.11.

Two screens of
the help index.

Colors	Line break	Small caps
Columns	Line drawing	Sort
Commands	Line spacing	Speed keys
Copy	Load document	Spell
Cross referencing	Macros	Spreadsheet link
Delete	Mailing labels	Strikethrough
Division break	Margins	Style sheets
Doc retrieval	Move text	Sub/Superscript
DOS, OS/2 and back	Mouse	Summary sheets
Double Space	Networks	Table of Contents
File formats	Numbering	Tables
Font	Outline	Tabs
Footers	Overtype	Text/Graphics mode
Footnotes	Page break	Thesaurus
Form letters	Position frame	Toggle case
Formatting	Printing	Underlining
Formatting-fast	Print Merge	Undo edit
Function Keys	Print Preview	Uppercase
Gallery	Quit	Windows

HELP INDEX: Gallery

Select Help topic; press PgDn for more topics
Pg26 Co37   {ip}   ?   2M   TTTCH3.DOC

Tip **Use the Tutorial program if you're really stuck and need a lesson.**

To use Tutorial help, highlight the command name or command option that's giving you trouble, and press Alt-H (or click the question mark). When the Quick Help screen appears, choose the Tutorial option from the help menu.

Chapter Summary

This chapter helped you to become oriented in the program by introducing you to all the screen features and status line codes. Learning about the features of the display screen is essential for productive writing with Word 5. In particular, you should be able to recognize the key indicator codes and know which keys you press to exit these modes (in case you enter them accidentally).

You also learned in this chapter about the cursor-movement keys and how to use those keys also for scrolling (with Scroll Lock on). You learned the difference between scrolling with the keys and scrolling with the mouse. (Remember that with the mouse you leave the cursor behind, so the screen may pop back when you enter more text.)

This chapter explained the various ways you can choose commands, and discussed the difference between choosing and carrying out commands. You learned that some function-key shortcuts give you fast ways to go directly to command options. And if you get stuck, you now know how to get help from Word 5's context-sensitive help program.

Now that you know how to find your way around Word 5, you're ready to customize the program for your own preferences and styles. To learn how, move on to Chapter 4.

4

Customizing Word 5: The Display Screen and Operating Characteristics

A terrific new feature of Word 5 is the much-improved Options menu. This menu combines the options formerly distributed between the Window Options and the old Options command menus. With this single menu, you can choose the display options and operating characteristics you want. Discussed here are the options that high-productivity Word users choose most often to speed and enhance their work. You also find in this section several Options macros that are designed to add even more functionality and speed to this impressive program.

This chapter discusses the following topics:

❑ Understanding the Options command

❑ Using the window options

❑ Using the general options

Understanding the Options Command

Conveniently grouped in a single menu, Word's options are now much easier to choose. Even so, you can lose your choices if you don't understand how Word saves them. That loss is no tragedy—you can restore your choices simply by making them again—but a little knowledge will help you avoid this problem.

79

Tip **The choices you make in the Options menu automatically become the program defaults the next time you use the program.**

When you use the **Q**uit command, Word creates or updates a file called MW.INI, which is always stored in the WORD program directory. This file stores (among other things) the choices made in the Options menu (see fig. 4.1). Whatever choices you make in this menu become the new program defaults, provided you have used the **Q**uit command to exit the program. The only exceptions are WINDOW OPTIONS choices you make for windows other than window 1. If you exit Word without choosing Quit (for instance, by simply turning off your computer while Word is running), your Options choices are not saved.

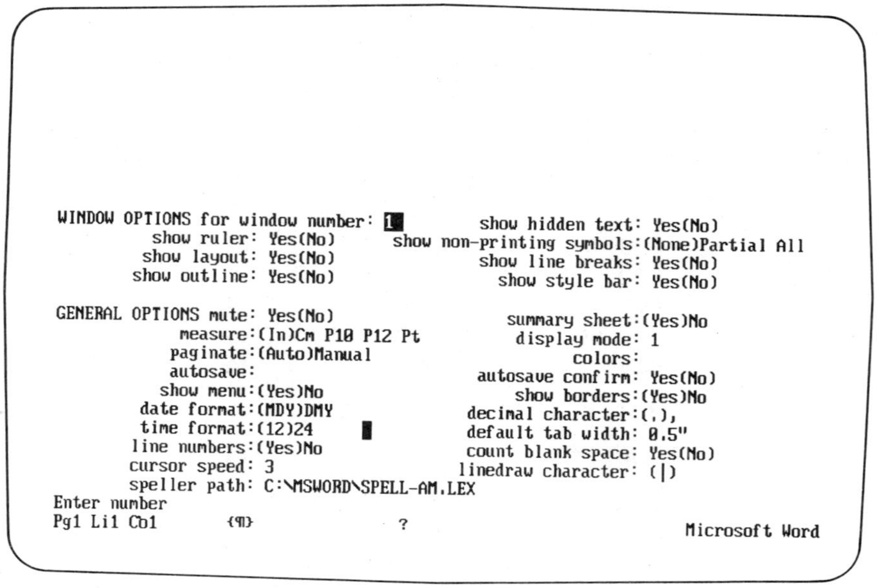

Fig. 4.1.

The Options command menu.

```
WINDOW OPTIONS for window number: 1        show hidden text: Yes(No)
         show ruler: Yes(No)    show non-printing symbols:(None)Partial All
        show layout: Yes(No)          show line breaks: Yes(No)
       show outline: Yes(No)          show style bar: Yes(No)

GENERAL OPTIONS mute: Yes(No)              summary sheet:(Yes)No
          measure:(In)Cm P10 P12 Pt        display mode: 1
         paginate:(Auto)Manual                   colors:
         autosave:                     autosave confirm: Yes(No)
        show menu:(Yes)No                 show borders:(Yes)No
      date format:(MDY)DMY             decimal character:(.),
      time format:(12)24       █       default tab width: 0.5"
     line numbers:(Yes)No               count blank space: Yes(No)
     cursor speed: 3                   linedraw character: (|)
     speller path: C:\MSWORD\SPELL-AM.LEX
Enter number
Pg1 Li1 Co1          {¶}              ?                    Microsoft Word
```

Trap **If you accidentally delete the MW.INI file or fail to copy it when reorganizing a hard disk, you lose your Options choices.**

Deleting the MW.INI file isn't a major disaster by any means; Word simply returns to its default settings. You easily can make the choices again with a few clicks in the Options menu.

Tip **The** WINDOW OPTIONS **command fields affect one window; the** GENERAL OPTIONS **command fields affect every document.**

The command fields grouped under the WINDOW OPTIONS heading in the Options menu affect only the window whose number appears in the for window number field. Because these options affect only one window at a time, this command gives you flexibility to set up multiple windows in different ways. When you display two windows on one document, for example, one can show an outline and the other can show the text.

When you make choices in the WINDOW OPTIONS fields for window 1 and quit Word, window 1 shows these choices the next time you start the program. However, Word does not save the choices made for window 2 and other windows.

The command fields grouped under GENERAL OPTIONS affect every document.

Using the Window Options

This section explains more about the fields affecting the display of individual windows. Options set for window 1 are saved as default options for window 1; options set for other windows are not saved for future sessions.

Trick **Display hidden text, but create a macro to hide text at a keystroke.**

Text formatted as hidden text can be displayed or hidden on the screen and printed or omitted from printouts. You can use hidden text to write comments to yourself or to collaborators. Hidden text also figures prominently in several advanced Word application techniques. Hidden text is used, for instance, to include in your document commands that link it to graphics files. You create hidden text by formatting with the Alt-E keyboard command or the Yes option in the hidden field of the Format Character command menu.

Normally, displaying hidden text is a good idea so that you can read the comments or check whether you have entered the commands properly. So choose the Yes option in the show hidden text field of the Options menu.

Having a keyboard command to toggle the hidden text display on and off is nice, however. Following is a macro that does the job:

```
«SET echo = "on"»
<ctrl esc>o<down 8>
Y<up 8><right>
«IF field = "Yes"»
«MESSAGE Hidden text display switched off»
«ENDIF»
«IF field = "No"»
«MESSAGE Hidden text display switched on»
«ENDIF»
«SET echo = "off"»
<space><left><down 8>N<enter>
```

To create and use this macro, follow the instructions in Chapter 13, "Macros." Save the macro with the macro name options_hidden.macˆ<ctrl o>h.

Trick **Display the ruler, which has many useful functions, but create a macro to toggle the ruler on and off if you find it distracting.**

Version 5's ruler is more functional than the rulers of previous versions of Word. As in previous versions, the ruler continues to show tab stops and paragraph indents. As you learn in Chapter 6, however, you now can use the mouse to format paragraphs and set tabs by manipulating the ruler directly, without using the Format Paragraph or Format Tab Set commands. Once you learn how easily you can use these features, you will want to display the ruler frequently.

Still, some users may find the ruler distracting. Following is a macro that toggles the ruler display on and off at a keystroke:

```
«SET echo = "off"»
<esc>o<down><space><enter>
```

To create and use this macro, follow the instructions in Chapter 13, "Macros." Save the macro using the macro name options_ruler.macˆ<ctrl o>r.

Trick **Use the** Partial **option in the** show non-printing symbols **field, but create a macro to choose among all three display options.**

As you learn in Chapter 4, a good idea is to display *paragraph marks*, the marks Word inserts in your document whenever you press Enter. If you accidentally delete these marks, you may inadvertently join two paragraphs and lose formatting. To avoid deleting paragraph marks accidentally, choose the Partial or All options in the show non-printing symbols field of the Options menu.

If you choose the Partial option, Word displays symbols showing where you press Enter (paragraph marks), Ctrl-Enter (newline characters), Ctrl-hyphen (optional hyphens), and Alt-E (to format hidden text). (You learn about these commands in the next chapter.) If you select the All option, Word displays all these symbols and, in addition, symbols representing Tab and space bar keystrokes (see fig. 4.2). If you choose the None option, Word hides all these symbols.

```
█ C[·······1·······2·······3·······4·······5·······6·····]·7····
                         ║NONPRINTING SYMBOLS║

    ┌────────────────────┬─────────────────┬──────────────────┐
    │ Symbol:            │ Displayed as:   │    Option:        │
    ├────────────────────┼─────────────────┼──────────────────┤
    │ Paragraph mark     │       ¶         │ Partial and All   │
    ├────────────────────┼─────────────────┼──────────────────┤
    │ Newline mark       │       ↓         │ Partial and All   │
    ├────────────────────┼─────────────────┼──────────────────┤
    │ Optional hyphen    │       -         │ Partial and All   │
    ├────────────────────┼─────────────────┼──────────────────┤
    │ Hidden text        │       •         │ Partial and All   │
    ├────────────────────┼─────────────────┼──────────────────┤
    │ Tab                │       →         │      All          │
    ├────────────────────┼─────────────────┼──────────────────┤
    │ Space              │                 │      All          │
    └────────────────────┴─────────────────┴──────────────────┘

  •                              █

Pg1 Li1 Co43      {¶}            ?                Microsoft Word
```

Fig. 4.2.

Nonprinting symbols.

Most writers prefer to use Word in the Partial setting, but occasions arise when you must see Tab and space bar keystrokes for critical formatting situations. When you're just reading your work on-screen, however, these symbols are distracting, so it's nice to hide all of them with the None option. The following macro presents a menu from which you can choose all three options.

```
«SET response = "N"»
«WHILE response = "N"»
    «ASK symbols=? Press (N)one, (P)artial, or (A)ll»
    «IF symbols="N"»
        <esc>o<right><down>«symbols»<enter>
        «SET response = "Y"»
    «ENDIF»
```

```
«IF symbols="P"»
    <esc>o<right><down>«symbols»<enter>
    «SET response = "Y"»
«ENDIF»
«IF symbols="A"»
    <esc>o<right><down>«symbols»<enter>
    «SET response = "Y"»
«ENDIF»
«ENDWHILE»
```

To create and use this macro, follow the instructions in Chapter 13, "Macros." Save the macro using the macro name options_symbols.mac^<ctrl s>r.

Tip **Because the** show layout **option slows Word considerably, toggle this mode on only when you need to view multiple columns or side-by-side paragraphs as you edit them.**

You learn more about the show layout option in Chapter 8. For now, avoid it unless you have a special reason to use it. If you do use the show layout option, toggle it on briefly by using Word 5's new Alt-F4 keyboard shortcut.

Trap **The** Yes **option in the** show line breaks **field displays line breaks as your printer prints them, but lines may run off the side of the screen.**

Word displays all type fonts and sizes using the 12-point, monospace font shown on the screen. Your printer, however, may actually print many more characters than Word can display in the 7.5-inch screen width, even if you use Word's default 6.0-inch line length. You may have formatted your text with a 10-point or smaller type size, for instance, or chosen proportional spacing, which packs more characters on a line. In any case, when you choose the Yes option in the show lines breaks field, lines may go past the right window border. If they do, you can still see them by scrolling right. But the constant scrolling back and forth slows Word's display, and following the screen as it shifts laterally is very hard on the eyes. Unless you have a special reason to see precisely where lines break, choose the No option in this field.

Trap **If you choose the** No **option in the** show line breaks **field, Word won't insert page breaks where they seem to occur on the screen.**

The page breaks you see on the screen are not necessarily accurate, and the line breaks you see on-screen aren't necessarily the ones that

Word will print. These differences can be confusing when you try to compare a printout with what you see on-screen. For example, page 17 of the printed copy may begin with "reservations," but the screen version's page 17 may begin with "advance." To see precisely where the page break is to occur, choose the Yes option in the show line breaks field. For convenient viewing, however, choose not to show the line breaks.

Trick   **Toggle the line-break option on and off with the Alt-F7 keyboard shortcut.**

Here's the answer to line-break display dilemmas: When you need to see precisely where Word breaks lines, use the Alt-F7 toggle key; then toggle the line-break display mode off by pressing Alt-F7 again.

Trick   **Use the Shift-F2 keyboard shortcut to toggle the outline edit mode on and off.**

To switch to the outline edit mode, you can choose the Yes option in the show outline field, but pressing Shift-F2 is faster. See Chapter 5 for more information on outlines.

Tip   **If you plan to use style sheets or running heads, choose the** Yes **option in the** show style bar **field.**

The *style bar* is a vertical column that appears at the left edge of the window when you set show style bar: Yes. You lose one column on the screen when the style bar displays, but as long as you use Word's default 6.0 inch length, that loss shouldn't be a problem. When you choose this option, Word displays the code of the style-sheet paragraph format currently attached to the document on the style bar. This feature does not have much significance until you create your own style sheets, but once you do, you will appreciate the style bar.

Another good reason to choose Yes in this field is that the style bar shows running head codes. These header and footer codes remind you what kind of header or footer you have chosen. See Chapter 6 for a list of these codes.

Using the General Options

The GENERAL OPTIONS group of fields in the Options menu affects all windows opened in Word. Any selections you make in this section of the Options menu are saved in MW.INI as defaults for future Word sessions. The tips, tricks, and traps in this section explain the GENERAL OPTIONS fields.

Tip   **Choose** No **in the** mute **field and** Yes **in the** summary sheet **field.**

Don't disable the beep that Word sounds when it cannot carry out a command—you need the warnings Word gives you. And don't choose the No option in the summary sheet field unless you use a two-floppy system. Doing so disables the summary sheet that appears after you save a document for the first time. Hard-disk users need the summary sheets to get full performance from Library Document-retrieval (discussed in Chapter 8).

Tip   **When you choose a measurement format for Word, the program makes that choice the default for all menus with measurement fields.**

Various Word options, such as margins and indents, are expressed in a specific unit of measure. The default unit is inches, but you can use the **O**ptions command to change the unit to centimeters, characters (10-pitch or 12-pitch), or points. When you change the default unit of measure, all fields containing a measurement are expressed automatically in that unit.

To see the effect of a change, select the Cm option in the measure field in the Options menu. Then choose the **F**ormat **P**aragraph command. As you see, the measurements are now expressed in centimeters. To change the default measurement back to inches, use the **O**ptions command again and choose the In option in the measure field.

The measurement choice you make affects the text fields of the Format and some other commands. You learn more about these commands in other chapters. Note here, though, that if you enter a measurement without including the measurement unit, Word assumes that you mean the default unit—the unit selected in the measure field of the Options command.

Tip   **Work in text mode for quick scrolling.**

The text mode, chosen by typing *1* in the display field in the Options menu, doesn't show all character formatting on-screen but is significantly faster than the graphics modes. Use the text mode for fast text entry, scrolling, and editing, and then switch to graphics mode when you need to see all your character formats.

Trap   **Alt-F9 doesn't necessarily toggle between text and graphics modes.**

In previous versions of Word, Alt-F9 toggled between text and graphics modes. In Word 5, however, Alt-F9 toggles between the two last modes chosen. Because many display adapters have three modes—one text mode and two graphics modes (including a high-resolution graphics mode)—it's by no means certain that pressing Alt-F9 toggles the screen between text and graphics modes. Alt-F9 could very well toggle the screen between the two graphics modes.

Trick **If your system displays three modes, including a high-resolution text mode, create a macro to choose among them.**

If you use a Hercules graphics adapter, you may choose between three display modes, as you discover when you press F1 in the display mode field of the Options menu. Other adapters offer four or five modes. In such cases, the Alt-F9 key toggles between the last two modes chosen—not necessarily between text and graphics modes. You can choose the mode you want simply by using the **O**ptions command. Following is a macro that presents an on-screen menu from which you can choose a display mode with a minimum of fuss and hassle.

```
«SET response = "N"»
«WHILE response = "N"»
«ASK display=? Press 1 for text, 2 for 25-line
    graphics, or 3 for high-res display»
«IF display="1"»
    «SET response = "Y"»
    <esc>o<right><down 5>«display»<enter>
«ENDIF»
«IF display="2"»
    «SET response = "Y"»
    <esc>o<right><down 5>«display»<enter>
«ENDIF»
«IF display="3"»
    «SET response = "Y"»
    <esc>o<right><down 5>«display»<enter>
«ENDIF»
«ENDWHILE»
```

To create and use this macro, follow the instructions in Chapter 13, "Macros." Save the macro using the macro name options_display^<ctrl o>d.

If your adapter uses more than three modes, you can expand this macro by adding additional «IF»....«ENDIF» statements and adding more options to the on-screen menu displayed by the «ASK» instruction.

Tip **Choose the** Auto **option in the** paginate **field so that Word displays page breaks actively.**

You can turn off active pagination if you want—and you may want to if you're writing a computer program or some other document that doesn't require pagination. Automatic pagination works smoothly and unobtrusively: Word waits until you pause and then puts in the page break at its correct location.

Word 5's automatic page breaks are especially handy when you're writing letters. With previous versions of the program, it was all too easy to write a letter that printed nothing but the complimentary close on the second page! Unless you deliberately repaginated your document with the Print Repaginate command (which still exists), you wouldn't know where the page break occurred.

Here is another reason to leave automatic pagination on: if you do, the page number indicator on the status line is actively updated and corrected, enabling you to move around in the document with the Jump Page command.

Tip **Word 5's control over color displays has been greatly enhanced.**

If you have a color monitor, you can choose precisely the colors you want for the following display features:

❏ Screen features such as the window background, command names and options, window borders, messages on the message line, and the status line. You can make command option names stand out on command menus, for instance, and disguise the status line by painting it in a faint color.

❏ Character emphases such as boldface, italic, superscript, and strike-through. You can give distinctive colors to characters formatted with two emphases, such as boldface and italic.

❏ Font sizes. This important new features gives you a way, for the first time, to see the font sizes chosen for the text displayed on the screen.

Word's preset color choices may suit you just fine. If so, use the colors option to find out what the colors mean.

To set or view colors, do the following:

1. Choose the **O**ptions command and highlight the colors field.

2. Press F1. When the color-selection list appears, highlight the feature you want to change.

3. Press PgUp or PgDn to cycle through the list of available options. Alternatively, choose a letter from the list displayed at the top of the screen.

4. Press Enter to carry out the command.

Tip **Hide the edit command menu to see a 23-line display.**

Most Word users prefer to hide the command menu (choose No in the show menu field) so that they can see more text on the screen (see fig. 4.3). The edit command menu reappears when you press Esc.

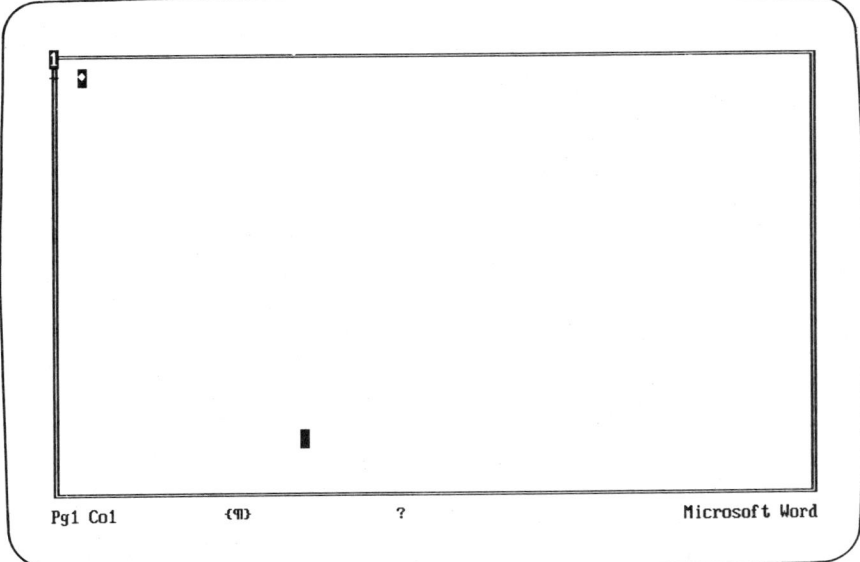

Fig. 4.3.

Enlarging the document window by hiding the command menu.

Pg1 Co1   {¶}   ?   Microsoft Word

Trap **If you use the mouse, you disable a convenient mouse feature if you hide the edit command menu.**

One advantage of using the mouse is that when the edit command menu is visible, you can just point to the command you want and click—you don't have to press Esc to activate the command menu. If you hide the menu by choosing No in the show menu field, you must press Esc before using the mouse to give commands. If you're a good typist, and if your Esc key is conveniently located, however, you may not mind this extra keystroke.

Tip **Hide the screen borders to see a 24-line display.**

Choose the No option in the screen borders field in the Options menu if you want to hide the screen borders. If you also hide the menu, a "clean screen" effect results (see fig. 4.4). After you choose this command, the borders disappear and room is available for more characters on a line. Note, however, that this command doesn't work if more than one window is open on the screen. If you open an additional window, the borders reappear.

Fig. 4.4.

"Clean screen" effect produced by hiding menu and borders.

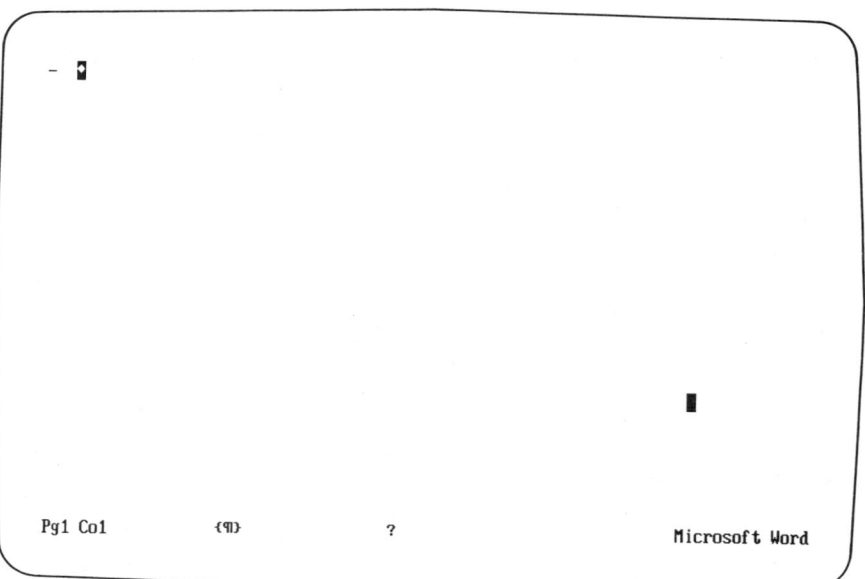

Pg1 Co1   {¶}   ?   Microsoft Word

Trap **Think twice about hiding the borders if you use the mouse.**

When you turn off the borders, you cannot scroll with the mouse. If you find the mouse-scrolling techniques discussed in Chapter 3 helpful, leave the borders displayed.

Tip **Vary the** default tab width **setting to suit your needs.**

When you open a new document, Word automatically sets tab stops every half inch. You can change this default width by modifying the measurement in the default tab width field in the Options menu. Word remembers the new measurement and uses it in all subsequent editing sessions, until you change the measurement.

Adjusting the `default tab width` is a useful technique when you work with documents, such as outlines or program listings, that use levels of indentation to emphasize their structure.

The `default tab width` setting is overridden by tab stops created with the Format Tab Set command and by the paragraph styles applied from the style sheet attached to the document.

Trick **Choose the** Yes **option in the** `line` numbers **field to add a line number indicator to the status line.**

You have no reason not to use this option—it doesn't slow down Word perceptibly. If you chose Yes in the `paginate` field, the status line shows line numbers for the current page. If you chose No for the `line numbers` field, line numbers run consecutively for the whole document, up to the maximum of 999.

You can control how Word counts lines: If you want the program to count blank lines, choose Yes in the `count blank space` field. If you want Word to skip blank lines, counting only the ones on which you have entered text, choose No for the `count blank space` field.

Note: The choice you make in the `count blank space` field affects the way Word prints line numbers when you turn on line-number printing with the Format Division line-Numbers command.

Trick **For non-North American applications, you can choose the appropriate date and time formats. You also can use commas instead of periods for decimal numbers.**

Choose the desired formats in the `date format`, `time format`, and `decimal format` fields. Word uses the format you choose whenever the program automatically inserts dates, times, and decimal numbers.

Tip **Set the cursor speed to suit your system.**

Word 5 is faster than previous versions and moves the cursor so quickly that many users find the speed disconcerting. The new version of Word has a cursor-speed adjustment that allows power typists to crank out text as fast as their fingers allow.

Setting the Options menu `cursor speed` field to 9 (the maximum) allows the cursor to careen around the screen at a speed difficult to control. Switch to text mode and backspace with a `cursor speed` setting of 9: you will probably decide that you prefer a slower pace. You can set the `cursor speed` to a value from 0 to 9. The default setting is 3.

Trick **If you prefer the overtype mode and want to make overtype mode the default, turn it on. Then use Quit to leave Word.**

Most word processing programs offer two text-entry modes: the insert mode and the overtype mode. In the insert mode, when you insert characters in text already typed, the inserted characters push existing text to the right and down. Word's default is the insert mode. In the overtype mode, however, the new characters that you type rub out existing text. Some people prefer to work in the overtype mode all the time. If you're one of these people, you can make overtype the default mode.

To turn on overtype mode, press F5. The message OT appears in the status line. Now quit Word by choosing **Q**uit from the edit command menu. Word notes your choice in the MW.INI file; overtype mode is in effect the next time you use the program.

Chapter Summary

The new Options command menu is your key to customizing Word's display screen and operating characteristics. Word saves the last choices you make in a session so that they become the new program defaults. (You can always change and resave them if you don't like the first choices made.) The WINDOW OPTIONS choices become defaults, however, only if you choose them for window 1.

Here's a summary of recommendations for the WINDOW OPTIONS: Display hidden text so that you can read comments and check commands using hidden text. Display the ruler, which has wonderful new functions in Word 5. Choose the Partial option in the non-printing symbols field so that you can see where you have pressed Enter. Toggle on show layout when you need it by pressing Alt-F4; toggle on line breaks by pressing Alt-F7. Use Shift-F2, rather than the Options menu, to shift to the outline edit mode. Turn on the style bar so that you can see style sheet and running head codes.

To summarize the GENERAL OPTIONS in the Options menu: Don't mute Word. Keep the Yes setting in the summary sheet field—you must fill out the summary sheets in order to get maximum performance from Library Document-retrieval.

When you choose a new unit of measure, it becomes the default in all menus requiring measurements; don't change the default unless you work with metric measures or printer's points.

With Word 5, your display adapter may have three or more display modes; you can choose among these modes with the `display` field. Use text mode for fast text entry, scrolling, and editing, and then switch to graphics mode when you need to see your character formats. Keep automatic pagination on so that you can see where Word breaks pages. If you want, customize the screen's colors—particularly if you use different font sizes. Always work with autosave switched on, using a 5-minute or 10-minute interval. Unless you work with the mouse, hide the command menu. You also can hide the window borders, but you disable mouse-scrolling techniques if you do so. Vary the default tab width if you want, and turn on the line number indicator. Modify the cursor-control speed if the cursor moves too fast.

5

Writing Strategies: Word and the Composing Process

Many word processing manuals, including Word's, neglect a crucial area of discussion: they give much attention to text editing (as well as formatting and printing) but little to text creation, which is treated as though it were no problem. Unless you're just typing someone else's work, however, text creation *is* a problem, as experienced writers know only too well. Beyond the age-old problem of writer's block, writers who use word processing programs find themselves confronting the possibilities and limitations of the computer while engaging in dialog with the muses.

Research on the composing process shows that this confrontation is inevitable. Experienced writers cycle through three distinct phases of the writing process: planning, translating (putting the plan down in words), and reviewing (revising and editing). Most writers do at least some editing as they write. Word processing adds an additional complication: thinking about formatting as you create your text is often useful and sometimes necessary.

This chapter presents a comprehensive approach to text creation with Word. Under the assumption that you do some editing and formatting as you write, this chapter also encourages you to develop a limited repertoire of simple editing and formatting commands. You can master these commands so that their use becomes next to automatic. That way, the commands don't intrude on your thinking as you write.

Covered in this chapter are the following topics:

- ❏ Creating text
- ❏ Editing as you write
- ❏ Formatting as you write

❑ Using tabs as you write

❑ Creating and formatting footnotes as you write

Creating Text

The basics of text creation are covered in this chapter, with special treatment of two topics not found in any other book on this subject: the editing-as-you-write and formatting-as-you-write methods.

❑ *Editing as you write.* As good writers compose, they transpose words, delete sentences, change the order of paragraphs, and perform other editing operations. The challenge here is that Word's editing commands are so numerous and powerful that you easily can lose track of your line of thought as you cope with the commands. For effective writing with Word, you will be well compensated for your efforts to identify a limited working subset of these commands.

❑ *Formatting as you write.* Many writers prefer to format their documents after composing the text—and for good reason. Formatting while writing introduces yet another complexity into the composition process (as if you don't have enough difficulties already). If you prefer, you can take this approach with Word and go back over your document to do the formatting later.

Formatting as you write with Word, however, offers a significant advantage: you can eliminate the major (and tedious) step of selecting text. If you learn a simple set of formatting commands, you reap a handsome dividend in saved time.

This chapter presents only some of Word's editing and formatting commands—the ones you will find most useful as you create text. You can find more extensive treatments of formatting and editing in Chapters 7, 8, and 9.

Tip **Simply start Word to create a new blank document.**

The blank document that appears in window 1 when you start Word has no name; you name the document when you save it with the Transfer Save command. Available to you by default are all the formatting options available in the default style sheet, NORMAL.STY.

For many writing applications, this blank document—and the default formatting commands—provide all you need to get the job done.

Chapter 9 discusses ways you can open existing documents.

Tip **To abandon a document without saving it, use the Transfer Clear Window command.**

If you have been experimenting or have written something you don't want to save, the Transfer Clear Window command clears the document window. When you see the message Enter Y to save, N to lose changes, or Esc to cancel, press N to abandon the document.

Tip **Enter text in text mode.**

Perhaps you are the kind of writer for whom the first step in creating a document is getting your thoughts down as fast as you can. Or perhaps you are typing a memo or report that you or someone else has scribbled out in longhand or dictated into a cassette recorder. Whatever the circumstances, and depending on the kind of system you are using, you may be able to enter text faster if you switch to text mode before you start typing. In text mode, Word does not show actual character formatting on the screen, and the program can keep pace with even the fastest typist.

To switch to text mode, choose **O**ptions and then choose the display field; press F1 and choose Text from the list. Alternatively, you can toggle between modes by pressing Alt-F9, although this command toggles between the two modes last chosen, which may not include the text mode. (Chapter 4 presents a macro that gets around this command's shortcomings.)

Tip **Press the Enter key only when you want to start a new paragraph.**

Like most word processing programs, Word automatically "wraps" a word to a new line when the word goes beyond the right margin. You don't need to press Enter at the end of every line. Press Enter only when you want to begin a new paragraph.

This point goes beyond mere convenience. Word's designers define a "paragraph" of text rather differently than most people do. In Word, a paragraph is set off by Enter keystrokes. When you press Enter, Word defines as a paragraph all the text that follows until you press Enter again. A paragraph, in Word's terms, could be one word or dozens of pages.

If you press Enter at the end of every line, Word cannot recognize the paragraphs you create. As far as Word is concerned, each separate line is a distinct paragraph. When you select a paragraph for formatting, the command affects only the line in which the cursor is positioned. Word formats what *it* defines as a paragraph but not the unit of text that *you* define as a paragraph.

Trap   **If you delete a paragraph mark accidentally, Word joins the two paragraphs.**

A common complaint of new Word users is that paragraph breaks seem to collapse for some mysterious reason during the editing process. But the reason is simple. Every time you press Enter, Word inserts a paragraph mark in your document. You can edit (copy, insert, and delete) these marks just as you can any other character. If you set the Options menu's show non-printing symbols field to None, you cannot see the marks. When you're editing, you may accidentally delete a mark that divides two paragraphs. If you do, the two paragraphs become one.

Trap   **If you delete a paragraph mark between two differently formatted paragraphs, Word joins the paragraphs and uses the second paragraph's format.**

Suppose that you have typed an extended quotation with a half-inch indentation on the left, and then typed a flush-left paragraph (see fig. 5.1). If you accidentally delete the paragraph mark that divides the two paragraphs, the half-inch indentation disappears, and the joined paragraph assumes the flush-left paragraph's formatting (see fig. 5.2). Such an event can be frustrating, especially if you're a new Word user.

Tip   **Use the Options command and choose the** Partial **option from the** show non-printing symbols **field to display paragraph marks.**

You can avoid unintended paragraph merges or formatting losses by displaying the Enter keystrokes. With these keystrokes visible, you can avoid removing them unintentionally. To display them, change the default setting, None, in the show non-printing symbols field of the Options command menu, as suggested in Chapter 4. Figure 5.3 shows a document displayed with the None option. Figure 5.4 shows the same document displayed with the Partial option; figure 5.5 shows the document with the All option.

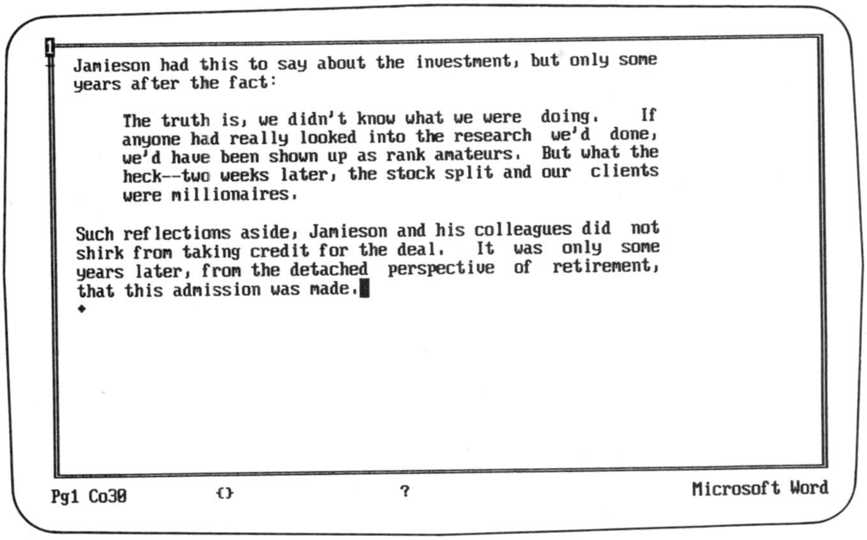

```
Jamieson had this to say about the investment, but only some
years after the fact:

     The truth is, we didn't know what we were doing.    If
     anyone had really looked into the research  we'd  done,
     we'd have been shown up as rank amateurs.  But what the
     heck--two weeks later, the stock split and our  clients
     were millionaires.

Such reflections aside, Jamieson and his colleagues did  not
shirk from taking credit for the deal.  It  was  only  some
years later, from the detached  perspective  of  retirement,
that this admission was made.█
◆

Pg1 Co30          {}                ?                  Microsoft Word
```

Fig. 5.1.

Two paragraphs formatted differently.

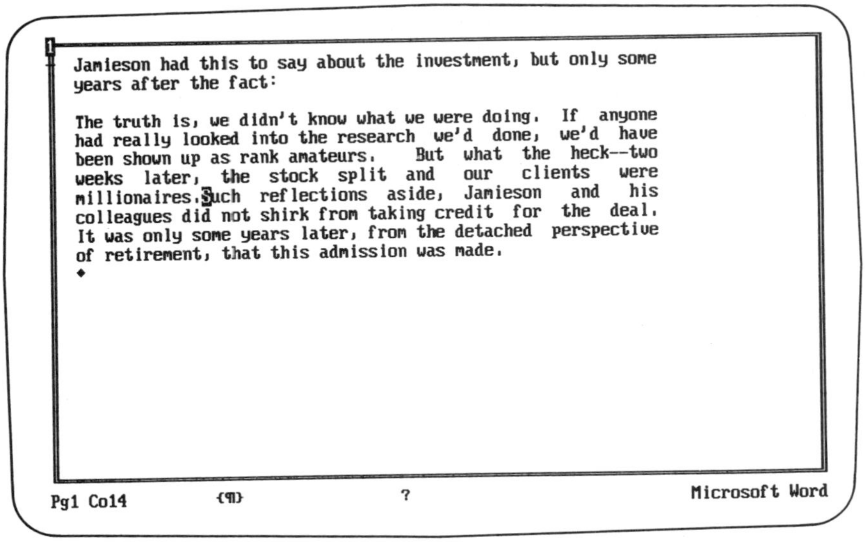

```
Jamieson had this to say about the investment, but only some
years after the fact:

The truth is, we didn't know what we were doing.  If  anyone
had really looked into the research  we'd  done,  we'd  have
been shown up as rank amateurs.    But  what  the  heck--two
weeks later,  the  stock  split  and  our  clients  were
millionaires.Such reflections aside, Jamieson  and  his
colleagues did not shirk from taking credit  for  the  deal.
It was only some years later, from the detached  perspective
of retirement, that this admission was made.
◆

Pg1 Co14          {¶}               ?                  Microsoft Word
```

Fig. 5.2.

Loss of the first paragraph's formatting after deleting the hidden paragraph mark.

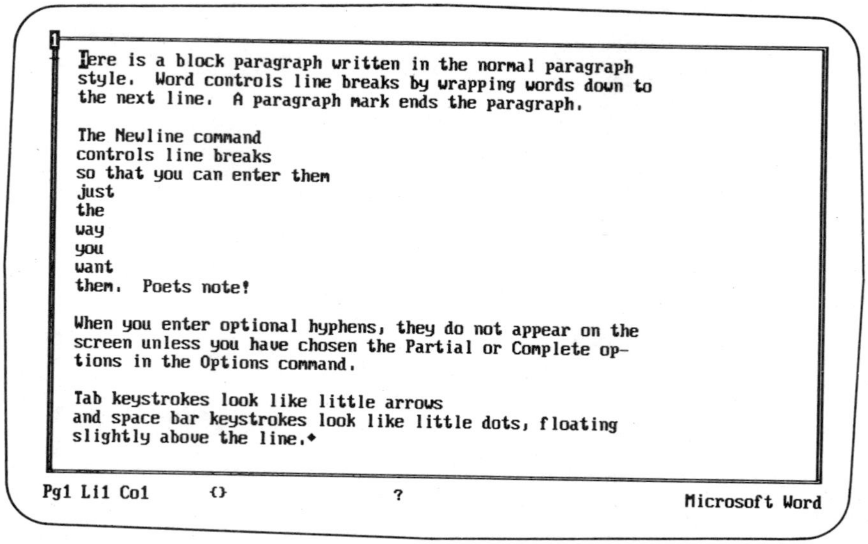

Fig. 5.3.

Document displayed after choosing None in the Option command's show non-printing symbols field.

```
Iere is a block paragraph written in the normal paragraph
style. Word controls line breaks by wrapping words down to
the next line. A paragraph mark ends the paragraph.

The Newline command
controls line breaks
so that you can enter them
just
the
way
you
want
them.  Poets note!

When you enter optional hyphens, they do not appear on the
screen unless you have chosen the Partial or Complete op-
tions in the Options command.

Tab keystrokes look like little arrows
and space bar keystrokes look like little dots, floating
slightly above the line.◆

Pg1 Li1 Co1        {}                ?                    Microsoft Word
```

Paragraph mark

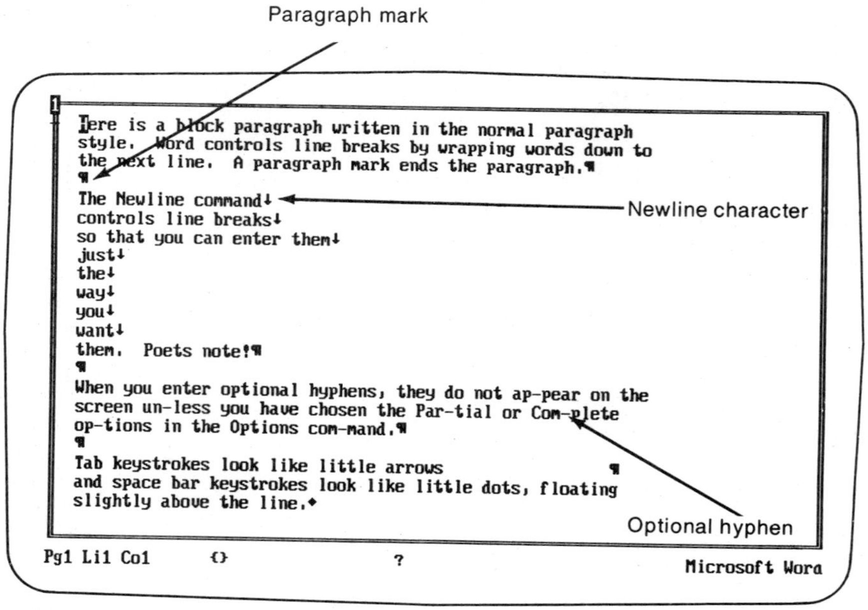

Fig. 5.4.

Document displayed after choosing Partial in the Option command's show non-printing symbols field.

```
Iere is a block paragraph written in the normal paragraph
style.  Word controls line breaks by wrapping words down to
the next line.  A paragraph mark ends the paragraph.¶
¶
The Newline command↓                                    ← Newline character
controls line breaks↓
so that you can enter them↓
just↓
the↓
way↓
you↓
want↓
them.  Poets note!¶
¶
When you enter optional hyphens, they do not ap-pear on the
screen un-less you have chosen the Par-tial or Com-plete
op-tions in the Options com-mand.¶
¶
Tab keystrokes look like little arrows              ¶
and space bar keystrokes look like little dots, floating
slightly above the line.◆

Pg1 Li1 Co1        {}                ?                    Microsoft Word
```

Optional hyphen

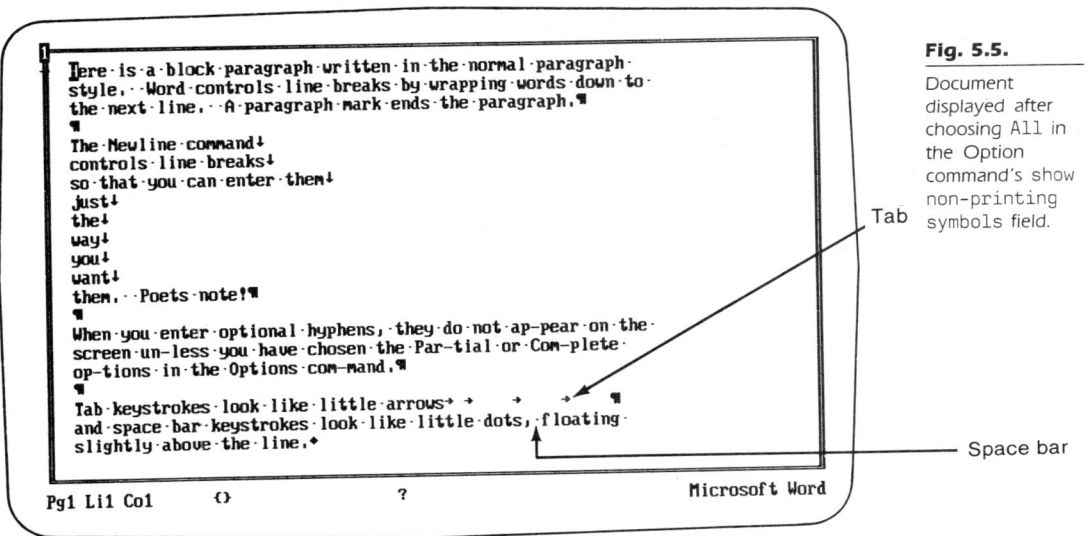

Here·is·a·block·paragraph·written·in·the·normal·paragraph·
style,··Word·controls·line·breaks·by·wrapping·words·down·to·
the·next·line,··A·paragraph·mark·ends·the·paragraph.¶
¶
The·Newline·command↓
controls·line·breaks↓
so·that·you·can·enter·them↓
just↓
the↓
way↓
you↓
want↓
them,··Poets·note!¶
¶
When·you·enter·optional·hyphens,·they·do·not·ap-pear·on·the·
screen·un-less·you·have·chosen·the·Par-tial·or·Com-plete·
op-tions·in·the·Options·com-mand.¶
¶
Tab·keystrokes·look·like·little·arrows→ → → → ¶
and·space·bar·keystrokes·look·like·little·dots,·floating·
slightly·above·the·line.◆

Pg1 Li1 Co1   {}   ?   Microsoft Word

Fig. 5.5.

Document displayed after choosing All in the Option command's show non-printing symbols field.

Tab

Space bar

Tip **Join and split paragraphs by removing and inserting paragraph marks.**

You can join or split paragraphs by deleting or inserting paragraph marks. To join two paragraphs, delete the paragraph mark at the end of the first paragraph. The first paragraph takes on the paragraph formatting of the second paragraph, and the two paragraphs become one.

To split one paragraph into two, insert a paragraph mark (simply press the Enter key) where you want the split to occur. The paragraph formatting of the two paragraphs does not change.

Trap **If you use Enter, Tab, or the space bar to indent paragraphs or add blank lines, you disable some of Word's most powerful formatting features.**

If you want to type paragraphs with a half-inch indentation of the first line and blank lines between paragraphs, you may be tempted to press Tab to begin the paragraph and Enter twice after finishing the paragraph. But this method greatly limits Word's capability to reformat the document quickly. For example, if you later decide that you don't want the indentation, you have to go through the whole document and delete all the Tab keystrokes, one by one. A much, much better way exists—as you will see.

If you use Word's paragraph-formatting commands to control first-line indentation and blank lines, Word automatically enters the indent and blank line whenever you press Enter. Obviously, this approach saves time. But even more significantly, all the paragraphs formatted this way can be reformatted with just two or three keystrokes. You can select your whole document, or as much of it as you want, and use the **F**ormat **P**aragraph command to adjust indentations, spacing, and other formats—and every selected paragraph is affected.

Don't enter blank spaces and lines with the Enter, Tab, or space bar keys. Format as you go, as explained later in this chapter, adding indentations and blank lines as part of your standard paragraph format.

Trick **If you want to control line breaks in a single paragraph, use the Shift-Enter keyboard command to start new lines.**

Ordinarily, Word starts new lines automatically with word wrapping. Word fills out the line before starting a new one—until you press Enter to start a new paragraph.

You can control line breaks, however, without starting a new paragraph, by using Shift-Enter. Figure 5.6 shows a section of text containing several lines of various lengths, all of which are included in one paragraph. All the lines you create with Shift-Enter are treated together as a single paragraph until you press Enter again. Using Shift-Enter has three big advantages:

❏ If you give a paragraph-formatting command anywhere in the lines, the command affects the whole paragraph, not just the line on which the cursor is positioned. Suppose that you type your name and address in three lines, using Shift-Enter. You then can use a single command (Alt-C) to center all the lines simultaneously.

❏ Because Shift-Enter does not start a new paragraph, the command doesn't use the space before or space after options (if any) attached to the current paragraph style. If you use the Alt-O (Open paragraphs) command, for instance, Word inserts 1 li (1 line) in the space before field of the Format Paragraph command. So every time you press Enter, Word puts a blank line before the paragraph. If you use Shift-Enter, however, Word starts the new line without inserting a blank line.

❏ If you sort text using the Library Autosort command, all the lines linked by Shift-Enter keystrokes are treated as a single unit.

When you use Shift-Enter, Word enters a newline character in your document (see fig. 5.6). If you have chosen the **O**ptions command and the `Partial` or `All` option for the `show non-printing symbols`, the character appears as a down arrow on the screen.

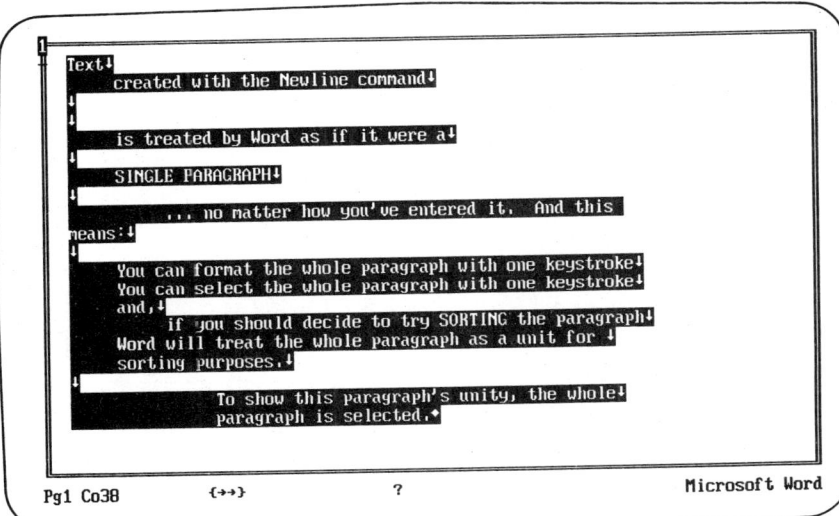

Fig. 5.6.

Paragraph created by pressing Shift-Enter to control line breaks.

Tip **Insert a nonbreaking hyphen when you want Word to keep a hyphenated word on one line.**

When wrapping lines of text, Word generally wraps whole words. Word makes no effort, however, to keep the parts of hyphenated words on the same line. Unless you tell the program otherwise, it assumes that hyphens are convenient places to break words like *high-rigging* and *short-tempered* if divisions are necessary to create acceptable line breaks. Usually, breaking on a hyphen causes little problem, but at times a line break at a hyphen is unacceptable, either because the break causes ambiguity or because the result is ugly. The first line of figure 5.7 is an example of an unattractive line break.

You can tell Word not to break a hyphenated word by inserting the hyphen with the Ctrl-Shift-hyphen key combination rather than just the hyphen key. This technique forces Word to keep the parts of the hyphenated word on the same line, as shown in figure 5.8.

Fig. 5.7.

A bad line break with a manual hyphen.

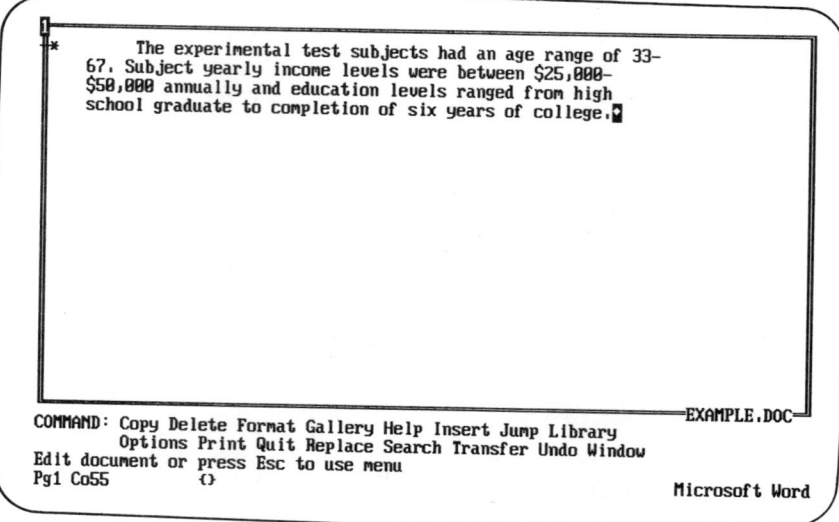

Fig. 5.8.

Controlling the line break with a nonbreaking hyphen.

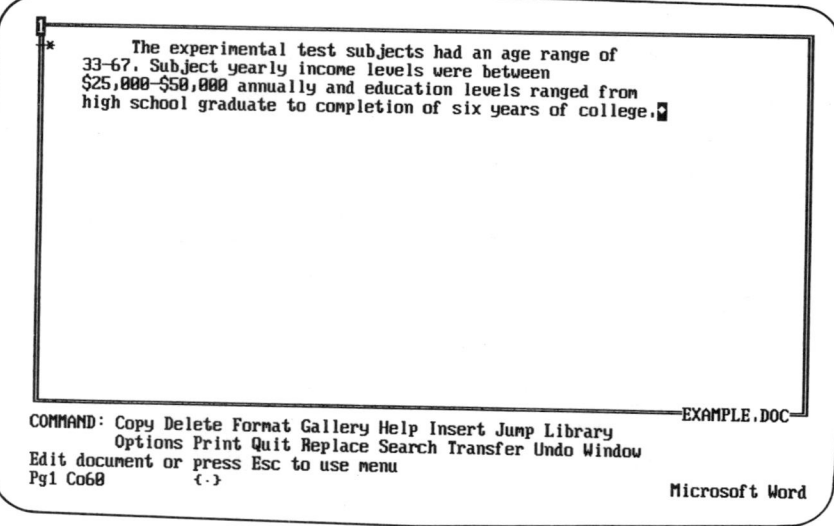

Trick   Toggle on the display of line breaks with Ctrl-F7.

Bear in mind that Word doesn't show precisely where line breaks occur unless you choose the Yes option in the show line breaks field of the Options menu (see Chapter 4). To find out whether hyphens will cause problems at the end of a line, toggle on the display of line breaks by pressing Ctrl-F7. Word breaks the lines on-screen where the lines will break when you print the document.

Tip **If you work with narrow columns of text, use optional hyphens in long words or hyphenate your document automatically.**

Word can print more than one column of text on the page. When columns are narrow (less than four inches), however, word wrap can produce ugly gaps along the right margin as long words are moved down to the next line. You can type long words with optional hyphens at the syllabic breaks (for example, *dis-con-tin-u-ance*). If the word occurs at the end of a line, Word splits the word in one of the places you have indicated. If the word doesn't appear near the end of a line, Word hides the hyphens and keeps the word together.

Enter an optional hyphen by pressing Ctrl-hyphen. (Use the hyphen key, not the minus key on the numeric keypad.) Optional hyphens appear on the screen when you choose the Partial or All option from the show non-printing symbols field of the Options menu. The optional hyphens disappear when you choose the None option in this field.

Another way to insert optional hyphens is to use Word's automatic hyphenation command (Library Hyphenate). This command automatically inserts optional hyphens in words that Word knows how to break. (The file HYPH.DAT on your Word Program disk contains the needed information.)

To hyphenate your document automatically, do the following steps:

1. Press Ctrl-PgUp to position the cursor at the beginning of your document.

2. Choose the **L**ibrary **H**yphenate command.

3. When the Library Hyphenate menu appears (see fig. 5.9), choose the Yes option to confirm each hyphen placement, or choose No to insert hyphens automatically.

    Word inserts hyphens correctly almost all the time, but confirming each placement is a good idea.

4. When Word proposes to insert a hyphen, press Y to confirm the placement of the hyphen, N to skip the word completely, or use the right-arrow and left-arrow keys to move the highlight where you want the hyphen to appear (see fig. 5.10).

Fig. 5.9.

The *Library*
Hyphenate
command menu.

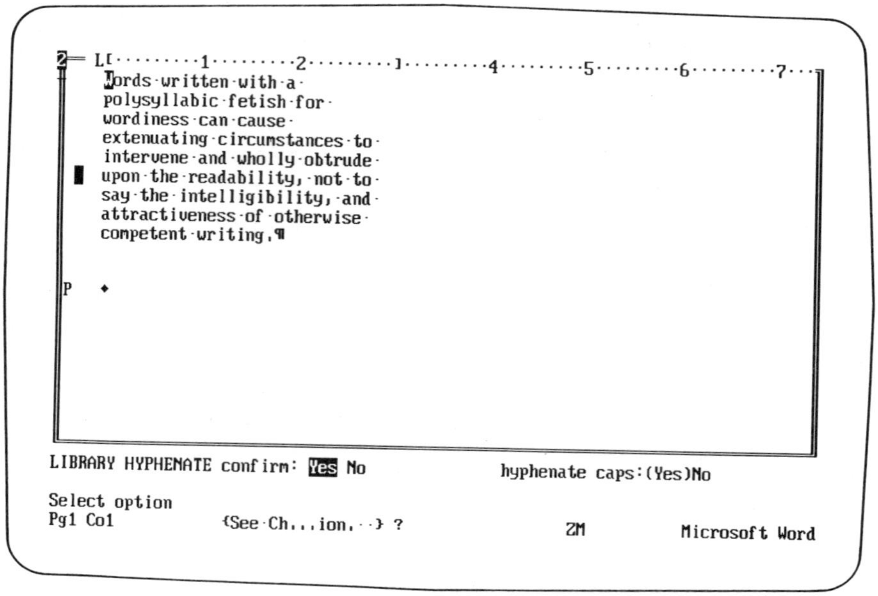

```
≣─ L[········1········2·······]····4·····5·····6·····7···
  ]ords·written·with·a·
  polysyllabic·fetish·for·
  wordiness·can·cause·
  extenuating·circumstances·to·
  intervene·and·wholly·obtrude·
█ upon·the·readability,·not·to·
  say·the·intelligibility,·and·
  attractiveness·of·otherwise·
  competent·writing.¶


P   ◆



LIBRARY HYPHENATE confirm: ▊Yes▊ No              hyphenate caps:(Yes)No
Select option
Pg1 Co1          {See·Ch...ion.··} ?              2M        Microsoft Word
```

Fig. 5.10.

Confirming
hyphen
placement.

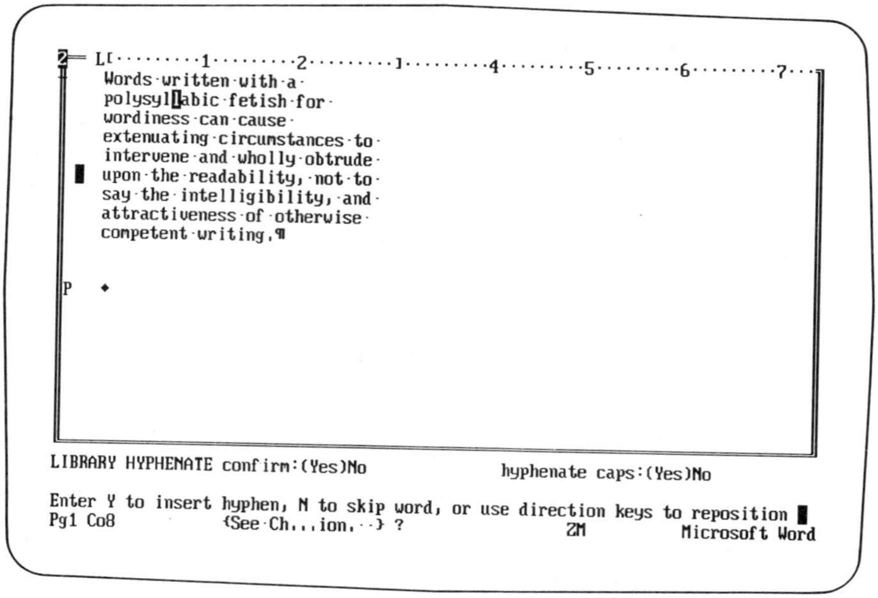

```
≣─ L[········1········2·······]····4·····5·····6·····7···
  Words·written·with·a·
  polysyll█abic·fetish·for·
  wordiness·can·cause·
  extenuating·circumstances·to·
  intervene·and·wholly·obtrude·
█ upon·the·readability,·not·to·
  say·the·intelligibility,·and·
  attractiveness·of·otherwise·
  competent·writing.¶


P   ◆



LIBRARY HYPHENATE confirm:(Yes)No              hyphenate caps:(Yes)No
Enter Y to insert hyphen, N to skip word, or use direction keys to reposition █
Pg1 Co8          {See·Ch...ion.··} ?              2M        Microsoft Word
```

When Word is finished hyphenating your document, line breaks are improved (see fig. 5.11).

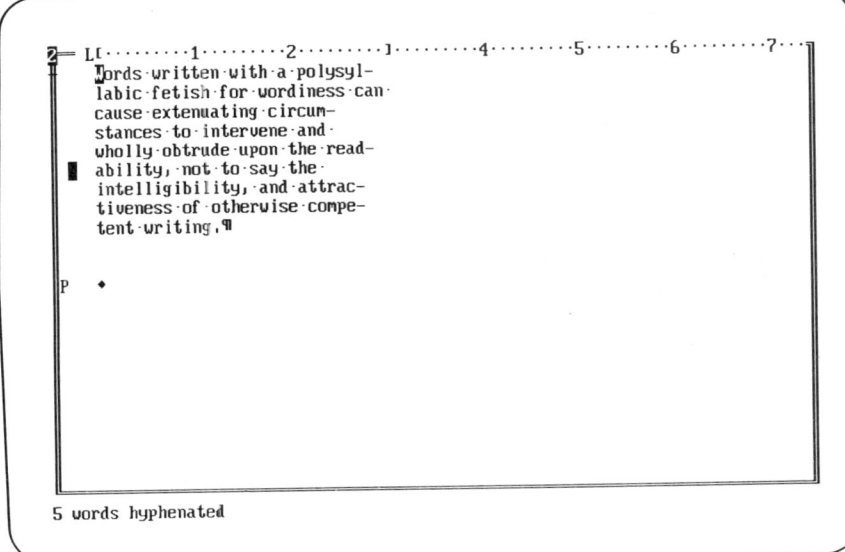

Fig. 5.11.

Document's appearance after hyphenating.

To remove the hyphens you just inserted, choose **U**ndo immediately. To remove optional hyphens after you have chosen another command or moved the cursor (thus disabling Undo), choose the **R**eplace command and in the text field type a caret followed by a hyphen (^-). Leave the with text field blank, and carry out the command by pressing Enter or clicking the command name.

Tip Insert a nonbreaking space when you want Word to keep two words on the same line.

You can keep two words together on the same line by pressing Ctrl-space bar between the words rather than just the space bar. Word then keeps these words together on one line. If the line does not have enough room, the program moves both words down to the next line. You can use this technique to improve the look of a page by ensuring that a paragraph does not end with only one word on the last line.

Tip Use Ctrl-Shift-Enter to force a page break.

If you write using the Yes option in the paginate field of the Options menu, Word inserts natural page breaks automatically. Natural page breaks are active; Word repositions them as you insert or delete text. Word doesn't insert a page break until you use up all the space on the page.

If you know that you want to start a particular piece of text on a new page, however, you can force a page break by pressing Ctrl-Shift-Enter. Word represents forced page breaks on-screen with a dense row of dots. The dots in natural page breaks are separated by spaces; the ones in forced page breaks aren't (see fig. 5.12)

Fig. 5.12.

A natural page break and a forced page break.

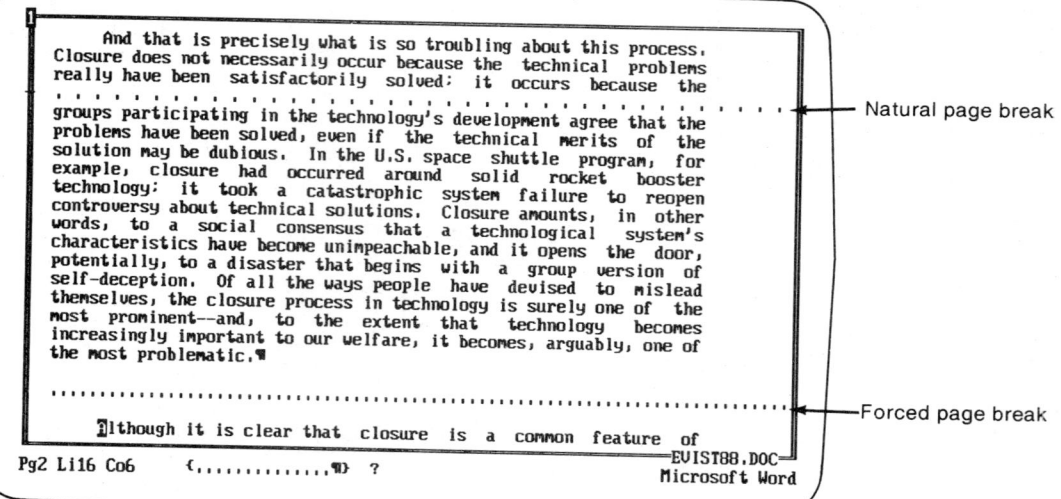

Natural page break

Forced page break

You can remove a forced page break the same way you remove any character—by placing the cursor on the forced page break and pressing Del.

Trap **When you force a page break, subsequent insertions or deletions above it may produce an unattractive result.**

When you force a page break, Word cannot reposition the page break as needed. If you insert or delete text above the forced page break, the page break you thought was necessary may suddenly become quite unattractive—such as a page with only two or three lines on it. In general, avoid forcing page breaks unless you are sure that you want the break to occur no matter what happens in subsequent edits. For example, a page break between chapters should remain even though further editing is done. To determine whether your document contains forced page breaks that you no longer need, choose the **P**rint **R**epaginate command and select the Yes option in the confirm page breaks field.

Trick   **To keep Word from inserting a page break below a heading, format the heading with the** keep follow **option in the Format Paragraph command menu.**

Later in this chapter you learn how to format as you go, but this keep follow trick is relevant to the preceding trap and deserves mention here. You can prevent Word from breaking a page below a heading, or any other paragraph of text, by choosing the Yes option in the keep follow field of the Format Paragraph command menu. When you choose this option by using the **F**ormat **P**aragraph command, Word keeps the selected paragraph with the paragraph immediately following (see fig. 5.13). To make sure that the heading stays with the text below it, always enter blank lines beneath the heading with the space after field of the Format Paragraph menu. If you enter a blank line under a heading by pressing Enter, Word keeps the blank line with the heading, not the text, and you may get a bad page break.

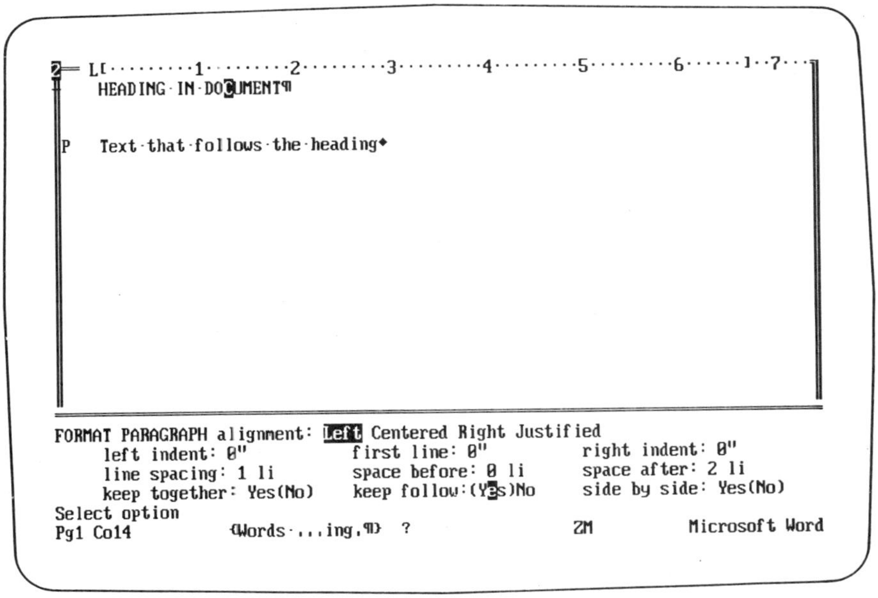

```
2═ L[········1········2·········3········4········5········6····]··7···]
│ HEADING·IN·DOCUMENT¶
│
│P   Text·that·follows·the·heading◆
│
│
│
│
│
│
│
│
│
│
│
│
FORMAT PARAGRAPH alignment: █Left█ Centered Right Justified
    left indent: 0"         first line: 0"        right indent: 0"
    line spacing: 1 li      space before: 0 li    space after: 2 li
    keep together: Yes(No)  keep follow:(Yes)No   side by side: Yes(No)
Select option
Pg1 Co14           ⟨Words·..,ing,¶⟩  ?              2M        Microsoft Word
```

Fig. 5.13.

Formatting a heading so that Word won't break a page under it.

Style-sheet entries for headings can do this formatting job automatically—and much more, as you will learn in Chapter 6.

Trick   Use ASCII codes to access special characters.

All the characters and control codes that your computer can create are represented by ASCII (American Standard Code for Information Interchange) codes. ASCII includes 256 possible codes, numbered 0 through 255. The first 32 codes are nonprinting control codes used for such things as carriage returns. The codes from 33 through 127 are printable characters from your keyboard—numbers, letters, and punctuation. The codes above 127 represent foreign-language characters and graphics symbols that are not directly accessible from the keyboard. These characters are called the *extended character set*. Figure 5.14 shows the IBM extended character set built into your computer and used to display characters on the screen.

Fig. 5.14.

The IBM extended character set.

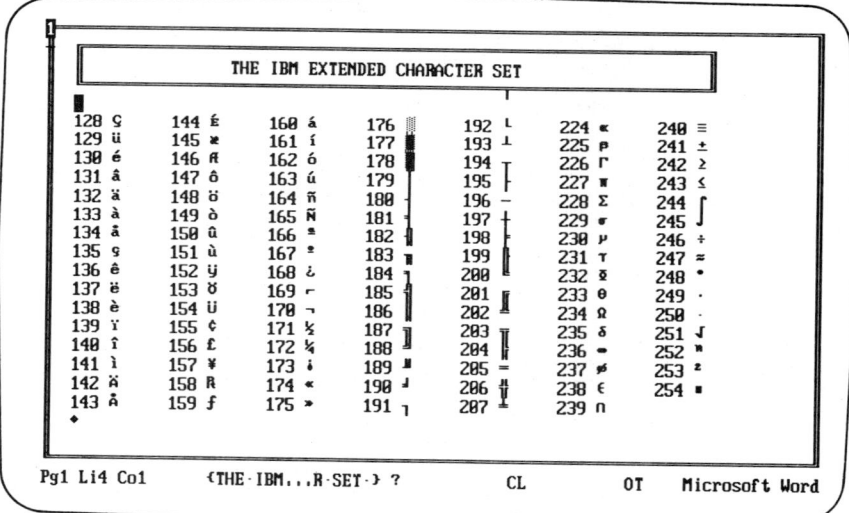

You can enter ASCII codes by holding down the Alt key and typing the number of the code on the numeric keypad (with or without pressing Shift or Num Lock). The number keys above the alphabet keys do not work for this purpose.

Trap   Entering an ASCII character may produce a symbol on your screen but a blank space in the printed document.

Not all printers can reproduce the characters represented by ASCII codes above 127. Before you go to the trouble of producing elaborate designs with extended characters, check the user's manual for your printer to find out whether it supports the extended character set.

Word 5

Trick **Find out which characters your printer has assigned to ASCII codes 128 through 255.**

Word 5 includes a macro called character_test.mac in the glossary file MACRO.GLY on Word Utilities disk 2. You can use this macro to test your printer's character-printing capabilities. For information on using Word's supplied macros, see Chapter 13.

Trap **Word frequently fails to align space bar keystrokes correctly when printing columns.**

If you're creating a table with aligned columns of numbers or text, use the Tab key—not the space bar—to align the text. For more information on using and setting tabs, see "Formatting as You Write," later in this chapter.

Tip **Use the Thesaurus to find the right word.**

Word comes equipped with what many users believe is the best computer-based thesaurus available. Chapter 10 covers Word's Thesaurus in detail. For now, however, here's a brief overview of its use: place the highlight on or just after the word you want to look up and press Ctrl-F6. If Word cannot find the Thesaurus software, you are prompted to insert the Thesaurus disk. When the Thesaurus appears, the screen splits into two windows, showing your document and a list of synonyms (see fig. 5.15). Select the word you want and press Enter. Word enters the new word in your document, replacing the original word. If you decide against replacing the original word, press Esc instead of Enter. The Thesaurus window closes, and you return to your document.

Editing as You Write

Most writers perform at least minor editing (and perhaps some more-than-minor editing) while composing a document. Ideally, such editing operations should be so effortless that you need not stop to think about them, leaving you free to concentrate on writing.

So selecting just a few of Word's many editing commands—a limited set of commands that you can memorize and use automatically—makes good sense.

Fig. 5.15.

Selecting
synonyms with
Word's Thesaurus.

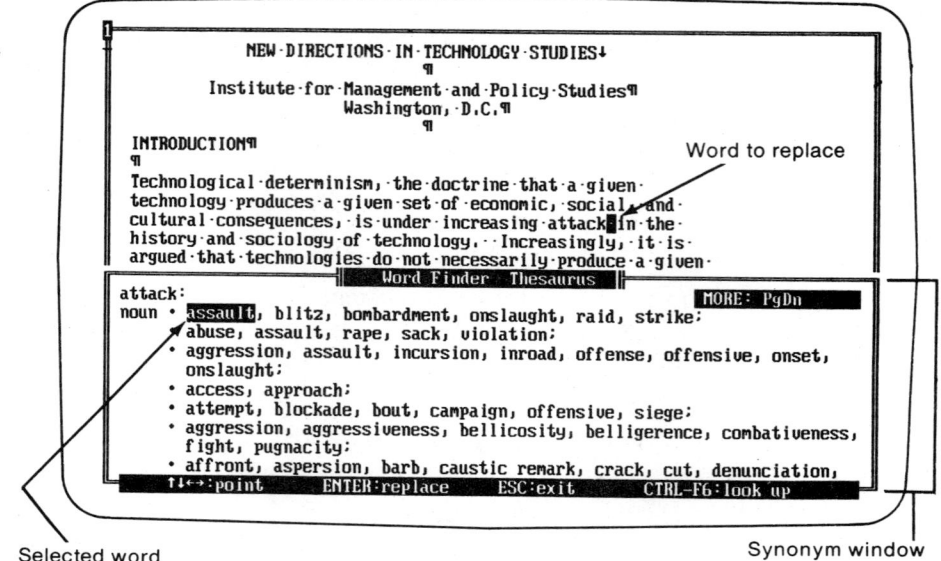

Editing commands fall into the following categories:

❑ *Commands for selecting text.* In general, these commands affect the text selected with the highlight. You can use keys or the mouse to select fixed amounts of text: words, lines, sentences, paragraphs, and even the whole document. You also can use keys and the mouse to select custom-tailored amounts of text, ranging from a few characters to dozens of pages.

❑ *Commands for copying, deleting, and inserting text.* You can delete text permanently if you prefer, or you can delete or copy text to the scrap, a temporary parking place for deletions. You also can delete or copy text to glossaries, a subject treated in the next chapter. Finally, you can insert text from the scrap or from glossaries.

❑ *Commands for copying and moving text with one command.* These commands simplify common editing operations. You can move text by deleting it to the scrap and reinserting the text elsewhere, for example, but you can perform the same operation with fewer keystrokes. To move text with the mouse, select the text to be moved, point to the place to which you want the text moved, hold the Ctrl key, and click either mouse button.

Selecting Text

Because Word offers a complete set of keyboard techniques for users who don't have a mouse, the program contains many more text-selection commands than you will need. Most Word users develop a repertoire of selection techniques that meet their needs. You will be wise to follow their example by exploring these techniques and choosing the ones you find especially useful. Tables 5.1 and 5.2 list the keys or mouse action that you can use to select various fixed amounts of text.

Table 5.1
Keyboard Commands for Selecting Fixed Amounts of Text

Key	Selects
F7	Word left
F8	Word right
Shift-F7	Preceding sentence
Shift-F8	Next sentence
F9	Preceding paragraph
F10	Next paragraph
Shift-F9	Current line
Shift-F10	Whole document

Table 5.2
Mouse Commands for Selecting Fixed Amounts of Text

Mouse Action	Selects
Click right button on word	Word
Click both buttons in sentence	Sentence
Click left button in selection bar	Line
Click right button in selection bar	Paragraph
Click both buttons in selection bar	Whole document

Tip **In Word, editing and formatting commands act on only the selected text.**

When you work in the document area, one character is always selected or highlighted: this is the cursor. You can expand the highlight by using text-selection techniques. In general, editing and formatting commands affect the selected text. To edit and format with Word, you select text and then choose a command.

Tip   **Some text-selection commands select fixed units of text, such as words or sentences; others select variable amounts of text.**

You have many options for both kinds of text selections. Choose techniques you find convenient from both the fixed-unit and variable-amount approaches—you need both.

Remember that you don't have to memorize all these text-selection commands in order to use Word effectively. You can make do by mastering just three or four commands and supplementing them with the keyboard or mouse methods for selecting variable amounts of text. Don't ignore the keyboard techniques just because you have a mouse. Even the most vociferous defenders of the mouse use some keyboard tactics. What's more, you may find yourself working with a computer (at the office, for instance) that isn't equipped with a mouse and then be obliged to rely exclusively on the keyboard techniques.

Tip   **Press F6 to turn on a mode that lets you highlight precisely the right amount of text.**

When you press F6, Word switches to the extend-selection mode, and the characters EX appear on the status line. When this mode is on, the direction or scrolling keys *expand* the highlight rather than *move* it. You can press additional keys to refine the highlight, either enlarging it or shrinking it as you want.

To turn off extend mode, press F6 again. Table 5.3 lists the keys you can use to select variable amounts of text in extend mode.

Table 5.3
Selecting Variable Amounts of Text with the Keyboard (in Extend Mode)

Key	Expands highlight
Up arrow	Up one line
Down arrow	Down one line
Left arrow	Left one character
Right arrow	Right one character
Home	To beginning of line
End	To end of line
PgUp	Up one window
PgDn	Down one window
Ctrl-up arrow	Up line-by-line (to entire line)
Ctrl-down arrow	Down line-by-line (to entire line)
Ctrl-left arrow	To word left

Table 5.3—Continued

Key	Expands highlight
Ctrl-right arrow	To word right
Ctrl-Home	To first line of window
Ctrl-End	To last line of window
Ctrl-PgUp	To beginning of document
Ctrl-PgDn	To end of document

Tip **You can extend the selection by holding the Shift key and pressing any cursor control key.**

You can use the Shift key with any of the keys listed in table 5.3 to select variable amounts of text. To expand the highlight to the first line of the window, for example, press Shift-Ctrl-Home. This technique differs from the F6 (extend mode) approach. When you press F6, you toggle on the extend mode. As long as the mode is on, you can expand the highlight. When you use the Shift key, however, the highlight freezes when you release the Shift key. As long as you hold the Shift key, you can expand the highlight by using any of the keys listed in table 5.3. Once you release the Shift key, pressing additional arrow or scrolling keys removes the highlight from the screen and moves the cursor.

Tip **Selecting variable amounts of text with the mouse is exceptionally easy.**

To select text with the mouse, simply click the left button and drag (hold the button and move the mouse), expanding the highlight as far as necessary. When you have highlighted the text you want to select, release the button.

In extend mode, clicking the mouse button instantly expands the highlight from the cursor to the pointer's location.

Deleting, Copying, Inserting, and Moving Text

Table 5.4 lists the keyboard techniques for common editing operations. Identify the techniques you want to include in your limited repertoire of tools for editing as you go.

Table 5.4
Keyboard Commands for Deleting, Copying,
and Inserting Text

Key	Effect
Backspace	Deletes character left
Del	Deletes selected text to scrap
Shift-Del	Deletes selected text permanently
Ins	Inserts text from scrap

Command	Effect
Delete	Deletes selected text to scrap or to a glossary
Copy	Copies selected text to scrap or to a glossary
Insert	Inserts text from scrap or glossary

Tip **Use the Backspace key to rub out mistakes as you make them.**

The simplest editing technique of all, the Backspace key is useful for correcting errors as you type. You can hold the Backspace key to rub out words and even whole lines. If the cursor moves backward too fast for you to control, use a lower number in the cursor speed field of the Options menu.

Trap **You press the Backspace key, but nothing is deleted.**

The Backspace key is disabled in overtype mode. If you press Backspace and nothing happens (other than a beep from your computer), check the status line. If the key status indicator shows the message OT, you're in overtype mode. Press F5 to return to insert mode and restore the Backspace key's function.

Tip **If you're performing editing operations with the scrap, use the Del and Ins keys rather than the menu commands.**

Pressing the Del key is the same as choosing the **D**elete command from the main menu and pressing Enter; pressing the Ins key is identical to choosing the **I**nsert command and pressing Enter.

When you use either the **D**elete or the **I**nsert command, Word displays two curly braces in the To command field. The curly braces represent the scrap, which is Word's proposed response to this command field. If you accept the proposed response by pressing Enter, Word cuts text to the scrap (Delete) or puts the scrap's contents into your text (Insert). Using the Del and Ins keys, however, is faster.

Tip **If you use the Del key or the Delete command to remove unwanted text, you can restore the deletion.**

When you select text and press the Del key (or use the **D**elete command) the deletion—no matter how big—is routed to the scrap. If you discover that the deletion wasn't a good idea, just position the cursor where the deletion occurred and press Ins (or use the **I**nsert command). The deleted text is replaced. Text cut with Backspace, however, isn't routed to the scrap and cannot be restored with the Ins key or Insert command.

Tip **The best way to restore a deletion is to use the Undo command, but you must give the command immediately.**

Using the **U**ndo command to restore a deletion is better than the Ins technique mentioned in the preceding tip because you don't have to make sure that the cursor is properly positioned. Moreover, Undo restores deletions made with the Backspace key. You cannot use Undo for this purpose, however, if you have added text or given a command since making the deletion.

Trap **The contents of the scrap are overwritten every time you copy or delete text.**

The contents of the scrap are replaced whenever you press the Del key or choose the Copy or Delete command (except when you use these commands to create a glossary entry). Remember: the scrap can hold only one unit of text at a time.

Trick **If you cut or copy something to the scrap and then accidentally overwrite the text, retrieve the old text with the Undo command.**

Suppose that you delete a brilliant paragraph to the scrap, planning to insert the text somewhere else in your manuscript. As you scroll to the place where you want to insert the text, you find a mistake. You forget what you're doing, delete something, and then discover to your dismay that your brilliant paragraph is gone. Despair not: you can recover the lost text. Immediately choose **U**ndo. The last deletion you made is canceled, and the "lost" text reappears in the scrap.

Trick **To avoid losing something of value stored temporarily in the scrap, use Shift-Del to delete text.**

You can delete selected text without storing it in the scrap by holding the Shift key when you press Del. Although you then cannot insert the deleted text elsewhere, you still can undo the deletion by choosing the **U**ndo command.

Trick   **If you use the keyboard version of Word, emulate WordStar's text-deletion commands.**

Table 5.5 lists macro names and codes for two popular WordStar® text-deletion commands.

Table 5.5
Macros To Emulate WordStar Text-Deletion Commands

Macro name	Macro code
del_word_right.mac^<ctrl t>	<ctrl right><f8><del>
del_line.mac^<ctrl y>	<shift f9><del>

To create and use these macros, follow the instructions in Chapter 13, "Macros."

Tip   **You can move text easily by deleting it to the scrap and then reinserting the text elsewhere.**

Simply select the text you want to move, press Del (or use the **Delete** command) to delete the text to the scrap, move the cursor to the place you want the text to appear, and press Ins. Before settling on this technique, however, try the mouse and macro techniques described in this section. Using the scrap, as the previous tips and traps make clear, has its risks.

Trick   **Use the scrap to repeat text.**

Word saves you the trouble of repeatedly entering the same text by allowing you to copy the text to the scrap and then reinsert the text wherever you need it. The scrap is easy to use, but because the contents of the scrap can be lost easily, you should use this trick only if you are going to insert copies of the text into the document immediately after copying the text.

Place a copy of the text in the scrap without removing the text from the document by choosing **C**opy and accepting the proposed response. The scrap's contents, enclosed in curly braces, are displayed on the status line at the bottom of the screen.

To reinsert the contents of the scrap into your document, select the location in the document where you want the copied text to appear and either press the Ins key or choose the **I**nsert command. Inserting the text from the scrap into the document does not delete the text from the scrap, so you can insert copied text as many times as you want.

Trick   **Copy text to the scrap with Alt-F3.**

Press Alt-F3 to copy selected text directly to the scrap. This shortcut is the equivalent of pressing Esc, choosing **C**opy, and then pressing Enter.

Trick   **Quickly replace text with the contents of the scrap with Shift-Ins.**

To replace selected text in the document with the contents of the scrap, press Shift-Ins. Word overwrites the selected text with the contents of the scrap, saving you the trouble of deleting the selected text manually.

Tip   **Use the mouse to copy text rapidly.**

If you have a mouse, you can easily copy text from one place to another. Simply select the text to be copied (see fig. 5.16). Next, move the mouse pointer to the spot where you want a copy of the selected text to appear (see fig. 5.17). Then hold the Shift key, and click either mouse button. The text is copied directly, not through the scrap, as shown in figure 5.18.

The only disadvantage to this technique is that because the scrap does not receive a copy of the text, you cannot repeat the insertion. If you want to insert the same piece of text elsewhere, you must repeat the entire procedure.

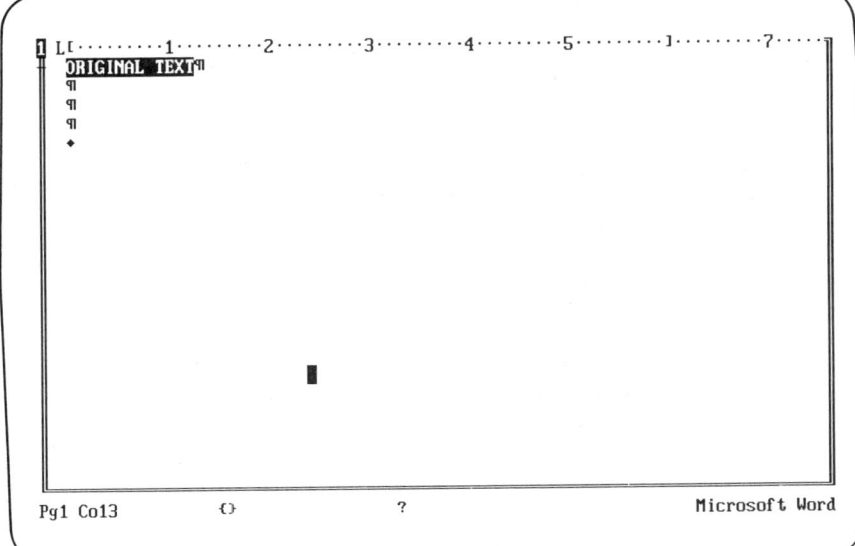

Fig. 5.16.

Using the mouse to select text to be copied.

Fig. 5.17.

Selecting the destination.

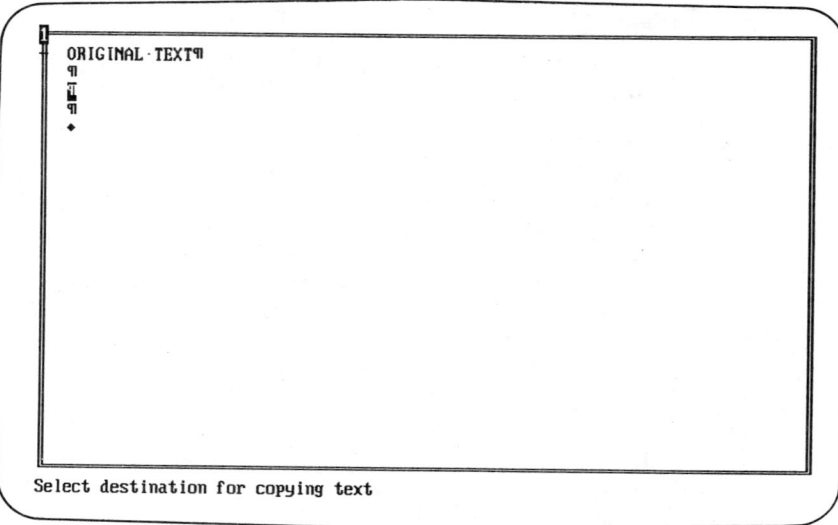

Fig. 5.18.

After copying the text with the mouse.

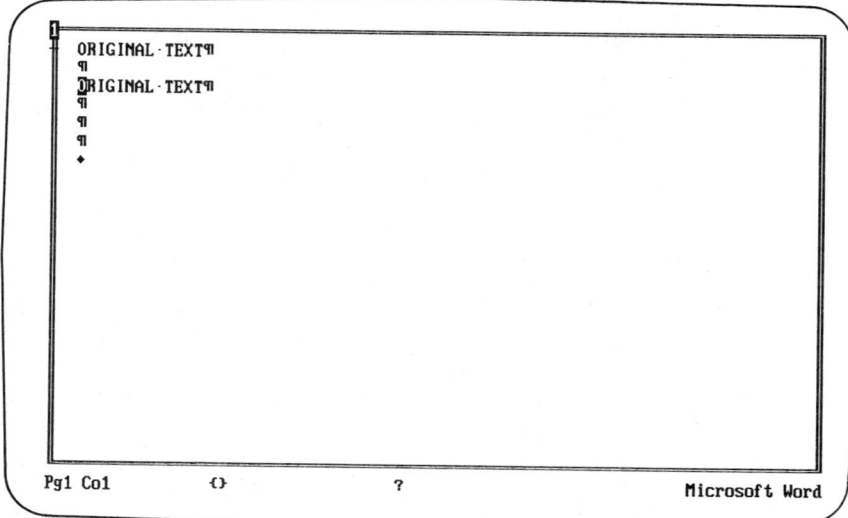

Tip   Move text quickly and safely with the mouse.

Mouse users can also move text rapidly and safely from one place to another. Select the text to be moved (see fig. 5.19). Move the mouse pointer to the location where you want the text to appear (see fig. 5.20). Hold the Ctrl key, and click the left mouse button. As shown in figure 5.21, the text is moved directly rather than through the scrap, which is precisely the advantage of this technique. You cannot possibly lose the text accidentally.

```
┌─────────────────────────────────────────────────────────┐
│ ▪                                                         │
│                      Washington, ·D.C.¶                   │
│                            ¶                              │
│ INTRODUCTION¶                                             │
│ ¶                                                         │
│ Technological·determinism,·the·doctrine·that·a·given·     │
│ technology·produces·a·given·set·of·economic,·social,·and· │
│ cultural·consequences,·is·under·increasing·attack·in·the· │
│ history·and·sociology·of·technology.···Whether·or·not·these· │
│ possibilities·are·realized·depends·on·the·social,·cultural,· │
│ and·economic·setting·in·which·the·innovation·occurs.··     │
│ Increasingly,·it·is·argued·that·technologies·do·not·      │
│ necessarily·produce·a·given·set·of·outcomes;·on·the·      │
│ contrary,·a·new·technology·merely·creates·a·new·set·of·   │
│ possibilities.·¶                                          │
│ ¶                                                         │
│ ¶                                                         │
│ ¶                                                         │
│ BACKGROUND¶                                               │
│ ¶                                                         │
│ The·Origins·of·Technological·Determinism¶                 │
│ ¶                                                         │
│ The·concept·of·technological·determinism·antedates·the·   │
│                                             ╌OUTLINE2.DOC╌ │
│ Pg1 Co15        {Increas...ties.·}·?        Microsoft Word │
└─────────────────────────────────────────────────────────┘
```

Fig. 5.19.

Using the mouse to select text to be moved.

```
┌─────────────────────────────────────────────────────────┐
│ ▪                                                         │
│                      Washington,·D.C.¶                    │
│                            ¶                              │
│ INTRODUCTION¶                                             │
│ ¶                                                         │
│ Technological·determinism,·the·doctrine·that·a·given·     │
│ technology·produces·a·given·set·of·economic,·social,·and· │
│ cultural·consequences,·is·under·increasing·attack·in·the· │
│ history·and·sociology·of·technology.·▪·Whether·or·not·these· │
│ possibilities·are·realized·depends·on·the·social,·cultural,· │
│ and·economic·setting·in·which·the·innovation·occurs.··     │
│ Increasingly,·it·is·argued·that·technologies·do·not·      │
│ necessarily·produce·a·given·set·of·outcomes;·on·the·      │
│ contrary,·a·new·technology·merely·creates·a·new·set·of·   │
│ possibilities.·¶                                          │
│ ¶                                                         │
│ ¶                                                         │
│ BACKGROUND¶                                               │
│ ¶                                                         │
│ The·Origins·of·Technological·Determinism¶                 │
│ ¶                                                         │
│ The·concept·of·technological·determinism·antedates·the·   │
│                                             ╌OUTLINE2.DOC╌ │
│ Select destination for moving text                        │
└─────────────────────────────────────────────────────────┘
```

Fig. 5.20.

Selecting the destination.

Fig. 5.21.

After moving the text with the mouse.

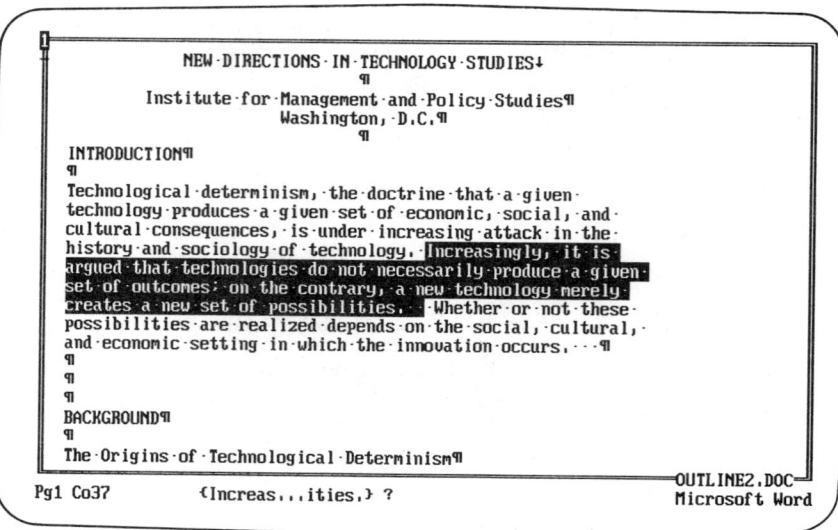

```
NEW·DIRECTIONS·IN·TECHNOLOGY·STUDIES↵
                    ¶
    Institute·for·Management·and·Policy·Studies¶
              Washington,·D.C.¶
                    ¶
INTRODUCTION¶
¶
Technological·determinism,·the·doctrine·that·a·given·
technology·produces·a·given·set·of·economic,·social,·and·
cultural·consequences,·is·under·increasing·attack·in·the·
history·and·sociology·of·technology.·Increasingly,·it·is·
argued·that·technologies·do·not·necessarily·produce·a·given·
set·of·outcomes;·on·the·contrary,·a·new·technology·merely·
creates·a·new·set·of·possibilities.··Whether·or·not·these·
possibilities·are·realized·depends·on·the·social,·cultural,·
and·economic·setting·in·which·the·innovation·occurs.···¶
¶
¶
¶
BACKGROUND¶
¶
The·Origins·of·Technological·Determinism¶
```

```
Pg1 Co37        {Increas...ities.} ?              OUTLINE2.DOC
                                                  Microsoft Word
```

Tip · Create a macro that moves text rapidly and safely.

If you don't have a mouse, you can use a macro to achieve the same degree of safety when moving text. Here's the text of a macro that prompts you each step of the way:

```
«PAUSE Select text to be moved. Press Enter when done»
«SET WORD = Selection»
<del>
«PAUSE Select destination point. Press Enter when done»
«WORD»
```

To create and use this macro, follow the instructions in Chapter 13, "Macros." Save the macro using the macro name quick_move.mac^<ctrl q>m.

This macro creates a variable called WORD and assigns the selected text to that variable. The macro stores the contents of this variable without depending on the scrap. After you select the destination and press Enter, the macro inserts the contents of the variable into your document.

Trap · Word scrolls down after you make an insertion.

Suppose that you move a block of text that doesn't fit on the screen where the block is inserted. Word scrolls to the end of the inserted text after it is pasted in. For some users, that movement is not a problem. Many writers, however, complain that after making an insertion, they need to work on the transition between the old text and the beginning of the inserted material and so must immediately scroll back to the beginning of the insertion. If you move many paragraphs, this scrolling can become tedious.

Trick   If you have a mouse, you can stop Word's downward scrolling after an insertion.

Here's an undocumented feature of Word: Cut a big paragraph to the scrap and place the cursor where you want the text to appear. Now position the mouse pointer one or two lines above the cursor. Press Ins to insert the text from the scrap and then immediately click the left mouse button. Word does not scroll the screen down to the bottom of the inserted text.

Trick   Transpose characters with the mouse.

To transpose characters written in the wrong order (such as *Ferd* rather than *Fred*), select the second character that is out of order. Then move the mouse pointer to the first character that is out of order. Hold the Ctrl key and click the left button.

Trick   Transpose words with the mouse.

Use the approach presented in the preceding tip to transpose words written in the wrong order (such as *ill mildly* rather than *mildly ill*). Select the second word and move the mouse pointer anywhere in the first word. Then hold the Ctrl key and click the right button.

Trick   Transpose sentences with the mouse.

You can transpose entire sentences in the same way that you transpose letters or words: Select the second sentence, move the mouse pointer anywhere in the first sentence, hold the Ctrl key, and click both buttons.

Fundamental Formatting Concepts

With Word, you can either format as you write or format later, whichever you prefer. The two techniques differ in the following ways:

- ❏ In the formatting-as-you-write approach, you use formatting commands to "program" the cursor. The text you type has the chosen format or formats until you give another formatting command. With this technique, you can "lay down" formats as you create text. The challenge is to develop a limited repertoire of simple techniques; then you can use the commands without allowing them to interfere with the composing process.

❏ If you prefer to format after your text is complete, you use text-selection commands to select (highlight) the text you want to format. Then you issue a formatting command that affects only the selected text. This approach is best suited to advanced formatting tasks, such as creating running heads, that you can do after you have written your document.

The advantage of formatting as you write is that you don't have to use text-selection commands before formatting. Selecting words, sentences, and paragraphs for formatting retrospectively is tedious and time consuming. When you format as you write, you give a formatting command and then type; Word enters the format with the text.

In this section, you will find a survey of some basic points about formatting, and in the following section, you will find a detailed examination of the formatting-as-you-write approach. Chapter 7 presents a more detailed examination of character and paragraph formatting, including the formatting-later approach.

Tip **Understand the distinctions Word draws between character, paragraph, and page style formats.**

Understanding these distinctions helps you grasp what is happening on Word's screen as you write.

❏ *Character styles* include the formats that affect the appearance of characters, such as boldface, italic, underlining, strike-through, uppercase only, small caps, double underlining, and position (superscript, normal, or subscript). With Word, you also can use all the fonts (type styles) and type sizes your printer can produce. You even can create hidden text, which you then can choose to display and print or to hide.

❏ *Paragraph styles* include the formats that affect the appearance of all the text in a paragraph, such as alignment (flush left, flush right, or justified), indentation (from both the right and left margins, as well as the paragraph's first line), line spacing (single-space or double-space), and blank lines before or after the paragraph. You also can tell Word whether you want to keep all the lines of the paragraph together on a page and keep the paragraph on the same page with the paragraph that follows.

❏ *Page styles* include the formats that affect the page design, including margins, footnotes, running heads, page number location, and others.

Table 5.6 lists the default character, paragraph, and page style formats in effect when you start Word. These formats come from the default style sheet, NORMAL.STY, that Word uses unless you choose the **F**ormat **S**tylesheet **A**ttach command to instruct Word otherwise.

Table 5.6
Word's Default Styles

Character Styles	Setting
Boldface	No
Italic	No
Underline	No
Strike-through	No
Uppercase	No
Small caps	No
Double underline	No
Position	Normal
Font name	*
Font size	*
Page numbers	Default font and size
Footnote reference mark	Normal position

Paragraph Styles	Setting
Alignment	Left flush
Left indent	0″
First line	0″
Right indent	0″
Line spacing	1 line
Blank lines before	0 lines
Blank lines after	0 lines
Keep lines together	No
Keep with following paragraph	No
Footnote text	Single space, left flush

Page Styles	Setting
Footnote position	Same page
Number of columns on page	1
Line numbers	Off
Top margin	1″

Table 5.6—Continued

Page Styles	Setting
Bottom margin	1"
Left margin	1.25"
Right margin	1.25"
Page length	11"
Page width	8.5"
Running head position from top	0●
Page numbers	No
Page number location from top	0.5"
Page number location from left	7.25"
Page numbering	Start at 1
Page number style	Arabic (1,2,3, etc.)
Running head position	0.5" from top
Running head on first page	No

* Depends on printer named in Print Options `printer` field

Tip **You can apply character styles to any group of characters. Paragraph styles apply to whole paragraphs. Page styles apply to whole documents, or divisions of a document.**

You can apply character styles to any group of characters, from 1 to 1,000,000 and more.

Paragraph styles always apply to the whole paragraph. If you choose a paragraph style, it applies to all the text within a paragraph. Remember that Word defines a paragraph as the text between two paragraph marks (or the text between the beginning of the file and the first paragraph mark). A paragraph can be a single-line heading.

Page styles normally apply to whole documents. As you learn in Chapter 8, however, you can divide your document into divisions. Each division then can have its own page style.

Trap **You lose formats when you delete paragraph and division marks.**

When you choose paragraph formats for a paragraph, Word stores the formats in the paragraph mark at the end of the paragraph. If you delete the paragraph mark, you lose the formats.

Similarly, Word stores the nondefault page style formats you choose in a *division mark*. A division mark is a double row of dots, automatically inserted at the end of your document or anywhere in the document where a new division begins. If you delete the division mark, you lose the formats for the preceding division.

If you accidentally delete a paragraph or division mark accidentally, choose the **U**ndo command immediately to restore the deleted material. If you have waited too long to use Undo (the command's function changes if you move the cursor, type something, or choose another command), press Ins to restore the mark from the scrap.

Formatting as You Write

Writing is something of a juggling act—you must think of many considerations at once, such as person, point of view, word choice, tense, unity, coherence, and so on. For many writers, those decisions are already too much to cope with—and if you're like them, you may prefer to put off formatting (yet *another* ball in the air) until you have finished writing the text. If you know what you're going to say, however, or if you're typing something you have already written, you may prefer to format as you write. If you do, you will save keystrokes and time because you won't have to select the text before formatting it.

Tip **To format your text as you write, the speed-key formatting shortcuts are best.**

You can choose formats from the Format Character, Format Paragraph, or Format Division command menus. By far the best way to format is to use the speed-key formatting shortcuts, entered by holding the Alt key and pressing another key to achieve a format attribute (for example, pressing Alt-B for boldface).

The speed-formatting shortcut keys are defined by Word's default style sheet, NORMAL.STY. A major reason for modifying NORMAL.STY (which you can do very easily with Word 5) is to change the speed keys. You learn how to change the speed keys in Chapter 12. Table 5.7 lists the default speed-key shortcuts.

Why should you prefer the speed-key formatting shortcuts over the Format menus? Following are several reasons:

❑ Word keeps the shortcuts in memory, so they're super fast.

❑ The shortcuts require fewer keystrokes than the Format menus.

❑ The shortcuts are mnemonic: the command letter reminds you of the command's function (for example, Alt-B is boldface, Alt-C is center), so the shortcuts are easy to memorize.

❑ You can build on the shortcuts later, adding modifications stored in your own style sheets.

Learn the speed-key formatting approach—it pays off handsomely now and later when you create style sheets.

Table 5.7
Speed-Key Formatting Shortcuts

Key	Format
Alt-B	Boldface character style
Alt-C	Centered paragraph style
Alt-D	Double underline character style
Alt-E	Hidden text character style
Alt-F	Indent first line of paragraph to next tab
Alt-J	Justified paragraph style
Alt-K	Small caps character style
Alt-L	Flush-left paragraph style
Alt-M	Reduce left indent one tab
Alt-N	Increase left indent one tab
Alt-O	Open paragraphs with blank line before
Alt-Q	Indent extended quotation
Alt-R	Flush-right paragraph style
Alt-S	Strike-through character style
Alt-T	Hanging indent paragraph style
Alt-U	Underline character style
Alt-2	Double-spaced paragraphs
Alt- =	Superscript character style
Alt--(hyphen)	Subscript character style

Tip **The Alt-key formatting commands are not toggle switches.**

Many word processing programs handle formatting by using toggle commands: a command like Ctrl-B turns on boldfacing, for instance, and the same command turns off boldfacing later. With Word, however, you cancel special paragraph formats by pressing Alt-P; you cancel special character formats by pressing Alt-space bar. Suppose that you turn on line centering with Alt-C and boldfacing with Alt-B, and then you type some text. To return to normal paragraph and character formatting, press Alt-P and Alt-space bar.

Trick **You can "program" the cursor so that it "lays down" several formats.**

If you press Alt-B, Alt-K, Alt-T, and Alt-U, the characters you type appear in boldface, underlined small caps, and the paragraph is formatted with a hanging indent (second and subsequent lines indented one tab stop). When you press Enter, Word copies all these formats to the next paragraph. To cancel these formats, simply press Alt-space bar to cancel all the character formats and press Alt-P to cancel the paragraph format.

Tip **One significant advantage of style sheets is that you can combine several formats in a single Alt-key command.**

As you learn in Chapter 12, a style sheet gives you—among other things—a way to create new formatting key codes or alter existing ones. When you create or alter key codes, you can combine several formatting commands in one Alt-key formatting command. You can create an Alt-key formatting command, for instance, that simultaneously enters all the formats mentioned in the preceding tip. (For more information, see Chapter 12, "Style Sheets.")

Formatting Characters and Paragraphs as You Write

You can put Word's formatting features to work as you create your text. This way you can see how your text will look when printed. You save time, too, because formatting as you write eliminates the need to select the text first, as you must do when you format retrospectively.

Trap **If you try to format a single character with a character style (such as superscript), the command doesn't work.**

When only one character is selected (highlighted), a character formatting command merely "programs" the cursor so that the next character you type has the format. New Word users frequently fall into this trap when attempting to superscript a number with Alt-= after typing the number. If you type a number, put the cursor on the number, and press Alt-=, nothing happens—until you type the next character, which is superscripted. Make a note of this method: use the Alt-key character-formatting command *before*, not after, you type the character to be formatted.

Trick **To format a single character with a character style, use the command twice.**

To format one character that has already been typed, use the command twice. To cancel character formatting on a single character, for example, highlight the character and press Alt-space bar twice.

Tip **When you press Enter, Word carries the formatting to the next paragraph.**

The character and paragraph formats in effect when you press Enter are carried to the next paragraph unless you deliberately alter them by issuing a formatting command. If you begin typing with the default normal paragraph style (flush left and single-spaced), the next paragraph has that style too.

Tip **Create a standard paragraph style to enter text in your document.**

Because Word copies the current formats when you press Enter, begin your document by creating a standard paragraph format. To create a document with single-spaced, justified paragraphs, each with a one-tab first-line indent and a blank line separating them, start your work session by giving the following Alt-key commands:

Alt-J (right-margin justification)
Alt-F (first-line indent of one default tab stop)
Alt-O (blank line before paragraph)

Every time you press Enter, this format is available for the following paragraph.

Using the formatting commands to format standard text paragraphs instead of using the Tab and Enter keys to create indents and blank lines is an excellent idea, as suggested in an earlier trap. If you use the Tab and Enter keys, you must reformat all the paragraphs manually if you change your mind about their appearance. If you create indents and spacing by choosing formats with speed keys or the Format commands, however, you can reformat them all by selecting them and using the Format command again.

If your printer can produce multiple fonts, you can expand your format by choosing a font and font size with the Format Character menu.

Trap **If you "lay down" a format that requires several commands to create, you may lose it when you start a new format.**

This possibility is one major drawback of formatting without style sheets. Suppose that you're working with the standard paragraph format just described, but then decide to enter an extended quotation. You press Enter; on the new paragraph mark, you press Alt-Q. When you resume standard paragraphs, however, you must specify all the formats again—an extremely tedious job.

Not all formatting choices cancel the current formatting. Alt-L and Alt-J, for instance, create, respectively, flush-left and justified alignments, and Alt-2 adds double-spacing, but these additions do not cancel other formats. The same effect is true of formatting choices you make in the Format menu. If you press Alt-P, Alt-T, or Alt-A, however, all current paragraph formats are canceled, and you will have to enter your standard paragraph formats again.

The best way to cure this problem is to create a style-sheet entry that automatically creates a complex standard character format. You can also copy formats from one place to another in your document. Chapter 7 discusses the techniques for copying formats.

Trap **If you work with nonstandard fonts, Word cancels the font choice every time you press Alt-space bar.**

Every printer has a standard character style. The Hewlett-Packard LaserJet™'s standard character style, for instance, is the monospace typewriter font Courier. If you have a printer that prints multiple fonts, you will probably want to take advantage of more dramatic fonts, such as Times Roman, Helvetica, or Schoolbook.

If so, you're in for an unpleasant surprise when you create and print your work. Your font choices, like other character formatting choices, are canceled every time you press Alt-space bar. Suppose that you're typing, thinking you're "laying down" text in 10-point Helvetica, which you chose from the Format Character command menu before you started typing. Then you turn on boldface character formatting by pressing Alt-B, and cancel boldface by pressing Alt-space bar. Without realizing what you have done, you have not only canceled boldface formatting, you have also canceled the 10-point Helvetica font. Because you cannot see fonts on the screen, you won't find out that the font changed until you print your document.

Note: If you have a color monitor, you can display font-size choices in different colors. To choose color, use the `colors` field in the Options menu. Although this welcome new Word 5 feature doesn't cure the problem, it helps.

Trick **Create a style-sheet entry to enter a standard paragraph and standard character format.**

You can get around the "unwanted font" problem by fussing with the keyboard, but by far the best solution is to waste no time before modifying the default style sheet, NORMAL.STY, to include a new default character format. To do this, record a new standard paragraph format with the **Format Stylesheet Record** command. Significant new Word 5 features make modifying existing NORMAL.STY key codes or adding new ones vastly easier and less costly to the user. Chapter 12 explains the procedures with an easy-to-follow, key-by-key tutorial. Don't hesitate to put style-sheet formatting to work for you right now.

Using Tabs as You Write

Word's default tab stops are placed at 0.5-inch intervals across the screen. You can change the default tab width by typing a new measurement in the `default tab width` field of the Options menu, as explained in Chapter 4. If you need to change the default tabs for just one section of text, however, you should create new custom tab stops.

Thanks to a major improvement in Word's tab-setting procedure, setting tabs with Word 5 is easy. Because you probably will want to set the tabs as you create and type tables and other units of text with custom tab stops, this section presents an overview of tab procedures.

Tip **Custom tabs are paragraph formats.**

Because custom tab settings are paragraph formats, the custom tabs you set apply to the currently selected paragraph or paragraphs—or the whole document if you select it with the Shift-F10 key. This fact also means that when you press Enter, Word copies the custom tabs to the next paragraph. Finally, if you accidentally delete the paragraph mark, the custom tabs go bye-bye along with all the other paragraph formats chosen for the paragraph.

Tip **When you set custom tabs, Word cancels all the default tabs to the left of the custom tab stop (but not the tabs to the right).**

When you set a custom tab, you want to be able to tab over to it unrestricted by intervening tabs. To allow this, Word cancels all the default tab stops to the left of the first new custom tab. The default tabs to the right of the custom tab stop, however, are still in place.

Tip **Understand your custom tab options.**

You can set five kinds of tabs with Word:

❑ Left-flush tabs align units of text by their first characters, with a ragged right edge.

❑ Right-flush tabs align units of text by their last characters, with a ragged left edge.

❑ Centered tabs align text centered at the tab stop. Use centered tabs to center text at several locations across the screen.

❑ Decimal tabs align numbers centered by their decimal points.

❑ Vertical tabs aren't tab stops at all. When you choose a tab, Word inserts a vertical line aligned with the tab stop. This line isn't a character—you cannot move it or erase it (unless you remove the tab stop itself). For this reason, vertical tabs are easy to work with. Use vertical tabs when you want to add vertical lines to tables.

Figure 5.22 shows the effects of these tab stops.

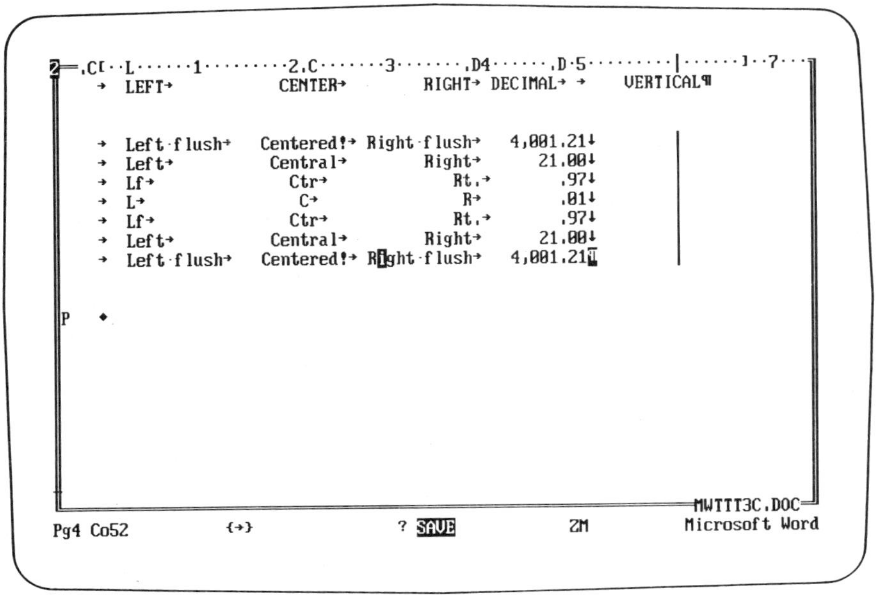

Fig. 5.22.

The five types of custom tab stops.

```
2=.C[··L······1········,2.C·····3······,D4······,D·5·········|·····]··7···]
      →  LEFT→           CENTER→       RIGHT→ DECIMAL→  →      VERTICAL¶

      →  Left·flush→  Centered!→ Right·flush→   4,001.21↓                │
      →  Left→        Central→        Right→       21.00↓                │
      →  Lf→          Ctr→              Rt.→         .97↓                │
      →  L→           C→                  R→         .01↓                │
      →  Lf→          Ctr→              Rt.→         .97↓                │
      →  Left→        Central→        Right→       21.00↓                │
      →  Left·flush→  Centered!→ Right·flush→   4,001.21↓                │

P   •




                                              ┌MWTTT3C.DOC┐
Pg4 Co52        {→}            ? SAVE       ZM    Microsoft Word
```

Tip **Set tabs with the keyboard.**

To set tabs with the keyboard, use the following steps:

1. Place the cursor in the paragraph for which you want to create custom tabs, or select the paragraphs (if you want tabs set in more than one).

2. Choose the **F**ormat **T**ab **S**et command. Alternatively, use the Alt-F1 keyboard shortcut.

    If the ruler isn't displayed, Word turns it on.

3. Press F1 to activate the special cursor on the ruler.

4. Press the right- or left-arrow key to move the cursor along the ruler. Alternatively, press PgDn or PgUp to move the cursor in 1-inch jumps; press Home or End to move to the beginning or end of the ruler.

    The `position` field displays the cursor's location.

5. To set a tab, press the first letter of the alignment you want (L for left-aligned or C for centered, for example).

    That's all you do to set the tab.

6. Set additional tabs if you wish.

7. Press Enter to carry out the command.

Tip **Turn on the ruler to set tabs with the mouse.**

The Format Tab Set command turns on the ruler if it isn't on already, but you are wise to keep the ruler on at all times if you use the mouse. You can set tabs directly on the ruler without using the Format Tab Set command. You also can perform some paragraph-formatting tasks directly with the ruler, as you learn in Chapter 8. Turn on the ruler by choosing the `Yes` option in the `show ruler` field of the Options menu, or use the ctrl-or macro described in Chapter 4. If you have a mouse, you can turn on the ruler by clicking both buttons in the upper right corner of the window.

Tip **Just click the ruler to set tabs with the mouse.**

Here's one of the best changes in Word 5: If you have a mouse, you can set tabs right on the ruler without using the Format Tab Set command. Use the following steps to set tabs with the mouse:

1. Place the cursor in the paragraph for which you want to create custom tabs, or select the paragraphs (if you want tabs set in more than one).

2. Point to the L to the left of the ruler and click it until the alignment you want is displayed. If you want left alignment, skip this step, because L is already displayed.

3. Click the left button on the ruler at the position where you want to set the tab. Word responds by displaying the alignment letter at that position.

4. To set additional tabs with the same alignment, click additional positions.

5. To set additional tabs with a different alignment, click a new alignment option and then click new positions.

Tip   **When you adjust custom tab positions, Word 5 displays the adjustment actively on the screen.**

Here's another new Word 5 feature that makes the program much easier to use: In preceding versions, you didn't see tab realignments until you carried out the Format Tab Set command. If the realignment wasn't right, you had to use the command again—and again and again, most likely. Now, you see realignments on the screen before carrying out the command.

Tip   **You can delete custom tab stops one at a time.**

If you use the keyboard, you can delete custom tab stops with the Format Tab Clear command, but using Format Tab Set or pressing Alt-F1 is actually better. Here's how to clear tab stops with the keyboard:

1. Select the paragraph or paragraphs containing the tabs you want to delete.

2. Choose the **F**ormat **T**ab **S**et command or press Alt-F1.

3. Press the down arrow to select the first tab.

4. Press Ctrl-Del to delete the selected tab and all the tabs to the right of that tab. Alternatively, press Del to delete only the selected tab.

5. Press the down arrow to select and delete additional tabs if you wish.

6. Press Enter to carry out the command.

Word restores the default tab stops to the right of the remaining custom tabs, if any. If all custom tabs have been removed, all the default tabs are restored.

If you use the mouse, you can delete tabs just by pointing to them on the ruler and clicking both buttons. Easy!

Trick **Delete all custom tabs at once with the Format Tab Reset-all command.**

The Format Tab Reset-all command removes all custom tab stops for the selected paragraph or paragraphs. If you change your mind, choose **U**ndo immediately after using this command.

Trick **Write a macro to help you set and delete tabs with the keyboard.**

You can easily set and delete tabs from the keyboard with Word 5, but you must remember some new functions for the cursor keys. That's why setting tabs is an excellent procedure for a menu-based macro. This macro doesn't require you to remember what the special keys do and walks you through the whole procedure. This nice, big macro demonstrates the power—and excellent structure—of Word's macro programming language. The macro presents the user with the choices of setting, moving, or deleting tabs, and then walks through the selected procedure:

```
«SET echo = "off"»
«SET response = "N"»
«WHILE response = "N"»
«ASK choice=?(S)et, (M)ove, or (D)elete custom tabs?»
    «IF choice = "S"»
        «SET response = "Y"»
        «SET continue = "Y"»
        «WHILE continue = "Y"»
            «ASK tab=? (L)eft, (R)ight, (C)entered, (D)ecimal, or
                (V)ertical?»
            <alt f1>
            «PAUSE Press Right, Left, PgUp, PgDn, Home, or End
                to choose position and press Enter»
            «tab»<enter>
            «ASK continue= ? Set another - (Y)es or (N)o?»
        «ENDWHILE»
    «ENDIF»
    «IF choice = "M"»
        «SET response = "Y"»
        <alt f1>
        «PAUSE Down or Up to select, Ctrl-Left or Ctrl-Right to
            move, Enter when done»
        <enter>
```

```
«ENDIF»
«IF  choice  =  "D"»
      «SET  response  =  "Y"»
      <alt  f1>
      «PAUSE  Down  to  select,  Del  to  remove,
            Ctrl-Del  to  remove  all  to  right»
      <enter>
«ENDIF»
«ENDWHILE»
```

To create and use this macro, follow the instructions in Chapter 13, "Macros." Save the macro using the macro name quick_tabs.mac^<ctrl q>t.

Creating and Formatting Footnotes as You Write

If you work in a professional or business writing situation, you may face one additional formatting-as-you-write challenge: creating and formatting footnotes. Word's footnoting capabilities are excellent. Word automatically inserts the footnote reference mark and a footnote number and adjusts the numbering automatically if you insert or delete footnotes. Footnote printing is completely automatic: Word very capably takes care of all the tedious footnote-placement problems. The program prints a rule to separate footnotes from the text, and long footnotes are automatically "floated" to the bottom of the next page. You also can choose to create endnotes if you don't want the footnotes to appear at the bottom of the page.

Although Word handles footnotes well, creating and formatting them correctly can be challenging. This section provides a quick overview of the problems—and the solutions.

Trap **You must use three different commands to create footnotes.**

You must follow this procedure carefully to create footnotes correctly.

1. Choose between footnotes or endnotes by choosing the Same-page or End option in the Format Division Layout command menu. If you choose End, Word prints the footnotes as endnotes at the end of the document. If you divide your document into divisions, the endnotes appear at the division break. See Chapter 8 for more information on divisions.

2. To create a footnote, use the **F**ormat **F**ootnote command. At the `reference mark` field, just press Enter so that Word automatically numbers the footnotes.

After you use the Format Footnote command, Word moves the cursor to the special footnote area, past the end mark. The reference mark appears automatically.

3. Type the text of the footnote.

4. Use the **J**ump **F**ootnote command to return to the footnote reference mark's location in the document.

Trap   **The footnote reference mark prints in normal position, not superscript.**

If you want the reference mark to be superscripted, you must format it manually using the Alt-= command. That formatting can be tedious if you're entering many footnotes.

To remedy this problem, you can create a macro. But by far the best way is to add to Word's default style sheet, NORMAL.STY, an entry that automatically superscripts footnote reference marks. For details, see Chapter 12.

Trap   **Word doesn't repeat the formats you choose for footnote text.**

Suppose that you enter a footnote; after typing it, you press Alt-J to justify the footnote text and Alt-O to add a blank line. Then you enter another footnote. Word doesn't repeat the formats you chose for the first footnote. You must give the formatting commands all over again.

To solve this problem, you can create a macro to do the formatting for you. The best solution, however, is to create a style-sheet entry that automatically formats footnote text precisely the way you want. For details, see Chapter 12.

Trap   **You cannot delete a footnote by deleting the footnote text.**

If you attempt to delete the footnote text's paragraph mark in the footnote area, you see the message, `Not a valid action for footnotes`. To delete the footnote, delete the reference mark.

Trick   **Move a footnote by moving the reference mark.**

To move a footnote, just select the reference mark in the text (not in the footnote area) and press Del to cut the reference mark to the scrap. Move the cursor to the mark's new location, and press Ins. Word automatically adjusts footnote numbering if necessary.

Chapter Summary

In this chapter, you have learned many ways to harness Word's power as you compose a document. To create text fast, use the text mode. Press Enter only when you want to start a new paragraph, and work with the `Partial` or `All` options for the display of nonprinting symbols so that you can see the paragraph marks you create. Join and split paragraphs by editing paragraph marks. Don't create indents or blank lines using Enter, Tab, or the space bar; instead, create a standard paragraph format to enter these formats automatically. If you need to even out lines, use automatic hyphenation. Use forced page breaks only when you always want the page break where you press Shift-Ctrl-Enter; use the `keep follow` option in the **F**ormat **P**aragraph command to guard against unwanted page breaks in other situations.

To edit or format text already typed, you must first select it so that it is highlighted on the screen. From all the text-selection techniques, choose the fixed-unit and variable-amount techniques that you find convenient. As you type, use Backspace and Del to fix errors immediately. Use **U**ndo right after the deletion if you change your mind and want to restore the deleted text. If you cut text with Del or the **D**elete command, Word stores the text temporarily in the scrap, which holds only one deletion at a time—new deletions wipe out the former contents. You can insert the contents of the scrap anywhere in your document by pressing Ins or using the **I**nsert command. To avoid erasing the scrap's contents, use Shift-Del to delete a selection. If you use the keyboard-only version of Word, create macros to emulate WordStar text-editing commands.

You can use the scrap to move text, but moving text with the mouse is easier—and safer—because you have no chance of accidentally erasing the scrap's contents and losing the text you're moving). If you don't have a mouse, create a macro to move text safely.

Word distinguishes between character, paragraph, and page style formats. The default formats are contained in the default style sheet, NORMAL.STY. Character styles apply to any group of characters, but paragraph styles apply only to whole paragraphs. Page styles apply to the whole document or to divisions in a document (if you have created divisions by entering a division break). Paragraph and page style formats are stored in the paragraph and division marks; if you delete the marks, you lose the formats.

When you format as you write, you "program" the cursor to "lay down" the formats you choose. To do so, you can use the **F**ormat **C**haracter or **F**ormat **P**aragraph commands, but the speed-key shortcuts, defined by NORMAL.STY, Word's default style sheet, are the best. As you learn in Chapter 12, you can easily modify these keys, so learning them now is an excellent idea.

When you press Enter, Word copies the current character and paragraph formats to the next paragraph. Because of this feature, you can create a document with a paragraph format you defined—a format that can include automatic first-line indents and blank lines after the paragraph. You lose your formatting choices, however, when you stop writing standard paragraphs and choose a new format, such as a heading or extended quote. To resume standard paragraphs, you must give all the formatting commands again. To solve this problem, learn how to copy formats, as described in Chapter 7, or create a new standard paragraph format by modifying NORMAL.STY, as suggested in Chapter 12. When you create a new standard paragraph format, Word uses its character format for all formats. If you want to use a nonstandard character font for printing, refer to Chapter 12.

You probably will want to set tabs and create footnotes as you type. With Word 5, setting, realigning, and deleting tabs with the mouse is extremely easy. With the keyboard version, these procedures are still easy, but a macro can save you the trouble of remembering some special commands. When you create footnotes, you must use three commands (Format Division Layout to specify footnote location, Format Footnote to create the footnote reference mark and type footnote text, and Jump Footnote to return to the text). You must format the reference mark and the footnote text manually each time you enter a footnote. If you add style-sheet entries to NORMAL.STY, however, you can get Word to enter the formats automatically. If you use footnotes, see Chapter 12.

6

More Writing Strategies: Using Outlines and Windows

When word processing programs for personal computers first were introduced, many people—including writing teachers—thought that using such software would automatically improve anyone's writing. By removing the time penalty for text revision, many people thought, word processing software would encourage writers to revise. The result could only be improved writing quality.

But word processing presents new problems for the writer. Because the display screen offers a limited view of the text, writers sometimes find it difficult to retain a grasp of their document's structure as they write. This problem is aggravated by the penalties imposed by scrolling, which becomes tedious and time consuming in lengthy documents. The result, all too often, is that long documents created on personal computers are poorly organized.

Here is where Word comes in. Word's outlining and windowing features provide the tools you need to sustain a grasp of your document's overall structure as you write. Most writing experts agree that the single most important factor in good writing is the quality of the document's organization. If you can learn how to use Word's features to create a well-conceived plan for your document's organization, and keep this plan in mind as you write, you will take a giant step toward quality writing.

Admittedly, planning before writing is a somewhat tedious business—and frankly, many writers are lazy and don't plan. When you write in business or professional situations, however, time is of the essence. You cannot afford to throw out a 45-page report because it's hopelessly disorganized and start over.

Even if you're dedicated to good planning, however, you run into a problem with even the best outline when you start writing. Writing is a form of thinking and of discovery. As you write, you discover new ways of thinking about, and organizing, your subject. You must therefore make changes to the outline. Soon keeping the outline up to date is a bigger chore than doing the writing, and you give up the outline.

If that's ever happened to you, here's some excellent news. You can use Word to create an outline before writing, but what's really significant about Word outlines isn't the advantage you get from planning. As you see in this chapter, Word automatically updates your outline to reflect changes you make as you write, even if they involve major reorganizations of your document.

You will grasp the significance of this feature when, after following this chapter's suggestions, you switch to the outlining mode and see your document's structure plainly and clearly displayed—even after you have performed major edits and reorganized large blocks of text. In an instant, your plan, your document's structure, and your next line of attack become crystal clear. This book suggests several pathways to high-productivity, but make no mistake: this is a 15-lane interstate.

In short, if you write business reports, academic articles, or any moderately lengthy or complex material, don't miss the approach to writing set forth in this chapter. You need a few tricks and ways around a trap or two (including a particularly valuable macro) in order to make these features work for you.

This chapter is concerned with the use of these features to aid and enhance the text-creation process. The following topics are discussed in this chapter:

- ❏ Creating outlines
- ❏ Viewing your outline's structure by collapsing and expanding headings
- ❏ Editing outlines
- ❏ Linking document headings and outline headings
- ❏ Numbering outlines automatically
- ❏ Using windows while creating text

A discussion of uses of outlines and windows for high-productivity editing purposes is found in Chapter 9.

Creating Outlines

In any outline, the first-level heading is logically superior to the others; it should state the subject being covered. Subordinate levels contain subtopics. Within a subtopic are additional subtopics, and so on. The level of a heading in the outline is shown by its indentation. First-level headings are not indented; second-level headings are indented one tab; third-level headings are indented two tabs; and so on.

High school and college composition instructors have long urged students to create outlines in this way, and for good reason: the more you think about your document's logical structure before you write, the more likely you are to achieve well-organized results.

In the early 1980s, computer programmers took this advice to heart and created *idea-processing programs*: stand-alone programs that help create, edit, and print outlines. These programs typically include commands for accomplishing the following tasks:

❏ *Typing outline headings*, each on its own line

❏ *Lowering or raising outline levels.* In idea-processing programs, the level of a heading is controlled not by tabs but by commands that *raise* a heading (that is, move it left) or *lower* a heading (move it right). You can use these commands to restructure an outline's logic.

❏ *Reorganizing outline headings.* Raising or lowering outline headings shifts them left or right. Idea-processing programs also provide commands that move headings up or down, letting you try different arrangements for topics.

❏ *Collapsing and expanding headings.* When an outline grows beyond the limits of the screen, its usefulness in providing a view of the document's structure is reduced. To solve this problem, idea-processing programs include commands that *collapse*, or hide, the subheadings under a heading. Later, if you want to see these subheadings again, you can *expand* them so that they reappear.

❏ *Printing the outline.* Many idea-processing programs let you print all levels of an outline or only the levels you specify.

Word's outlining features include all these commands and more. But Word also has another significant advantage over other idea-processing programs. Most other programs are stand-alone programs. After you finish an outline, you can print it and use it as a guide for writing. But as you write and learn more about how you want to make your point, you probably will change your document's structure. The outline you made, therefore, becomes an increasingly unreliable guide to your document's structure.

Word's outlining features, however, can be used to create a dynamic link between the document and the outline. As you make changes to your document, the changes are reflected in the outline. Changes to the outline can restructure the sections of your document.

With Word, outlining is no longer unrelated to the writing process. Because a document and its outline are connected, you can outline your document and write it at the same time. The headings you type in the outline become the headings of the document, and vice versa. There is no wasted effort. The outline processor merely offers you another way of examining and manipulating your document—a way that allows you to keep track of its overall structure, even as you write.

This chapter discusses outlining as an aid in text creation and in sustaining a grasp of your document's organization. Table 6.1 summarizes Word's key combinations and commands for outlining. Notice in this chapter that K+, K−, and K* refer to the plus, minus, and asterisk keys on the *numeric* keypad. Pressing the keyboard keys does not produce the same results. When a command uses a number, however, you must use the numbers on the top row of the main keyboard: for example, Alt-9 and Alt-0.

Table 6.1
Keys and Commands for Outlining

Key(s)	Effect
Shift-F2	Toggle between document view and outline view
Alt-0	Lower the selected heading's level
Alt-9	Raise the selected heading's level
K−, Alt-7, or F11	Collapse subheadings and body text below selected heading
K+, Alt-8, or F12	Expand subheadings (not body text) below selected heading

Table 6.1—Continued

Shift-K +, Shift-Alt-7, or Shift-F12	Expand body text below selected heading
Shift-K −, Shift-Alt-8, or Shift-F11	Collapse body text below selected heading
K*, PrtSc, or Ctrl-F12	Expand all headings below the selected heading
Ctrl-K +	Display headings to specified level (n = 1, 2, 3, etc.)
Shift-F5	Toggle between outline edit and outline organize mode

Command	Effect
Library Autosort	Sorts selected headings at one level
Library Number	Numbers all headings or selected headings in an outline
Print Printer	Prints outline as shown on-screen (in outline view only)

Tip **Think of the outline and the document as two ways of viewing the same text.**

You can view any document in two ways: document view and outline view. So far, you have looked at documents only in document view. If you press Shift-F2, Word switches to the outline view, which gives you another way of looking at the same document. Figure 6.1 shows how a document looks in outline view. Figure 6.2 shows how the same document looks in document view.

Tip **Distinguish between outline headings, document headings, and body text.**

To use Word's outline view effectively, you must understand three terms:

❑ *Outline headings.* the headings you create when you create an outline in outline edit mode. These headings appear as topics and subtopics in an outline; the first-level heading is flush left; the second-level heading is indented one tab, and so on (see fig. 6.3).

Fig. 6.1.

The outline view
of a document.

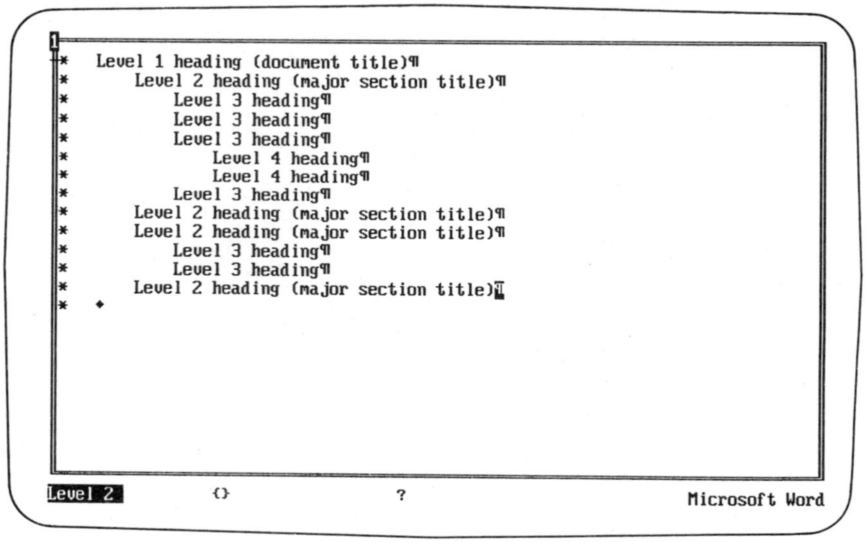

```
┌─────────────────────────────────────────────────────────┐
│ ⌐                                                        │
│ *   Level 1 heading (document title)¶                    │
│ *      Level 2 heading (major section title)¶            │
│ *         Level 3 heading¶                               │
│ *         Level 3 heading¶                               │
│ *         Level 3 heading¶                               │
│ *            Level 4 heading¶                            │
│ *            Level 4 heading¶                            │
│ *         Level 3 heading¶                               │
│ *      Level 2 heading (major section title)¶            │
│ *      Level 2 heading (major section title)¶            │
│ *         Level 3 heading¶                               │
│ *         Level 3 heading¶                               │
│ *      Level 2 heading (major section title)█            │
│ *   ♦                                                    │
│                                                          │
│ Level 2        {}              ?          Microsoft Word │
└─────────────────────────────────────────────────────────┘
```

Fig. 6.2.

The document
view.

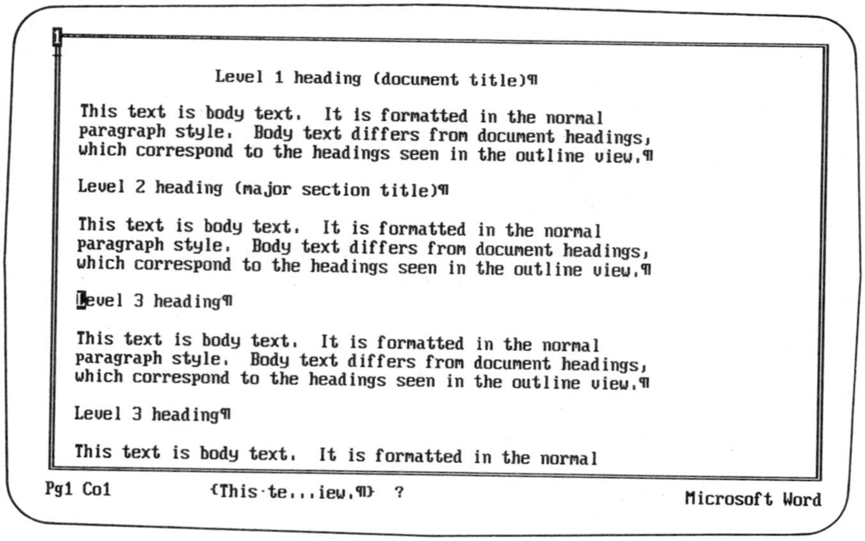

```
┌─────────────────────────────────────────────────────────┐
│ ⌐                                                        │
│              Level 1 heading (document title)¶           │
│                                                          │
│   This text is body text.  It is formatted in the normal │
│   paragraph style.  Body text differs from document headings, │
│   which correspond to the headings seen in the outline view.¶ │
│                                                          │
│   Level 2 heading (major section title)¶                 │
│                                                          │
│   This text is body text.  It is formatted in the normal │
│   paragraph style.  Body text differs from document headings, │
│   which correspond to the headings seen in the outline view.¶ │
│                                                          │
│   █evel 3 heading¶                                       │
│                                                          │
│   This text is body text.  It is formatted in the normal │
│   paragraph style.  Body text differs from document headings, │
│   which correspond to the headings seen in the outline view.¶ │
│                                                          │
│   Level 3 heading¶                                       │
│                                                          │
│   This text is body text.  It is formatted in the normal │
│ Pg1 Co1        {This·te...iew.¶}  ?       Microsoft Word │
└─────────────────────────────────────────────────────────┘
```

☐ *Document headings.* the outline headings as they appear in
document view. When you switch to document view after
creating an outline, these headings lose their indentations and
appear flush left. You can format them any way you want; the
formatting does not affect placement in the outline view. If

you are writing a book, first-level document headings are chapter titles, and second-level document headings are the titles of major sections within the chapter.

❏ *Body text.* the text written under the headings in normal paragraph form. You can display the body text in outline view if you want, but it's better to hide body text so that you can see the outline (see fig. 6.3).

Fig. 6.3.

Headings and body text in outline view.

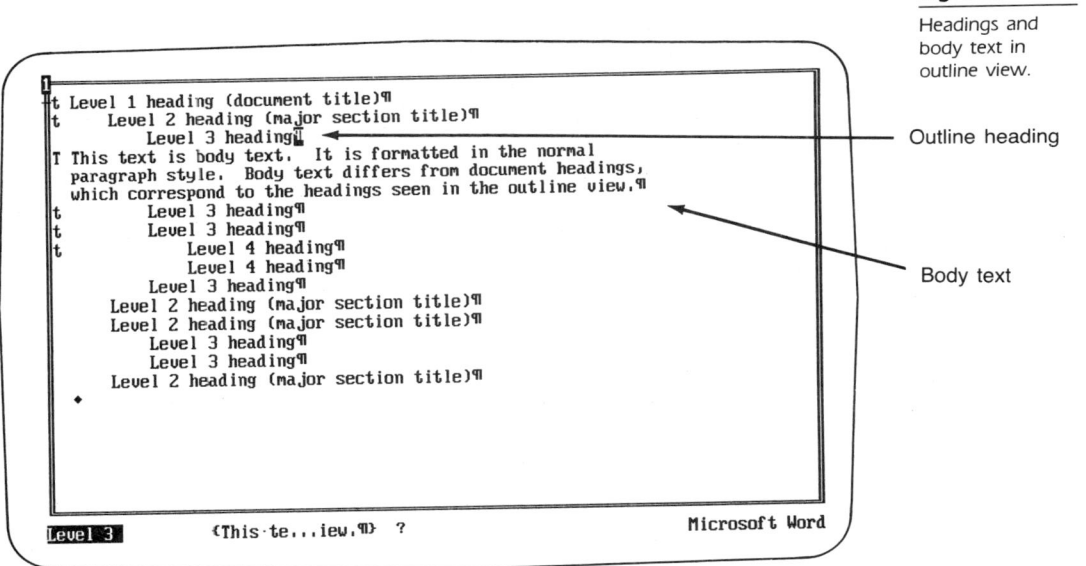

Outline heading

Body text

As you see, outlining is best suited for creating documents that use headings for different sections (such as a book, with chapter titles and section headings). You still can use outlining even if you don't want to divide your document with headings. Simply create your outline using hidden text, which you can choose to display and print if you want (or to hide if you don't). This trick is explained in "Linking Document Headings and Outline Headings" in this chapter.

Tip **Understand the difference between outline edit mode and outline organize mode.**

The outline view has two modes, and their differences are important. The *outline edit* mode is the one you use to create outlines and edit individual headings (see fig. 6.4). In *outline organize* mode, the minimum unit of selection is an entire heading, and you can select more than one heading at a time (see fig. 6.5). You use this mode to reorganize your outline after you have created it.

Fig. 6.4.

The outline edit mode.

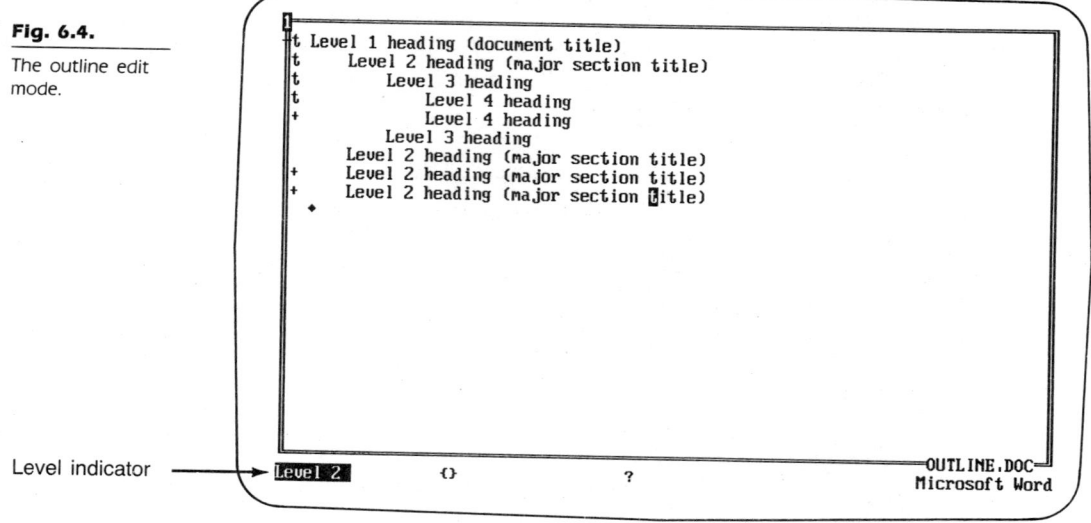

Level indicator

Fig. 6.5.

The outline organize mode.

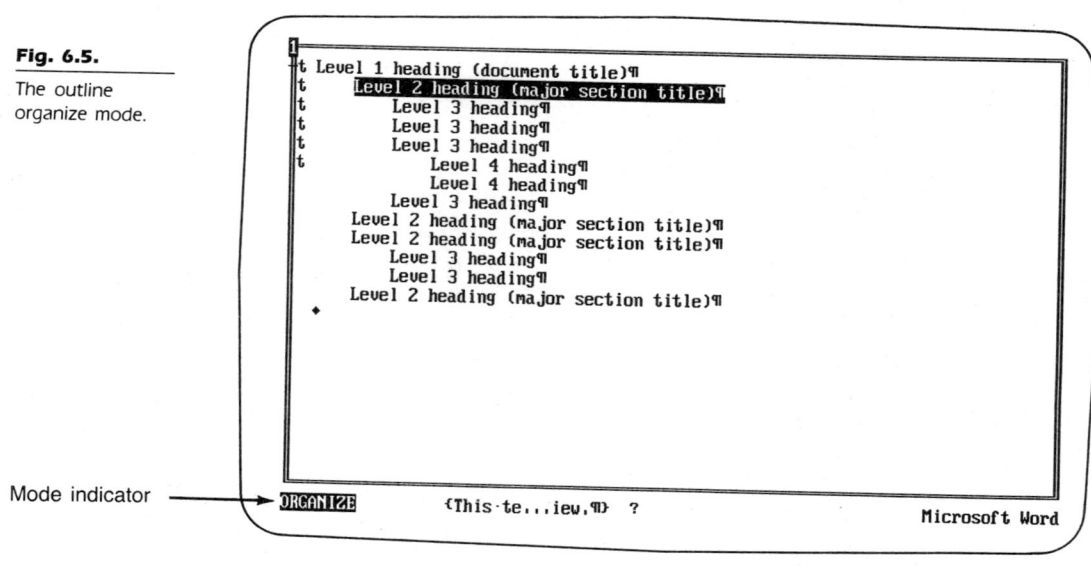

Mode indicator

Tip   **By default, Word is in outline edit mode when you press Shift-F2.**

After you press Shift-F2 to enter outline edit mode, you must press Shift-F5 to enter outline organize mode. Shift-F5 is a toggle key; pressing Shift-F5 again returns you to outline edit mode. To return to document view, press Shift-F2 again.

Trap   **You cannot go directly from your document to the outline organize mode.**

If you press Shift-F5 in the document mode, nothing happens (except a beep). To enter the outline organize mode, first press Shift-F2 and then press Shift-F5.

Tip   **To create a subheading, press Enter to move the cursor down one line. Then press Alt-0.**

When you start a new outline, Word positions the cursor at Level 1. You can use this level for the document's topic or title. When you press Enter, Word creates a new heading with the same level as the preceding one. Press Alt-0 to lower the heading one level to the right, and type a new heading. Continue in this way, pressing Enter to start new headings, Alt-0 to lower the heading's level, and Alt-9 to raise it.

Tip   **Use the parentheses on the keyboard's 9 and 0 keys to remind you which key raises heading levels and which key lowers them.**

In uppercase, the 9 and 0 keys enter the left and right parentheses, respectively. You can use these symbols to remind yourself which keys change a heading level. When you want to raise a heading level, that is, move the heading to the left, press Alt-9 (or the left parenthesis). When you want to lower a heading level, that is, move the heading to the right, press Alt-0 (or the right parenthesis).

Trick   **Use Alt-9 or Alt-0 to raise or lower several headings at once.**

When you want to raise or lower a block of several headings, don't waste time adjusting each heading. Press Shift-F5 to enter the outline organize mode from the outline edit mode, and select all the headings you want to adjust (see fig. 6.6). Then press Alt-9 to raise the headings or Alt-0 to lower them (see fig. 6.7). The headings can be the same or different levels, but all are raised or lowered one level.

Fig. 6.6.

Selecting several
headings to lower
at once.

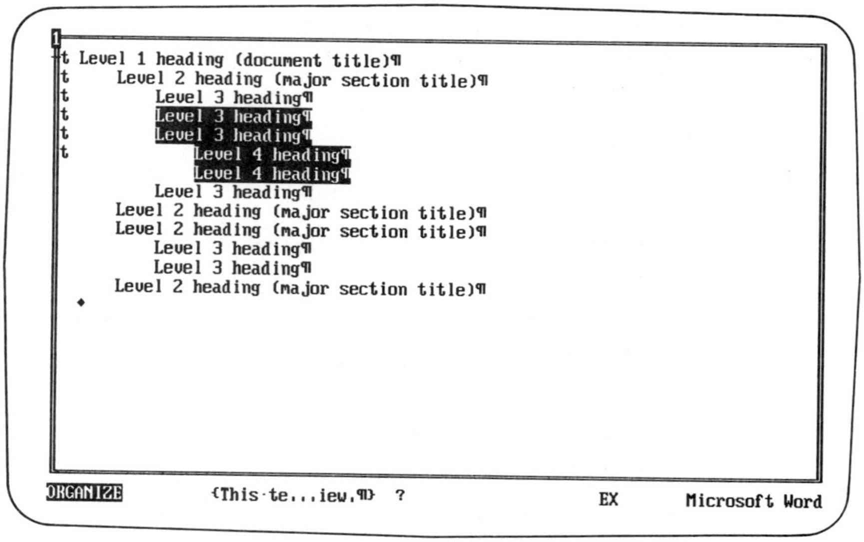

```
t Level 1 heading (document title)¶
t    Level 2 heading (major section title)¶
t       Level 3 heading¶
t       Level 3 heading¶
t       Level 3 heading¶
t          Level 4 heading¶
t          Level 4 heading¶
        Level 3 heading¶
    Level 2 heading (major section title)¶
    Level 2 heading (major section title)¶
       Level 3 heading¶
       Level 3 heading¶
    Level 2 heading (major section title)¶
◆

ORGANIZE        {This·te...iew.¶}  ?                    EX      Microsoft Word
```

Fig. 6.7.

Selected headings
have been
lowered one
level.

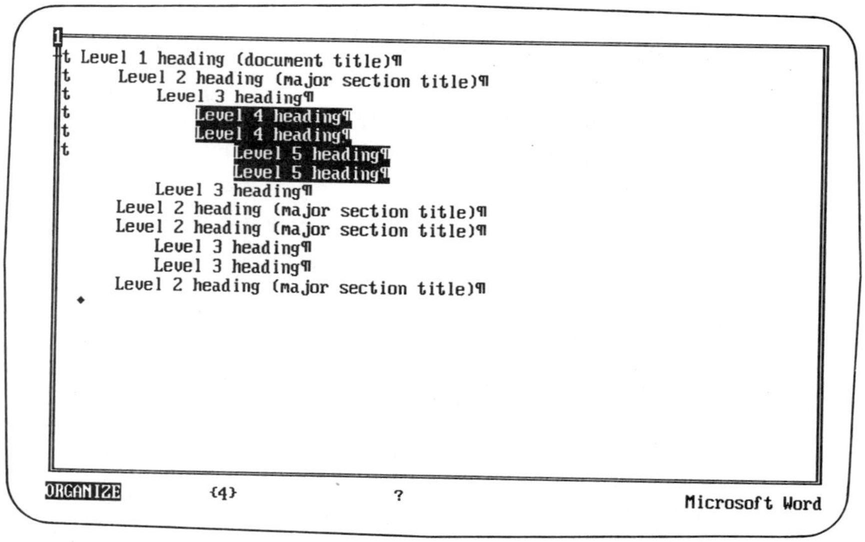

```
t Level 1 heading (document title)¶
t    Level 2 heading (major section title)¶
t       Level 3 heading¶
t          Level 4 heading¶
t          Level 4 heading¶
t             Level 5 heading¶
t             Level 5 heading¶
        Level 3 heading¶
    Level 2 heading (major section title)¶
    Level 2 heading (major section title)¶
       Level 3 heading¶
       Level 3 heading¶
    Level 2 heading (major section title)¶
◆

ORGANIZE        {4}                    ?                      Microsoft Word
```

To add body text beneath a heading, select the desired heading's
paragraph mark and press Enter. Then press Alt-P, and start typing.
Word indicates that whatever you type is a text paragraph by
displaying an uppercase T in the left margin. (If you collapse the body
text, the uppercase T changes to a lowercase t.)

If you want to enter another heading after typing the text, press Enter at the end of the paragraph and then press Alt-9. If you decide to make the text you have typed into a heading, press Alt-9 while the cursor is positioned anywhere in the text paragraph.

Viewing Your Outline's Structure by Collapsing and Expanding Headings

When your outline grows beyond the bounds of the screen or window, you should collapse headings so that you can keep the overall structure in view. When you collapse the subheadings and text under a heading, Word hides them from view and inserts a plus sign (+) in the selection bar, indicating that subheadings have been hidden. As you collapse body text and third-level or fourth-level headings, your document's overall structure—indicated by first-level and second-level headings—comes into view on one screen so that you can see the entire structure easily.

Tip **To collapse all the subheadings and body text under a heading, select the heading and press the K− key.**

Move the cursor to the heading under which you want to collapse subheadings and body text, selecting the heading (see fig. 6.8). Collapse the subheadings beneath this heading by pressing the K− key. (Do not use the hyphen key.) If your keypad does not have a minus key, press Alt-8. Figure 6.9 shows the result. The plus sign in the selection bar (+) indicates where subheadings have been collapsed. A t indicates where body text has been collapsed.

Tip **Collapse body text so that you can see the structure of your outline.**

After you create your outline, switch back to document view to flesh out your outline with text. When you switch back to the outline to view your document's structure, however, you see the body text as well as the headings. To collapse all the body text in the whole outline, press Shift-F10 to select the entire outline. Then press Shift-K− to collapse all the text.

Fig. 6.8.

Selecting a
heading to
collapse its
subheadings.

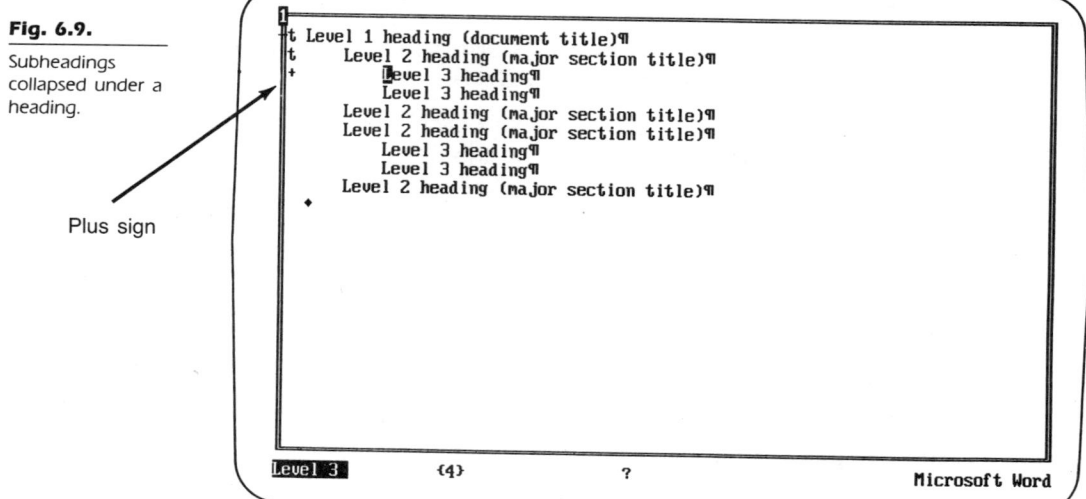

```
t Level 1 heading (document title)¶
t     Level 2 heading (major section title)¶
t         Level 3 heading¶        ◄─────────── Selected heading
t             Level 4 heading¶
t             Level 4 heading¶
t                 Level 5 heading¶
t                 Level 5 heading¶
          Level 3 heading¶
    Level 2 heading (major section title)¶
    Level 2 heading (major section title)¶
          Level 3 heading¶
          Level 3 heading¶
    Level 2 heading (major section title)¶
  ◆
```

```
Level 3         {4}              ?              Microsoft Word
```

Fig. 6.9.

Subheadings
collapsed under a
heading.

Plus sign

```
t Level 1 heading (document title)¶
t     Level 2 heading (major section title)¶
+         Level 3 heading¶
          Level 3 heading¶
    Level 2 heading (major section title)¶
    Level 2 heading (major section title)¶
          Level 3 heading¶
          Level 3 heading¶
    Level 2 heading (major section title)¶
  ◆
```

```
Level 3         {4}              ?              Microsoft Word
```

Tip   Collapse body text and show headings to a level you specify.

To collapse all body text and subheadings below a specific heading,
press Ctrl-K+ from anywhere in the outline. The message Enter a
number from 1 to 7 appears in the message line, as shown in figure
6.10. This message prompts you for the number of levels you want to

see. To display only the first-level and second-level headings, press 2. The body text and all headings lower than Level 2 disappear, as shown in figure 6.11.

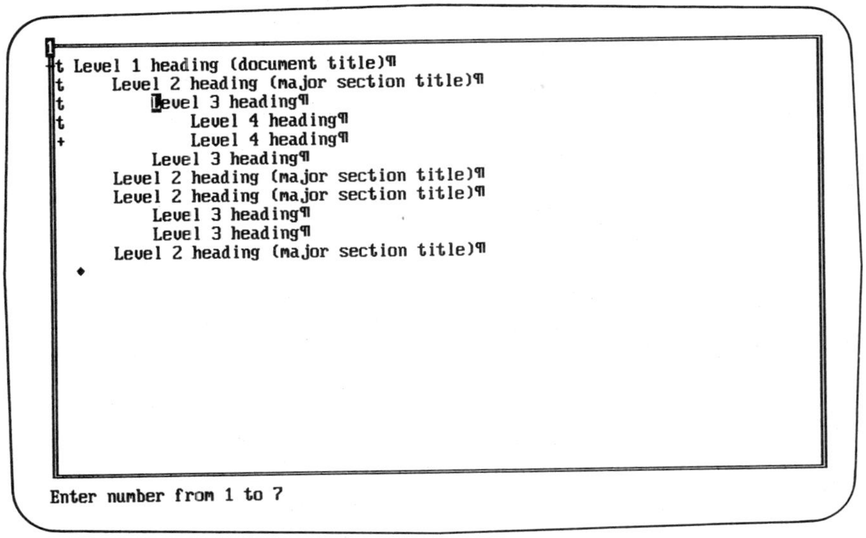

```
t Level 1 heading (document title)¶
t     Level 2 heading (major section title)¶
t         Level 3 heading¶
t             Level 4 heading¶
+             Level 4 heading¶
          Level 3 heading¶
      Level 2 heading (major section title)¶
      Level 2 heading (major section title)¶
          Level 3 heading¶
          Level 3 heading¶
      Level 2 heading (major section title)¶

    ♦

Enter number from 1 to 7
```

Fig. 6.10.

Entering the heading levels you want to see.

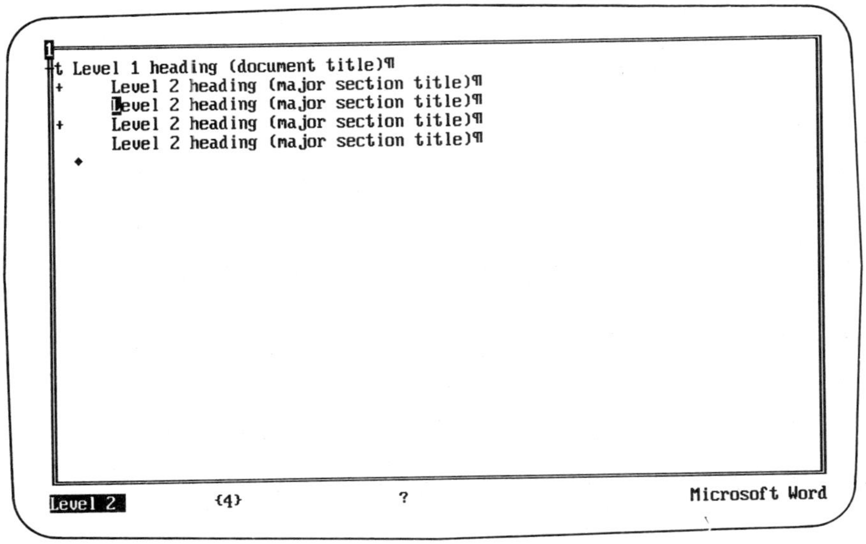

```
t Level 1 heading (document title)¶
+     Level 2 heading (major section title)¶
      Level 2 heading (major section title)¶
+     Level 2 heading (major section title)¶
      Level 2 heading (major section title)¶
    ♦




Level 2        {4}              ?                    Microsoft Word
```

Fig. 6.11.

Headings collapsed to the level you specified.

Tip **You can tell when you have collapsed subheadings under a heading by the plus sign that appears in the selection bar.**

Without the plus sign in the selection bar, you have no way of knowing that subheadings are hidden from view. If you see a plus sign (+) in the selection bar (just inside the left window border), as in figure 6.12, you know that at least one heading is hidden. The hidden material may or may not also contain some body text.

Fig. 6.12.

Symbols that indicate collapsed headings or body text.

Collapsed body text

Collapsed headings

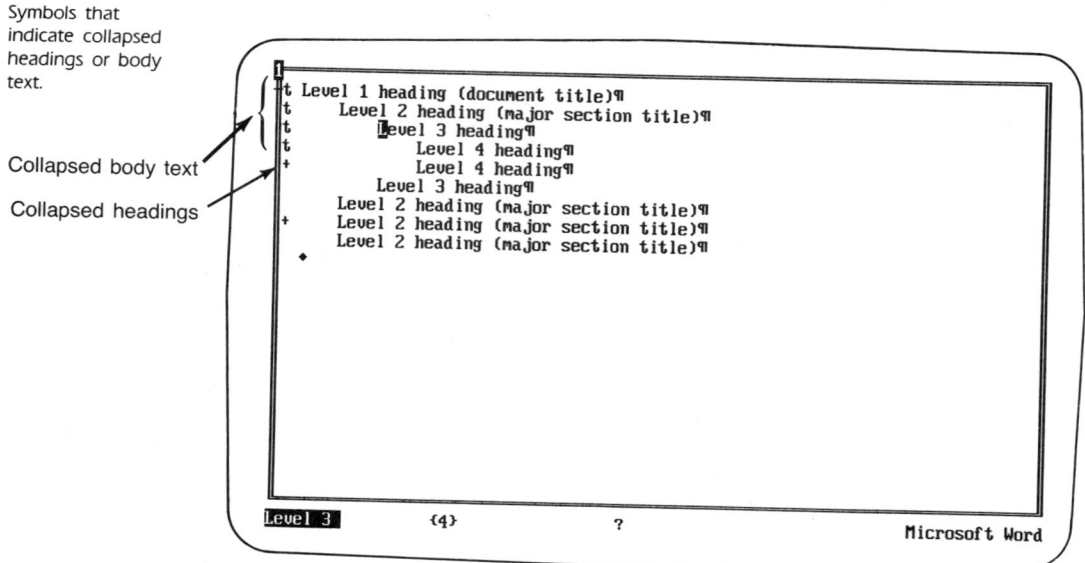

Tip **If a lowercase t appears in the selection bar, the only collapsed material is body text.**

Normally, you want to hide body text from view in your outline. When the t appears in the selection bar, you know that the only hidden material is body text; no headings are hidden. If a plus sign (+) appears in the selection bar, at least one heading is hidden from view (again see fig. 6.12); body text may also be hidden.

Trap **You can use the mouse to expand and collapse headings, but you must first switch to outline organize mode.**

If you try to select more than one heading in outline edit mode, nothing happens. In this mode, you can work on only one heading at a time. To select more than one heading, press Shift-F5 to switch to outline organize mode. Click both buttons to collapse all headings and body text below a heading. Click the right button to expand the next level below a heading. Clicking the left button simply selects a heading. You can drag to select several headings at once.

Tip **To expand the next-level subheadings beneath a heading, press the K+ key.**

If your keypad does not have a plus key, press Alt-7. This command expands only the next level of subheadings. If you select a second-level heading, for example, pressing K+ reveals only the third-level headings.

Tip **To expand all the subheadings beneath a heading, select the heading and press the K* key.**

If you don't have a numeric keypad, press the PrtSc (Print Scrn) key. Do not use the asterisk on the main keyboard.

Tip **To expand all headings, press Shift-F10 to select the entire outline and then press the K* key.**

Word shifts to the outline organize mode when you press Shift-F10. Pressing K* expands all the headings but does not expand the body text. If you want to see the body text too, press Shift-K+.

Trick **On an extended keyboard, use the extra function keys to collapse and expand headings and body text.**

Word can take advantage of the extra function keys on an extended keyboard. Press F11 to collapse headings and Shift-F11 to collapse body text. Press F12 to expand headings and Shift-F12 to expand body text.

Trap **You try to collapse a selected part of an outline but you cannot.**

Make sure that you use K−, the minus key on the numeric keypad, to collapse headings and text in outline view. The minus key on the standard keyboard simply enters a hyphen to the left of the first character in the selection. If you have an extended keyboard, you can press F11 instead of K− to collapse a selection.

Trap **You try to collapse or expand headings with the mouse but you cannot.**

You can use the mouse to collapse and expand headings only if you are in outline organize mode. To switch from outline edit to outline organize mode, press Shift-F5. Then try again.

Trap **You cannot collapse and expand text with the mouse.**

If you want to collapse or expand a text paragraph, you must use the Shift-K − and Shift-K + techniques. The mouse works only with headings.

Editing Outlines

Word gives you the ability to edit your outline to correct minor mistakes in the wording or arrangement of headings. And after you have added large amounts of body text beneath the headings, you can edit in another, much more powerful, way. When you move a heading on your outline, Word automatically moves any subheadings or body text beneath the outline, too. Thus, you can restructure your document with just a few keystrokes.

Tip **Choose the most appropriate mode for the kind of editing you want to do.**

You can edit an outline in document view or in the outline view's outline edit or outline organize mode. You use the same general editing procedures in all three modes. However, editing in each mode has its advantages and disadvantages:

❑ *Document view*. The obvious disadvantage of editing in document view is that the structure of the document is buried in the text, only a portion of which appears on-screen at any moment. When you are making changes to words in text paragraphs, however, editing in document view makes sense because you can see the words in their context. To keep your document's overall structure in mind, however, toggle back and forth between the outline view and the document view. In outline view, collapse all body text and third-level or fourth-level headings, if needed, so that you can see the organization you have chosen in just one screen.

❑ *Outline edit mode*. Edit in this mode only when you want to change the wording of a heading or a visible text paragraph. The text-selection keys work just as they do in document view, so editing outline text—headings and subheadings—is easy in outline edit mode. Remember that you can select only one heading at a time; you therefore should switch to outline organize mode to make major adjustments to the structure of an outline.

❑ *Outline organize mode.* The cursor-control keys work differently in this mode: they select headings, not characters. For this reason, outline organize mode is best when you want to reorganize a document's structure by deleting, moving, or copying whole sections. In addition, you can select several headings at once by using standard techniques, such as F6 (Extend). Table 6.2 lists the cursor-control keys and what they select in outline organize mode.

Table 6.2
The Cursor-Control Keys in Outline Organize Mode

Key	Selects
Up arrow	Preceding heading at current level (skips lower-level headings)
Down arrow	Next heading at current level (skips lower-level headings)
Left arrow or F9	Preceding heading, regardless of level
Right arrow or F10	Next heading, regardless of level
Home	Nearest heading at next higher level physically above the selected heading
End	Last heading at next lower level physically below the selected heading

Tip **In outline organize mode, use the Home and End keys to move quickly up and down the levels of your outline.**

The Home key selects the nearest higher-level heading physically above the currently selected heading. If a Level 3 heading is selected, for example, pressing Home selects the first Level 2 heading up from the selected heading. The End key selects the last subheading among the subheadings directly below the selected heading. If a Level 3 heading is selected, for example, pressing End selects the last Level 4 heading directly under the selected heading. Repeatedly pressing these keys moves you quickly through the logical levels of your outline.

Tip **Use the up-arrow and down-arrow keys to move to headings at the same level, skipping all higher-level and lower-level headings.**

The up-arrow and down-arrow keys let you move quickly up and down through the same-level headings. When you reach the last heading at that level, however, you cannot go any farther. Press Home to go to the next-higher level or End to go to the next-lower level. You also can use the left-arrow or right-arrow key to move, respectively, to the preceding or next heading level.

Tip   **To scroll vertically through all headings of your outline, use the right-arrow and left-arrow keys.**

The right-arrow key moves you up and the left-arrow key moves you down. The use of these keys for this purpose has less to do with logic than with the influence of a famous idea-processing program that defined the keyboard in this way.

Tip   **Use standard editing techniques to edit outlines.**

You can use Word's standard editing techniques to rearrange your outline. Simply press the Del key to put a selected heading and any collapsed subheadings or text in the scrap, and press Ins to insert the contents of the scrap above a selected heading. When you insert a heading, Word automatically adjusts its level to be the same as the heading that follows.

Trick   **Use mouse techniques to move headings in outline organize mode.**

The mouse offers a simple method for moving headings in outline organize mode:

1. Select the heading you want to move.

2. Press and hold the Ctrl-left mouse button combination. The message Select destination for moving text appears on the message line.

3. Move the pointer to where you want the heading to appear.

4. Release the Ctrl key and the button. Any collapsed subheadings or body text moves with the heading.

Trap   **Deleting a heading in outline view also deletes all collapsed headings and text beneath the heading.**

When you delete a heading in outline view, you also delete all collapsed headings and text beneath the heading. Unless you know what this collapsed material is, the best procedure is to expand the material and make sure that you really want to dispose of the text before "pulling the plug."

Trap   **Word sorts the headings at the highest selected level but leaves subheadings undisturbed.**

If you select a series of second-level headings that have Level 3 subheadings, Word sorts only the Level 2 headings. The Level 3 subheadings move with their Level 2 headings, but the program won't sort them. To sort the Level 3 headings, select them and use **L**ibrary **A**utosort again.

Linking Document Headings and Outline Headings

One of the most powerful and useful aspects of Word's outline view is the dynamic link Word creates between document headings and outline headings. If you create an outline before you write your document, the headings you type in your outline appear as headings in your document. In your document, you should format them so that they look like document headings. If you add new headings while writing your document, you must take special steps to make sure that the heading appears in your outline. You will need a macro to make sure that the outline always reflects your document's structure accurately. This section covers these topics.

Trick **Create your document's headings as outline headings in outline edit mode.**

You have probably been creating headings in this way already, but keep this point clearly in mind: when you create a document heading, always do so by making it an outline heading (as distinguished from body text) in your outline. That way the link between the document headings and outline headings is automatic.

To convert document headings into outline headings, press Shift-F2 to enter the outline edit mode. Select the document heading, and press Alt-9 to raise the heading to Level 1. Then press Alt-0 to lower the heading level, if you wish.

Tip **If you format headings in document view, the formats you choose do not affect the way the headings are indented in the outline.**

This feature is a benefit because you can set up your document headings in any way you want. In your document, for example, you can center a Level 1 heading and have Level 2 headings positioned flush left (see fig. 6.13). In the outline view, however, the way the headings are displayed shows no change, even after all the formatting you have done. The original pattern of indentation remains intact (see fig. 6.14).

In document view, the indentations of the outline's headings disappear, and all the headings appear at the left margin (flush left). In document view, you can format these headings as you want. The first-level headings, for instance, can be centered with a blank line below, and the second-level headings can be flush left with a blank line above and below, as in figure 6.13. Use the **F**ormat **P**aragraph command to attach these formats to the headings (including the blank lines above and below). When you press Shift-F2 to return to outline view, the blank lines and centering disappear, and the headings appear at the correct levels (see fig. 6.14).

Trap   **If you add new headings while writing your document in document mode, the headings do not automatically appear in the outline.**

Suppose that while you're writing, you decide to divide a section by inserting a new heading. You center the text and boldface it, so it looks just like all the other headings. But when you switch to outline view, your new heading is nowhere to be seen: the new heading is still body text as far as Word is concerned. You must format the text as a heading, as the following tip suggests. But by far the easiest way to solve this problem is to add heading entries to your NORMAL.STY style sheet. (For instructions, see Chapter 12, "Style Sheets.")

Trick   **Modify NORMAL.STY so that it includes speed-formatting keys for headings automatically inserted in outlines.**

Here's one of the most important high-productivity tricks in this book. The style-sheet entries described here produce new speed-formatting key codes for headings. Following is a quick overview of what the codes do:

❑ *Heading 1st-level* (Alt-H1). This style-sheet entry formats a centered, boldfaced heading, with blank space above and below, and prevents page breaks beneath the heading. The style sheet automatically copies the heading's text to your outline and formats the heading as a Level 1 heading.

❑ *Heading 2nd-level* (Alt-H2). This style-sheet entry formats a flush-left, boldfaced heading, with blank space above and below, and prevents page breaks beneath the heading. The style sheet automatically copies the heading's text to your outline and formats the heading as a Level 2 heading.

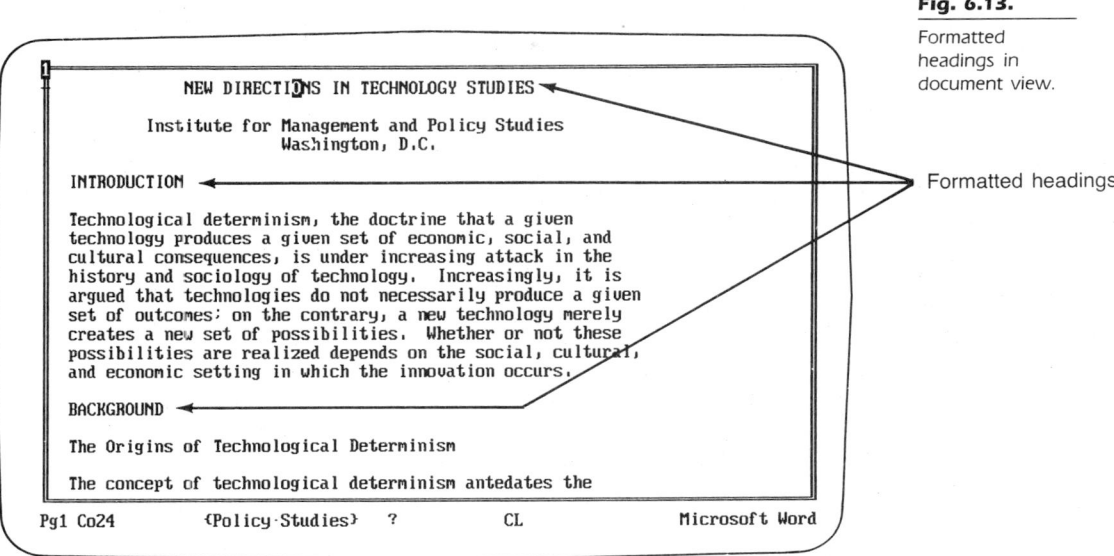

Fig. 6.13.

Formatted headings in document view.

Formatted headings

Fig. 6.14.

The same formatted headings in outline view.

❑ *Heading 3rd-level* (Alt-H3). This entry formats a flush-left, italicized heading, with blank space above and below, and prevents page breaks beneath the heading. The style sheet automatically copies the heading's text to your outline and formats the heading as a Level 3 heading.

Chapter 12 explains how to create these speed keys—and how to modify them to suit your formatting needs. If you create reports or proposals with headings and want to use outlining, don't hesitate to update NORMAL.STY with these extremely useful speed keys (see Chapter 12 for the information you need).

Trap **As you add body text to your document, Word adds the text to your outline.**

When you switch back to outline view to see your document's structure, you see any new body text you have added. In most cases, that means the outline's structure is no longer completely visible. To view the outline's structure, you must collapse all the headings and expand them again down to a specified level, omitting body text.

Trick **Write a macro to eliminate body text by collapsing and expanding your outline to a level you specify.**

Here's another important macro, one that adds significantly to Word's usefulness for high-productivity applications. This macro collapses body text and displays headings to a level you specify. In addition, the macro ensures that the outline is updated to include all the headings in your document. Use this macro every time you want to view your document's structure.

```
«SET echo = "off"»
«SET response = "N"»
«WHILE response = "N"»
     «ASK level =? Collapse outline to level 2, 3, or 4?»
     «IF level = "2"»«SET response = "Y"»«ENDIF»
     «IF level = "3"»«SET response = "Y"»«ENDIF»
     «IF level = "4"»«SET response = "Y"»«ENDIF»
«ENDWHILE»
<ctrl esc>o<down 3>y<enter>
<ctrl pgup>
<ctrl keypad+>«level»
«PAUSE View outline and press Enter to return to  document»
<Shift F2>
```

To create and use this macro, follow the instructions in Chapter 13, "Macros." Save the macro using the macro name quick_outline.mac^<ctrl q>o.

Trick **You can use outlining even if you don't want to add headings to a document.**

Some documents don't require document headings, although you may want to add headings to better organize your document. If you create an outline, however, Word leaves the outline headings as text in document view. To hide the headings in your document, format them as hidden text. To create an outline as hidden text, do the following steps:

1. Press Shift-F2 to enter outline view.

2. Before you start creating your outline, choose the **F**ormat **C**haracter command and choose the Yes option in the hidden field.

3. Choose the **O**ptions command and choose the Yes option in the show hidden text field.

4. Create your outline in the usual way (see fig. 6.15).

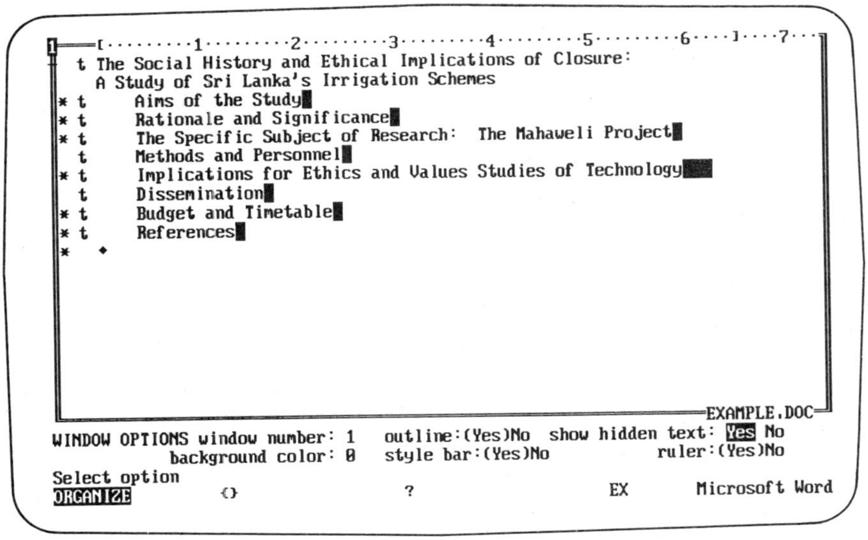

Fig. 6.15.

Creating an outline with hidden text.

When you shift to the document view, display or hide your headings by choosing the Yes or No option in the **O**ptions command's show hidden text field. When you print your document, you can print or hide the headings by choosing the Yes or No option in the **P**rint **O**ptions command's hidden text field.

If you create a style sheet, you can attach the hidden text format to your headings. When you define the key code, use the **F**ormat **C**haracter command and select the Yes option in the hidden field.

Tip **Use windows to switch back and forth between document view and outline view.**

A major advantage of outlining, as you have seen, is that you can create and maintain a dynamic link between document headings and outline headings. If as you write, you frequently use the outline to refresh your memory of the document's overall structure, you almost certainly will produce better-organized work.

But switching views creates a problem. When you switch to outline view using Shift-F2, the highlight jumps to the next heading up from the text you are working on. Therefore, when you switch back to the document view, the cursor may be positioned some distance from where you were working, making you waste time scrolling back to your original location.

If you open two windows on the screen, however, you can display one in outline view and one in document view. If you turn on the zoom mode, you can press the F1 key to change instantly between outline view and document view without affecting the location of the cursor in your document. For more information on windows and zooming, see the section "Using Windows While Creating Text," in this chapter.

Numbering Outlines

Numbering an outline can serve you and your readers. Some documents you write may require a numbered heading format; numbering also reinforces the order of headings for you. If you want, you can use the Library Number command to number an outline's headings automatically. Word inserts the numbers before the outline headings in outline view. The numbers appear in the document as well. If you decide you don't like the numbers, you can remove them by selecting the Remove option in the Library Number command. Word offers two numbering formats for you to choose from: a default format and a legal format.

Tip **By default, Word numbers outlines following the style guidelines recommended in _The Chicago Manual of Style_.**

When you issue Library Number, Word uses the following formats for the levels of an outline:

❏ Level 1 headings: Roman numerals (I, II, III, and so on)

❏ Level 2 headings: uppercase letters (A, B, C, and so on)

❏ Level 3 headings: Arabic numerals (1, 2, 3, and so on)

❏ Level 4 headings: lowercase letters and right parentheses [a), b), c), and so on]

❏ Level 5 headings: Arabic numerals enclosed in parentheses [(1), (2), (3), and so on]

❏ Level 6 headings: lowercase letters enclosed in parentheses [(a), (b), (c), and so on]

❏ Level 7 headings: lowercase Roman numerals and right parentheses [i), ii), iii), and so on]

Word numbers only to the seventh level. You can create additional outline levels with Alt-0, but Word numbers them using the Level 7 format. Figure 6.16 shows how the default heading levels appear in an outline.

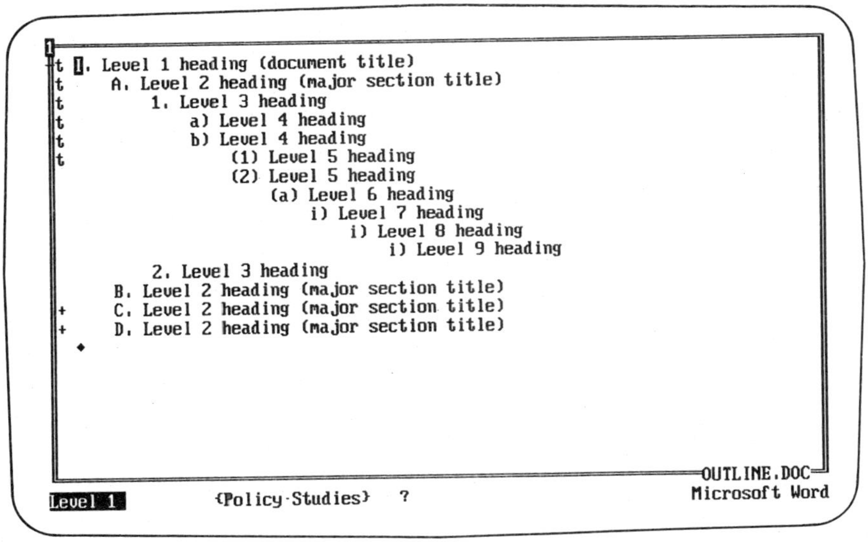

Fig. 6.16.

Numbered headings (default format).

```
t  I. Level 1 heading (document title)
t     A. Level 2 heading (major section title)
t        1. Level 3 heading
t           a) Level 4 heading
t           b) Level 4 heading
t              (1) Level 5 heading
t              (2) Level 5 heading
                  (a) Level 6 heading
                     i) Level 7 heading
                        i) Level 8 heading
                           i) Level 9 heading
        2. Level 3 heading
     B. Level 2 heading (major section title)
+    C. Level 2 heading (major section title)
+    D. Level 2 heading (major section title)
     ◆
                                          ═OUTLINE.DOC═
 Level 1        {Policy·Studies}   ?       Microsoft Word
```

Trick **If you type 1. before the text of your first Level 1 heading, Word uses legal numbering format.**

Word's default format places Roman numerals (I, II, III) before Level 1 headings, following *The Chicago Manual of Style* format. Replacing the first Roman numeral with *1.*, however, produces legal numbering format for the document. Following is how the numbers appear in legal format:

❑ Level 1 headings: 1.

❑ Level 2 headings: 1.1.

❑ Level 3 headings: 1.1.1.

❑ Level 4 headings: 1.1.1.1.

❑ Level 5 headings: 1.1.1.1.1.

❑ Level 6 headings: 1.1.1.1.1.1.

❑ Level 7 headings: 1.1.1.1.1.1.1.

Figure 6.17 shows how an outline looks in legal format (compare it with Word's default format in fig. 6.16). Word numbers only to the seventh level. You can create additional outline levels with Alt-0, but Word numbers them using the Level 7 format.

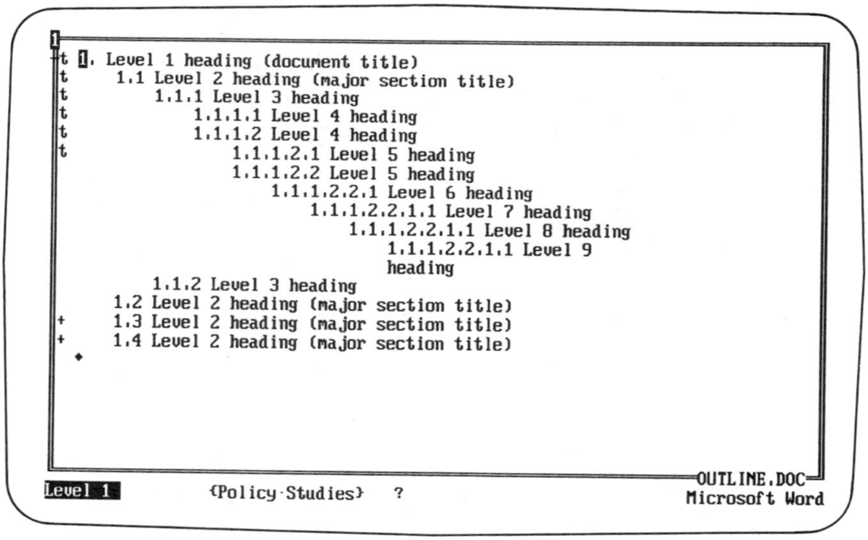

Fig. 6.17.

Numbered headings (legal format).

```
t  ▯. Level 1 heading (document title)
t      1.1 Level 2 heading (major section title)
t         1.1.1 Level 3 heading
t             1.1.1.1 Level 4 heading
t             1.1.1.2 Level 4 heading
t                 1.1.1.2.1 Level 5 heading
                  1.1.1.2.2 Level 5 heading
                      1.1.1.2.2.1 Level 6 heading
                          1.1.1.2.2.1.1 Level 7 heading
                              1.1.1.2.2.1.1 Level 8 heading
                                  1.1.1.2.2.1.1 Level 9
                                  heading
          1.1.2 Level 3 heading
      1.2 Level 2 heading (major section title)
+     1.3 Level 2 heading (major section title)
+     1.4 Level 2 heading (major section title)
    ◆
```

```
Level 1        {Policy·Studies}    ?        OUTLINE.DOC
                                             Microsoft Word
```

Trap   The outline numbers Word inserts are not updated automatically.

After you make changes to an outline or document, the level numbers are not updated automatically. You need to use the Update setting in the **Library Number** command to restore the numbers' accuracy.

Trick **If you have made changes under only one heading, you can update it without renumbering the whole outline.**

For especially large documents, updating the heading formats in an outline with Library Number can consume large amounts of memory and time. Fortunately, you can renumber just the section in which you have made changes. To do this, use the following procedure:

1. Select the heading above the changes you have made.

2. Choose the **Library Number** command.

3. Set the `restart` sequence field to No.

4. Press Enter to carry out the command.

Trick **You can tell Word not to include certain headings in the numbering sequence.**

If you want to exclude specific headings from the numbering sequence, simply type a hyphen or an asterisk in front of those headings. When you choose **Library Number**, Word skips headings preceded by either of these characters, continuing the numbering sequence with the next "unflagged" heading.

Tip **You can remove numbers from headings as easily as you can add them.**

If you have added numbers to an outline only for your own benefit and don't need the numbers in the final draft, you can remove the numbers by selecting the **Library Number** command's Remove option. If you select the first character or paragraph of the outline when you choose **Library Number**, Word removes the numbers from the entire outline. If you select part of the outline before choosing **Library Number**, Word removes the numbers from just the selected part.

Using Windows While Creating Text

Word can display up to eight different windows at a time. You can use windows in two ways:

❏ To display up to eight different documents

❏ To display different parts of the same document, or one document in different modes (such as document view and outline view). When you look at two or more windows on the same document, each window scrolls independently. Changes you make in one window, however, affect the text displayed in the other windows.

You can combine these techniques if you want. You can display two windows on a document, for example—one showing the outline view and one showing the document view. At the same time, you can open a third window, containing another document.

Word's window commands provide ways to split windows in two different ways: vertically or horizontally. Vertical splits are of limited use unless you are working with columns or short lines. For most purposes, horizontal splits are more useful.

After splitting the screen, you can zoom one of the windows to full size with a click of the mouse or a keystroke; a second click or keystroke shrinks the window (and reveals the hidden windows). You can open several documents or several windows on one document and shift among them with ease, without sacrificing the full-screen view vital to good writing.

This section covers the use of windows for text-creation purposes. See Chapter 9 for information on using windows for editing. For a summary of window-related keys and commands, see table 6.3 (for keys and commands) and table 6.4 (for mouse techniques).

Tip **Turn off the menu to clear space on-screen.**

Before you start splitting the document area into windows, you may want to turn off the menu to create as much work space as possible. Choose **O**ptions and select No in the menu field.

You may be tempted to turn off the screen border as well, but the screen border can be useful when splitting windows with the mouse. After you split the document area once, the borders reappear anyway, so turning them off does not give you more space.

Table 6.3
Keys for Windows

Key(s)	Effect
F1	Makes the next window active
F1 (while using Window commands)	Displays special cursor to locate window split or window move
Ctrl-F1	Zooms window to full size (if zoomed, exits zoom mode)

Table 6.4
Mouse Techniques for Windows

Mouse operation	Effect
Click left button on top or right window border	Splits window and shows two views of the same document
Click right button on top or right window border	Splits window and clears new window
Click right button on window number	Toggles on and off zoom mode
Click left button on window number	In zoom mode, switches to next window (when not in zoom mode, makes clicked window active)
Drag on lower right corner of window	Resizes window
Click both buttons on top or right window border	Closes window

Tip **Use the mouse to control window operations.**

You can open, size, move, and close windows with the keyboard, but using the mouse is much faster.

Trick **To split a window, using the keyboard, move the cursor to where you want the split to occur. Then choose Window Split.**

If you are splitting the window horizontally, place the cursor on the line where you want the split to occur. If you are splitting the window vertically, place the cursor on the column where you want the split to occur. Then when you use the Horizontal or Vertical options of the **W**indow **S**plit command, Word automatically inserts this location in the at line field.

Trick **If you didn't move the cursor before choosing Window Split, you can use other techniques to determine where the split occurs.**

If you forgot to position the cursor where you want to split a window, when you choose the Horizontal or Vertical option of the **W**indow **S**plit command, you may specify at the at line field the line or column number where you want the split to occur.

Alternatively, you can press F1, activating a special cursor (see fig. 6.18). Press the arrow keys to move the cursor up or down along the left border of the window, or right or left along the top border, to visually determine the location of the split.

Fig. 6.18.

Special cursor for choosing window split location.

Special cursor ————

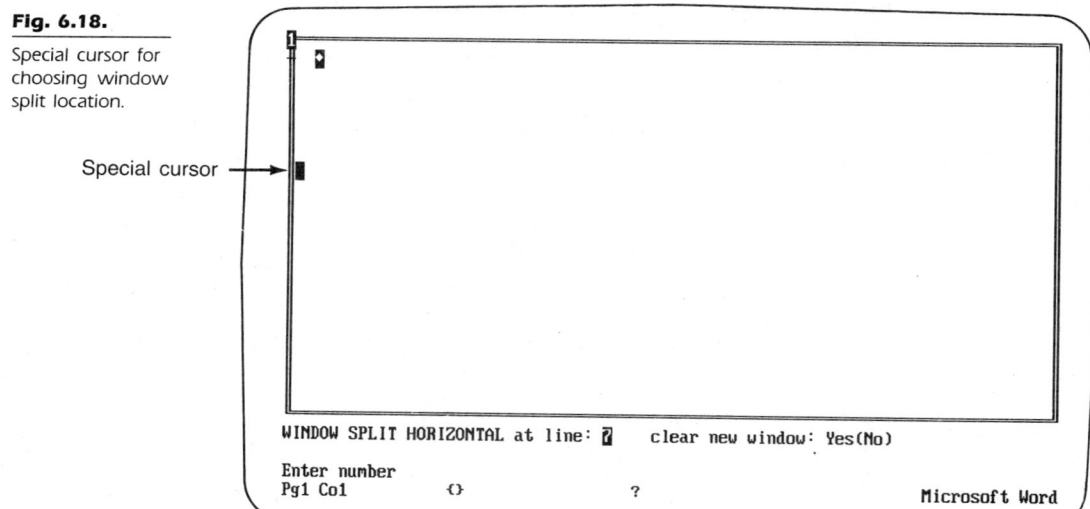

```
WINDOW SPLIT HORIZONTAL at line: 7    clear new window: Yes(No)

Enter number
Pg1 Co1           {}                 ?                  Microsoft Word
```

Tip **Split the screen with the mouse to provide two views of the same document.**

If you have a mouse, move the pointer to the right or top window border until the shape changes. In graphics mode, you see a box with a horizontal line (at the right border) or a vertical line (at the top border). In text mode, you see a rectangle the same size as the cursor. When you have positioned the pointer where you want the split to occur, click the left mouse button.

If you do not have a mouse, use the Horizontal or Vertical option of the **W**indow **S**plit command. In the at line field, Word inserts the cursor's line number (for a horizontal split) or column number (for a vertical split). Then press Enter to split the screen.

Tip **Split the screen and clear the new window with one command.**

If you have a mouse, split the window by clicking the right mouse button. If you do not have the mouse, choose the Yes option in the clear new window field of the **W**indow **S**plit command.

Trick   **If you forgot to clear a new window when you opened it, use the Transfer Clear Window command.**

The Transfer Clear Window command clears all text and formatting from the active window, giving you a new, blank document. This command does not affect inactive windows.

Choose this command carefully. If you choose Transfer Clear All by accident, and choose No in response to Word's query about saving your work, you may wipe out your document.

Tip   **Use the F1 key to make the next window active.**

Each window has an identifying number (1 through 8), which Word assigns in order as you create the windows. The number of the currently active window is highlighted in the upper right corner of the window.

To make a different window active, you must cycle through the windows to the one you want, by pressing the F1 key. If window 2 is active and you want to work in window 4, for example, press F1 twice to go from window 2 to window 3 and then to window 4. If you have a mouse, simply click the left button on the window you want to work in to make it active.

Trap   **In previous versions of Word, Shift-F1 made the preceding window active. In Word 4 and 5, Shift-F1 is a shortcut to the Undo command.**

If you are used to this key combination from previous Word versions, watch out! You could wipe out important editing changes without understanding what happened. To restore all or at least most of the changes, use the Undo command again.

Tip   **Zoom a window to full size to work in it.**

Word 4.0 added a zoom feature to Word's windowing capabilities. If you want to see more of the contents of a particular window but don't want to bother with closing and reopening all the other windows on your screen, you can simply press Ctrl-F1 to zoom the active window to full size, temporarily hiding the other windows. If you have a mouse, click the right button on the window number. After you zoom the window to full size, you see the message ZM in the key indicator in the status line. Press Ctrl-F1 again (or click the right mouse button on the window number again) to switch back to the tiled window mode.

Trick **Press F1 to move from window to window in zoom mode.**

When you have chosen the zoom mode, pressing F1 (or clicking the left mouse button on the window number) opens the next window at full size. If window 2 is active, for example, you can press F1 twice to zoom to window 3 and then to window 4.

Tip **You can change the size of windows on-screen.**

When you are working with tiled windows (two or more windows on-screen at once), you can resize them to show more of a particular document.

To resize a window with the mouse, point to the window's lower right corner until the pointer changes shape. In graphics mode, the pointer changes to arrows pointing in four directions. In text mode, the pointer changes to a rectangle the same size as the cursor. Drag, using either button. Let go when you have moved the pointer to the new location of the split.

You can use this technique to resize windows vertically as well as horizontally. To resize a vertical split, click the window's lower right corner and drag horizontally. If you move vertically, Word moves the split up or down as well as left or right.

To resize a window with the keyboard, use the **Window Move** command. The command's fields require you to specify the line number and column number of the screen location where you want the window's lower right corner moved.

Trick **To resize a window with the keyboard, press F1 to activate the special cursor.**

To resize a window with the keyboard using the special cursor, perform the following steps:

1. Issue the **Window Move** command and highlight the to row field.

2. Press F1.

3. Move the special cursor to the line to which you want the split to move.

4. Highlight the column field.

5. Press F1 again.

6. Move the special cursor to the column to which you want the split to move.

7. Press Enter.

Trap **You try to resize a window with the mouse in text mode but open a new window or turn on a ruler instead.**

Using a mouse makes it much easier to handle window splits in graphics mode, one of Word's two screen display modes. But in text mode, the shape changes that signal a window split, the ruler switch, and a window move are indistinguishable. You may therefore have difficulty telling whether a click will split the window again, turn on the ruler, or let you move the window.

The action Word takes depends on your position. If you missed the lower right corner of the window when you clicked, Word responds as if you are trying to split the window or turn on the ruler. If you are on the ruler switch, the ruler appears. If you want to turn off the ruler, choose the No option in the ruler field of the **O**ptions command, or click both buttons with the mouse pointer in the upper right corner of the window—where the pointer was when you accidentally turned on the ruler.

If you are not on the ruler switch, Word responds as if you are trying to split the window. If you are three lines or columns (or fewer) away from the split, Word does not split the window and you see on the message line the message Not a valid window split. If you are more than three lines or columns away, however, a split occurs. See some of the following tips for ways to close the unwanted window. Use Alt-F9 to toggle on the graphics mode when splitting or sizing windows with the mouse in order to make the mouse cursor shapes easier to identify.

Trap **You cannot split a window in zoom mode.**

You must press Ctrl-F1 or click the right button on the window number to switch back to the tiled screen mode, where you can split the window.

Tip **Close a window quickly with the mouse.**

To close a window with the mouse, simply position the pointer anywhere in the window's right or top border and click both buttons. If you have closed the only window on a document you haven't saved, Word asks whether you want to abandon the text, save it, or cancel the command.

If you don't have a mouse, move the cursor to the window you want to close. Then use the **W**indow **C**lose command.

Trick **Create a macro to handle window-management tasks.**

If you're using the keyboard version of Word, you must remember several special commands and techniques as you manage windows. As a result, the subject of window management is grist for the macro mill. Here's a nice big macro that handles all window-management tasks. This macro presents you with a menu asking whether you want to split the screen, resize an existing window, or close a window.

```
«SET echo = "off"»
«SET response = "N"»
«WHILE response = "N"»
«ASK choice=?(S)plit screen, (R)esize a window, or (C)lose window?»
«PAUSE Press Ctrl-F1 if ZM on; place cursor in window to modify
      and Enter to continue»
   «IF choice = "S"»
        «SET response = "Y"»
        «SET test = "N"»
        «WHILE test = "N"»
        «ASK clearnew=?Clear new window (Y/N)?»
            «IF clearnew="Y"»
                «SET test = "Y"»
                <ctrl esc>wsh<f1>
                «PAUSE Press Down or Up to choose line for window
                      split and press Enter»
                <tab>y<enter>
            «ENDIF»
            «IF clearnew="N"»
                «SET test = "Y"»
                <ctrl esc>wsh<F1>
                «PAUSE Press Down or Up to choose line for window
                      split and press Enter»
                <tab>n<enter>
            «ENDIF»
        «ENDWHILE»
   «ENDIF»
   «IF choice = "R"»
        «SET response = "Y"»
        <ctrl esc>wm<tab><f1>
        «PAUSE Press Down or Up to choose new line for window split and
              press Enter»
        <enter>
   «ENDIF»
```

```
«IF  choice  =  "C"»
     «SET  response  =  "Y"»
     «SET  confirm  =  "N"»
     «WHILE  confirm  =  "N"»
          «ASK  preserve = ?(S)ave  work  or  (A)bandon?»
          «IF  preserve =  "S"»
               «SET  confirm  ="Y"»
               <ctrl f10>
               <ctrl esc>wc<enter>
          «ENDIF»
          «IF  preserve =  "A"»
               «ASK  check  =  ?Are  you  sure  (Y/N)?»
               «IF  check  =  "Y"»«SET  confirm  =  "Y"»«ELSE»«QUIT»
               «ENDIF»
          <ctrl esc>wc<enter>N
          «ENDIF»
     «ENDWHILE»
«ENDIF»
«ENDWHILE»
```

To create and use this macro, follow the instructions in Chapter 13, "Macros." Save the macro using the macro name quick_window.macˆ<ctrl q>w.

Trap **Word saves only the window option choices you make in window 1.**

Word stores most of the choices you make using the Options command in the file MW.INI (see Chapter 2 for more information on MW.INI). Word saves only the Options choices you make for window 1, however. If you make Options choices for other windows, Word doesn't save them.

Tip **Put your outline in one window and your document in another, and switch between them instantly in zoom mode.**

Open two windows on your document. Leave window 1 in document view. To put the outline in the second window, take the following steps:

1. Make the second window active by pressing F1 or clicking the mouse in the window.

2. Choose the **O**ptions command and select the Yes option in the `outline` field. Then press Enter.

3. Press Ctrl-F1 or click the right button on the window number to enter zoom mode.

Press F1 or click the left button on the window number to move instantly between outline view and document view in zoom mode.

Chapter Summary

The outline mode's chief benefit is to provide another way of looking at your document. To be sure, you can use the outline mode to plan your work—and you should. But the real benefit of outlining is the active link between document headings and outline headings. When you shift to outline view, you hide the body text and see your document's structure.

Use outline edit mode to create outlines and edit individual headings. Use outline organize mode to rearrange the outline. As you learn in Chapter 9, you can rapidly reorganize a huge document by reorganizing the outline in the outline organize mode.

To see your outline's structure when the outline grows larger than the screen, collapse subheadings. To see subheadings again, expand them.

Link your document headings and outline headings. Create the document headings as outline headings in outline edit mode; if you add new document headings in document mode, be sure to format them as outline headings by shifting to outline edit mode and pressing Alt-0 and Alt-9. If you plan frequently to create complex documents with headings, don't waste any time before adding outline entries to the NORMAL.STY style sheet.

View your document's structure as the document evolves by switching to outline edit mode. Use a macro to collapse body text and refresh the outline's structure.

You can use windows to display two or more parts of the same document or up to eight different documents at once. If you zoom a window to full size, you can move from one full-size window to the next just by pressing F1. If you use the keyboard version of Word, create a macro to handle window-management tasks.

7

Formatting Your Document: Character and Paragraph Styles

Word's most impressive capabilities lie in the user's control over the appearance of text on the printed page. Unlike most word processing programs (some of which are little more than glorified electric typewriters), Word was designed with many of the characteristics of a scaled-down typesetting program. Word's strength is evident in many areas, particularly in the way the program handles character and paragraph formatting, the subjects of this chapter.

As powerful as Word is, however, the designers created the program within the constraints of the IBM Personal Computer environment and its display adapters and printers. As a result, character and paragraph formatting with Word is sometimes a tricky and confusing business. In this chapter, you learn how to chart a clear course through Word's intricacies and idiosyncrasies. As in all the chapters of this book, the goal is to disclose the techniques high-productivity, professional writers have developed to get the most out of Word.

Chapter 5, "Writing Strategies: Word and the Composing Process," introduced character and paragraph formatting in the context of formatting-as-you-write. This chapter builds on and broadens your character and paragraph formatting knowledge by surveying the following topics comprehensively:

- ❑ Formatting characters and paragraphs with Word 5
- ❑ Understanding Word's measurement options
- ❑ Formatting character styles

177

❏ Formatting paragraph styles

❏ Formatting lines and boxes

❏ Formatting side-by-side paragraphs

❏ Searching and replacing character and paragraph formats

Understanding Character and Paragraph Formatting with Word 5

If you have used previous versions of Word, you will not find major changes in the way Word 5 handles character and paragraph formatting. Word 5 has a few new features, to be sure, but the overall approach is the same.

Word's default formats are determined by the default style sheet, NORMAL.STY, which Word uses unless you specifically instruct it otherwise (you learn how to work with style sheets in Chapter 12). The default style sheet formats a document with the following styles:

❏ The default character style of the printer named in the Print Options menu printer field (usually a fixed-width Pica font).

❏ Paragraphs formatted flush left and single-spaced.

❏ Tab stops every 0.5 inches, with left alignment.

❏ Paper size of 8.5 by 11 inches, with margins at 1.0 inch top and bottom, and 1.25 inches left and right.

You change these formats by giving formatting commands. You can give formatting commands in three ways:

❏ *Using the speed keys.* Word's default style sheet, NORMAL.STY, includes many speed-key commands for formatting purposes. Use these keys as often as possible for formatting purposes; they're fast, and you can modify and expand them as you create style sheets.

❏ *Using the Format command menus.* Use the Format Character and Format Paragraph command menus when you want to use a format not available with a speed-key command or when you want to attach several formats at once to a selection.

❏ *Using style sheets.* The most powerful method of all, style sheets provide a way actually to change the default formats. You can modify some styles, such as the footnote reference-mark style, the footnote paragraph style, and the page-number style, just by creating a style-sheet entry for these formats. You also can modify existing NORMAL.STY speed keys so that they enter precisely the formats you want. You can create new speed keys, too. Finally, you can create several alternative versions of a style sheet, each appropriate for specific functions, such as writing letters or reports.

You can use formatting commands in two ways:

❏ *Format as you write.* Before you start to write, choose a format using one of the three formatting techniques (speed keys, the Format commands, or a style-sheet format). You have then "programmed" the cursor so that as you type, Word enters the formats selected. Chapter 5 introduces this formatting technique.

❏ *Format later.* To format text you have already typed, select it, using one of the text selection methods discussed in Chapter 5, which explains them in the context of editing-as-you-write. Use the same techniques to select text for formatting purposes.

This chapter explores the default speed keys and the Format commands in detail. For information on style sheets, see Chapter 12.

Understanding Word's Measurement Options

Word wasn't designed just for desktop computers in Tehachapi, Tucson, and Tonapah; Word was also designed for the international market and for print shops where the program is used to drive sophisticated typesetting machinery. For this reason, you can select a measurement format in metric units or in printer's points, as well as in inches. As you learned in Chapter 3, you change the program's default unit of measure by choosing an option in the measure field in the Options menu. After you choose a measure, Word uses the selected measurement as the default in all command menus containing measurement fields.

Trap **If you choose printer's points or some other measure and forget you have done so, you may enter a measurement inappropriately.**

Suppose that you choose printer's points as the default measurement format and then forget that you have done so. You select several paragraphs and choose the **Format Paragraph** command. Thinking in inches, you type *1.5* in the left indent field of the Format Paragraph menu. Word, however, assumes that you mean 1.5 points, which is only about two one-hundredths of an inch.

Trick **Override the default measurement format by typing a measurement code.**

You can override the default measurement format by using the codes shown in table 7.1. If you have selected inches as the default measurement, for instance, you still can enter measurements in printer's points if you use the abbreviation *pt* after the number.

Word converts the measurement to the format specified in the measure field of the Options menu, and the converted measurement is displayed in the current field.

Table 7.1
Measurement Options

Measurement Format	Field Entry
Inches (default)	in or "
Centimeter (2.54 per inch)	cm
10 pitch (10 characters per inch)	p10
12 pitch (12 characters per inch)	p12
Printer's points (72 per inch)	pt
Lines (6 per inch; 1 li = 12 pts)	li (or enter measurement in points)

Trap **No matter which measurement format you choose, the** line spacing, space before, **and** space after **fields treat numbers as lines.**

The line spacing, space before, and space after fields are on the Format Paragraph menu. These three fields always translate any number you enter to a number of lines.

Suppose that you choose printer's points as the default measurement format. You want to leave one blank line before a paragraph, so you enter *12* in the `space before` field. You figure that 72 points (1 inch) divided by 6 (the standard number of lines per inch) equals 12 points—the measurement corresponding to Word's standard line height. When you carry out the command, you find—to your surprise—that Word leaves a space of 12 lines and shows 144 pt in the `space before` field.

You can override the line measurement default in these fields by using the abbreviations shown in table 7.1. If you type *12 pt* in the `line spacing` field, for instance, Word accepts this measurement.

Formatting Character Styles

Word provides a variety of ways to shape the appearance of characters on the printed page. You can emphasize with boldface, underlining, and other formats; control a character's position on the line (subscript or superscript); put a line through text to be deleted from a document (strike-through); control your printer's font and font size options; and use hidden text.

Word approaches character formatting in two ways, and both have their drawbacks:

❑ *Formats displayed on-screen* (boldface, italic, underline, strike-through, uppercase, small caps, double underline, superscript, subscript, and hidden). If your video adapter has a graphics mode, you can see all these formats on-screen. This capability doesn't necessarily mean that your printer can *print* these formats. Some printers cannot print italic, for instance, or cannot do so unless you set a switch or insert a special font cartridge.

❑ *Formats not displayed on-screen* (font and font size). Word can take full advantage of your printer's fonts and font sizes, but you cannot see these formats on the screen. (As noted in Chapter 3, however, if you have a color monitor, you can assign distinctive colors to font sizes.)

Tip **Of the formats Word displays on-screen, use only the ones your printer can print.**

Don't waste your time formatting a document with double underline and italic if your printer cannot produce these formats. In most cases,

Word substitutes another character format, such as underlining, when your printer cannot produce the one you want. In other cases, the formatting disappears entirely.

Tip **Use the Print Options command to name a printer before you format characters so that you can see the available formatting options.**

Only after you have issued the Print Options command do your printer's fonts and sizes become available for formatting purposes. After you use the Print Options command to name a printer, the Format Character command menu's font name and size fields contain your printer's default font and size settings. You can see a list of the available options by pressing F1 when the field is highlighted (see figs. 7.1 and 7.2).

Trap **Even after you use the Print Options command, Word does not disable the character formats your printer cannot support.**

If your printer cannot handle italic, for instance, Word does not stop you—or even beep at you—as you go through your document italicizing here and there. But you're wasting your time. Word either substitutes another format or ignores the formatting completely when you print.

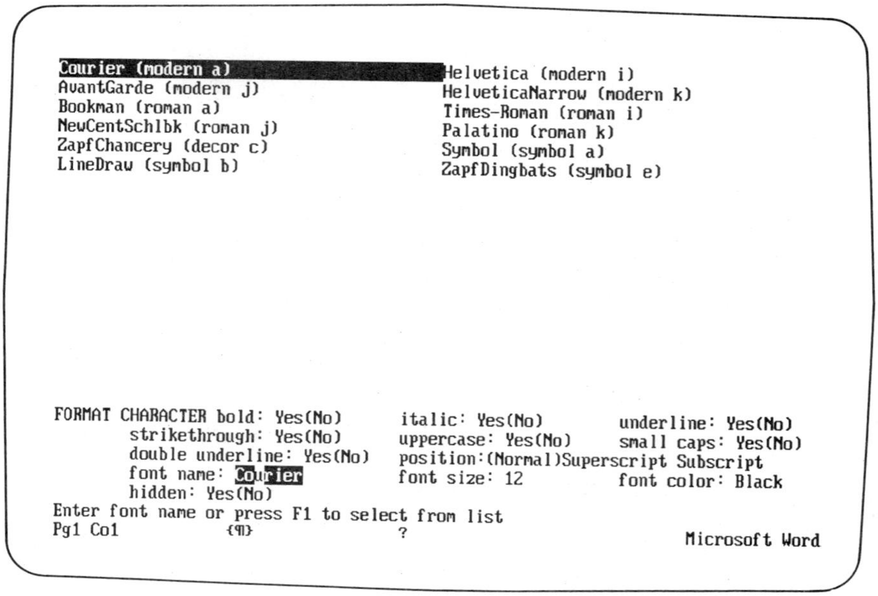

Fig. 7.1.

Displaying the list of available fonts.

```
Courier (modern a)                    Helvetica (modern i)
AvantGarde (modern j)                 HelveticaNarrow (modern k)
Bookman (roman a)                     Times-Roman (roman i)
NewCentSchlbk (roman j)               Palatino (roman k)
ZapfChancery (decor c)                Symbol (symbol a)
LineDraw (symbol b)                   ZapfDingbats (symbol e)




















FORMAT CHARACTER bold: Yes(No)      italic: Yes(No)         underline: Yes(No)
              strikethrough: Yes(No)  uppercase: Yes(No)     small caps: Yes(No)
          double underline: Yes(No)   position:(Normal)Superscript Subscript
              font name: Courier      font size: 12          font color: Black
              hidden: Yes(No)
Enter font name or press F1 to select from list
Pg1 Co1              {¶}              ?
                                                            Microsoft Word
```

```
2              4              6              8
10             12             14             16
18             20             22             24
26             28             30             32
34             36             38             40
42             44             46             48
50             52             54             56
58             60             62             64
66             68             70             72
74             76             78             80
82             84             86             88
90             92             94             96
98             100            102            104
106            108            110            112
114            116            118            120
122            124            126

FORMAT CHARACTER bold: Yes(No)      italic: Yes(No)       underline: Yes(No)
         strikethrough: Yes(No)     uppercase: Yes(No)    small caps: Yes(No)
         double underline: Yes(No)  position:(Normal)Superscript Subscript
         font name: Palatino        font size: 2          font color: Black
         hidden: Yes(No)
Enter font size in points or press F1 to select from list
Pg1 Co1          {¶}                 ?                     Microsoft Word
```

Fig. 7.2.

Displaying the list of available font sizes.

Trap **You begin a new document by choosing character formats; but after you press Enter, you see the message** End mark cannot be edited.

Even though you have chosen character formats from the Format Character menu, you may get this error message in a new document. To avoid this trap, enter at least one character—a space will do— and then move the cursor on top of that character before issuing any character-formatting commands.

Trap **You format characters with the** Yes **option in the** uppercase **field of the Format Character menu, but the uppercase formatting disappears when you save your document as an ASCII text file.**

Formatting the case of characters with this option is lost when you save your document with the Text-only or Text-only-with-line-breaks options in the Transfer Save menu.

Trick **To change the case of letters permanently, use the new Ctrl-F4 toggle.**

New to Version 5, this function key permanently changes case; the changes aren't lost if you save your file as an ASCII text file. To use this toggle, select the letters you want to change. Then press Ctrl-F4.

Keep pressing Ctrl-F4 until you obtain the result you want. If you start with all lowercase letters, this key formats the selection as all uppercase, then as lowercase with initial capitals, and finally as all lowercase.

Tip **Not all formats are available with speed keys.**

Table 7.2 shows the formats available with speed-key formatting and with the Format Character command. As the table shows, the `font name` and `font size` fields are available only through the Format Character command. Another advantage of using the command instead of speed-key shortcuts is that you can enter two or more formats at the same time.

Table 7.2
Character Formats
Speed Key and Format Character Command

Format	Speed Key Command Field	Format Character
Boldface	Alt-B	bold
Italic	Alt-I	italic
Underline	Alt-U	underline
Strike-through	Alt-S	strikethrough
Capital letters		uppercase
Small capital letters	Alt-K	small caps
Double underline	Alt-D	double underline
Superscript	Alt-= (equal)	position
Subscript	Alt-- (hyphen)	position
Font style		font name
Font size		font size
Font color*		font color
Hidden text	Alt-E	hidden

*Color printers only.

Trap **When you press Tab, you may get unwanted underlining.**

Suppose that you type a word at the beginning of a line and underline that word. Then you decide to indent the word one tab stop; you press Home (to go to the beginning of the line) and then press Tab (to indent the word one tab stop). The word moves over, but the underlining stretches so that it is under the tab spaces and the word (see fig. 7.3).

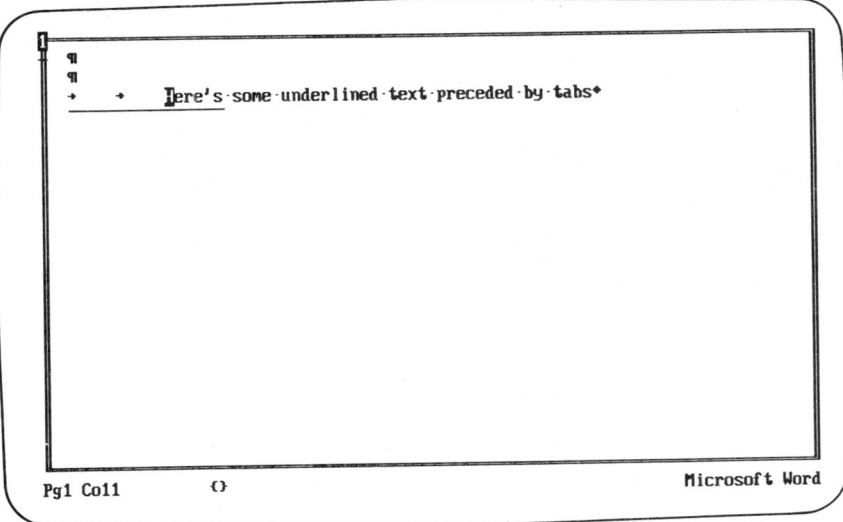

Fig. 7.3.

Underlining extended inappropriately after Tab is pressed.

To grasp what's happening, imagine that character styles are attached to single characters (just as paragraph styles are attached to paragraph marks). If you select that character and press Tab or any other key that enters a character, Word gives any new text the format of the selected character. If the character is underlined, Word underlines any new text you type after selecting that character—including tabs and spaces.

To use the Tab key on formatted text, press Alt-space bar, the command that cancels all character formatting, before you press Tab.

Trick **When you add text after a word that already has the desired character format, repeat the formatting command.**

Word continues formatting only if you start typing *within* the formatted characters. If you select the first character *after* the text you underlined, for instance, the new characters you type are not underlined. You have to give the formatting command again.

Trap   You must give the same command twice to format a single character.

If only one character is selected (the cursor), giving a speed-key formatting command once merely "programs" the cursor to enter the chosen format. To format a single character, issue the command twice.

Note: This trap doesn't apply to formats chosen through the Format menus.

Tip   To cancel character formats for a single character, press Alt-space bar twice.

The principle given in the preceding trick also applies to the command that cancels character formatting. Pressing Alt-space bar once cancels special character formats for the next character you type, not for the character on which the cursor is positioned. Issue the command twice to cancel the formatting at the cursor.

If you have selected more than one character, however, press Alt-space bar just once.

Trap   A character style, such as underlining, pops up where you don't want it—without your having given a formatting command at that point.

Suppose that you are formatting text after it has been typed. When you select some text for character formatting, you inadvertently include a paragraph mark in the selection. (A paragraph mark, like any other character that can be displayed, can receive formatting.) The character format has been attached to the paragraph mark without your realizing what has happened.

When you press Enter to make a new paragraph, the formatted paragraph mark is copied. As you know, when you start typing on top of a character with a character format, Word extends the character format. So you get underlining (or whatever formatting is contained by the paragraph mark) where you don't want that formatting.

If you don't understand what's happening, you can push the paragraph mark all over your document, with frustrating results—especially if you cannot see the mark on the screen.

Suppose that a paragraph mark has boldfacing inadvertently attached. When you start a new paragraph, you see boldfaced text after typing a few characters and pressing the space bar to start a new word. To get rid of the unwanted formatting, you select the words and the space—but not the paragraph mark—and press Alt-space bar. The boldface format reappears after you press Enter and start a new paragraph. Boldface reappears because you canceled the boldfacing only for the space just before the paragraph mark, not for the mark itself. You pushed the mark down line by line until you pressed Enter, at which time you made a fresh copy of the mark and started the vexing process all over again.

To remove all extra character formats from a paragraph mark, select it. Then press Alt-space bar twice.

Tip **The Format Character menu has different displays, depending on what is selected. You can put these differences to work.**

This capability is an undocumented but very useful feature of Word. The following list explains the three different Format Character displays that you may see:

❏ If you select an unformatted character or a series of unformatted characters, the Format Character menu shows the default formatting settings (see fig. 7.4).

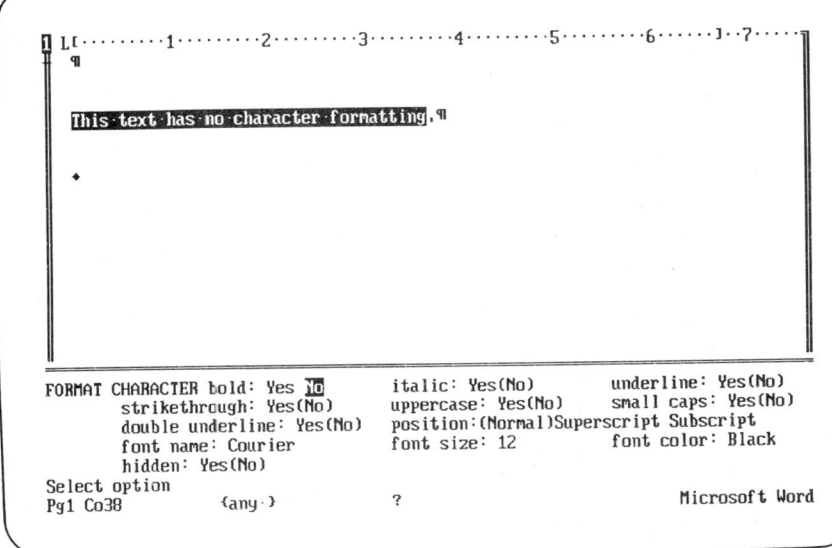

Fig. 7.4.

The Format Character menu after unformatted text has been selected.

❏ If you select a formatted character or two or more characters that share the same formats, the Format Character menu shows the current formats. You can use this display to find out which formats are attached to a particular character (see fig. 7.5).

Fig. 7.5.

The Format Character menu after a unit of text with the same formatting has been selected.

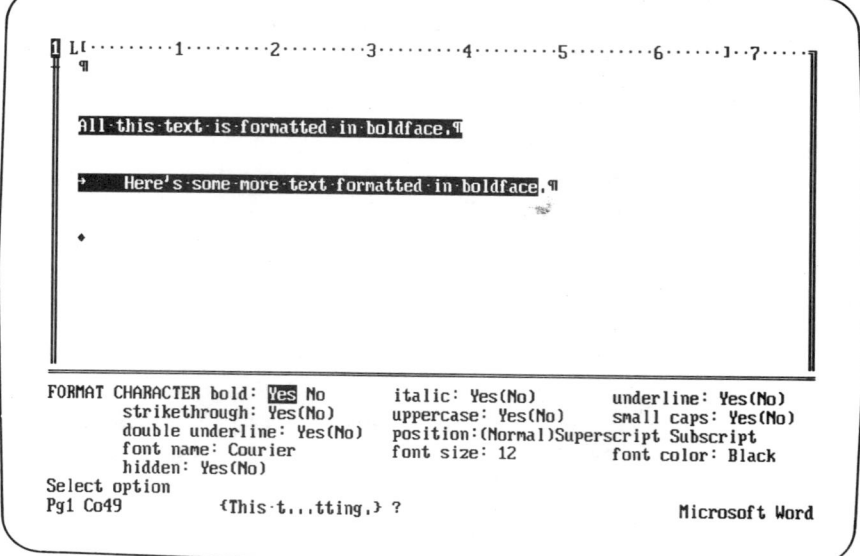

If you select text with two or more different formats (or one part of the text is formatted but the other is not), the Format Character menu shows no options selected (see fig. 7.6).

As you can see, when Word detects that a selection has two or more formats, the program removes the parentheses around options in the command fields. These parentheses normally indicate which options are selected (including the defaults if you have made no choices). When the command menu shows no parentheses, the Format Character command affects only the formats selected with the command. If you choose bold: Yes, for instance, that's the only format the command enters. All the other formats are neutral, meaning that whatever formatting was in effect is still in effect, but boldface has been added to these other formats.

Tip **Learn the many commands and options available for viewing and printing hidden text.**

Table 7.3 lists these options. If you wish, you can display hidden text and print it, or you can display it and switch it off when printing (see fig. 7.7). You also can collapse hidden text so that only a two-headed

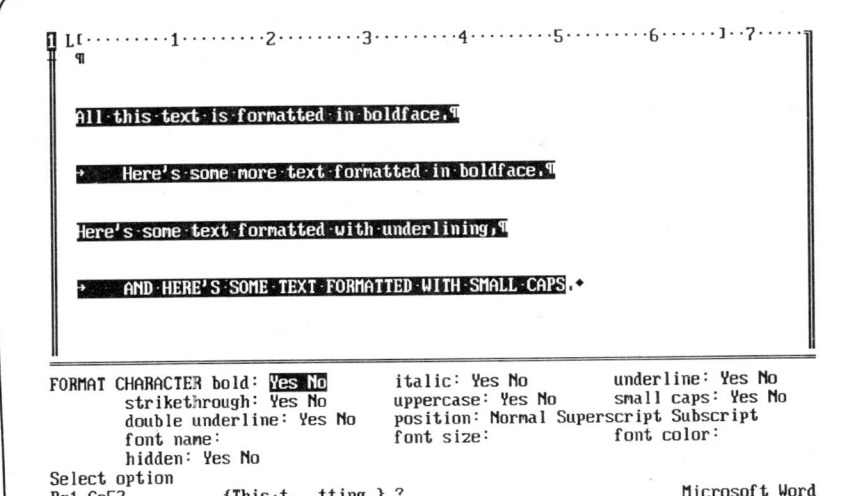

Fig. 7.6.

The Format Character menu after selecting text with two or more different formats.

arrow shows where you have placed the hidden text (see fig. 7.8). If you want, you can hide even the two-headed arrow marks so that the screen looks as though nothing is there.

Tip   **If you are using hidden text extensively, switch to graphics mode.**

In text mode, Word displays hidden text with underlining, so you may have difficulty distinguishing hidden text from surrounding text.

In graphics mode, hidden text is displayed with a distinctive big-dot-little-dot underlining, which is easy to see on the screen.

Trap   **Paragraph marks can receive hidden text formatting.**

Already discussed in this chapter was an unwelcome adventure in extra underlining and boldfacing caused by an inadvertently formatted paragraph mark. Just imagine the damage Word can do if you inadvertently format a paragraph mark with hidden text. You can write several paragraphs that don't print without your realizing what has happened.

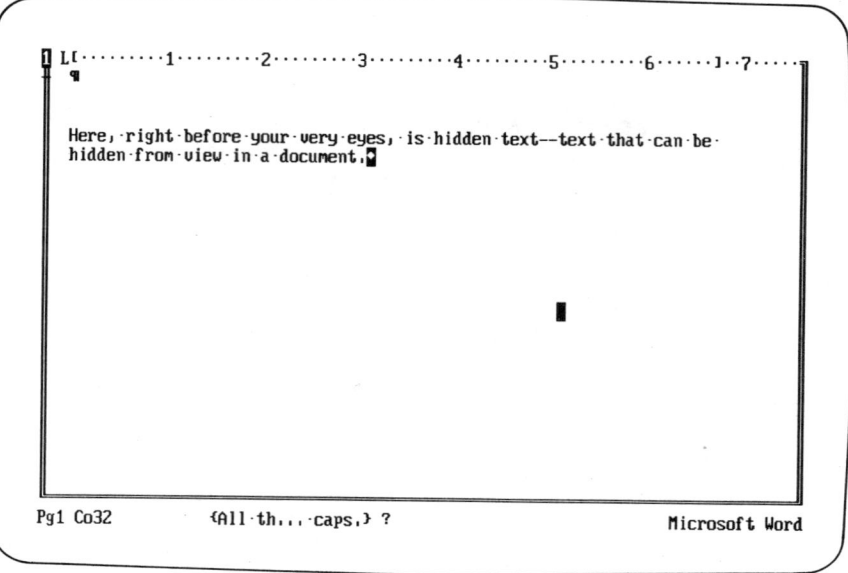

Table 7.3
Commands That Affect Hidden Text

Command	Effect
Alt-E (cursor selected)	Format following text as hidden text
Format Character hidden: Yes	Format selection as hidden text
Alt-E	Format selection as hidden text
Options show hidden text: Yes	Display hidden text in window
Options show hidden text: No	Hide hidden text in window
Options non-printing symbols: None	If hidden text is hidden, display no symbol showing its location
Options non-printing symbols: Partial or All	If hiddden text is hidden, display double arrow showing its location

Table 7.3—Continued

Command	Effect
Print Options hidden: No	Do not print hidden text
Print Options hidden: Yes	Print hidden text, whether it is visible or not

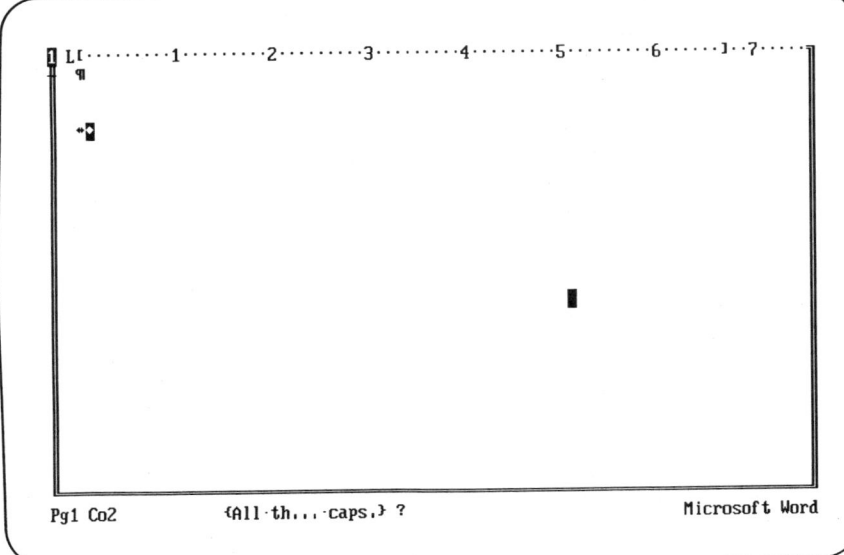

Fig. 7.8.

Two-headed arrow shows hidden text's location.

Trap **Some printers do not adjust line height properly when you change fonts.**

Most printers adjust line spacing so that bigger fonts are accommodated automatically. Others don't. To find out whether your printer automatically adjusts line spacing for all fonts, run a simple test. Create a document with one line for each font and font size your printer supports. Format each one with a different font and font size. If your printer supports Pica 8, 10, 12, and 16 and Elite 10 and 16, for instance, create your document with six lines formatted as follows:

Pica 8
Pica 10

Pica 12
Pica 16
Elite 10
Elite 16

Now test your printer by printing the document. If your printer adjusts the lines properly, the larger fonts are not squashed together, and the smaller ones are not separated by too much white space.

Trick **If your printer doesn't adjust for varying font sizes, enlarge or decrease line height by typing measurements in points in the Format Paragraph menu's** line spacing **field.**

When you single-space a document, the measurement in the line spacing field is normally 1 li, or 12 points. If you create a heading with 16-point type, however, format the heading by typing *16 pt.* in this field.

Trick **Use the mouse to copy formats quickly.**

You can use the mouse to copy character formatting quickly from one area to another. Simply select the characters you want to format, point to a character with the format you want to copy, hold the Alt key, and click the left mouse button.

Trick **To repeat the last formatting command entered, press F4.**

The F4 (repeat edit) key repeats the actions of the last formatting command you gave. Use F4 to repeat a formatting command in several locations that you cannot select at the same time.

Formatting Paragraph Styles

The speed keys for paragraph formatting and the Format Paragraph command provide the tools you need to format paragraphs in the following ways:

❑ Align the paragraph's margins (flush left, flush right, centered, and right-justified)

❑ Indent the right margin, the left margin, both margins, or just the first line

❑ Create a hanging indent (first line normal and all following lines indented)

❑ Control line spacing with precision

❏ Keep lines of a paragraph together on one page

❏ Keep a paragraph with the following paragraph on the same page

❏ Place paragraphs side by side

Figure 7.9 shows the effects of all these formats (except keep together and side-by-side paragraphs) on the screen. A later section of this chapter covers side-by-side paragraphs; all the other types of paragraph formatting are covered in this section.

Note the following points about paragraph formatting:

❏ Word defines a paragraph as any unit of text that ends with a paragraph mark. For Word, then, a paragraph can be dozens of pages long—or it can be just one character. In fact, a single paragraph mark with no text attached is a full-fledged paragraph as far as Word is concerned—even if all the mark does is enter a blank line in your document.

❏ A paragraph includes its paragraph mark. If you select just the mark, you can attach a paragraph format to the entire paragraph.

❏ Think of the paragraph mark as the place where Word stores paragraph-formatting information. If you delete the mark, the paragraph formats are lost, and the paragraph takes on the format of the following paragraph. To recover the deleted mark, press Ins or choose **U**ndo from the edit menu.

❏ Not all paragraph formats are controlled by speed-key commands or the Format Paragraph command. Other commands suppress widows (a paragraph's final line left alone at the top of a page) and orphans (a paragraph's first line left alone at the bottom of a page). Widows and orphans are controlled by the widow/orphan control field of the Print Options menu. Although you can control line lengths by adjusting the paragraph indentation fields, a better method is to set line length with the Format Division Margin command, discussed in Chapter 6.

Tip   **Use the speed keys when you can.**

The speed keys require fewer keystrokes to accomplish a goal than using the Format Paragraph command. To format a paragraph with flush-right alignment, for instance, you can simply press Alt-R. To accomplish the same alignment with the Format Paragraph command, however, you need six keystrokes.

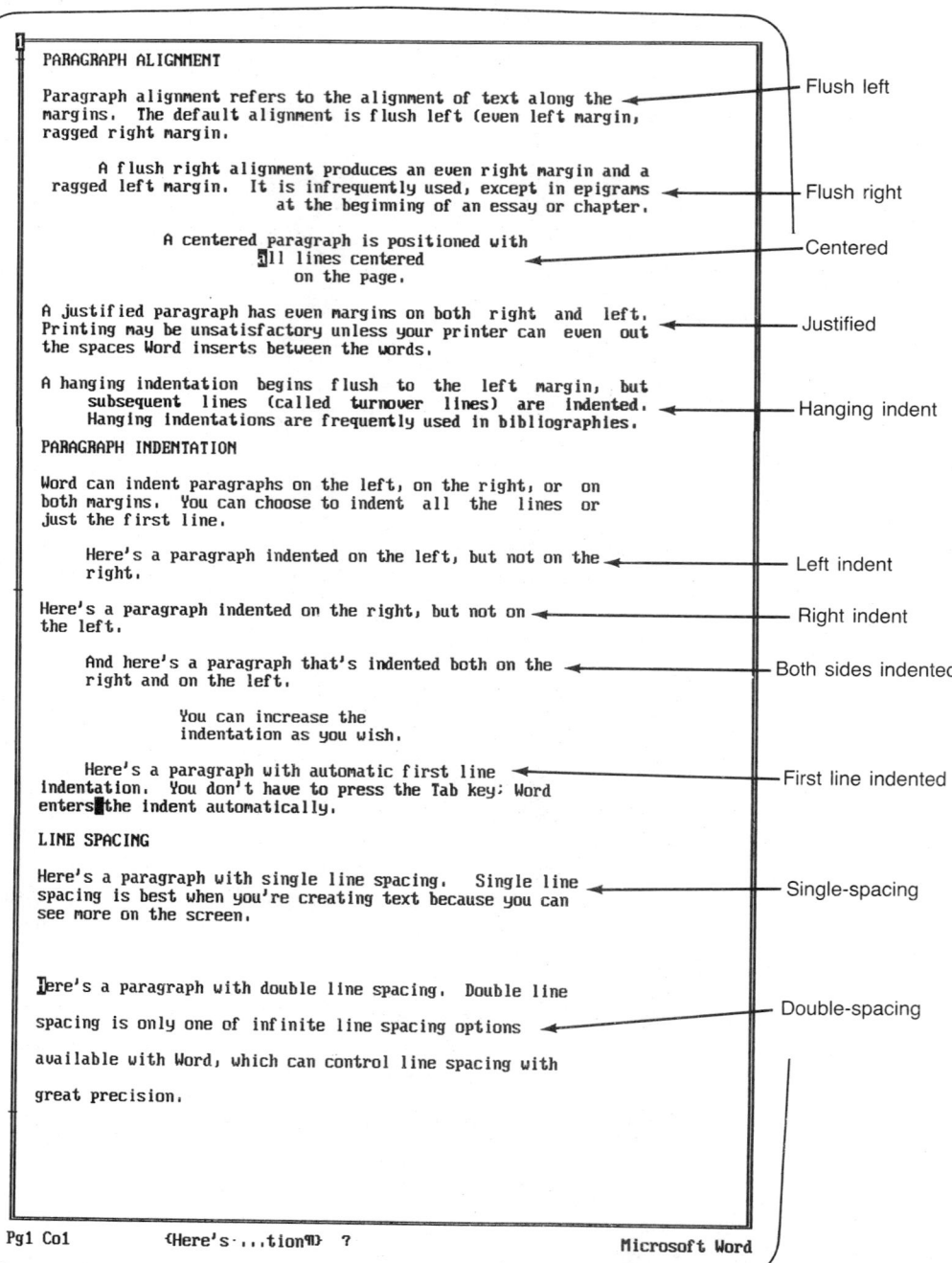

PARAGRAPH ALIGNMENT

Paragraph alignment refers to the alignment of text along the — Flush left
margins. The default alignment is flush left (even left margin,
ragged right margin.

A flush right alignment produces an even right margin and a
ragged left margin. It is infrequently used, except in epigrams — Flush right
at the beginning of an essay or chapter.

A centered paragraph is positioned with
all lines centered — Centered
on the page.

A justified paragraph has even margins on both right and left.
Printing may be unsatisfactory unless your printer can even out — Justified
the spaces Word inserts between the words.

A hanging indentation begins flush to the left margin, but
subsequent lines (called turnover lines) are indented. — Hanging indent
Hanging indentations are frequently used in bibliographies.

PARAGRAPH INDENTATION

Word can indent paragraphs on the left, on the right, or on
both margins. You can choose to indent all the lines or
just the first line.

Here's a paragraph indented on the left, but not on the — Left indent
right.

Here's a paragraph indented on the right, but not on — Right indent
the left.

And here's a paragraph that's indented both on the — Both sides indented
right and on the left.

You can increase the
indentation as you wish.

Here's a paragraph with automatic first line — First line indented
indentation. You don't have to press the Tab key; Word
enters the indent automatically.

LINE SPACING

Here's a paragraph with single line spacing. Single line — Single-spacing
spacing is best when you're creating text because you can
see more on the screen.

Here's a paragraph with double line spacing. Double line

spacing is only one of infinite line spacing options — Double-spacing

available with Word, which can control line spacing with

great precision.

Pg1 Co1   {Here's·...tion¶} ?   Microsoft Word

Tip **You must use the Format Paragraph command to choose certain paragraph formatting options.**

The options that must be selected from the Format paragraph menu include line spacing options other than single-spacing or double-spacing, and options to indent the right margin, keep the lines of a paragraph together on a page, keep a paragraph with the following paragraph, and control spacing after a paragraph. In addition, you need the Format Paragraph menu to choose formats with measurements other than the ones linked to speed keys. If you want a 0.75-inch hanging indent, for instance, Alt-T does not work; Alt-T indents the second and subsequent lines in increments of 0.5 inch each time you press the key combination. See table 7.4 for a comparison of Alt-key and Format Paragraph command options.

Table 7.4
Paragraph Formats
Speed Key and Format Paragraph Command

Format	Speed Key Command Field	Format Paragraph
Left alignment	Alt-L	alignment: Left
Centered	Alt-C	alignment: Centered
Right alignment	Alt-R	alignment: Right
Right-justified	Alt-J	alignment: Justified
Left-margin indent	Alt-N (1 tab)	left indent: 0.5"
First-line indent	Alt-F (1 tab)	first line: 0.5"
Right-margin indent		right indent:
Left-margin and right-margin indent	Alt-Q	left indent: 0.5" right indent 0.5"
Double line spacing	Alt-2	line spacing: 2
Blank line before	Alt-O	space before: 1
Blank line after		space after:
Keep lines together		keep together: Yes
Keep with following paragraph		keep follow: Yes
Format side-by-side		side-by-side: Yes

Tip **You don't have to select the entire paragraph to format it with paragraph formats.**

As long as you position the cursor anywhere in the paragraph (including on the paragraph mark itself), the command you give affects the whole paragraph. Don't bother selecting the whole paragraph.

Tip **You can select several paragraphs at once for paragraph formatting.**

Use the mouse or the F6 extend mode to select more than one paragraph for paragraph formatting. When you have extended the highlight to the last paragraph you want to change, you need not select the whole paragraph, just part of it.

Tip **You can select the entire document for paragraph formatting.**

Press Shift-F10 to select the entire document. Then use an Alt-key formatting command or the **F**ormat **P**aragraph command.

Tip **The Format Paragraph command menu has different displays, depending on what is selected. You can put these differences to work.**

The Format Paragraph menu, like the Format Character menu, appears three different ways, depending on what is selected. The following list describes the three displays:

❑ If you select an unformatted paragraph or a series of unformatted paragraphs, the Format Paragraph menu shows the default formatting settings (see fig. 7.10).

❑ If you select a formatted paragraph or two or more paragraphs that share the same formats, the Format Paragraph menu shows the formats in effect (see fig. 7.11). You can use this display to find out which formats have been attached to a particular paragraph.

❑ If you select text with two or more different formats (or one part is formatted but the other is not), the Format Paragraph menu shows no options selected (see fig. 7.12). You can attach paragraph formats to existing paragraphs without losing the options already chosen.

Text with no formatting

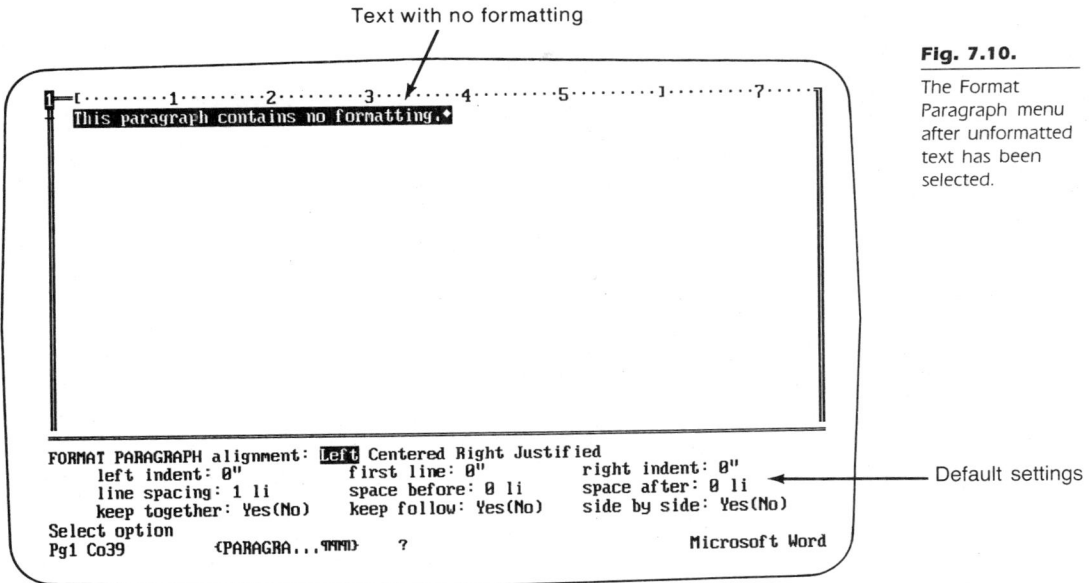

Fig. 7.10.

The Format
Paragraph menu
after unformatted
text has been
selected.

Default settings

Text all one format

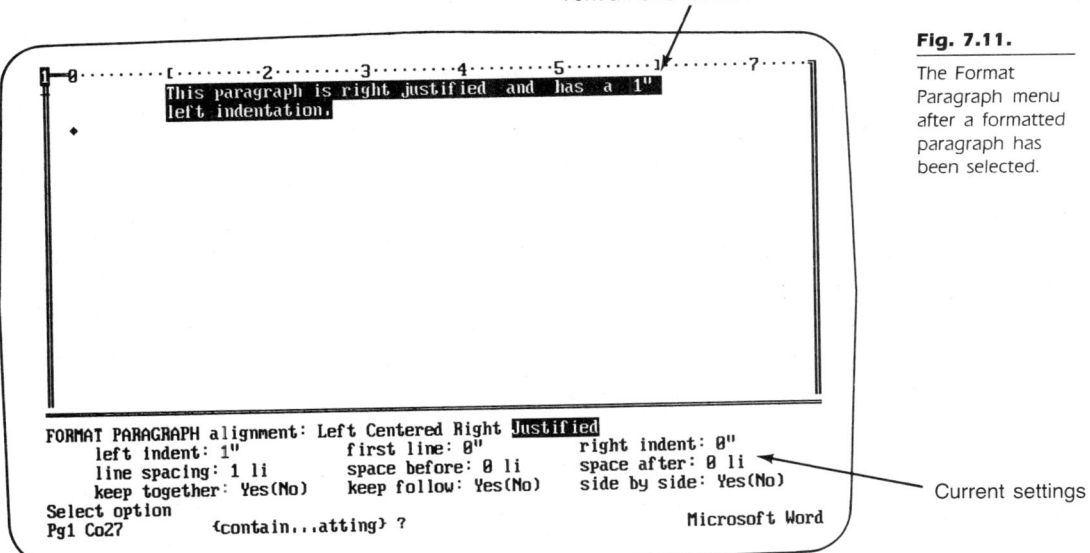

Fig. 7.11.

The Format
Paragraph menu
after a formatted
paragraph has
been selected.

Current settings

Fig. 7.12.

The Format Paragraph menu after text with two or more different paragraph formats has been selected.

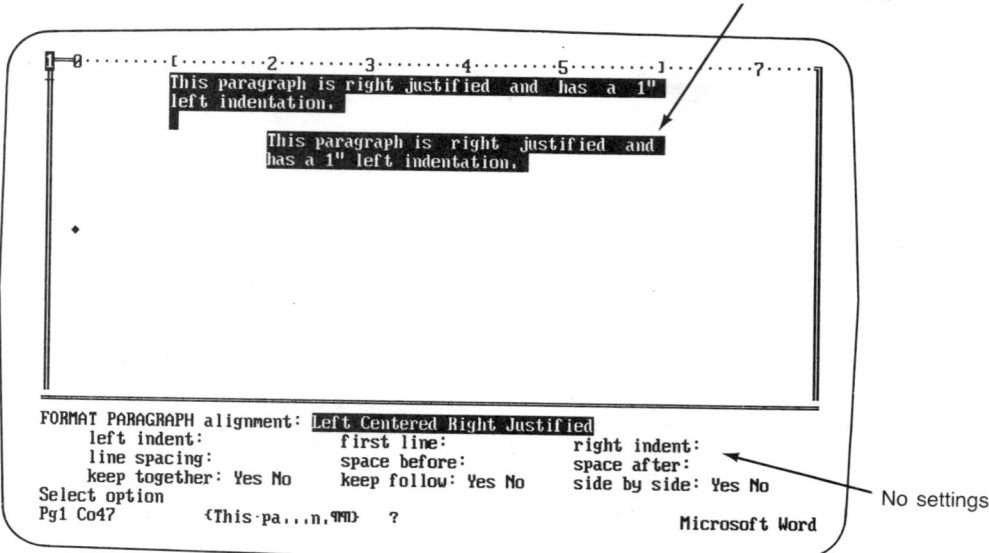

Text with varied formats

No settings

Trap **If you press Alt-P to cancel one paragraph format when you have attached other formats, Word cancels all the paragraph formats.**

When you press Alt-P, you cancel all the paragraph formats, not just the one you want to eliminate. Here's an extreme example: Suppose that you have created a document with a variety of paragraph formats, including hanging indents, first-line indents of 0.75 inch, a right-justified margin, and double-spacing. Then you find out that you must print your manuscript with single-spacing. So you select the whole document with Shift-F10 and press Alt-P to remove the double-spacing. The double-spacing disappears, but so do all your other paragraph formats. You can restore all the lost formats by choosing the **U**ndo command.

Trick **To delete one paragraph format and leave others intact, use the Format Paragraph command.**

This command, like the Format Character command, appears with no options selected if the text you are formatting contains different formats. You can use Format Paragraph, therefore, to delete just one format and leave the others. To change double-spacing to single-spacing throughout an entire complex manuscript, press Shift-F10 to select the entire manuscript. Then choose the **F**ormat **P**aragraph command and type *1 li* in the line spacing field. Leave all the other fields as they are unless you want additional formats to apply to the entire document.

Trick **You can alter a format entered with a speed key by using the Format Paragraph command.**

Suppose, for instance, that you have just used Alt-T to create a hanging indent, but you want to increase the amount of the indent. Position the cursor in the paragraph and choose **Format Paragraph**. When the Format Paragraph menu appears, select the left indent field and increase the number.

Tip **Create your documents with single-spacing. When you finish editing, format the whole document with double-spacing.**

Style guidelines often call for double-spacing throughout the document, but writing with double-spacing in effect is not a good idea. Getting a good view of your document's structure is hard enough with just 19 lines displayed (with the edit command menu shown) or 23 lines displayed (with the menu hidden and the borders removed). Use single-spacing so that you can see complete paragraphs.

To double-space your entire document, first select it by pressing Shift-F10. Then press Alt-2 or use the **Format Paragraph** command and type 2 *li* in the line spacing field.

Tip **You can vary the width of the first-line indent.**

Assuming that you are using Word's default tab stops, pressing Alt-F applies a first-line indent of 0.5 inch to the paragraph containing the cursor. If you choose the **Format Paragraph** command, however, you can control the width of this indent by specifying the desired width in the first line field.

You also can change the indentation by altering the default tab width setting in the Options menu.

Tip **In effect, Alt-N increases the left indent by one tab stop; Alt-M decreases the left indent by one tab stop.**

The Alt-N command indents the left margin one tab stop. If you are using Word's default tab stop setting of 0.5 inch, Alt-N enters a 0.5-inch indent. If you press Alt-N again, the left margin is indented another 0.5 inch.

Think of this command as if it adds 0.5 inch per keystroke to the left indent field of the Format Paragraph menu. If you press Alt-N once, the field reads 0.5". If you press Alt-N twice, the field reads 1.0". You can keep pressing Alt-N until you squeeze all the text close to the right margin. You cannot push the text past the margin, however.

Alt-M does just the opposite; it decreases the figure in the `left indent` field by 0.5 inch per keystroke. You cannot go beyond the left margin, however.

You can use these commands to organize a document quickly with a logical pattern of successive indentations. A better practice, however, is to use Word's outline view for these purposes.

Tip **Use Alt-Q to enter an extended quotation.**

Style guidelines frequently call for extended quotations to be set off from the text by left-margin and right-margin indents of one-half to one inch. Alt-Q, a new Word 5 speed key, accomplishes this job. This new command indents the left and right margins by one default tab (0.5 inch unless you changed the default tab width setting in the Options menu).

Tip *Avoid a right-justified margin when you use short line lengths.*

With extremely narrow columns of text (three inches or less), Word has problems justifying the right margin (see fig. 7.13). The program leaves unsightly gaps in the right margin and may even fail to justify some lines. To avoid this problem, format the columns flush left or use hyphenation extensively.

Fig. 7.13.

The right-justified margin problem.

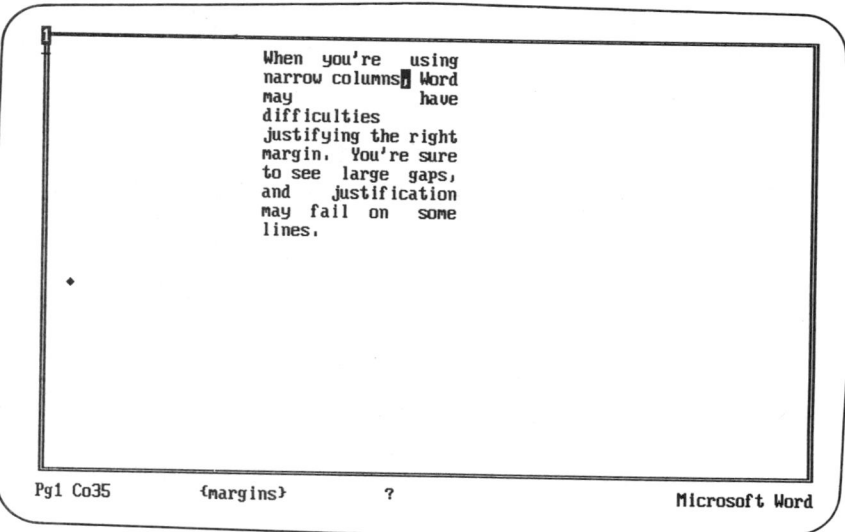

Tip   **Format hanging indents with a negative number in the** first
line **field of the Format Paragraph menu.**

If you format a paragraph using the Alt-T command and inspect the
Format Paragraph menu, you see that left indent has been set at
0.5 inch, and the first line field contains a negative number: -0.5"
if 0.5 is the default tab setting (see fig. 7.14). This negative number
tells Word to place the first line 0.5 inch to the left of the left-margin
setting chosen in the left indent field. To increase the hanging
indent to 1 inch, type *1.0* in the left indent field and *-1.0* in the
first line field.

```
=!····[···1·········2·········3·······4·········5·········]········7····
  Hanging indentations are useful for many applications, such
     as typing bibliographic references.  In a hanging
     indent, the first line is typed flush to the left
     margin.  Subsequent lines, called turnover lines, are
     indented.  The Alt-T command formats hanging
     indentations with a 0.5" indentation.█

  ◆




FORMAT PARAGRAPH alignment: Left Centered Right Justified
     left indent: 0.5"          first line: -0.5"      right indent: 0"
     line spacing: 1 li         space before: 0 li     space after: 0 li
     keep together: Yes(No)     keep follow: Yes(No)   side by side: Yes(No)
Select option
Pg1 Co43          {When·yo...nes.¶}  ?                 Microsoft Word
```

Fig. 7.14.

Formatting a
hanging indent
by entering a
negative number
in the first
line field.

Trick   **Indent paragraphs with the mouse and the ruler.**

This feature is another nice Word 5 change. In previous versions, you
could format paragraph indents by dragging the indent symbols on the
ruler, but you had to use the **Format Paragraph** command first, and
you couldn't see the effects of your changes until you carried out the
command. Now, as long as the ruler is displayed, you can manipulate
the symbols directly, and the selected text reformats immediately. You
can change the position of the symbols until you get them just right.
Table 7.5 lists the symbols that appear on the ruler.

To change the position of an indent symbol, click the right button and
drag.

Table 7.5
Paragraph Indent Symbols on the Ruler

Symbol	Type of Indent
[	Left indent
]	Right indent
|	First line indent

Trap **The left-indent symbol hides the first-line indent symbol.**

To set the first-line indent, first drag the left-indent symbol to the right. Then drag the first-line indent symbol to the position you want and drag the left-indent symbol back.

Trap **Do not control margins with the Format Paragraph command's** left indent **and** right indent **fields or with the indent symbols on the ruler.**

These fields and symbols refer to indentations from the current margins, which are set in the Format Division Margins command. If you need to change the margins, do not do so by adjusting paragraph indents. Use the **Format Division Margins** command instead. See Chapter 8 for instructions. If you control margins with the correct command, changing them is easy. If you try to set them with indents, however, you may have to reformat much of your document manually if you decide to change the margin settings.

Use the indent fields and symbols only to set up a special, temporary format for text you want to set off from the rest of your document.

Trap **Creating blank lines with Enter keystrokes can cause formatting problems.**

Every time you press Enter, Word inserts a paragraph mark in your document. As you learned at the beginning of this section, Word treats even a single paragraph mark as a full paragraph. If you change your formatting after you create your document, these extra paragraph marks can get in the way. In figure 7.15, paragraphs have been created with single-spacing. A paragraph mark follows each paragraph.

Watch what happens in figure 7.16. The whole document was selected with Shift-F10 and the Alt-2 (double-spacing) command was used. Because Word treats a paragraph mark as a full paragraph, the program formats the marks with double-spacing as well. The result, as you can see, is unattractive: the document has too much space between paragraphs. In situations like this, you have to scroll through your whole document and remove the paragraph marks one by one.

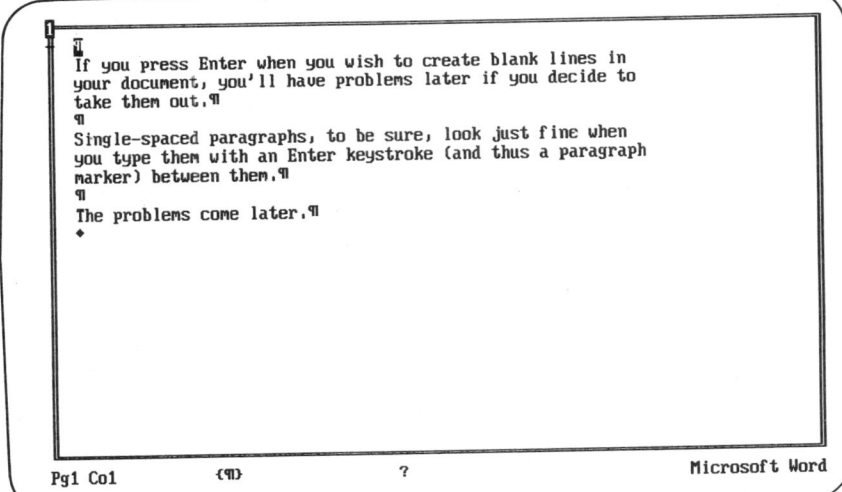

Fig. 7.15.

Enter keystrokes used to create blank lines.

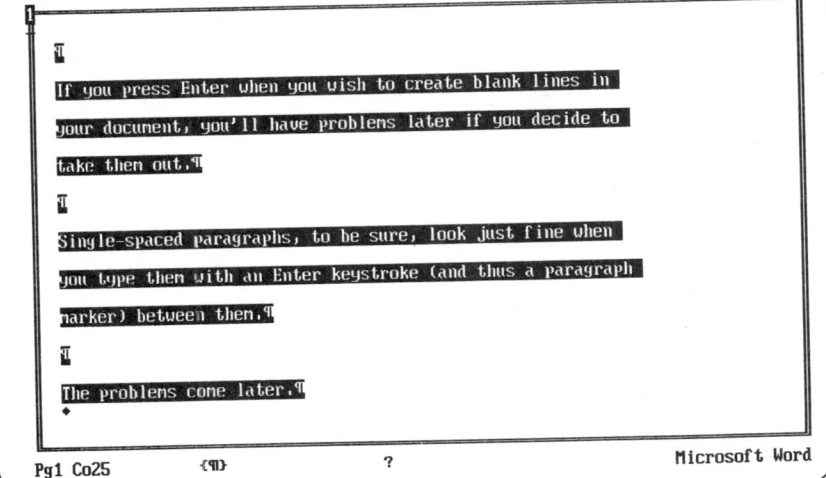

Fig. 7.16.

Paragraph marks with double-spacing paragraph formatting.

Tip **Format paragraphs so that blank lines are included in the paragraph format (open spacing).**

You can format the paragraphs in a document so that they are separated by one-line spaces, by using Word's Alt-O (the letter O, not zero) formatting command. Pressing Alt-O is the equivalent of entering *1 li* in the Format Paragraph menu's space before field.

Trap **The** space before **and** space after **fields are cumulative.**

Suppose that you are creating a document which follows rigid company style guidelines. These guidelines insist on four blank lines—no more, no less—after a chapter title. So you create a heading format with *4 li* in the space after field. The guidelines also call for single-spaced paragraphs separated by one blank line. You format your paragraphs with the Alt-O command. The Alt-O command, however, is the equivalent of entering *1 li* in the Format Paragraph menu's space before field. After your heading, then, you get five blank lines, not four: four from the heading format and one from the paragraph format (see fig. 7.17).

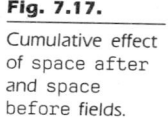

Fig. 7.17.

Cumulative effect of space after and space before fields.

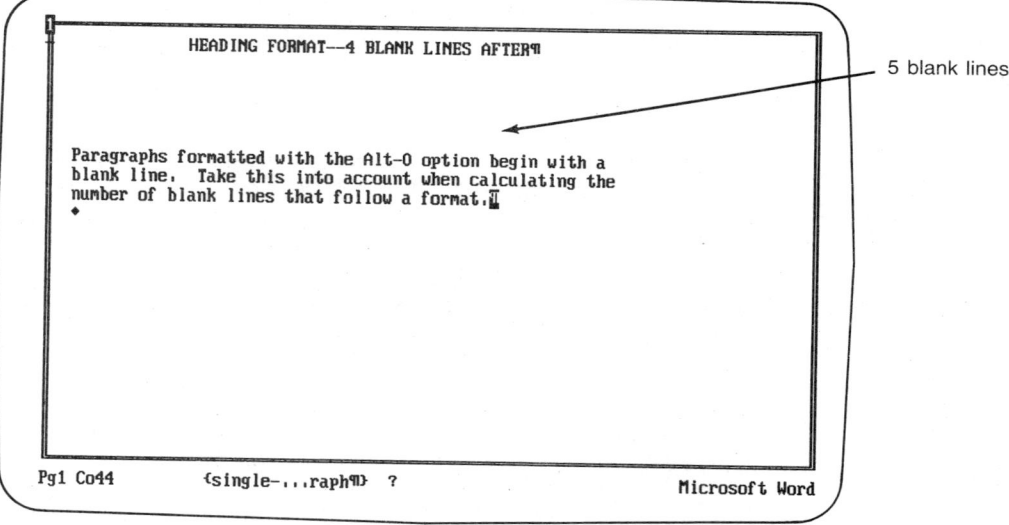

HEADING FORMAT---4 BLANK LINES AFTER¶

Paragraphs formatted with the Alt-O option begin with a blank line. Take this into account when calculating the number of blank lines that follow a format.¶

5 blank lines

Pg1 Co44   {single-...raph¶}   ?   Microsoft Word

Tip **If you choose a line spacing other than 1 li, Word starts each new paragraph with one or more blank lines.**

Consider this fact when you compute the number of blank lines after headings. Word places one blank line before a double-spaced paragraph, two blank lines before a triple-spaced paragraph, and so on (see fig. 7.18). These blank lines are added to any blank-line instructions contained in the preceding paragraph's space after field (as well as the current paragraph's space before field).

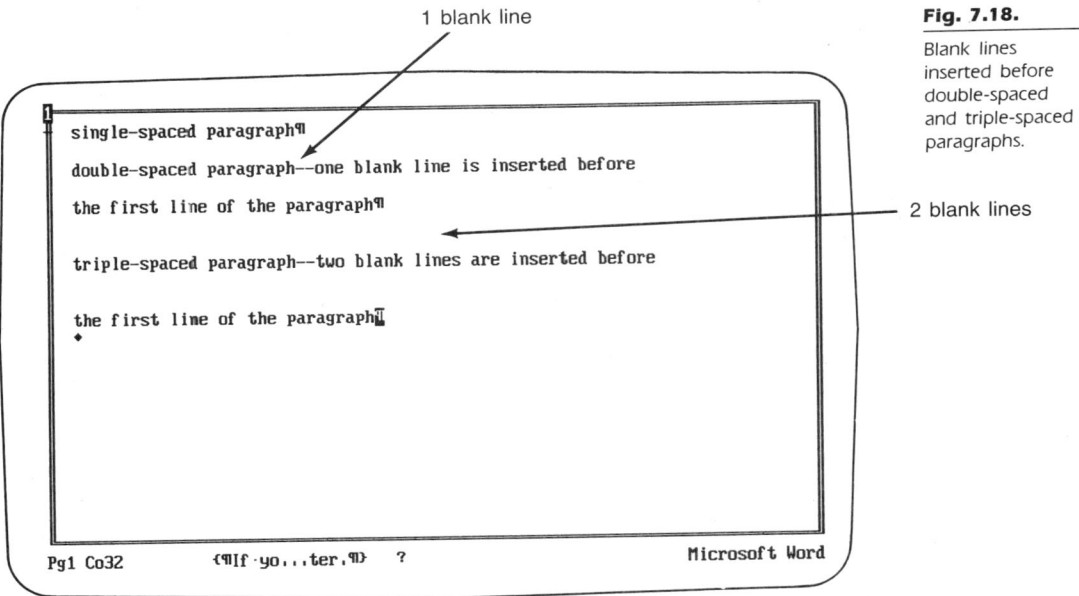

1 blank line

2 blank lines

Fig. 7.18.

Blank lines inserted before double-spaced and triple-spaced paragraphs.

Tip   **Eliminate widowed headings by using the** keep follow **field.**

A widowed heading is a heading left by itself at the bottom of a page. With most word processing programs, your only choice is to scroll through the document page by page before printing in order to eliminate this unattractive error. Word gives you a way of preventing widowed headings. Although this fact remains unknown and uncelebrated, the feature is one of the biggest time-savers in the whole program. When you create a heading, format it with the number of blank lines you want after that heading. Then choose the Yes option in the keep follow field. (Don't enter blank lines by pressing Enter; otherwise, Word keeps your heading with the blank-line paragraph mark and not necessarily with the text that follows. Remember that as far as Word is concerned, a paragraph mark, all by itself, is a full paragraph.)

Tip **Keep tables, bibliographic references, and addresses together by using the** keep together **field.**

Any paragraph formatted with the keep together field is kept on one page when printed. If Word finds that it must insert a page break within the paragraph, Word moves the whole paragraph to the next page and begins printing there.

Tip **Use the newline key sequence to create complex paragraphs that you want to keep together on a page.**

The newline key sequence (Shift-Enter) is useful for creating tables and other complex text that you can define as a single paragraph. Use the keep together field to make sure that such text is kept on one page.

Trick **Copy formats quickly with the mouse.**

You can use the mouse to copy paragraph formatting quickly from one area to another. Simply select the paragraph or paragraphs you want to format, point to a paragraph with the format you want to copy, hold the Alt key, and click the right mouse button.

Formatting Lines and Boxes

The Format Border command menu provides options for creating lines and boxes for paragraphs (see fig. 7.19). If you choose the Lines option, you can specify where you want the lines (and which ones to use): above, below, left, or right. You can choose single-width (normal) lines, boldface lines, double lines, or—new to Word 5—thick lines. If you choose the Box option, Word automatically draws a box around the selected paragraph, giving you the same line options. New to Word 5, too, are options for choosing colors (if you have a color printer) and background shading.

Fig. 7.19.

The Format
Border command
menu.

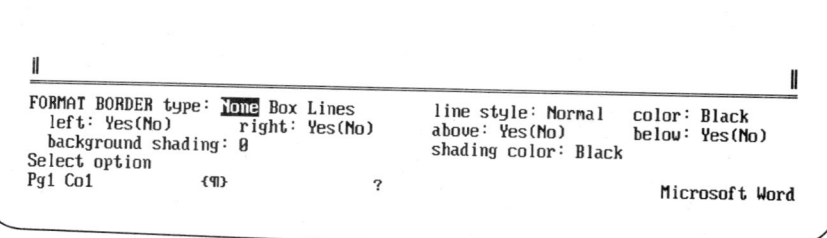

Tip Use the Format Borders command to create business forms quickly.

You can create an attractive form with Format Border in short order. Figure 7.20 shows a form created with several Format Border options.

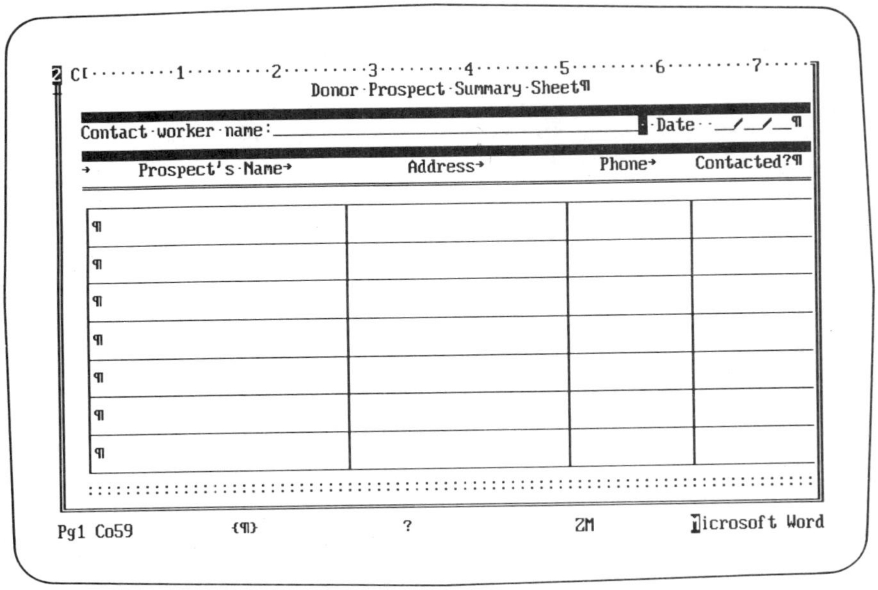

Fig. 7.20.

A business form created with the Format Border command.

Tip Use vertical tabs to create vertical lines within boxes.

The vertical lines in the boxes in figure 7.20 were created by selecting the boxes and setting vertical tabs with the Format Tab Set command. For more information on tabs, see Chapter 5.

Trap When you press Enter, you get lines or boxes you don't want.

Whenever you press Enter, Word copies the formats currently in effect, including any choices made in the Format Border command menu. To cancel the lines and boxes, select the paragraph and use the Format Border command. Choose None in the type field to cancel lines and boxes. Type 0 in the background shading field to cancel background shading.

Formatting Paragraphs Side by Side

You can create multiple columns with Microsoft Word in two ways:

❏ Type 2 or a larger number in the number of columns field of the Format Division Layout command menu.

❏ Format paragraphs side by side by choosing the Yes option in the side-by-side field of the Format Paragraph menu.

The two methods differ. The Format Division Layout method creates newspaper-style columns: the text in each column is independent and the columns' positions relative to one another are decided by the accidents of page size and formatting. You can format unlimited amounts of text this way. The side-by-side method, in contrast, links pairs of paragraphs. Paragraph 1 always prints to the left of Paragraph 2, Paragraph 3 always prints to the left of Paragraph 4, and so on. You can format only 16 consecutive pairs of paragraphs this way. (You can start another 16 pairs after creating a paragraph with normal paragraph formatting.)

Tip **Use side-by-side paragraph formatting when you want to show the relationship between the text in two paragraphs.**

The virtue of Word's side-by-side paragraph formatting capability is that you can link two paragraphs so that they always are printed next to each other. (The Format Division command's multiple-column options create two or more independent columns of text.) Examples of such applications are words and their definitions, product names and their descriptions, or objectives and implementation strategies.

Tip **If you want to type only a few words in the left column and provide a lengthy explanation in the right column, don't bother with side-by-side formatting. Set up a definition format with the Format Paragraph command.**

To set up a definition format, create a big hanging indent by typing a large left indent (say, 3.5") in the left indent field of the Format Paragraph command menu. Then type the same number, expressed as a negative number (-3.5") in the first line field. Carry out the command and create a flush left tab at the left indent (3.5"). When you enter text with this format, the first line is flush to the left margin, allowing you to type a few words. Press Tab and start typing the definition or explanatory text. Subsequent lines, called *turnover lines*, start at 3.5 inches.

Tip **Plan your formatting strategy before you use the Format Paragraph command for side-by-side paragraphs.**

Sketch your plan on paper before formatting side-by-side paragraphs. Plan to leave a space of 0.5 inch between the side-by-side paragraphs. If you use Word's default margins, 1.25 inch on the left and right, you can work with a 6-inch line length. If 0.5 inch is required for the space between the paragraphs, 5.5 inches remain. You therefore can create two 2.75-inch paragraphs. If you want Paragraph 1 (the left paragraph) to be narrower than Paragraph 2, you can choose 2 inches for Paragraph 1's width, and 3.5 inches for Paragraph 2.

Trap **When you enter the text for side-by-side paragraphs, do not separate them by pressing Enter twice.**

As you know, Word defines a lone paragraph mark as a paragraph. If you insert an extra paragraph mark after the text of Paragraph 1, Word prints the mark as Paragraph 2, and you have a mess when you print your document.

Trap **If you format side-by-side paragraphs before entering the text, they may not align correctly.**

Word copies the paragraph formats in effect when you press Enter. If you choose to place blank lines in front of the side-by-side paragraphs, you may be tempted to format Paragraph 1 as you type it by entering a number in the space before field of the Format Paragraph menu. Here's the problem: When you press Enter to type Paragraph 2, the right paragraph, Word continues the paragraph format in effect—the blank line before—to the new paragraph. Your paragraphs do not align correctly when you print them.

Tip **After you type the two paragraphs, decide whether you want blank lines before or after the pair.**

To leave a blank line or lines before the side-by-side paragraphs, enter the number of lines in the space before and space after fields of the Format Paragraph command menu, and format both paragraphs the same way.

Tip **Control the width of Paragraph 1 through the** right indent **field of the Format Paragraph menu.**

To specify the width of Paragraph 1, type in the right indent field of the Format Paragraph menu a number including the space to be inserted between the paragraphs. If you want Paragraph 1 (the left paragraph) to be 2.75 inches wide, type *3.25* in the right indent field:

a 2.75-inch indent from the right margin plus a 0.5-inch blank space between the two paragraphs. (These figures are based on a 6-inch line length.)

Tip **Control the width of Paragraph 2 through the left indent field of the Format Paragraph menu.**

To specify the width of Paragraph 2 (the right paragraph), type in the left indent field of the Format Paragraph menu Paragraph 1's width plus the blank space. If you want the right paragraph to be 2.75 inches wide, type *3.25* in the left indent field: a 2.75-inch indent from the left margin plus a 0.5-inch blank space between the two paragraphs. (These figures are based on a 6-inch line length.) Refer to table 7.6 for examples of right-indent and left-indent settings and their effects on side-by-side paragraphs.

Table 7.6
Side-by-Side Paragraphs
(Assuming a 6-Inch Line Length and 0.5 Inches between Paragraphs)

Paragraph Options	For 1 (Left) Type in right indent Field	For 2 (Right) Type in left indent Field
Paragraphs of equal size	3.25″	3.25″
Smaller left paragraph	4.5″	2.0″
Smaller right paragraph	2.0″	4.5″

Trick **Check your formatting visually with Word's new Show Layout mode (Alt-F4).**

New to Word 5 is the Show Layout mode, controlled by the show layout field of the Options menu (or toggled with Alt-F4). Although this mode slows down Word's screen updating, Show Layout mode permits you to view and edit most page formats, including side-by-side paragraphs, right on the screen. After creating side-by-side paragraphs, press Alt-F4 to view your work. Figure 7.21 shows side-by-side paragraphs in normal display mode; figure 7.22 shows the same paragraphs in Show Layout mode.

```
2 L[········1·······2········3········4·······5········]·······7···]
  Here's·the·text·above·[]he·paragraph.···It·doesn't·have·the·
  two-column,·side-by-side·layout.¶


  This·is·paragraph·one·of·
  text.··This·is·paragraph·
  one·of·text.··This·is·
  paragraph·one·of·text.··
  This·is·paragraph·one·of·
  text.··This·is·paragraph·
  one·of·text.··This·is·
  paragraph·one·of·text.··
  This·is·paragraph·one·of·
  text.··This·is·paragraph·
  one·of·text.··¶                                    █



                    This·is·paragraph·two·of·
                    text.··This·is·paragraph·
                    two·of·text.··This·is·
                                              ═TEST.DOC═
  P1 D1 C23        {below·}        ?              2M   Microsoft Word
```

Fig. 7.21.

Side-by-side
paragraphs
(normal display
mode).

```
2 L[········1·······2········3········4·······5········]═
  []ere[]s·the·text·above·the·paragraph.··It·doesn't·have·the·
  two-column,·side-by-side·layout.¶

  This·is·paragraph·one·of·     This·is·paragraph·two·of·
  text.··This·is·paragraph·     text.··This·is·paragraph·
  one·of·text.··This·is·        two·of·text.··This·is·
  paragraph·one·of·text.··      paragraph·two·of·text.··
  This·is·paragraph·one·of·     This·is·paragraph·two·of·
  text.··This·is·paragraph·     text.·This·is·paragraph·two
  one·of·text.··This·is·        of·text.··This·is·paragraph
  paragraph·one·of·text.··      two·of·text.··This·is·
  This·is·paragraph·one·of·     paragraph·two·of·text.··
  text.··This·is·paragraph·     This·is·paragraph·two·of·
  one·of·text.··¶               text.¶

  Here's·the·text·below·the·paragraph.··It·doesn't·have·the·
  two-column,·side-by-side·layout.¶

  ::::::::::::::::::::::::::::::::::::::::::::::::::::::::::::::::
                                              ═TEST.DOC═
  P1 D1 C1         {¶}            ?              2M   Microsoft Word
```

Fig. 7.22.

Side-by-side
paragraphs (Show
Layout display
mode).

Trick **Formatting side-by-side paragraphs requires many keystrokes and commands—so create a macro to guide you through the process.**

Use this macro after typing the two paragraphs to be formatted side-by-side.

```
«SET done = "n"»
<ctrl esc>o<down>Y<enter>
«PAUSE Place cursor in MIDDLE of first paragraph and
    press Enter»
<f10><f6><f10><ctrl esc>fpl<tab>0<tab>0<tab>0<tab>1 li<tab>0
li<tab>0 li<end>Y<enter><f6><f9><f6>
«WHILE done<> "y"»
    «ASK width1 = ?Right indent for 1st paragraph (try 3.25)?»
    «ASK width2 = ?Left indent for 2nd paragraph (try 3.25)?»
    «ASK spacebefore = ?Number of blank lines to insert above
        paragraphs (0 for none)?»
    «ASK spaceafter = ?Number of blank lines to insert
        below paragraphs (0 for none)?»
    <ctrl esc>fp<tab 3>«width1»<tab 2>«spacebefore»<tab>
        «spaceafter»<enter><ctrl down>
    <ctrl esc>fp<tab>«width2»<tab 4>«spacebefore»<tab>
        «spaceafter»<enter>
    <ctrl esc>o<down 2>Y<enter>
    «ASK done = ?Is this OK (Y/N )?»
«ENDWHILE»
```

To create and use this macro, follow the instructions in Chapter 13, "Macros." Save the macro using the macro name quick_side.mac^<ctrl q>s.

Searching and Replacing Character and Paragraph Formats

Suppose that you have just created a 40-page document, and you remember that you used double underlining somewhere, but you don't remember just where. The style guidelines you're using forbid this kind of emphasis. Alternatively, suppose that you have just formatted your whole document with italic character emphasis here and there, only to discover that your printer cannot handle italic and you must use underlining. In such situations, don't despair: use the **Format sEarch**

Character, Format sEarch Paragraph, Format repLace Character, or Format repLace Paragraph commands.

Trick   **Search for character formats with the Format sEarch Character command.**

When you choose the Format sEarch Character command, you see a version of the Format Character menu (see fig. 7.23). To search from the cursor up in your document (toward the beginning), choose the Up option in the direction field. To search down in your document (toward the end), choose Down. Then choose the format or formats for which you want to search. When Word finds the first characters to which this format is attached, the program highlights them. Repeat the search by pressing Shift-F4, if necessary.

```
FORMAT SEARCH CHARACTER direction: Up Down
    bold: Yes No              italic: Yes No          underline: Yes No
    strikethrough: Yes No     uppercase: Yes No       small caps: Yes No
    double underline: Yes No  position: Normal Superscript Subscript
    font name:                font size:              font color:
    hidden: Yes No
Select option
Pg1 Col         {¶}                ?                   Microsoft Word
```

Fig. 7.23.

The Format Search Character menu.

Trick   **Search for paragraph formats with the Format sEarch Paragraph command.**

When you choose the Format sEarch Paragraph command, you see a version of the Format Paragraph menu (see fig. 7.24). To search from the cursor up in your document (toward the beginning), choose the Up option in the direction field. To search down in your document (toward the end), choose Down. Then choose the format or formats for which you want to search. When Word finds the first paragraph to which this format is attached, the program highlights the paragraph. Repeat the search by pressing Shift-F4, if necessary.

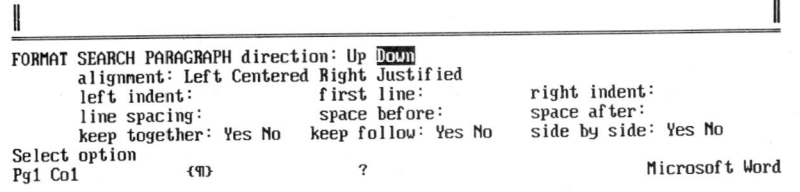

```
FORMAT SEARCH PARAGRAPH direction: Up Down
    alignment: Left Centered Right Justified
    left indent:           first line:          right indent:
    line spacing:          space before:        space after:
    keep together: Yes No  keep follow: Yes No  side by side: Yes No
Select option
Pg1 Col         {¶}                ?                   Microsoft Word
```

Fig. 7.24.

The Format Search Paragraph menu.

Trick   **Replace character formats automatically with the Format repLace Character command.**

When you choose the **F**ormat rep**L**ace **C**haracter command, you see a version of the Format Character menu (see fig. 7.25). Choose Yes in the confirm field unless you're sure that you know what you're doing. Then select the existing format or formats you want to replace and press Enter. To search for italic, for example, choose Yes in the italic field. Then press Enter.

Fig. 7.25.

Choosing the character format to search for.

```
FORMAT REPLACE CHARACTER confirm: Yes No
       bold: Yes No              italic: Yes No          underline: Yes No
       strikethrough: Yes No     uppercase: Yes No       small caps: Yes No
       double underline: Yes No  position: Normal Superscript Subscript
       font name:                font size:              font color: Black
       hidden: Yes No
Select option
Pg1 Co1            {¶}                   ?                       Microsoft Word
```

Word then presents a second menu, which prompts you to choose the format or formats you want to substitute (see fig. 7.26). To substitute bold for italic, for example, choose Yes in the bold field. Press Enter.

Fig. 7.26.

Choosing the character format to replace preceding format.

```
REPLACE WITH CHARACTER FORMAT
       bold: Yes No              italic: Yes No          underline: Yes No
       strikethrough: Yes No     uppercase: Yes No       small caps: Yes No
       double underline: Yes No  position: Normal Superscript Subscript
       font name:                font size:              font color: Black
       hidden: Yes No
Select option
Pg1 Co1            {¶}                   ?                       Microsoft Word
```

If you choose Yes to confirm each substitution, you have the option of making the substitution, skipping this case and continuing, or canceling the command. Word continues until no more instances of the format are found (or until you press Esc).

Trick   **Replace paragraph formats automatically with the Format repLace Paragraph command.**

When you choose the **F**ormat rep**L**ace **P**aragraph command, you see a version of the Format Paragraph menu (see fig. 7.27). Choose Yes in the confirm field unless you're sure that you know what you're doing.

```
 ‖                                                                     ‖
 ══════════════════════════════════════════════════════════════════════
 FORMAT REPLACE PARAGRAPH confirm: Yes No
       alignment: Left Centered Right Justified
       left indent:              first line:              right indent:
       line spacing:             space before:            space after:
       keep together: Yes No     keep follow: Yes No      side by side: Yes No
 Select option
 Pg1 Co1          {¶}             ?                        Microsoft Word
```

Fig. 7.27.

Choosing the paragraph format to search for.

Select the format or formats you want to replace and press Enter. To search for right-justified text, for example, choose Right in the alignment field. Press Enter.

Word then presents a second menu, which prompts you to choose the format or formats you want to substitute (see figure 7.28). To substitute left flush for right flush, for example, choose Left in the alignment field. Press Enter.

```
 ‖                                                                     ‖
 ══════════════════════════════════════════════════════════════════════
 REPLACE WITH PARAGRAPH FORMAT alignment: Left Centered Right Justified
       left indent:              first line:              right indent:
       line spacing:             space before:            space after:
       keep together: Yes No     keep follow: Yes No      side by side: Yes No
 Select option
 Pg1 Co1          {¶}             ?                        Microsoft Word
```

Fig. 7.28.

Choosing the paragraph format to replace preceding format.

If you choose Yes to confirm each substitution, you have the option of making the substitution, skipping this case and continuing, or canceling the command. Word continues until no more instances of the format are found (or until you press Esc).

Chapter Summary

You can change Word's default formatting settings for characters and paragraphs by formatting as you write or formatting later. You can format with speed keys, the Format command menus, or with style sheets.

In graphics mode, Word displays many character formats such as boldface, underlining, superscript, and strike-through—but your printer may not be able to print these formats. Find out which formats your printer can print and don't waste time formatting those that your printer cannot handle. In contrast, formats Word cannot display on-screen, such as fonts and font sizes, can be printed by printers with multiple-font capabilities. If you want to take advantage of multiple fonts, investigate style-sheet formatting immediately.

Unlike character formats, Word displays most paragraph formats on-screen the way they print. Use the speed keys whenever possible, but remember that some formats are available only in the Format Paragraph command menu.

Use the Format Border command to create attractive-looking business forms. After printing them, you can duplicate them inexpensively. Don't forget that you can use vertical tabs to put vertical lines in boxes. If you want to format paragraphs side-by-side so that the two paragraphs are kept together, simplify the process by creating and using a macro. If you need to find or change formats in your document, don't waste time hunting for them manually—let Word do the procedure automatically with the Format sEarch and Format repLace commands.

8

Formatting Pages and Page Styles

Every word processing program is essentially a bag of tricks for turning computer-based text into printed text. Just keep this point in mind the next time someone tells you about the "paperless office"— which, not surprisingly, has failed to materialize. In fact, paper manufacturers are enjoying an unprecedented sales boom!

The earliest word processing programs were designed with exactly this function in mind: computer programmers created these programs to crank out documentation and technical reports about the software the programmers wrote. Almost always, the documentation developed was reproduced directly (and informally) from printouts, so the developers included in these programs features that would help them with this task, such as automatic page numbering, automatic indexing, and table-of-contents features. The goal wasn't to produce anything fancy—the end product was a decently printed document or report, but you wouldn't enter it in a design contest.

Word shows its ancestry in such software. Word has always been an excellent program for generating documentation and reports for in-house reproduction. You can quickly prepare and print a multisection business report with Word, and with knowledge of a few advanced features, you can crank out a table of contents and an index automatically.

But word processing programs now wend their way far beyond the confines of programming labs, and new user demands have created a new genre of software: desktop publishing programs. A desktop publishing program provides the tools needed to do the job of a professional layout artist, preparing well-designed pages that incorporate graphics, multiple fonts, and well-arranged lines.

217

Desktop publishing programs, however, really aren't programs for writing—they lack the tools that an outstanding writing program like Word offers, such as outlining, multiple windows, a spelling checker, a thesaurus, and many other excellent features for text creation and editing. And word processing programs—Word included—really aren't desktop publishing programs—they cannot do all the fancy things that a desktop publishing program can do. But a new generation of improved word processing software provides most users with the features they need for page design. With Version 5 of Word, there's no question that Word is among the top programs in this category, with features like the following:

❑ Version 5's new Show Layout mode displays many page-design formats right on the screen while you're editing. These formats include running heads, side-by-side paragraphs, multiple columns, and areas set aside for printing graphic images.

❑ Print preView displays a graphic representation of each page of your document, showing how Word is to print all page-design features, such as margins, footnotes, and page numbers.

❑ The Format pOsition command "anchors" a paragraph of text or an imported graphic image so that text "floats" around it.

Word isn't the most powerful program on the market for page design, but you surely will find the tools it provides to be adequate for most business and professional writing purposes. With Word 5, you can create handsome-looking newsletters, brochures, handouts, illustrated reports, and other relatively simple documents. Let graphics experts and layout artists fuss with the fancy stuff! Word gets the job done quickly—and you will be surprised at how nice the results look.

You will be even more surprised at how easily you can make Word's features work for you. Of all the material discussed in this book, some of the most amazing improvements to Word are discussed in this chapter. What's more, many of Word's older features that were formerly a big chore to use, such as multiple-column text and running heads, have been greatly improved, and they're much easier to use. If you have hesitated in creating running heads, using newsletter columns, importing graphics, or "floating" text around illustrations, the wait's over.

Covered in this chapter are the following topics:

❑ Fundamentals of page-style formatting

❏ Setting margins and page sizes

❏ Adding page numbers

❏ Creating headers and footers

❏ Using line numbers

❏ Creating documents with multiple divisions

❏ Creating newsletter columns

❏ Importing graphics

❏ Anchoring text frames and graphic images

Mastering the Fundamentals of Page-Style Formatting

Microsoft Word handles most page-style formatting with the Format Division command. You use this command to add page numbers to your document, change margins, choose between footnotes and endnotes, and create newspaper columns.

Like a few other Word commands, the Format Division command name is misleading. Usually you use this command to create a single page style that runs through a document. Of course, you can use this command to create sections (called *divisions*) within a document, and this feature is highly useful. Because such uses are uncommon, Word's documentation is forced to speak of a "single division" in a document, which is a contradiction. This awkward nomenclature is one reason why some people find Word difficult to learn.

The Format Division command is easier to remember if you keep in mind that its purpose is almost always to set up a single page format for your whole document. If you think of this command as the "Format Page" command, it shouldn't give you much trouble.

When you choose the **F**ormat **D**ivision command, the menu shown in figure 8.1 appears. Format Division includes the following four commands:

❏ Format Division Margins. Use this command to set margins (top, bottom, left, and right), to create a *gutter* (a special margin for binding pages), to specify special page sizes (other than the standard 8.5 by 11 inches), and to specify the location of running heads.

❏ Format Division Page-numbers. Use this command to turn on automatic page numbering, to specify the location of page numbers, to control the sequence of numbering, and to choose the type of numbers you want to use (such as Arabic or Roman).

❏ Format Division Layout. Use this command to choose between footnotes and endnotes, to turn on multiple-column formatting, and to control page breaks between sections of a document. Parts of this command are discussed in "Creating a Document with Multiple Divisions," in this chapter.

❏ Format Division line-Numbers. Use this command to print line numbers in the left or right column of your document.

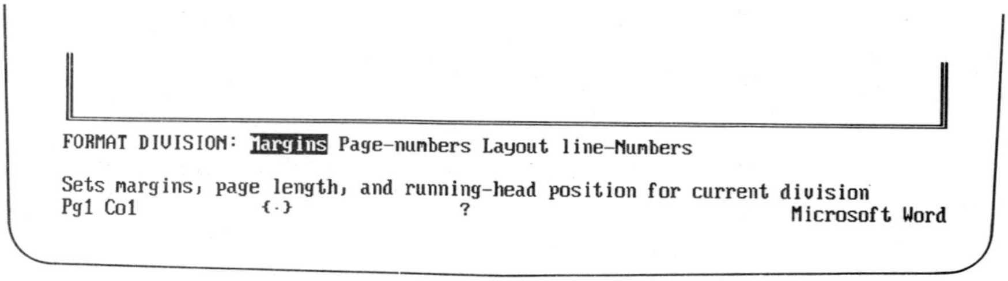

Fig. 8.1.

The Format Division command menu.

```
FORMAT DIVISION: margins Page-numbers Layout line-Numbers

Sets margins, page length, and running-head position for current division
Pg1 Co1              {·}             ?                    Microsoft Word
```

Tip   **When you select an option other than the default settings in Format Division, Word enters a division mark above the end mark.**

The division mark, a double row of dots, automatically appears just above the end mark even if you have chosen the None setting in the Option command's show non-printing symbols field (see fig. 8.2).

If you use the Format Division command again and choose additional options, Word does not insert additional division marks. It stores the new formats in the division mark that already exists—just as Word stores paragraph formats in the paragraph mark.

Trap   **The division formats you choose affect only the text you type above the division mark.**

Suppose that you start a session with a fresh, blank Word document and you choose the Format Division command to turn on page numbering and set new margins. You then select the end mark and start typing. But when you print your document, page numbers do not appear and the margins are not correct.

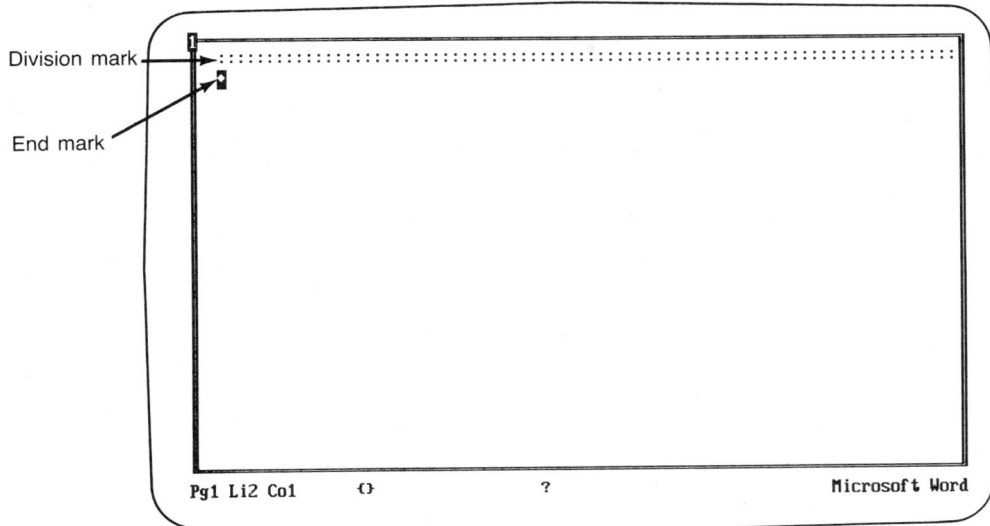

Division mark

End mark

Pg1 Li2 Col   {}   ?   Microsoft Word

Fig. 8.2.

The division mark.

To avoid this problem, remember that the division mark affects only the text *above* the mark. If the division mark is the first character in your document, select the division mark and press Enter to create space to work in.

Trap   **If you delete the division mark, you delete the division formats you have chosen.**

The division mark stores division formatting, just as paragraph marks store paragraph formatting. If you delete the division mark, Word reverts to the division formatting specified in the style sheet attached to the document. If you have not attached one of your own style sheets, using the Format Stylesheet Attach command, Word uses the default division settings in NORMAL.STY, the default style sheet. If you delete a division mark in a document with multiple divisions, the division above the deleted mark takes on the formats of the following division.

Setting Margins and Page Sizes

The Format Division Margins menu is shown in figure 8.3. If you are working with nonstandard page sizes, you can use this command to tell Word to use any page size you specify. In addition, you can easily set the top, bottom, left, and right margins.

Fig. 8.3.

The Format
Division Margins
command menu.

```
‖                                                                            ‖

FORMAT DIVISION MARGINS
      top: 1"                    bottom: 1"
      left: 1.25"                right: 1.25"
      page length: 11"          width: 8.5"        gutter margin: 0"
      running-head position from top: 0.5"         from bottom: 0.5"
      mirror margins: Yes(No)                      use as default: Yes(No)
Enter measurement
Pg1 Co1              {§}              ?                    Microsoft Word
```

Tip **You can change Word's default page size to accommodate your needs.**

Word can adjust to any page size, including European sizes, up to 22 inches by 22 inches. Note, however, that changing the page size changes the width of lines. To determine line width, subtract the total of the specified margin settings from the page width.

Tip **Word's default page size and margin settings create a 6-inch line.**

If you do not alter Word's default page width and margin settings, your lines are 6 inches in length. Word specifies a default page width of 8.5 inches with 1.25-inch right and left margins, resulting in a line length of 6 inches.

Trap **Many printers cannot handle right or left margins of less than 0.5 inch.**

At times you may want to use margins less than 0.5 inch; but print a test copy first. Many laser printers, for example, cannot print within 0.25 inch of the paper's edge because the printer uses these margins to guide the paper.

Trap **If you change the margins in the middle of a document, the change affects the whole division.**

Many word processing programs let you change the margins as you write so that only the text you enter has those margins. Not so with Word. If you change the margin settings in the Format Division Margins command, all the text in the current division is affected, not just the text entered after you make the change.

Tip **To change the margin settings in the middle of a document, press Ctrl-Enter to start a new division.**

One good reason to start a new division within a document is to change the margin setting without affecting the margins of text already typed. To start a new division, press Ctrl-Enter. Then position the cursor within the new division and use the Format Division Margins command to set the new margins. For more information on starting new divisions, see "Creating a Document with Multiple Divisions," in this chapter.

Trap **Don't confuse margins and paragraph indentations.**

The paragraph indentations you set in the Format Paragraph command's `right indent` and `left indent` fields (see Chapter 5) are measured in from the margins. Margins, on the other hand, are measured in from the edge of the page. Control margins with the Format **D**ivision **M**argins command.

Tip **Add a gutter if you plan to print your document on both sides of the page and bind the pages.**

A *gutter* is an extra margin on the right side of even-numbered pages and the left side of odd-numbered pages. Gutters are needed when printing two-sided documents to facilitate binding. To add a gutter, type a number (*0.5″* is a common size) in the `gutter margin` field of the Format Division Margins command.

Another way to add a gutter is to choose `Yes` in the `mirror margins` field of the Format Division Margins menu. This option prints the left and right margins you have chosen on odd pages and reverses them on even pages. If you choose a 1.5-inch left margin and 1.0-inch right margin, for instance, Word prints a 1.5-inch *left* margin on the odd pages and a 1.5-inch *right* margin on the even pages.

Trick **Save your margins and page size choices as defaults.**

In previous versions of Word, the only way to set new default margins and page sizes was to create a style sheet. With Version 5, however, you can save all the choices in the Format Division Margins menu as the new defaults. Just choose the `Yes` option in the `use as default` field of the Format Division Margins command menu.

Adding Page Numbers

The Format Division Page-numbers command provides one of the two ways to turn on automatic page numbering (see fig. 8.4). You also can turn on page numbering by creating a running head with a *page glossary* (a symbol that tells Word where you want the page numbers to appear). If you want to omit the page number from the first page of your document, you must use the running heads, which have other advantages, as discussed in the "Creating Running Heads" section in this chapter.

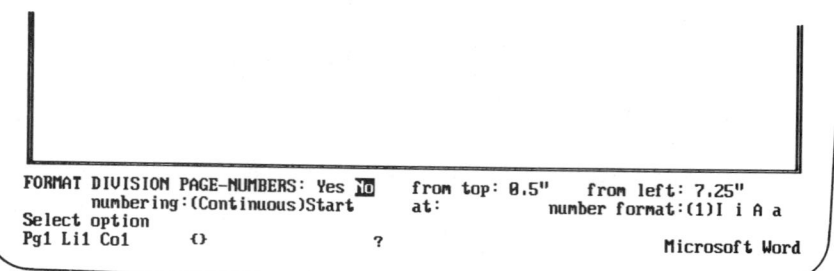

Fig. 8.4.

The Format Division Page-numbers command menu.

```
FORMAT DIVISION PAGE-NUMBERS: Yes No   from top: 0.5"    from left: 7.25"
   numbering:(Continuous)Start   at:         number format:(1)I i A a
Select option
Pg1 Li1 Co1     {}                  ?                      Microsoft Word
```

Trap **Word does not print page numbers unless you use a command.**

In Word, page numbers are turned off by default—an odd choice, because most people prefer to use them. Almost every time you create a new document, then, you have to remember to turn on page numbering. Eventually you will forget to do so and print a lengthy document only to find that you have omitted page numbers. The tips and tricks that follow suggest ways to turn on page numbers.

Trick **Create for the default style sheet, NORMAL.STY, a style-sheet entry that automatically turns on page numbering for all documents.**

One good reason (among many) for creating a style sheet is that you can include a standard division format. When you create this format, you can include instructions that print page numbers in all documents. See Chapter 12 for more information. But before you turn on page numbering this way, note the limitations of page numbers inserted with the Format Division Page-numbers command, listed in the next trap.

Trap **If you turn on page numbers with the Format Division Page-numbers command, you have no way to omit page numbers on page 1.**

Normally, page numbers do not appear on the first page of a document—it doesn't look right to see a *1* on the first page of a two-page letter, for instance. Microsoft, how about suppressing first-page number printing for Version 6—or at least giving us the option?

For now, the only way you can print page numbers on all pages except page 1 is to add page numbers with running heads. Because you may have several other reasons to prefer the running head approach to page numbers, you should choose this approach. For more information, see the section entitled "Creating Running Heads," in this chapter.

Tip **You can print page numbers anywhere on the page.**

By default, Word positions page numbers at the top right of the page (0.5 inch from the top and 7.25 inches from the left edge). You can change this position. To center page numbers at the bottom of a standard page, for instance, type *10.5* in the from top field and *4.25* in the from left field of the Format Division Page-numbers command.

Trap **Some printers cannot handle page numbers positioned too close to the top or bottom of the page.**

Allow at least 0.25 inch from the top or the bottom of the page for the page number. For the best appearance, try to position the page numbers in the center of the margin. For example, if you use a 1-inch top or bottom margin, position the page number 0.5 inch or 10.5 inches in the from top field of the Format Division Page-numbers command.

Tip **You can start page numbering with any number you want.**

If you plan to combine several documents into a final report, you may want page numbers of the documents to start with a number other than 1. To do so, choose the Start option in the numbering field of the Format Division Page-numbers command and in the at field type the number at which you want page numbering to begin.

Trap **You type a number in the at field of the Format Division Page-numbers command to start page numbering at a number other than 1, but Word ignores your request.**

You must also choose the Start option in the numbering field. Microsoft, fix this for Version 6, OK?

Tip **Select a page number format from five options.**

You can choose from the following five page-number formats:

- ❏ Arabic: 1, 2, 3
- ❏ Roman uppercase: I, II, III
- ❏ Roman lowercase: i, ii, iii
- ❏ Alphabetic uppercase: A, B, C
- ❏ Alphabetic lowercase: a, b, c

The default format, Arabic, is used most often. Roman lowercase numbers are often used in front matter and prefaces, however, and alphabetic options are sometimes used in appendixes of technical reports. To change the page-number format, choose the **F**ormat **D**ivision **P**age-numbers command and select an option in the number format field.

Trap **You must use the Format Division Page-numbers command menu to control page-number format.**

Even if you control page numbering with running heads and choose the No option in the first field of the Format Division Page-numbers command, you still need to use the Format Division Page-numbers command menu to control page-number format.

Think of the first Page-numbers field as serving a restricted function: turning on or off Word's automatic page numbering feature. If you turn off the feature, you still can number pages with running heads. If you number pages with running heads, you still use the number format field to control the format (Arabic, Roman, and so on) of the numbers in the running head.

Trap **You format your document to print in a fancy, nonstandard font, but page numbers print in the default font.**

Word's default style sheet, NORMAL.STY, sets the character style of page numbers to the default font for your printer. You cannot change this setting in your document. To get around this problem, you must either add page numbers with running heads or modify NORMAL.STY. You learn how to add page numbers with running heads in this chapter; see Chapter 12 for information on modifying the default character style for page numbers in NORMAL.STY.

Creating Headers and Footers

With Word's Format Running-head command, you can create a *running head:* a line (or several lines, if you want) of text repeated on consecutive pages of a document. A commonly used running head is a short version of a document's title. You can position running heads in the top margin or bottom margin of your document. A top-margin running head is called a *header*; a bottom-margin running head is called a *footer*.

Word's header and footer options are unusually flexible, as summarized by the following points:

- ❏ You can create running heads that print on all the pages in your document, on all but the first page, or on only the first page.

- ❏ You can specify one running head for odd pages and another for even pages.

- ❏ You can have Word print a particular running head on only a specific group of pages.

- ❏ You can set up one running head to print in one part of a document and another to print in another part.

- ❏ You can set up a running head so that page numbers are printed precisely where and how you want them.

Version 5 users have much to celebrate when it comes to running heads. Although the intelligent hand that guided Version 5's revision unfortunately seems to have forgotten the Format Division Page-numbers command, no such neglect was given to the Format Division command's next-door neighbor on the edit menu. Many of the traps mentioned in the preceding edition of this book have been remedied. You will find it quite easy now to create good-looking headers and footers with Word 5.

Trick **Turn on the style bar before creating running heads.**

If you choose the Yes option in the style bar field of the Options menu, Word displays codes defining the kind of running head chosen. You learn more about these codes later in this chapter. For now, turn on the style bar before experimenting with running heads so that you can identify the running heads you create.

Tip **Create a header or footer by formatting a one-line paragraph with the Format Running-head command.**

After typing the text you want to appear in your running head, press Enter to make the text a separate paragraph. Then press the up arrow key to select the paragraph and use the **F**ormat **R**unning-head command. When the command menu appears (see fig. 8.5), choose either the Top (header) or Bottom (footer) option and carry out the command. A caret (ˆ) appears in the left margin to tell you that the paragraph has been formatted as running head text. If you turned on the style bar, a code appears as well. The codes beginning with t indicate headers (top); the codes beginning with b indicate paragraphs formatted as footers (bottom). See table 8.2 for a complete list of codes.

Fig. 8.5.

The Format
Running-head
command menu.

```
 ║                                                                    ║
 ║                                                                    ║
 FORMAT RUNNING-HEAD position: Top Bottom None
          odd pages:(Yes)No  even pages:(Yes)No  first page: Yes(No)   ▮
          alignment:(Left-margin)Edge-of-paper
 Select option
 Pg1 Co1              {§}               ?                  Microsoft Word
```

Tip **The default settings in the Format Running-head menu command fields print your header and footer on all pages except the first.**

The default settings are fine for most applications. As you learn elsewhere in this section, however, you can print different running heads on the odd and even pages of your document. On very few occasions, if any, will you want a running head on the first page.

Trick **Because the default settings in the Format Running-head command fields are fine for most purposes, use the Ctrl-F2 and Alt-F2 shortcuts to mark text as header or footer text.**

Press Ctrl-F2 to define a paragraph as a header; press Alt-F2 to define a paragraph as a footer. The default settings are used to format headers and footers marked in this way.

Tip **Version 5 formats running head paragraphs with the margins chosen for the rest of the document.**

This welcome change eliminates the fussing and calculations that were once necessary to align running heads with the margins. (You still can create headers or footers that are wider than the text margins, by formatting the running head with negative indents in the right indent and left indent fields of the Format Paragraph menu.)

Trap **The Format Running-head command doesn't actually format the running head text; the command just defines the text as a header or footer.**

The command really ought to be called "Define Running-head," because that's what it does. To format your running head, you must use other commands to do the following:

❏ Format the vertical position of headers and footers by typing measurements in the running head position from top and from bottom fields of the Format Division Margins command. The default setting for both fields is 0.5 inch, an appropriate measurement for Word's 1.0 inch default top and bottom margins.

❏ Format the horizontal, or lateral, position of the header or footer text by using the Format Paragraph or Format Tab Set command or their equivalents.

Trick   Include page numbers in a running head.

Word comes equipped with seven built-in glossary entries that serve various purposes. One glossary, page, automatically prints the current page number wherever this entry is inserted into your document. If you insert this glossary entry into your running head, Word prints the current page number each time the program prints the running head. Following is the procedure for inserting the page glossary into your running head:

1. Position the cursor where you want the page number to appear in your running head.

2. Type *page* and press F3.

Word automatically inserts the page glossary. The page number does not appear until the document is printed, but you can tell the glossary has been inserted because the word *page* is shown in parentheses.

Tip   Using running heads to print page numbers has several advantages over the Format Division Page-numbers method.

Following are the advantages of using running heads to print page numbers:

❏ You can precede or follow the page number with other text, such as the word *Page* or hyphens or asterisks.

❏ You can format the page-number character style in any way you want with a minimum of hassle. Just highlight the characters (page) and use any character formatting you wish, including fonts and font sizes.

❏ If you used the default settings in the Format Running-head command menu, Word does not print page numbers on the first page of your document. This fact alone makes this approach all but mandatory for business letters.

Trick **Use additional built-in glossary entries to incorporate the date and time into your running head.**

In addition to page, Word offers four other permanent glossary entries you might want to use in running heads. These glossary entries are listed in the following chart.

Glossary Name	Usage
date	If you type *date* and press F3, Word inserts the current system date, using the format selected in the date format field of the Options menu.
time	If you type *time* and press F3, Word inserts the current system time, using the format selected in the time format field of the Options menu.
dateprint	If you type *dateprint* and press F3, Word surrounds the word with parentheses. When you print the document, Word inserts the current system date at the time of printing.
timeprint	If you type *timeprint* and press F3, Word surrounds the word with parentheses. When you print the document, Word inserts the current system time at the time of printing.

Tip **To format a running head to print flush right, format the running head with the flush-right paragraph format.**

To format a paragraph flush with the right margin, use the Alt-R keyboard command or select the Right option in the alignment field of the Format Paragraph command.

Trick **Create a macro to add a header with page numbers to your document.**

This macro duplicates the page-number formatting inserted by the Format Division Page-numbers command, except the macro prints the page numbers in a font you specify and does not print a page number on page 1. You can use this macro anywhere in your document. This macro creates a *bookmark*, or a named location, to which the macro can scroll when it's finished. The macro then scrolls to the top of your document and inserts the page glossary, defines it as a flush-right running head, and formats it with the character font you chose. Finally, the macro returns the cursor to the location at which you invoked the macro, and erases the bookmark.

```
«ASK font  =  ?Font for page numbers?»
<shift f8><ctrl esc>fkjump1<enter>
<ctrl pgup><enter><ctrl-up>
<ctrl esc>fpR<tab>0<tab>0<tab>0<tab>1 li<tab>0
   li<tab>0li<end>N<enter>page<f3>
<f7><alt f8>«font»<enter>
<ctrl f2>
<ctrl esc>jkjump1<enter>
<ctrl esc>fk<del><enter>Y<shift f7>
```

To create and use this macro, follow the instructions in Chapter 13, "Macros." Save the macro using the macro name quick_pagenumbers.mac^<ctrl q>p.

Trick **Use tabs to set up a running head with three elements, positioned flush left, centered, and flush right.**

You easily can create a running head that prints your name flush left, the date at printing in the center of the header or footer, and the page number flush right. Just create a centered tab in the middle of the running head and a flush-right tab at the right margin. Then add the text, the `dateprint` glossary, and the `page` glossary.

Tip **Take advantage of Word's capability to place different running heads on odd and even pages.**

You can use this feature to increase the information in running heads. If you divide your document into chapters, for instance, you can place the document title on even-numbered pages and the chapter title on odd-numbered pages.

If you plan to have your Word document duplicated on an offset printing press, you may want to have the document printed on both sides of the paper. Printing on both sides reduces the bulk of a document and achieves a more professional look with the two-sided format generally used in commercial publications. If your document is to be printed in this way, consider formatting the even-numbered pages' running heads flush left and the odd-numbered pages' running heads flush right. This format is usually pleasing to the eye. Table 8.1 shows the settings used to create odd-page and even-page running heads; figure 8.6 shows their appearance on the screen.

Table 8.1
Settings for Right and Left Running Heads
for Two-Sided Printing

Odd-Page Running Head (Right Side after Binding)		
Command	*Field*	*Setting*
Format Paragraph	alignment	Right
Format Running-head	position	Top
	odd pages	Yes
	even pages	No
	first page	No

Even-Page Running Head (Left Side after Binding)		
Command	*Field*	*Setting*
Format Paragraph	alignment	Left
Format Running-head	position	Top
	odd pages	No
	even pages	Yes
	first page	No

Header for even page   Header for odd page

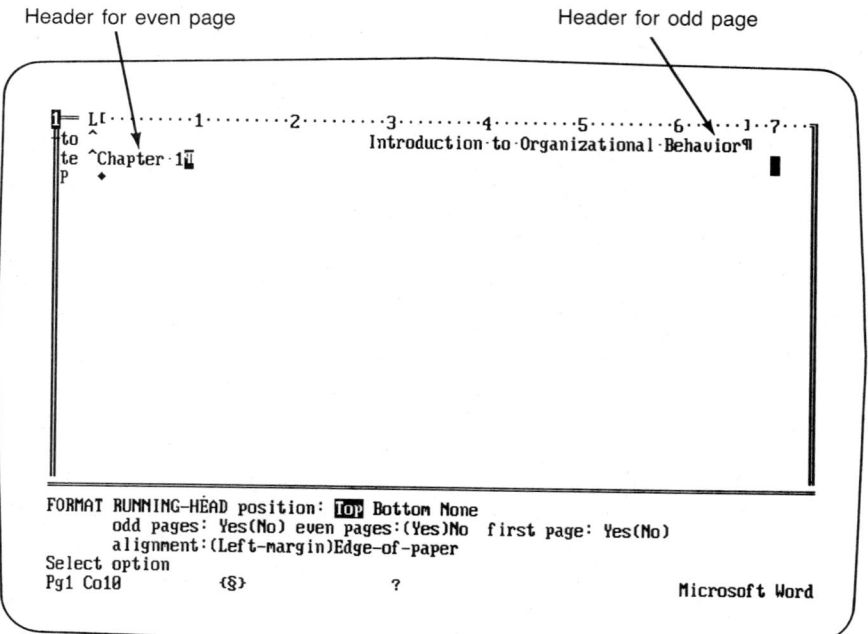

Fig. 8.6.

Odd-page and
even-page
running heads.

Tip **Check the style bar to see where a running head is to be printed.**

The *style bar* is a special on-screen column that displays paragraph styles and running head formatting. If you turn on the style bar by setting the Options command's style bar field to Yes, you can tell where a running head is to be printed. In figure 8.7, the to indicates that the running head prints at the top of odd-numbered pages; the te indicates that the text prints at the top of even-numbered pages. Table 8.2 lists the running-head codes and where the running-heads are printed.

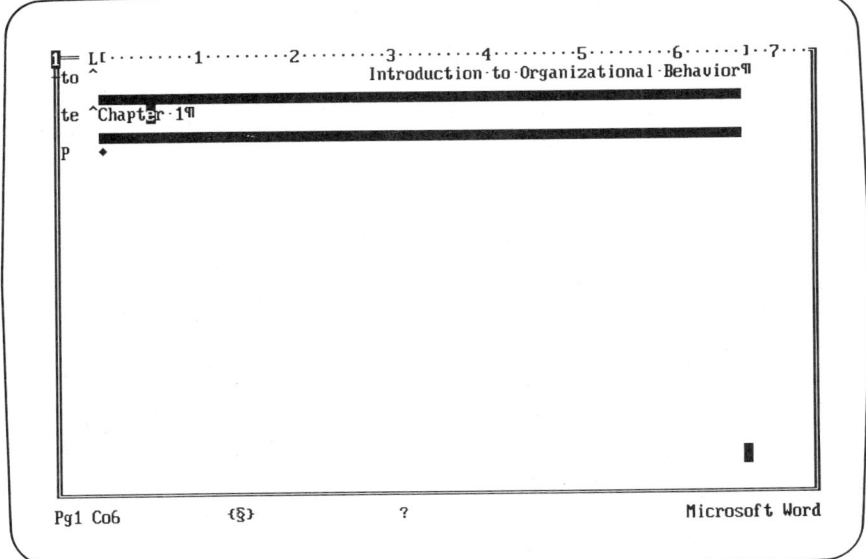

Fig. 8.7.

The running-head codes in the style bar.

Trick **You can change running heads in the middle of a document.**

When Word encounters a running head in a document, the program assumes that the running head is to stay in effect until the end of the division (which could be the end of the document). This statement is true unless you have formatted a subsequent running head with the same Format Running-head command settings. Thus, you can have Word print any number of running heads in a single document.

In a report with four distinct sections, for example, you may want each section to have its own running head. All you do is enter and format the new running head as the first paragraph of the first page on which

Table 8.2
Running-Head Codes in Style Bar

Code	Position on Page	Pages Printed On
t	Top	Odd and even pages
tf	Top	First page only
te	Top	Even pages only, or even pages and first page
to	Top	Odd pages only, or odd pages and first page
b	Bottom	Odd and even pages
bf	Bottom	First page only
be	Bottom	Even pages only, or even pages and first page
bo	Bottom	Odd pages only, or odd pages and first page

you want the running head to appear, using the Format Running-head command. To change a running head in the middle of a Word document, perform the following steps:

1. Select the first character of the first page on which you want the new running head to appear.

2. Press Enter to create a new paragraph.

3. Type and format the new running head using the **F**ormat **R**unning-head command.

Another way to change running heads in your document is to start a new division. For more information, see "Creating a Document with Multiple Divisions," in this chapter.

Tip You can cancel a running head by deleting it.

After you use the Format Running-head command, a caret (ˆ) appears in the style bar. If you change your mind about using a running head, however, no command deletes the running head. Instead, delete the whole paragraph—including the paragraph mark.

If you want to convert a running head back to a plain text paragraph without losing the running-head text, simply position the cursor anywhere in the running head, choose the **F**ormat **R**unning-head command, and select the None option in the position field.

Trap   **You print a document, but the running head is omitted.**

Word does not print a running head if insufficient space is reserved for it in the top or bottom margin. Unfortunately, Word gives no on-screen indication that the running head will not print.

Using a running head may require some planning. A one-line running head easily fits into the default one-inch top or bottom margin. If your running head is more than one line, however, you may need to change the Format Division Margins command's top or bottom setting.

Trick   **Add interest to a running head with paragraph borders.**

You can apply any of Word's formatting capabilities in a running head, including lines and borders created with the Format Border command (again see fig. 8.7). For more information on the Format Border command, see Chapter 7.

Tip   **Preview running-head formatting with the Print preView command.**

Print preView, new to Word 5, presents an on-screen graphic simulation of your document's appearance when printed. It shows, among other features, whether you have positioned running heads correctly. Unless you have limitless stores of paper, patience, and ink, preview your running head formatting before printing your document. For more information on Print preView, see Chapter 11.

Using Line Numbers

Word can print line numbers in the left or right margins of a document; this feature makes Word much more useful to legal professionals. To turn on line numbering, use the Format Division line-Numbers command (see fig. 8.8). By default, Word prints the line numbers 0.4 inch from the left edge of the page, and restarts the numbering at each page break. By default, all line numbers are printed.

Tip   **You can print line numbers in any increment.**

To print every other line number, enter 2 in the increment field of the Format Division line-Numbers command. To print every fifth line number, enter 5.

Fig. 8.8.

The Format Division line-Numbers command menu.

```
FORMAT DIVISION LINE-NUMBERS: Yes No            from text: 0.4"    ▊
        restart at:(Page)Division Continuous    increments: 1
Select option
Pg1 Co1              {§}                  ?                  Microsoft Word
```

Tip   **You can restart line numbering at page breaks, division breaks, or continue numbering through your document.**

Ordinarily, Word restarts line numbering at each page break. If you choose Division in the restart at field of the Format Division line-Numbers command, however, Word restarts the line numbers each time it encounters a division mark. If you choose Continuous, Word numbers the lines consecutively through the entire document, even if it is divided into multiple divisions.

Trick   **You can tell Word to skip blank lines when it prints line numbers.**

To skip blank lines, choose the No option in the count blank lines field of the Options menu.

Creating a Document with Multiple Divisions

Given its ancestry in programs designed by programmers to help crank out documentation, Word's incorporation of features ideal for multisection documents is not surprising. After all, a good manual or technical report is divided into chapters—but the whole document should fit into a single file so that automatic operations can be used to generate a table of contents and an index.

Word's capability to break a document into divisions reflects this ancestry. Division breaks, created by pressing Ctrl-Enter, are ideal for sectioning a document into chapters: at each division break, running heads and the footnote sequence are cancelled, which is appropriate for chapter breaks. Moreover, you can use a new page format after a division break. You can change any format controlled by the Format

Division commands, including the page-number style, the margins, and single-column or multiple-column formatting.

Should you use division breaks? Division breaks are essential, of course, if you're creating a huge, 500K document with several distinct chapters. But unless you're working on a fast 80386 system with a great deal of memory, you may run into insufficient memory problems if you try to compile an index from a 500K file. For most users, the advisable technique is to break lengthy documents into separate disk files.

Even so, occasions arise when division breaks come in handy. Use them, for example, when you want to switch from single-column to multiple-column formatting (discussed later in this chapter). You can use division breaks whenever you want to switch page formats in your document.

Tip   **To start a new division, press Ctrl-Enter.**

When you press Ctrl-Enter, Word inserts a new division mark, and the cursor jumps down below the mark (see fig. 8.9). Your document now has two divisions. To format a division, position the cursor in the new division and use the **Format D**ivision commands. Repeat these formatting steps for other divisions.

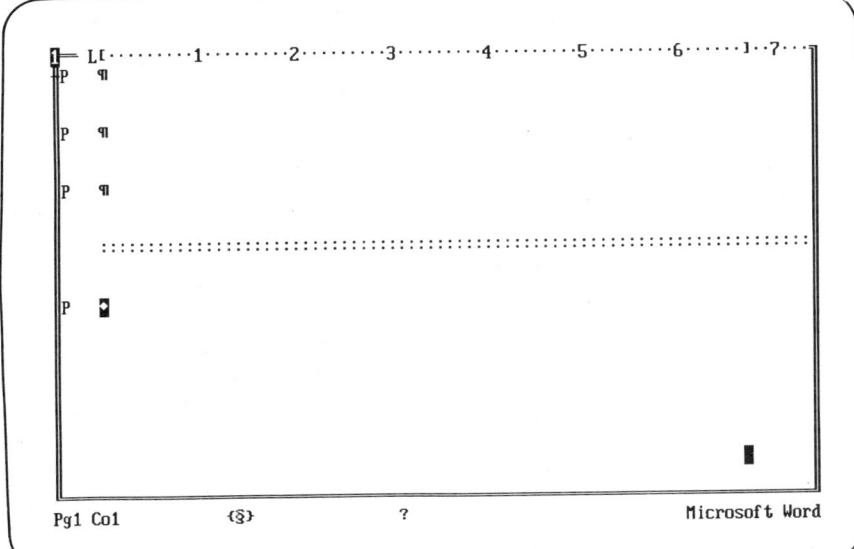

Fig. 8.9.

A division mark.

Trap   **When you create a new division by pressing Ctrl-Enter, both divisions have the division formats of the whole document.**

Creating a division break isn't the same thing as formatting the new division. When you insert a division break, Word uses the division formats already in effect. To change the page-style formats in the new division, you must place the cursor in the new division and use the Format Division command.

Tip   **Control page breaks with the Format Division Layout command.**

By default, Word starts a new page when the program encounters a division mark. However, you can control how page and other breaks occur when a new division starts. Move the cursor to the new division and choose the Format Division Layout command (see fig. 8.10). In the division break field, select one of the following options:

- ❏ Page (the default). Starts a new page at the division mark.

- ❏ Continuous. Continues printing the new division's text without a break of any kind.

- ❏ Column (if you are using multiple-column formatting). Starts a new column.

- ❏ Even. Starts printing the text of the new division at the top of an even-numbered page.

- ❏ Odd. Starts printing the text of the new division at the top of an odd-numbered page.

Tip   **After you divide your document by pressing Ctrl-Enter, Word's page-number indicator changes to tell the currently selected division.**

Next to the page number indicator at the bottom of the screen is a division indicator, which uses the code D to indicate divisions (see fig. 8.11). Divisions are counted sequentially from the beginning of the document (1, 2, 3, etc.).

Creating Newsletter Columns

Word has always done a good job of printing multiple-column text, but until Version 5, using Word's multiple-column features required more than a few tricks. You couldn't mix single-column and multiple-column

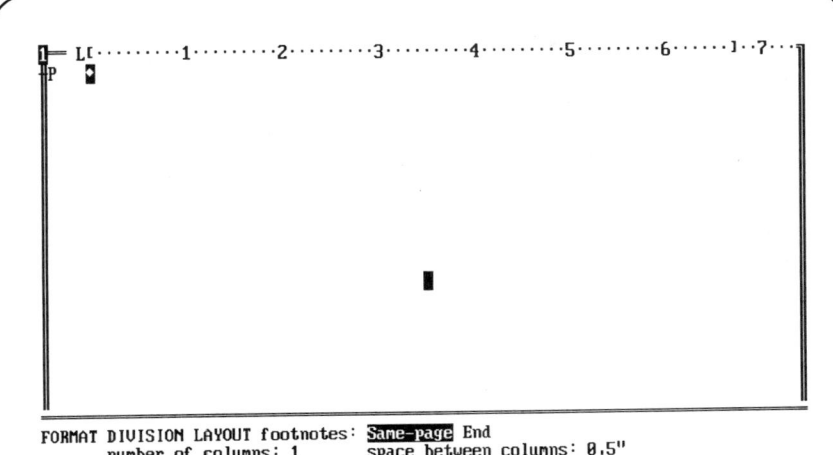

Fig. 8.10.

The Format
Division Layout
command menu.

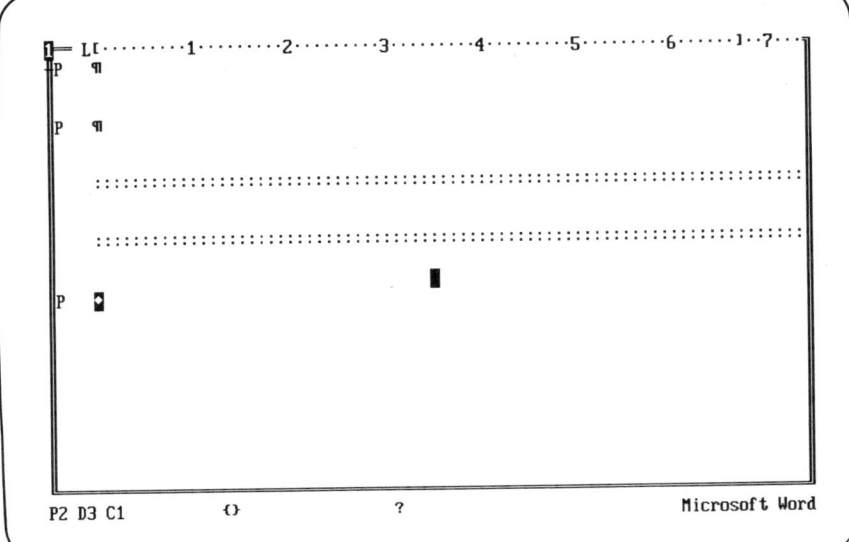

Fig. 8.11.

The division
indicator appears
on the status line
after you divide a
document with a
division break.

text on a page, and you couldn't see the columns until you printed your document—only to find, in most cases, that you had made some kind of formatting error. All that's history, thanks to some very nice Version 5 changes.

Tip **To create newspaper columns, type 2 or 3 in the** number of columns **field of the Format Division Layout command menu.**

That's all it takes to turn on automatic multiple-column formatting. The multiple-column format applies to the whole document, unless you divide the document by pressing Ctrl-Enter to create a division break. If you divide the document, the multiple-column format applies to the division in which the cursor is positioned when you give the command.

Tip **Toggle Alt-F4 to view multiple columns as they are to print, but return to the normal mode to edit.**

New to Version 5 is the Show Layout mode, which displays multiple-column text on the screen as you're editing (see figs. 8.12 and 8.13). Note, however, that you must pay a price for the screen display of multiple-column text: Word's display speed slows considerably. Unless you really need to see the columns on the screen, you may prefer to edit with Show Layout switched off. Toggle the mode on to view placement and effect, but toggle off Show Layout for editing.

Fig. 8.12.

Multiple columns displayed without Show Layout.

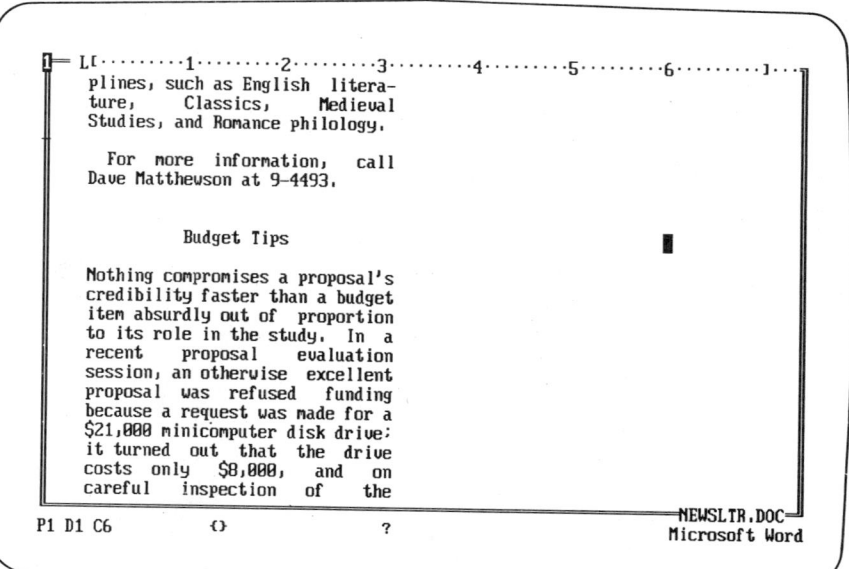

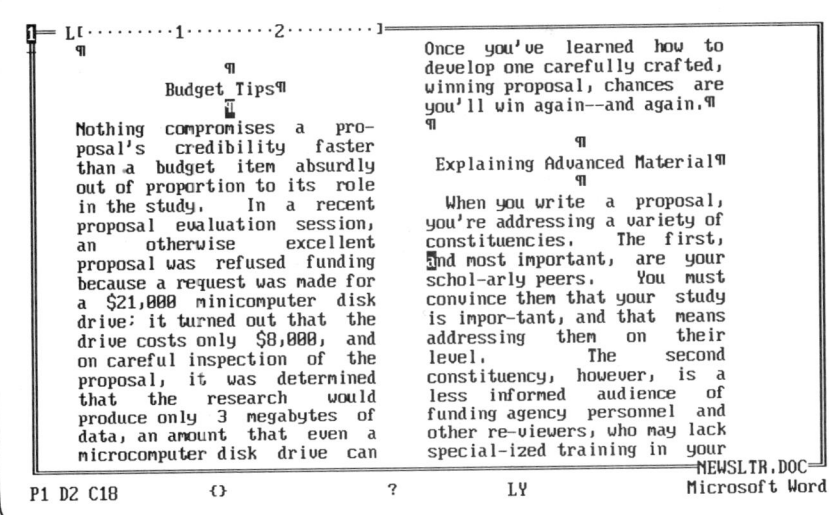

Fig. 8.13.

Multiple columns displayed with Show Layout.

Trick **Press Ctrl-5-right arrow to move to the next column right in the Show Layout mode; press Ctrl-5-left arrow to move left.**

When you're viewing multiple columns in Show Layout mode, you need a special command to move the cursor to the next column right or left. Word 5 includes two new cursor-control keys for this purpose. If you use a mouse, however, it's simpler just to click the cursor in the column you want to edit.

Trick **Press Alt-Ctrl-Enter to create a hard column break.**

This keyboard command is another very welcome new feature of Version 5. In previous versions of Word, you couldn't easily create a hard column break, which is like a hard page break except that the column break forces Word to start a new column. The earlier versions had a way to make a column break by creating a division break, but the process was cumbersome and had the unwanted effect of canceling all your footnotes and running heads. With the new Alt-Ctrl-Enter keyboard command, however, you can force Word to start new columns whenever you please.

Trick **Separate newspaper columns with vertical lines.**

Here's a Format Border trick for double-column newsletters: When you create a multiple-column format, type *0* (zero) in the space between columns field of the Format Division Layout command menu. Normally, this setting causes your columns to run up against one another unattractively, but go ahead and type the multiple-column text anyway. Now select all the multiple-column text. Choose the **Format Border** command. Select the Lines option in the type field, and choose Yes in the left and right fields. Carry out the command. Word prints the multiple columns with three vertical lines—one down the middle, one on the left, and one on the right sides of the text (see fig. 8.14).

Fig. 8.14.

Print preView of double-column newsletter with vertical lines.

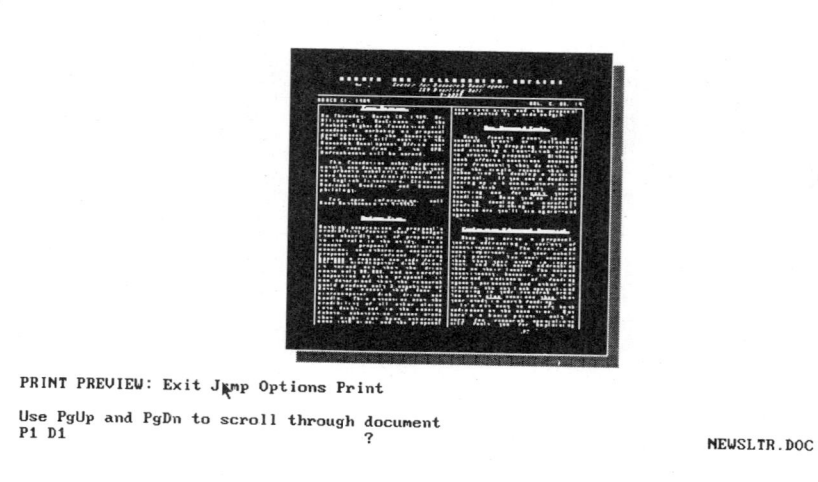

Trick **You can easily blend single-column and multiple-column formatting on a single page.**

In previous versions of Word, blending single-column and multiple-column text on a single page was close to impossible. You could do it, but the procedure is not worth remembering. Now, it's easy. To change the layout from single-column formatting to double (or triple), just create a division break by pressing Ctrl-Enter. Format the new division as multiple-column text; be sure to choose the Continuous option in the division break field of the Format Division Layout command. The division break can occur anywhere on the page, and you can use division breaks as often as you like.

Trick **_Create a single-column banner over multiple-column text._**

When you blend single-column and multiple-column text, chances are you're creating a banner (a single-column headline and title) for a newsletter or circular. To make the banner, create it using a single-column division format. Then press Ctrl-Enter to create a division break. Position the cursor beneath the break and choose the **F**ormat **D**ivision **L**ayout command. Select multiple columns by typing a number larger than *1* in the number of columns field and choose the Continuous option in the division break field. As you see in the next trap, positioning running heads just below the division break is a good practice (see fig. 8.15).

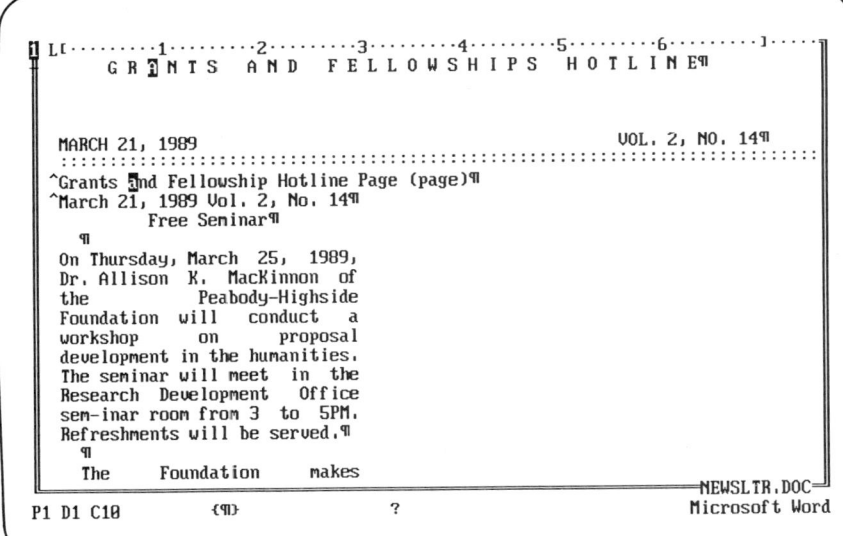

Fig. 8.15.

Formatting a newsletter banner.

Trap **_Division breaks cancel running heads and footnotes._**

Bear in mind that if you enter a division break to change from single-column to multiple-column formatting, you cancel running heads and restart the footnote-numbering sequence. That isn't necessarily a problem, because you can echo the running heads at the beginning of the next page. If you're using the division break to create a banner, put the running heads directly below the break (and just above the text).

Trick **To create within multiple-column text a single-column format that doesn't cancel running heads, use the Format pOsition command.**

The Format pOsition command is discussed in more detail in the next section. You can use this command to create and format a paragraph of single-column text, which you can insert anywhere in a multiple-column document without affecting running heads or footnotes. Use this technique if you want to change briefly from multiple-column to single-column formatting and then back again to multiple-column formatting.

Tip **Preview multiple-column formatting and other page styles with Print preView.**

Word 5's new Page preView command, like Show Layout, displays multiple-column text as it prints. Unlike Show Layout, Print preView also shows footnotes, endnotes, page numbers, and running heads. Use Print preView to give your document a final preview before printing (again see fig. 8.14).

Importing Graphics

An exciting new feature of Word 5 is the capability to import and print a variety of graphic images. Word 5 can import and print Lotus 1-2-3 graphics, PC Paintbrush files, any graphics file saved with the HPGL plotter standard, PostScript files, the TIFF files created by many scanners, and files created with Word 5's own screen-capture utility, CAPTURE.COM (on Word Utilities Disk 3). When you import these images into Word files, you don't see them on the screen in normal document mode. You can see them if you use the Print preView command, however, and Word prints them along with the rest of the document text.

Tip **Use the Library Link Graphics command to import graphics images into a Word file.**

To import a graphic image, do the following steps:

1. Press Enter to create a new, blank paragraph where you want the graphic to appear.

2. Choose the Library Link Graphics command (see fig. 8.16). Select the `filename` field and press F1. Word lists all files in the directory. Choose the graphic you want to import.

3. Press Enter to carry out the command with the proposed settings in the other command fields.

Fig. 8.16.

The Library Link Graphics command menu.

```
LIBRARY LINK GRAPHICS filename: C:\MSWORD\USING5\US5PIX\BARGRAPH.PIC
               file format: Lotus PIC      alignment in frame: Centered
               graphics width: 6.75"       graphics height: 4.874"
               space before: 0"            space after: 0.167"
Enter filename or press F1 to select from list
Pg1 Co64          {BAR.PI...re-19}  ?                    Microsoft Word
```

After you use Library Link Graphics, Word enters a command, including hidden text codes, into your document at the paragraph mark entered to "hold" the graphic. You don't see the image until you use **P**rint pre**V**iew (see fig. 8.17).

You can move the graphic simply by moving the command that Library Link Graphics inserted in your document. Delete the command to remove the illustration completely from your document.

Fig. 8.17.

Viewing the imported image with Print preView.

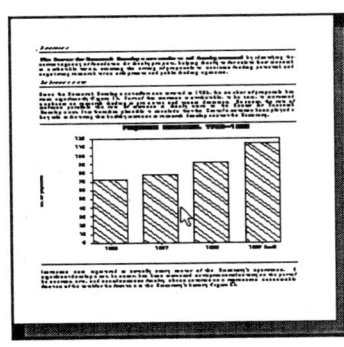

```
PRINT PREVIEW: Exit Jump Options Print

Use PgUp and PgDn to scroll through document
Pg1                          ?                REPORT.DOC
```

Trick   **Add borders to the graphic with the Format Border command.**

You can improve the graphic image's appearance in your document by surrounding the image with a box or positioning lines above and below it. To do so, simply select the paragraph containing the code inserted by Library Link Graphics and choose the Box option in the Format Border command menu. Using the current paragraph's width, Word draws a box around the graphic.

Trick   **Add a caption to the graphic.**

To position the caption within the lines or box added with the Format Border command, just place the cursor on the paragraph mark after the text inserted by the Library Link Graphics command and press Shift-Enter to start a new line. Type the caption.

Trick   **Type a series code name to number the illustrations in your document automatically.**

A new Word 5 feature makes it easy to automatically number any element in a series, such as illustrations or tables. Here's how:

1. Type *Figure* and press the space bar to enter one space.

2. Type *figno:* (do not forget the colon).

3. Position the cursor after the colon and press F3. Word places parentheses around the series code name.

Word doesn't display the figure number; you won't see it until you print your document. The parentheses (surrounding the code name) tell you, however, that the series code has been accepted and that Word will remove the *figno:* code and print a number in its place.

That's all it takes to number the illustrations in your document automatically! You can use the same techniques to number other series, such as tables. Just type any series code name of up to 31 characters followed by a colon, and press F3.

Anchoring Text and Graphics with Format pOsition

Word 5's new Format pOsition command is one of Version 5's most useful new features. With it, you can fix the position of a paragraph anywhere on the page so that the paragraph stays put even if you add more text above it.

Paragraph is used here in Word's sense. The paragraph you anchor can be a paragraph of text, for example, a sidebar like the ones that magazines use to emphasize a given passage. A paragraph also can be a graphic image imported with the Library Link Graphics command. Remember that any paragraph can be formatted with lines and boxes from the Format Border command, so the paragraph can have a box around it—and the box is anchored too. An anchored paragraph is called a *frame*. The term is a good one because it conveys the idea of a rectangular shape of fixed size and position.

Once you anchor the paragraph, the text you add to your document "floats" around the frame automatically. If room is left on the sides of the anchored frame, Word automatically splits the flow of text to flow past the frame to the left and right. You can place frames within multiple-column text, too, with very good results.

Tip **Understand your options for anchoring frames vertically and horizontally.**

When you use the Format pOsition command, you must specify how you want the frame anchored (see fig. 8.18). To do so, you specify a horizontal position and a vertical position. You also can control the amount of white space around the frame.

```
FORMAT POSITION
      horizontal frame position: Right        relative to: Column(Margins)Page
      vertical frame position: Centered        relative to:(Margins)Page
      frame width: Width of Graphic           distance from text: 0.333"
Enter measurement or press F1 to select from list
Pg1 Co22          {4}              ?                    Microsoft Word
```

Fig. 8.18.

The Format pOsition command menu.

The following list explains the various fields in the Format pOsition command menu.

❏ horizontal frame position. You may choose from the following frame-alignment options: Left, Centered, Right, Outside (on the outside of facing pages for documents printed on both sides of the page), or Inside (on the inside of facing pages). The position can be determined relative to the edges of the page, the page margins, or the column margins. In this field, you also can type a measurement from the left edge of the page, the left page margin, or the left column margin.

❏ vertical frame position. You may choose from the following frame-alignment options: In line (not anchored vertically), Top, Centered, or Bottom. The position can be fixed relative to the top and bottom edges of the page or the top and bottom margins.

❏ distance from text. Word's default response is 1/6th (0.333) inch. You can increase this measurement if you wish. Note that the value you specify determines the distance from the text on all four sides of the frame, not just the top and bottom. If the frame is narrower than the text column, text "floats" around the frame to the left and right.

❏ frame width. The proposed response is Width of Graphic (if you're anchoring a graphic), but you can also press F1 to choose Single column (spanning two columns) or Double column (if you're using multiple columns). Use these choices for graphics. To specify the width of a text frame, type a measurement, for example 2 in.

Trick **Anchor a graphic so that text "floats" around it.**

When you import the graphic with the Library Link Graphics command, be sure to choose in the graphics width field a measurement narrower than the line length you're using. Sizing the frame also sizes the graphic (instead of cropping it). If you're using 6.5-inch lines, for instance, choose a graphics width from the Library Link Graphics menu of about 3.5 inches. After importing the graphic, use the Format pOsition command to anchor the graphic vertically and horizontally, relative to the margins (see figure 8.19).

Trick **Add explanatory text or headings to the margins of a document.**

You have seen this layout technique in textbooks. It's easy to emulate this technique with Word 5 (see fig. 8.20). Use the Format Division Margins command to create a right margin of 3.0 inches. Then type the document's text. To add text to the margins, type it just before the paragraph adjacent to which you want the new text placed. Select the explanatory text and use the Format pOsition command; set horizontal frame position: Left and relative to: Page. Next, choose the In line option in the vertical frame position field. In the frame width field, type 2.5". Press Enter to carry out the

command. To format additional marginal comments or headings, copy
the formatting, using one of the techniques suggested in Chapter 7.

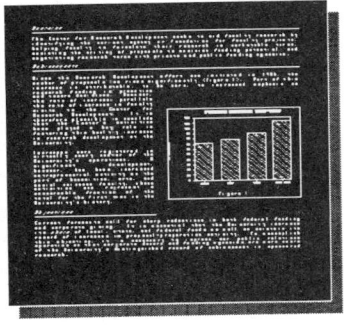

PRINT PREVIEW: Exit Jump Options Print

Use PgUp and PgDn to scroll through document
Pg1   ?   REPORT.DOC

Fig. 8.19.

Text "floats" around a graphic narrower than the line length.

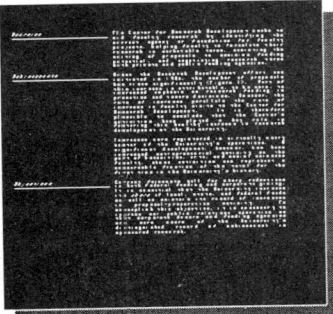

PRINT PREVIEW: Exit Jump Options Print

Use PgUp and PgDn to scroll through document
Pg1   ?   REPORT.DOC

Fig. 8.20.

Adding explanatory text to margins.

Trick   ***Echo important passages of text in sidebars.***

To create a sidebar, type the text on the page where you want the sidebar to appear. Then format the text with the **F**ormat p**O**sition command, choosing a vertical and horizontal alignment. (Try `Left` horizontal alignment relative to the margins, and `Bottom` vertical alignment relative to the margins.) Set a frame width (try 3.0″), and carry out the command. Add thick lines above and below the sidebar with the **F**ormat **B**order command and preview the results with **P**rint pre**V**iew (see fig. 8.21).

Fig. 8.21.

Creating a sidebar to emphasize important text.

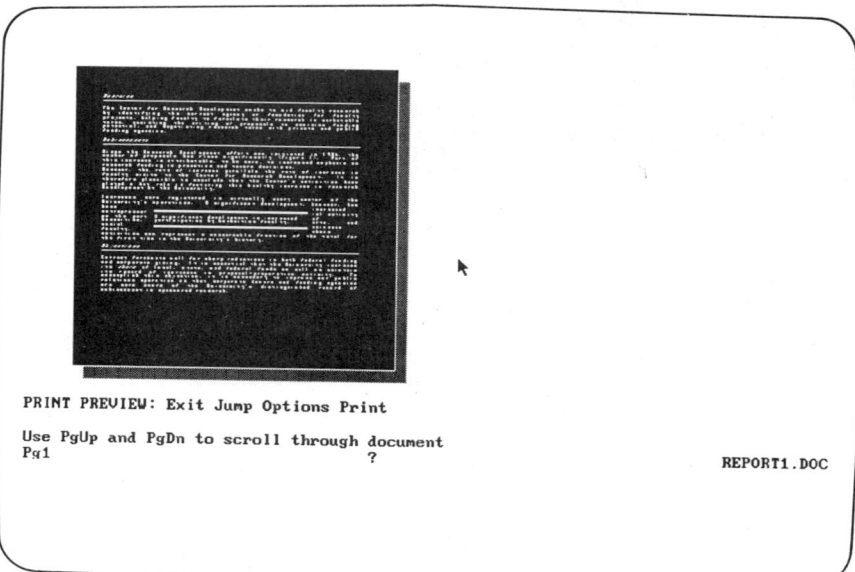

```
PRINT PREVIEW: Exit Jump Options Print

Use PgUp and PgDn to scroll through document
Pg1                                    ?                    REPORT1.DOC
```

Chapter Summary

Every word processing program, Word included, is designed to transform computer-based text into paginated, attractively printed hard copy. In Word, most page-style elements are controlled by the Format Division commands. Think of *division* as if it were synonymous with *page style.* When you choose an option from one of the Format Division menus, Word inserts a division mark at the end of your document. Don't delete the division mark; it contains your page-style formatting choices and affects the text positioned above the mark.

If you want to change Word's default margins and page-size settings, you can do so easily with the Format Division Margins command. By default, Word doesn't print page numbers. You can turn on page numbers in two ways: by choosing Yes in the Format Division Page-numbers menu, or by creating a running-head with the page glossary. Of the two methods, the latter is best. Running-head page numbers can be formatted just the way you want, and they don't print on page 1. Create a macro to add page numbers with the running-head technique.

To create a running head, use the Format Division Running-head command or the Ctrl-F2 or Alt-F2 shortcut. By default, Word aligns running heads at the left and right margins you defined for the document or division. To change the position of headers or footers vertically within the top or bottom margins, use the Format Division Margins command. Preview running heads with the Print preView command.

Legal professionals will appreciate Word's capability to print line numbers. You can set up Word to print all line numbers, to skip blank lines, to print in increments, and to restart line numbering wherever you please.

To divide your document into sections called divisions, press Ctrl-Enter to create a division break. Enter a division when you want to restart the footnote numbering sequence, stop running heads and start new ones, or change the page-style format. By default, Word breaks the page at a division break, but you can override this setting.

To create newspaper columns, type 2 or 3 in the number of columns field of the Format Division Layout command menu. Your choice affects the whole document unless you have divided it into divisions. If you have divisions, the choice applies only to the division in which the cursor is placed when you give the command. With Word 5, you can print single-column and multiple-column formatting on the same page. Toggle on the Show Layout mode to preview the column layout, but toggle back to the normal mode for quicker text entry and editing.

To import graphics into Word documents, use the Library Link Graphics command. You can import graphics files directly from many programs. The graphic doesn't appear in your document on-screen, however, until you use the Print preView command. If you like, you can enclose the image in a box using the Format Border command.

Word 5's new Format pOsition command anchors a paragraph in any position you specify. An anchored paragraph, called a frame, doesn't move when you insert or delete text. To anchor a frame, choose a horizontal and vertical position from the Format pOsition command menu. You can create a variety of interesting page designs with this command.

9

Strategies for Effective Editing

Once you have created a document, the time has come for a new kind of editing: *retrospective editing*. As you edit retrospectively, you use many of the same techniques and commands used when you wrote (see Chapter 5), including the text selection, insertion, and deletion commands. When you're editing retrospectively with a document that's many pages long, however, new challenges arise:

❑ *Keeping the text's structure in mind as you edit.* In a lengthy document, you easily can lose track of your document's overall structure when you view the document on the screen. Even if you hide the command menu, you see fewer than two dozen lines of text. This problem becomes particularly acute when the time comes to edit your document's large text domains. Such text domains, which may range from a paragraph to several pages in length, form your document's logical structure. If the domains are arranged illogically, your document lacks coherence.

❑ *Locating the text to be edited.* Another problem with lengthy documents is that you can waste significant amounts of time just trying to find the text to be edited. No matter how fast a program scrolls, locating text by scrolling through the document window by window is tedious and time consuming, not to mention hard on the eyes.

If you have ever struggled with these challenges while writing with a word processing program, take heart: this chapter contains good news. Word offers excellent tools for retrospective revision with high rates of productivity. In this chapter, you learn how to put these tools to work in a comprehensive revision strategy that helps you produce well-

253

organized work. Also covered are important new Word 5 features that make the program ideal for collaborative writing. Here's an overview of this chapter's contents:

❑ Finding and loading existing documents

❑ Moving around in a large document

❑ Searching for text and replacing text automatically

❑ Editing with multiple windows

❑ Editing with glossaries

❑ Editing with outlines

❑ Using the Undo command

❑ Using Word 5 for collaborative writing

Finding and Loading Existing Documents

Loading an existing document means that you move it from disk, where the document is saved, to the screen, where you can work on the document with Word. You can load a document in three basic ways:

❑ *Starting Word and loading a document at the same time.* Use this approach when you start a work session. Starting and loading simultaneously is faster than starting Word and then using the Transfer Load command to load a document. See Chapter 2 for information on loading a file this way.

❑ *Loading a document after Word is already started.* Use this approach to change documents when you are working with Word.

❑ *Loading a document with the Library Document-retrieval command.* With Library Document-retrieval, you can search a huge hard disk to find all the files that meet criteria you specify, including document text contained within the files themselves. No more hunting for a file when you cannot remember its name or where you stored it!

Loading Documents with the Transfer Load Command

If you know where a document is located and if you know its file name, use **T**ransfer **L**oad to load the file. New Word 5 features, however, make searching for a document easy even if you don't remember the document's location or name.

Tip   **Always make sure that the** setup **field in the Transfer Options command contains the name of the document directory in which you're working.**

When you start Word from a document directory, that directory is automatically the default. Check the Transfer Options command after starting Word to make sure that the document directory name you want appears in the setup field. If you want to work with a document from another directory, later in your work session, change the Transfer Options command setting first.

Trap   **If you chose the** Yes **option in the** save between sessions **field of the Transfer Options command menu, Word overrides the default directory choice made when you started Word in a document directory.**

Unless you always work in a single document directory, don't choose the Yes option in the Transfer Options save between sessions field. You can make good use of this command's capability to change the default directory for Word operations; by choosing Yes in the save between sessions field, you disable some of this command's usefulness.

Trap   **You try to load a file with the Transfer Load command, but you see the message** Enter Y to create file.

If you see this message, either you have typed the file name incorrectly, or else the document isn't in the default drive or directory.

Trick   **If you're having trouble finding a file, use the new Version 5 features that show you the names of other directories and drives.**

When you press F1 in the blank filename field of the Transfer Load command, you see the following (depending on what's on your disk):

❑ File names with Word's default extension DOC. Word does not display files with other extensions, or with no extension, unless you take special steps (described in a later trick). To choose a file, highlight the file name and press Enter.

❑ Subdirectories "beneath" the current default directory—that is, the one from which you started Word or the one chosen in the Transfer Options setup field. Subdirectory names are always shown in parentheses. To choose a subdirectory, highlight the directory name and press Enter. A new file list appears. If you don't find the file you want, move back to the parent directory by highlighting the [..] symbol and pressing Enter.

❑ The parent directory symbol, enclosed by brackets [..]. To move to the parent directory, highlight the [..] symbol and press Enter. A new file list appears, together with additional directory names.

If you keep pressing directory names or the parent directory symbol, you keep seeing new file lists. Word doesn't carry out the command until you select a file name and press Enter. So you can explore your entire hard disk this way—all without having to remember a single file name or directory name!

Trick **Use Transfer Load to load files that do not have the DOC extension.**

To load a file with an extension other than DOC, include the extension in the filename field of the Transfer Load command: for example, *PROFIT.TBL*. To load a file with no extension, type the file name followed by a period.

Trick **If you cannot remember the extension for a file, use wild cards to display all files in a directory, regardless of extension.**

The question mark wild card (?) replaces any single character; the asterisk wild card (*) replaces any number of characters. If you type *.* in the filename field of the Transfer Load command and press F1, for example, Word displays a list of all files on the disk or current directory, including program files. No matter what extension you gave a file, it appears on this list.

Trick **Limit the list of documents by using wild cards.**

You can use DOS wild cards to limit the list of documents you see after pressing F1 in the filename field of the Transfer Load command. If you type *.TXT* in the filename field of the Transfer Load command and press F1 (or a direction key in Word versions prior to 4), Word displays all the documents with the TXT extension, but no others. If you enter *CHAPTER?.** in this field, Word displays CHAPTER1.DOC, CHAPTER1.BAK, CHAPTER2.DOC, CHAPTER2.BAK, and so on.

Tip   **Use Ctrl-F7 to load documents—especially when you want to see the F1 file name display.**

Pressing Ctrl-F7 is a shortcut for loading a document. Using this shortcut is the same as choosing **T**ransfer **L**oad and then pressing the F1 key to list all the DOC files in the default directory. You then can choose the document you want from this list.

Tip   **Don't bother to clear the screen before loading a new document.**

If you have just saved the document on which you have been working and you want to switch to a new document, save keystrokes by not clearing the screen before you choose **T**ransfer **L**oad. As long as the current document has no unsaved changes, Word automatically clears the screen before loading the new document. If you have unsaved changes in the document or its style sheet, the program prompts you to save the changes before carrying out the Transfer Load command.

If you are creating a new window intending to load a document into it, you can leave the Window Split Horizontal and Window Split Vertical commands' clear new window fields set at their default, No. Again, Word automatically clears the window when you choose the **T**ransfer **L**oad command. As long as the current document remains loaded in one of the open windows, you are not prompted to save any unsaved changes.

Trick   **Write a macro to open a new window and load a document at the same time.**

Here's a macro that splits the screen, loads a file, and zooms the new window to full size.

```
«PAUSE Press Ctrl-F1 to unzoom windows if zoomed; Enter to continue»
<ctrl esc>wsh<F1>«PAUSE Move cursor to window split line and
    press Enter when done.»<tab>y<enter>
<ctrl esc>tl<f1>
«PAUSE Highlight filename and press Enter»
«SET filename=field»
<ctrl esc>tl«filename»<enter>
<ctrl f1>
```

To create and use this macro, follow the instructions in Chapter 13, "Macros." Save the macro, using the macro name quick_zoomload.mac^<ctrl q>z.

Trick **Combine two documents using Transfer Merge.**

When you use Transfer Merge in a document you have already loaded, Word inserts the second file at the cursor's location. If you are working on a file named CHAPTER1.DOC and you want to include a file called NOTES.TXT within CHAPTER1.DOC, for example, position the cursor where you want NOTES.TXT to appear. Then use **T**ransfer **M**erge and type the file name, NOTES.TXT, in the `filename` field. Carry out the command by pressing Enter or clicking the command name.

Before you load a document in a different directory, an excellent idea is to change the default directory by typing a new directory name in the `setup` field of the Transfer Options command. Here's why:

❏ *Path names*. If you have changed the default directory, you don't have to type path names when you load and save files to the new directory. Typing path names can be tedious, and you may make a mistake—and in so doing, inadvertently lose or even destroy your work.

❏ *Style sheets*. When you change default directories, Word automatically uses the new directory's NORMAL.STY style sheet, if it exists. As Chapter 12 explains, you can make use of this feature to create a whole series of customized NORMAL.STY style sheets, one for each directory on your hard disk. You can create a NORMAL.STY for letters, for instance, and put it in the directory called \MSWORD\LETTERS. You can create another, different NORMAL.STY for business reports, and put it into the directory called \MSWORD\REPORTS, and so on.

❏ *Document-retrieval*. In Version 5 of Word, the Library Document-retrieval Query command's `path` field automatically contains the directory named in the `setup` field of Transfer Options. So that the Document-retrieval file list always shows the files in the directory you're working with, you should change the default directory with **T**ransfer **O**ptions before loading or saving a file in a different directory.

If you equip each directory with its own, customized NORMAL.STY file, you will want to switch style sheets when you load a file in a different directory. Suppose that you started Word in the directory called

\MSWORD\LETTERS, for example—and you wrote a letter, naturally. The NORMAL.STY style sheet in that directory contains formats appropriate to letters—single-spaced paragraphs, the Courier typeface, and flush-left paragraph formatting. But now you want to write a business report. To do so, use the **T**ransfer **O**ptions command to switch to the directory called \MSWORD\REPORTS. When you do, Word automatically uses the NORMAL.STY in that directory—and this NORMAL.STY file is for business reports. It formats a document with double-spaced, right-justified paragraphs, using the Helvetica font.

Trick **Write a macro that automatically changes the default directory, loads a new style sheet, and displays a list of files.**

To take full advantage of Word's capability to load a directory's default style sheet automatically, you must remember to change default directories by using the **T**ransfer **O**ptions command every time you load a file from a different directory. But that change is hard to remember. And so—it's a job for a macro!

The following macro saves all open files, asks for confirmation before it starts, moves up to the parent directory, asks the user to select a new directory, chooses the Transfer Load command, and presents the F1 file list.

```
«SET response = "N"»
«WHILE response = "N"»
«ASK confirm = ?OK to save all files, change directories,
      and load new file (Y/N)?»
«IF confirm = "Y"»
      «SET response = "Y"»
      <ctrl esc>ta
      <ctrl esc>to..<enter>
      <ctrl esc>to<f1>
      «PAUSE Choose new directory and press Enter»<enter>
      <ctrl f7>
      «PAUSE Choose a file and press Enter»<enter>
«ELSE»«QUIT»
«ENDIF»
«ENDWHILE»
```

To create and use this macro, follow the instructions in Chapter 13, "Macros." Save the macro, using the macro name quick_loadchange.mac^<ctrl q>l.

Finding and Loading Documents with Document-retrieval

Given the restrictions of DOS file names (only 8 characters, plus three for a cryptic extension)—not surprisingly—many users get lost in a wilderness of files on their hard disks. Somehow, a file name like 88IRTRPH.GUT makes sense when you assign the name—but after a year during which the file whirls around mutely on your hard disk, you probably have no idea what's in that file.

For this reason, several software companies have made big bucks selling hard-disk search-and-retrieval programs to go hunting among your documents to find just the ones that meet criteria you specify. With such a program, you can ask, "Show me all the documents that contain the text, 'Blow me to Bermuda'," and after much gnashing of disks, a list of files appears. Such programs are limited in their usefulness, however, because they're stand-alone applications; you have to exit them and start another program to load the files and use them.

That's why Word's Library Document-retrieval command is such an important and useful addition to Word. This command gives you all the power of a stand-alone program plus some special Word features. As long as you fill out summary sheets when you save your document, you can retrieve documents by using any of the following summary-sheet information entries as a guide for retrieval operations:

- ❏ A descriptive document title of up to 40 characters
- ❏ The date of the document's creation
- ❏ The date of the document's last revision
- ❏ A version number you can assign to your document
- ❏ The document's author
- ❏ The document's typist, if different from the author
- ❏ A list of keywords you assign to your documents

If this information isn't rich enough to help you identify the document you want, you can even search the full text of all the documents created. Obviously, this feature is powerful, and it's well worth your attention if you create many files on a big hard disk.

With Version 5 of Word, Library Document-retrieval has become much more than a disk-searching utility: the new Copy and Delete commands in the Document-retrieval menu have transformed this command into a complete file-management system. You don't need to buy an expensive hard-disk management program for your computer because Library Document-retrieval has all the power you need to manage your Word files. In fact, some of the new Version 5 features are reminiscent of popular hard-disk management programs.

Tip **When you choose Library Document-retrieval, the command searches for files in the default directory.**

The default setting in the Library Document-retrieval Query command's path field is the directory from which you started Word or the directory named with the Transfer Options command (see fig. 9.1).

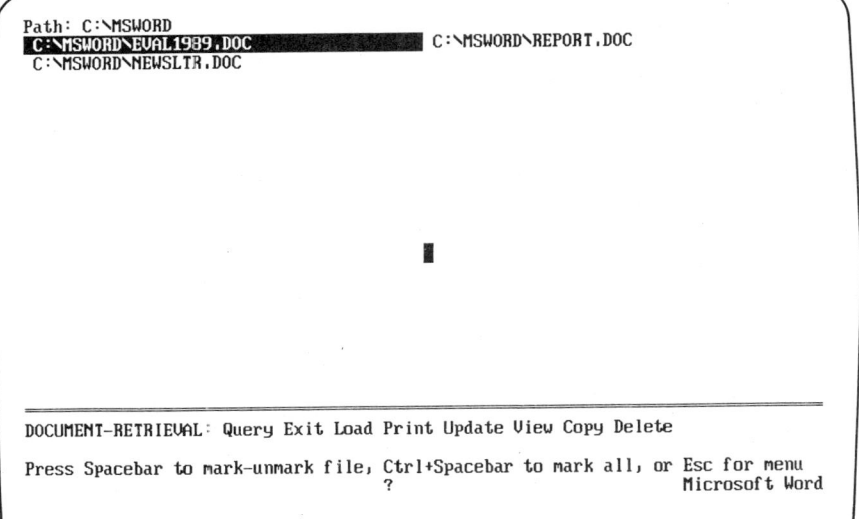

```
Path: C:\MSWORD
C:\MSWORD\EVAL1989.DOC                     C:\MSWORD\REPORT.DOC
C:\MSWORD\NEWSLTR.DOC




                              █




DOCUMENT-RETRIEVAL: Query Exit Load Print Update View Copy Delete

Press Spacebar to mark-unmark file, Ctrl+Spacebar to mark all, or Esc for menu
                          ?                          Microsoft Word
```

Fig. 9.1.

The Library Document-retrieval command menu.

Trap **Like Transfer Save, Document-retrieval displays DOC files only—unless you specifically instruct it otherwise.**

Bear this point in mind if you're searching for a file without the DOC extension. You can use wild cards to get around this problem. You can enter *.BAK* in the Query path field, for example, to find in the default directory all the files with the extension BAK.

Tip **To broaden the list of files, enter additional path names in the Query path field.**

Highlight the Query path field and press F1 to display the list of files, directories, and disks. To construct a Query statement that includes several directories, highlight a drive or directory name and press the comma key. Continue highlighting drive or directory names until you have included all the drives and directories you want to search (see fig. 9.2). Then press Enter. Word searches all the directories and drives named and presents a list of all files with the extension DOC.

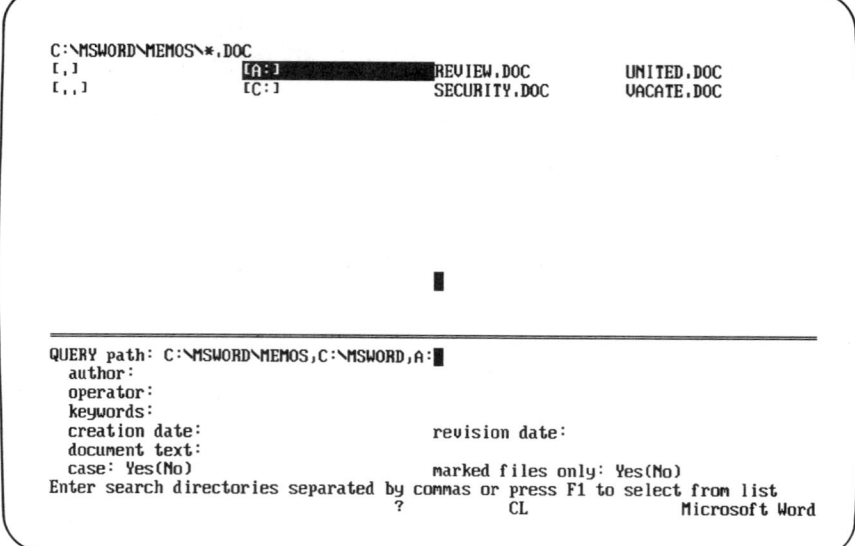

Fig. 9.2.

Expanding the list of directories in the path command field.

Trap   Version 5 does not save the directory choices made in the Query command fields.

In Version 4, the choices made in the Query fields were saved to the MW.INI file along with other options and customization choices. Version 5 doesn't save these choices. If you type drive or directory names in the Query field, they remain in effect for the editing session (unless you change them), but when you quit Word, they are not saved. Instead, Word reverts to the default setting (the setting in the setup field of the Transfer Options menu).

This change isn't a problem unless you're used to using the preceding version's Query command. A good argument exists for the changes to this command. With Version 5, as you have already learned, the Transfer Options command has finally become a useful way of controlling the default directory, and you can save the setting you make in the Transfer Options command's setup field. The place to specify the default document directory is Transfer Options, not the Library Document-retrieval Query menu.

Trick **Narrow the search by filling out additional fields in the Query command menu.**

When you fill out additional fields in the Query command menu, Word doesn't list the file unless it meets all the criteria you specify. Suppose that you type *Melissa* in the author field, *2/17/89* in the revision date field, and *Acme Disposal Services, Inc.* in the keywords field (see fig. 9.3). Word retrieves only the document or documents that meet all these criteria. In other words, to qualify for listing, all the documents must contain exactly the same information in their summary sheets.

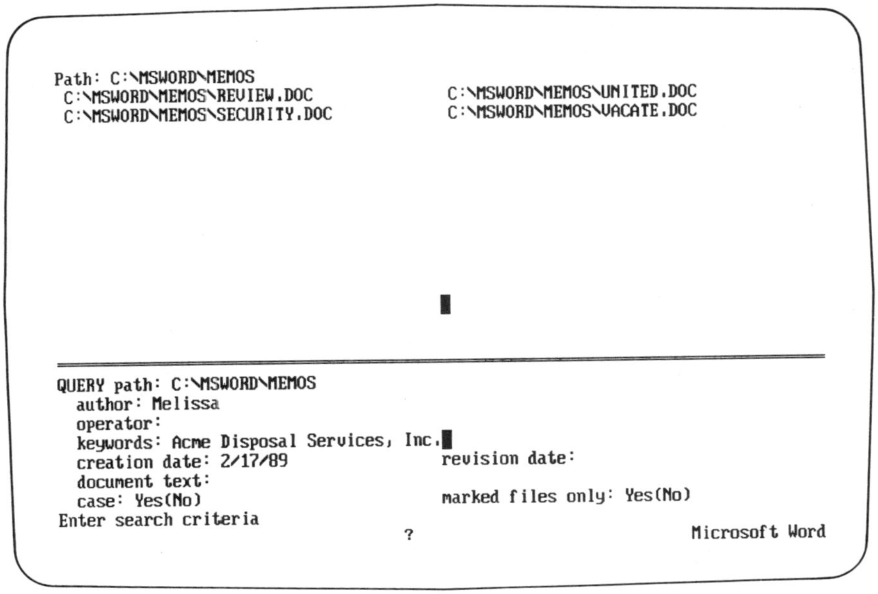

```
Path: C:\MSWORD\MEMOS
  C:\MSWORD\MEMOS\REVIEW.DOC              C:\MSWORD\MEMOS\UNITED.DOC
  C:\MSWORD\MEMOS\SECURITY.DOC            C:\MSWORD\MEMOS\VACATE.DOC




                                ▌


  ─────────────────────────────────────────────────────────────
QUERY path: C:\MSWORD\MEMOS
  author: Melissa
  operator:
  keywords: Acme Disposal Services, Inc.▌
  creation date: 2/17/89              revision date:
  document text:
  case: Yes(No)                       marked files only: Yes(No)
Enter search criteria
                        ?                          Microsoft Word
```

Fig. 9.3.

Narrowing the search.

A search this specific would probably retrieve just one document—you would get the letter Melissa wrote to Acme Disposal Services, Inc., on February 17, 1989, complaining about the fact that they hadn't picked up the garbage. However, if you typed just *Acme Disposal Services*, leaving the other fields blank, you would find all documents pertaining to Acme Disposal Services, perhaps revealing a long series of complaints!

You can see why filling out the summary sheets accurately and supplying plenty of information is so important. The more information you put in summary sheets, the more ways you have to fish documents out of that big hard disk. With 40-megabyte and 80-megabyte drives becoming more common, finding lost files becomes an even more significant time-waster in business contexts. That problem is why Document-retrieval is such a nifty and important feature of Word.

Tip   **Learn how to use logical operators in Query searches.**

Logical operators in Query fields provide a variety of ways to specify precisely which documents you want Word to retrieve. Following is a list of the operators you can use when you search for documents:

Symbol	Comment
,	The *OR* operator is inclusive; it retrieves documents that meet either of two criteria specified. In the author field, for instance, the query *SMITH,JONES* searches for documents created either by Smith or by Jones.
& or space	The *AND* operator is exclusive; it retrieves only those documents that meet both criteria specified. In the author field, for instance, the query *SMITH & JONES* searches for only those documents created by Smith and Jones as coauthors.
~	The *NOT* operator also is exclusive, but in a different way from the AND operator. The NOT operator retrieves all the documents that meet the first criterion specified, except the ones that also contain the second criterion. In the author field, for instance, the query *SMITH~JONES* searches for all the documents Smith has authored, except the ones co-written with Jones.
<	The *LESS THAN* operator is used only in the creation date and revision date fields. It causes Word to search for all documents created before a specified date.

Symbol	Comment
>	The *GREATER THAN* operator is used only in the `creation date` and `revision date` fields. It causes Word to search for all documents created after a specified date.

Logical operators can be used with great precision to retrieve documents. In figure 9.4 for example, the query searches only for those documents written by Smith or Jones after 5-8-87, that contain the text *Final* but not the text *Preliminary*. Any document retrieved must contain the text *Annual Report* in the `keyword` field.

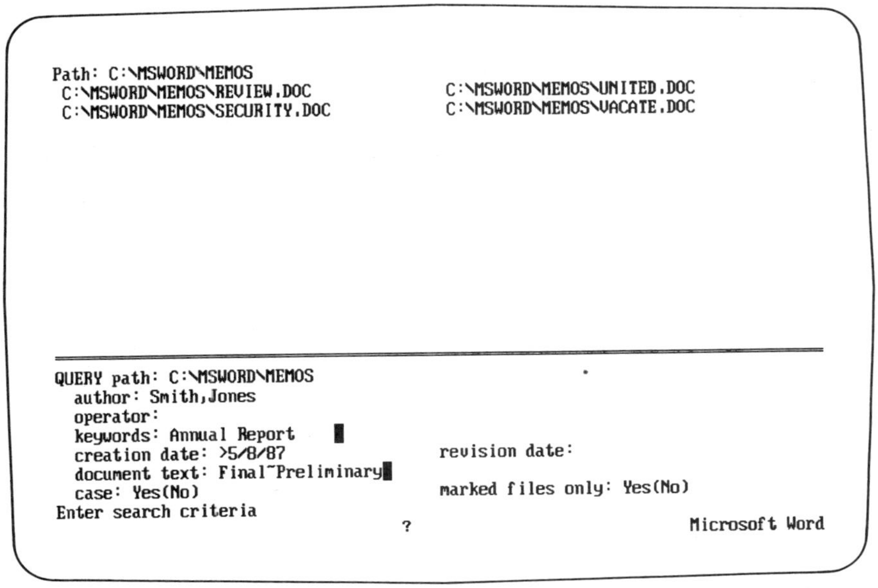

```
Path: C:\MSWORD\MEMOS
 C:\MSWORD\MEMOS\REVIEW.DOC          C:\MSWORD\MEMOS\UNITED.DOC
 C:\MSWORD\MEMOS\SECURITY.DOC        C:\MSWORD\MEMOS\VACATE.DOC




QUERY path: C:\MSWORD\MEMOS
  author: Smith,Jones
  operator:
  keywords: Annual Report      █
  creation date: >5/8/87            revision date:
  document text: Final~Preliminary█
  case: Yes(No)                     marked files only: Yes(No)
Enter search criteria
                          ?                    Microsoft Word
```

Fig. 9.4.

Searching with logical operators.

Tip **To search for all documents containing a specific word or phrase, type the word or phrase in the Query command menu's** document text **field.**

This command is very powerful, but it has its price. Instead of just searching summary sheets, which Word accomplishes quickly, this command actually searches through the full text of the documents themselves. As such things go, the search is quite fast, but if you have displayed many documents on the Document-retrieval screen, Word searches each of them. The search may tie up your computer for a minute or two—or longer if you're using a very basic system.

Trap **You still cannot find your document.**

Possibly you haven't included the right directory in the Query command menu. If you're really having trouble finding a file, the best procedure to follow in finding a document is this:

1. Add the names of all the directories in which you store Word documents to the Query command's path field.

2. Add additional criteria to the Query command menu, but do so sparingly and make sure that you have typed the information correctly and that it actually applies to the document.

If you're trying to find the letters to Acme Disposal, Inc., when the company is actually named Zackney Disposal, Inc., Document-retrieval won't find the documents!

In general, it's a good idea to cast your net wide at first, adding as many path names to the path field as you can. Then narrow the search one criteria at time. About when was the document created? What words or phrases would it surely contain? Ask questions such as these and transform them into Query field statements.

Tip **Increase the amount of information in the document list by choosing the** Long **or** Full **options in the View command submenu.**

By default, Document-retrieval lists documents in the Short form, which includes only the file name. One of the major benefits of Document-retrieval, however, is that it can provide much more information about files than does DOS. To take advantage of this feature, choose the Long or Full options of the **Library Document-retrieval View** command. The View command offers three choices:

❏ Short (the default). Shows the path name and file name. Use this option to display the most possible document names (see fig. 9.5).

❏ Long. Shows the path name, file name, author, and title (see fig. 9.6).

❏ Full. Displays the summary sheet for the currently selected document (see fig. 9.7).

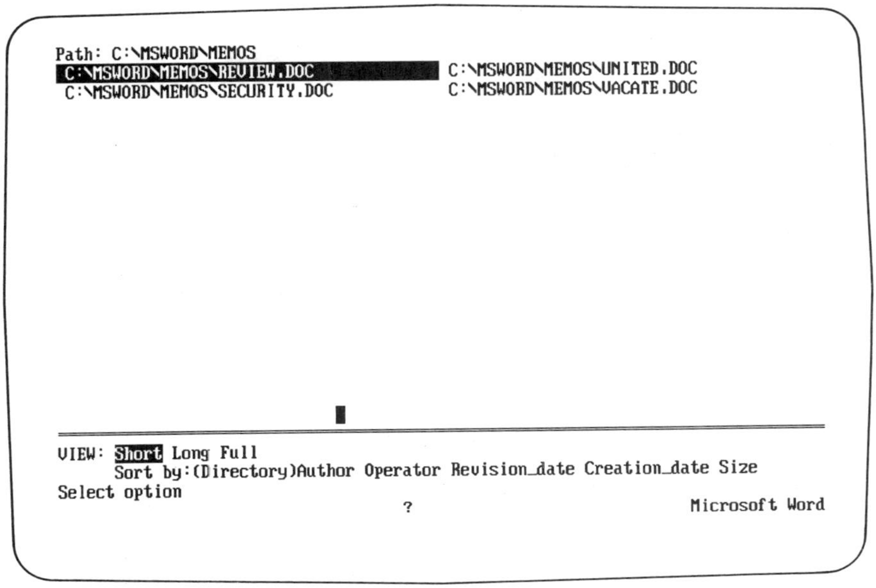

Fig. 9.5.

The Short display
option.

```
Path: C:\MSWORD\MEMOS
C:\MSWORD\MEMOS\REVIEW.DOC              C:\MSWORD\MEMOS\UNITED.DOC
C:\MSWORD\MEMOS\SECURITY.DOC           C:\MSWORD\MEMOS\VACATE.DOC








                              ▌

VIEW: Short Long Full
      Sort by:(Directory)Author Operator Revision_date Creation_date Size
Select option
                           ?                        Microsoft Word
```

Fig. 9.5.

The Short display
option.

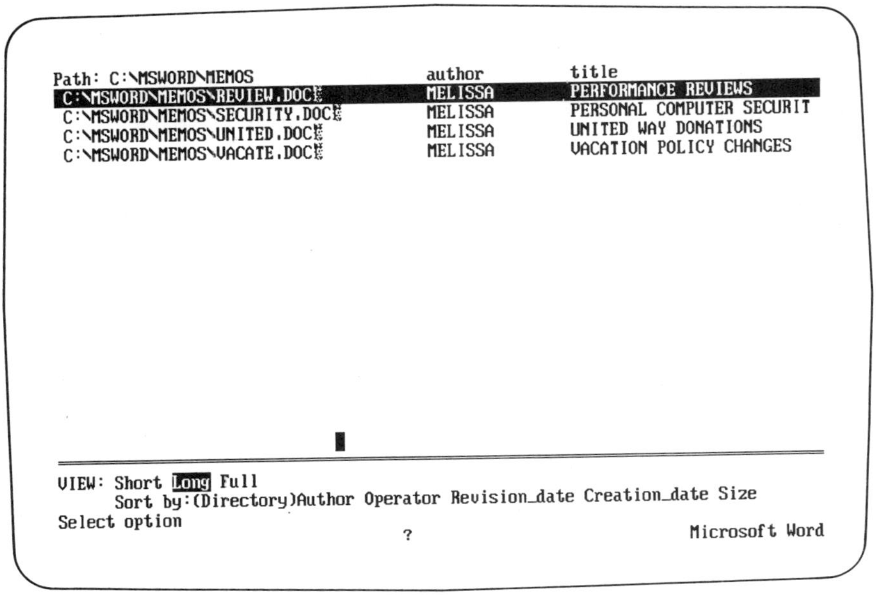

Fig. 9.6.

The Long display
option.

```
Path: C:\MSWORD\MEMOS                  author      title
C:\MSWORD\MEMOS\REVIEW.DOC             MELISSA     PERFORMANCE REVIEWS
C:\MSWORD\MEMOS\SECURITY.DOC          MELISSA     PERSONAL COMPUTER SECURIT
C:\MSWORD\MEMOS\UNITED.DOC            MELISSA     UNITED WAY DONATIONS
C:\MSWORD\MEMOS\VACATE.DOC            MELISSA     VACATION POLICY CHANGES









                              ▌

VIEW: Short Long Full
      Sort by:(Directory)Author Operator Revision_date Creation_date Size
Select option
                           ?                        Microsoft Word
```

Fig. 9.7.

The Full display option.

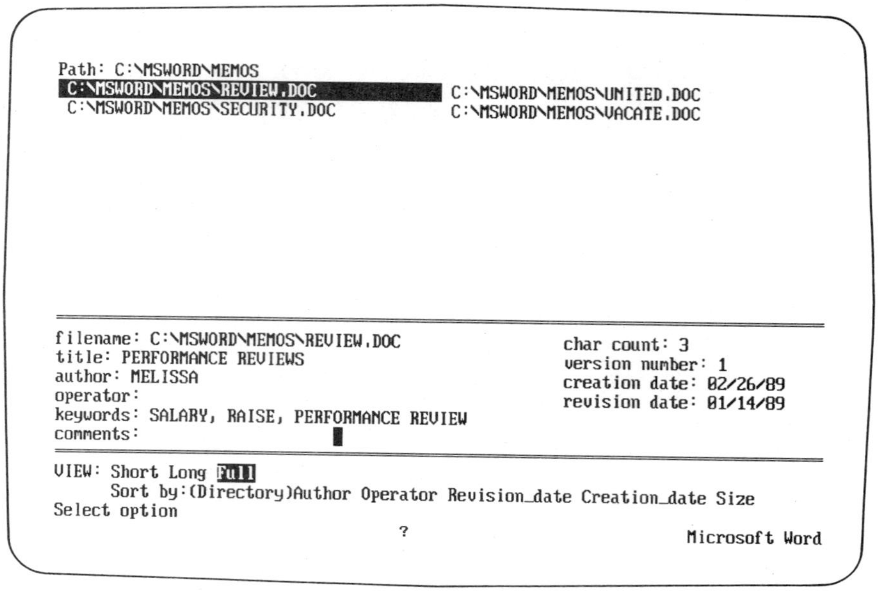

```
Path: C:\MSWORD\MEMOS
C:\MSWORD\MEMOS\REVIEW.DOC            C:\MSWORD\MEMOS\UNITED.DOC
C:\MSWORD\MEMOS\SECURITY.DOC         C:\MSWORD\MEMOS\VACATE.DOC




filename: C:\MSWORD\MEMOS\REVIEW.DOC           char count: 3
title: PERFORMANCE REVIEWS                     version number: 1
author: MELISSA                                creation date: 02/26/89
operator:                                      revision date: 01/14/89
keywords: SALARY, RAISE, PERFORMANCE REVIEW
comments:

VIEW: Short Long Full
      Sort by:(Directory)Author Operator Revision_date Creation_date Size
Select option
                              ?
                                                        Microsoft Word
```

Tip   Sort the directory by using the View command.

By default, Word sorts the displayed documents alphabetically by
directory. You can change the default sort order by choosing an option
in the sort by field of the View command, which offers several sorting
options. By choosing the Creation_date option in this field, for
example, you can display your documents sorted by creation date,
allowing you to differentiate among various versions of a file.

**Tip   You can change the summary sheet by using the Library
Document-retrieval Update command.**

Outside of the Document-retrieval command, you see the summary
sheet only once: the first time you save your document. If you make a
mistake when you fill out the summary sheet or if you got lazy and
didn't fill it out, you can have another chance. Use **L**ibrary **D**ocument-
retrieval, highlight the desired file name, press Enter, and use the
Update command.

Tip   Load a document from the list with the Load command.

After you have decided which document to load, choose the **L**ibrary
Document-retrieval **L**oad command and highlight the document's name
from the list that appears. Word inserts the name of the selected
document in the filename field of the Load command. Press Enter to
load the file.

Tip **Copy and archive documents with Document-retrieval.**

A very welcome new feature of Version 5 is a series of file-management aids in Document-retrieval. To copy a file to another directory or archive the file to a floppy disk, highlight the file and press Enter to mark it. (An asterisk appears next to the file name to inform you that it's marked.) You can mark additional files in this way, if you wish. If you change your mind and want to unmark a file, highlight the file name and press Enter again. If you wish, you can mark all the displayed files by pressing Ctrl-space bar. Then choose the **C**opy command (see fig. 9.8). As you can see from the Copy command menu, you can delete the files after Word copies them; you can copy the style sheets attached to the document, too.

```
COPY marked files to drive/directory: █
      delete files after copy: Yes(No)        copy style sheets: Yes(No)
Enter path or press F1 to select from list
                             ?                        Microsoft Word
```

Fig. 9.8.

Library Document-retrieval Copy command menu.

This command is excellent news for anyone who has wanted an intelligent way to clean up a hard disk. Because you can copy several files at once, this utility is fast and convenient. Because it automatically deletes files only after they have been successfully copied, it's safe and easy to use.

The quick_backup and quick_archive macros presented in Chapter 2, incidentally, make use of this command. The backup macro doesn't delete the file after backing it up to a floppy; the archive macro does.

Moving Around in a Large Document

With Version 5's new features, moving around in a large document is substantially easier than in previous versions. As before, you can use the outline mode to scroll quickly to a heading's location. With Word 5's new automatic pagination feature, the Jump Page command is much more useful than it was in previous versions of Word, which didn't repaginate automatically as you typed and edited. A new feature called bookmarks provides a way to define named units of text, to which you can jump at a keystroke.

Tip **In a large, complex document, use the outline view to move around in the text.**

If you have outlined your document (see Chapter 6), you can shift to the outline mode to scroll quickly to a section heading. With the cursor anywhere in your document, press Shift-F2 to switch to outline view. Place the cursor on the heading to which you want to scroll and press Shift-F2 again to switch back to the document view. The cursor is at the beginning of the section whose heading you selected.

Trick **Designate text as a bookmark and then scroll to it immediately whenever you wish.**

If you know that you're going to return to a section of a long document and edit that section further, define it as a bookmark. To define a bookmark, select a unit of text—a sentence or a paragraph—and use the **F**ormat bookmar**K** command. When the command menu shown in figure 9.9 appears, type a distinctive, one-word name, using up to 31 letters or numbers (you can also use the underscore and hyphen characters within the name). That's all there is to it!

To return to the bookmark, use the **J**ump bookmar**K** command. When the name field appears, type the bookmark name or press F1 to choose the name from a list.

You can define as many bookmarks as you wish, as long as each one has a unique name. If you want to remove a bookmark, select the text again, use the **F**ormat bookmar**K** command, and leave the name field blank. Carry out the command, and press Y to confirm the bookmark name's erasure.

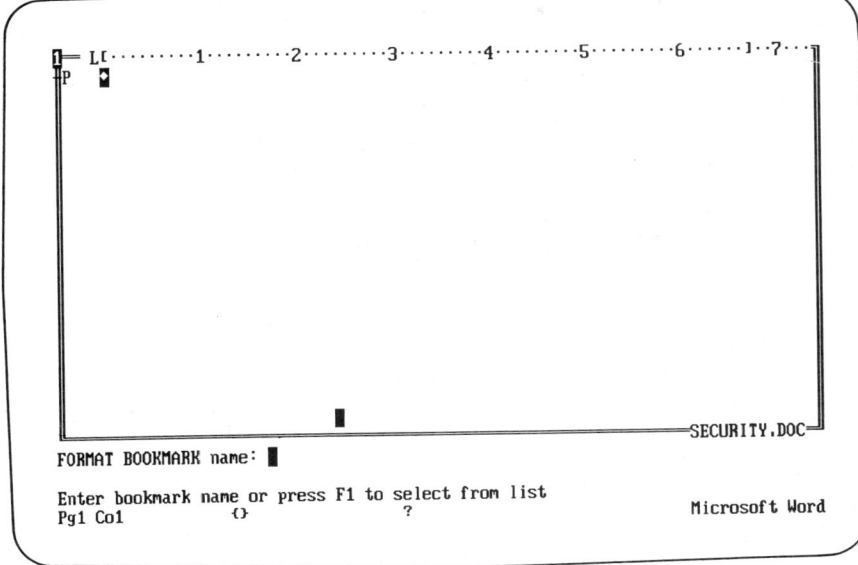

Fig. 9.9.

The Format bookmarK command menu.

Editing with Multiple Windows

Windows are useful for editing purposes. Splitting the screen makes moving text within a document and between documents easier and safer. For more information on the basics of opening, sizing, and closing windows, see Chapter 6.

Tip   Use windows to simplify moving text.

If you open a second window with the Window Split Horizontal command, you can display the text to be moved in the top window and locate the destination in the bottom window. To move the text, select the text in the top window, press Del to move the text to the scrap, press F1 to activate the bottom window, select the text's destination, and press Ins.

Using windows eliminates the necessity of scrolling through the document while the text is stored in the scrap. Any sidetracks during scrolling can result in the unintentional overwriting of the scrap's contents and, potentially, the loss of the text you were in the process of moving. Using windows also eliminates the need to scroll back through the document to resume editing. You can simply close the bottom window and continue working in the area of your document displayed in the top window.

Tip **Move text between windows with the mouse.**

Mouse copying and moving techniques work between windows as well as within them. To copy text with the mouse, select the text to be copied. Move the pointer to the window where you want the text to appear. Hold the Shift key and click the left button. (This method leaves a copy of the text in the original location.)

To move text between windows with the mouse, select the text to be moved. Move the pointer to the place in the other window where you want the text to appear. Hold the Ctrl key and click the left button. (This method deletes text from the original location.)

Tip **Use windows to transfer text from one document to another.**

Removing or copying text from one document and inserting that text into another document is easy with Word. You simply load the documents into separate windows and transfer the text from one window to the other in the usual way.

Usually, you are already working on one document when you decide to move a section to another document or insert a section from another document. In either case, open a second window and load the other document into it. (You don't have to clear the second window before loading the new document. When you choose Transfer Load, Word automatically clears the window for you.) Scroll through the first document until the text's target location is displayed. Move to the second window, select the text, and delete it to the scrap. Complete the process by returning to the original window and pressing the Ins key. You can then close the second window, responding appropriately to Word's prompts to save the changes to the document.

Editing with Glossaries

Glossaries deserve mention here because of their usefulness when you need to move large blocks of text.

Tip **When editing, cut text to a glossary, not the scrap.**

A glossary is much like the scrap, which is a temporary parking place for text. You can copy or cut text to the scrap and later insert that text elsewhere in your document (or in another document). The scrap, however, has one major liability: the scrap can hold only one unit of text at a time. When you cut some new text to the scrap, the new text wipes out the text stored there.

The scrap therefore isn't the best location for a large unit of text (such as several pages) that you're moving in a document. If you move the text by cutting it to the scrap, thinking that you will insert the text later, you may stop to do some editing as you scroll to the new location. Accidentally deleting the scrap's contents by cutting new text to it is much too easy, making several pages of typing disappear.

To avoid this catastrophe, cut the text to a glossary instead. Think of glossaries as scraps—a whole series of them—that you can name and store, temporarily or permanently. In an editing session, you can use glossaries to set up several alternative scraps, each of which can hold a block of text without the danger of loss.

Here's how to cut text to a glossary: After selecting the text to be moved, choose the **D**elete command from the main menu. Rather than pressing Enter immediately, type a name for the cut text. (Choose a descriptive name. If you're moving text about artichokes, for example, type *artichokes*.) After you type the glossary name, press Enter. Word cuts the text to a special storage place.

You cannot wipe out the text stored in this glossary unless you do so deliberately. If you select some new text and try to cut it to the *artichokes* glossary, Word displays the message Enter Y to overwrite glossary, N to retype name, or Esc to cancel.

Tip **Insert stored text from glossaries by using the Insert command or pressing F3.**

After you scroll to the text's destination, you can enter the glossary-stored text in two ways. The first way is to use the **I**nsert command and type the glossary's name. If you have forgotten exactly what you called it, press F1 to see a list of the glossaries created. Select the glossary you want and press Enter.

The second way is to type the glossary's name where you want to insert the text stored in that glossary and immediately press F3. The F3 key replaces the glossary's name with the text stored in the glossary.

When you quit Word, the program prompts you to save the glossaries you created. If you use glossaries to move text, however, you will probably prefer not to save them (after all, you moved the text from point A to point B in your document, so the text is still in your document). Just Press N to abandon the new glossaries you have created.

Tip **If you have used glossaries as substitutes for the scrap, you probably don't need to save them when you quit Word.**

You can save glossaries to disk if you want. When you quit Word without saving glossaries, you see the message Enter Y to save glossary, N to lose edits, or Esc to cancel. Press Y to save the glossaries if you prefer. If you have used glossaries as temporary parking places to store text while moving it around your document, however, you don't need to store the glossaries—provided, of course, that you remembered to put all the text back in your document. (If you haven't, press Esc and you have another chance to restore the text to the document.) In fact, saving unneeded glossaries is a bad idea. They take up disk space; and if you create too many glossaries, you cannot see all their names on one screen when you press F1 to retrieve them with the Insert command.

Editing with Outlines

By reorganizing your outline with outline organize mode, you can achieve major reorganizations of your text's structure in just a few keystrokes. As you move headings on the outline, Word moves all the text stored under the headings too. This capability is an exceptionally powerful editing technique.

Tip **Restructure large text domains with outline organize mode.**

To restructure your document, press Shift-F2 to move to the outline edit mode and then press Shift-F5 to switch to the outline organize mode. Select the heading or headings you want to move and press Del. Next, select the heading that should immediately *follow* the ones you're moving and press Ins. Word moves the headings you selected, together with any subheadings and text stored under the headings.

Trap **In outline edit mode, Word moves only the headings, not the accompanying text.**

If you use the technique described in the preceding tip to move a heading in outline edit mode, Word does not move the text stored under the heading. Use the outline organize mode instead. For more information on outlining, see Chapter 4.

Using the Undo Command

As you perform major editing operations with commands such as Replace, the chances grow that you will make unwanted or accidental major changes. As table 9.1 shows, the Undo command can restore your document to the way it was before you gave the command. Undo can wipe out even the ill effects of a poorly conceived Replace operation that inserted the wrong word throughout a document.

Table 9.1
Using the Undo Command

Last Editing Operation	Effect of Pressing Undo
Copied text to scrap	Preceding contents of scrap restored
Inserted text from scrap	Insertion canceled
Copied text with mouse	Copied text disappears
Moved text with mouse	Move canceled; text reappears in original location with highlighting
Deleted text to scrap	Text restored and highlighted; preceding contents of scrap restored
Deleted text with Backspace key	Text restored

Last Command Used	Effect of Pressing Undo
Copy	Preceding contents of scrap reappear
Format	Formatting canceled; text returns to the format in use before the Undo command was given
Format Replace	Operation canceled; text returns to formats used before the Format Replace command was given
Gallery	No effect; use the Exit command to return to document

Table 9.1 — Continued

Last Command Used	Effect of Pressing Undo
Help	No effect; use the Resume command to return to document
Insert	Insertion canceled
Jump	No effect
Library Autosort	Sort canceled; text returned to the sequence in effect before the Library Autosort command was given
Library Hyphenate	Hyphens that were just inserted are removed
Library Index	Index that was just created is removed
Library Number	Numbering is canceled; text is returned to the numbering in effect before the Library Number command was given
Library Run	No effect
Library Spell	No effect; choose the Quit command to return to document
Library Table	Table that was just created is removed
Library thEsaurus	Cancels word substitution and restores original word
Options	No effect; use the Options command and reset the settings in the command menu
Print	No effect; press Esc to stop printing
Quit	No effect
Replace	Replacements are removed; original text reappears

Table 9.1—Continued

Last Command Used	Effect of Pressing Undo
Search	No effect; cannot return to original search location
Transfer Load	No effect
Transfer Merge	Cancels merge
Transfer Save	No effect
Undo	Undoes effect of last Undo command; the change is restored

Tip **Experiment with the Undo command so that you're familiar with it.**

On a test document, perform various editing operations and **U**ndo them. Work with the command until you understand what it can do.

Trap **The Undo command doesn't work on all operations.**

Undo cannot reverse the actions of the Jump, Library Run, Library Spell, Options, Print, Quit, Search, and Transfer commands (with the exception of Transfer Merge). Think twice before using these commands.

Trap **You cannot undo a command if you type new text or give another command before using Undo.**

In general, Undo cancels the effect of the last editing command you gave or action you performed (including typing new text). If you issue another command or type text after giving a command, you cannot Undo the first command. Make sure that you're happy with the effects of a major Replace operation or some other significant change before you proceed to another task.

Trick **You can undo the effects of Undo.**

If you use **U**ndo to cancel a change, you can use the command again to restore the change. Suppose that you move some text, and when you see it in its new location, you're not sure whether you want the text there. So you choose **U**ndo. Having canceled the change, you see that the move was a good idea after all. Choose **U**ndo again to restore the insertion.

You can continue in this way as long as you like, toggling back and forth so that the change appears and disappears.

Searching for Text

The Search command in the edit command menu moves the cursor through your document with speed and precision. To use the Search command, you simply type the search text (the text you want to find) in the text field. After you press Enter, Word moves through your document. When Word finds text that matches the search text, the program highlights the text and returns control to you. This section contains suggestions for using the Search command to your best advantage.

Tip **Use Search to locate text for editing.**

After you have marked revisions on your printed copy, use **S**earch to move through your document sequentially, locating the next unit of text you're planning to revise. This method is much faster (and less fatiguing for the eyes) than reading through your whole document on the screen. Let Word do the work for you.

Tip **Begin a search by pressing Ctrl-PgUp to move to the beginning of your document.**

By default, Word searches from the highlight down. If you want to search the entire document, press Ctrl-PgUp before starting the search.

Tip **You can search up if you choose the** Up **option in the** direction **field of Search.**

Suppose that you're editing page 19 and you realize that you forgot to make a change on page 16. Instead of scrolling up manually, you can Search up, using this option.

Trap **After you make choices from the Search menu, the choices remain in effect until you change them or quit Word.**

The Search menu contains several options (discussed later in this section) in addition to the Up and Down direction options (see fig. 9.10). Be forewarned that the choices you make from this command menu remain in effect even after you complete the search. If you search up, for example, the direction field shows that Up is selected (with parentheses) the next time you use the Search command. If you fail to notice this setting, you may search in a direction that differs from the one you intend.

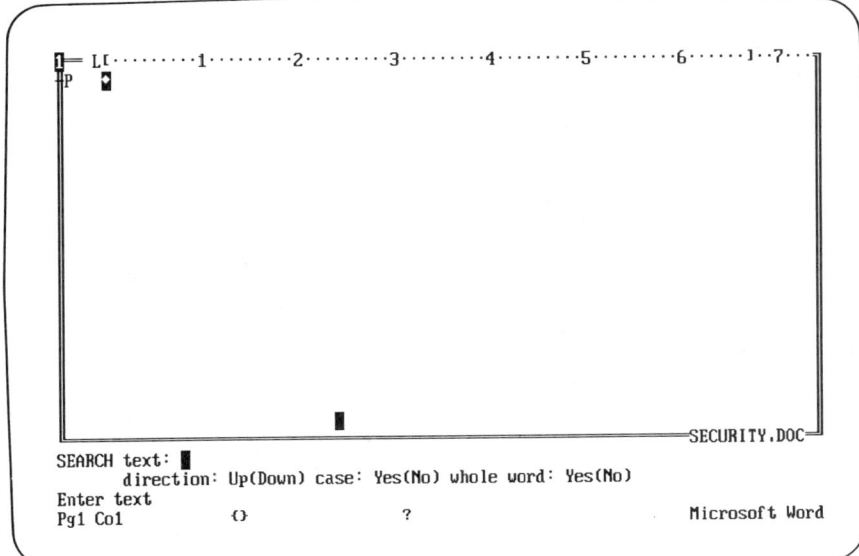

Fig. 9.10.

The Search command menu.

```
L[·········1·········2·········3·········4·········5·········6·····]··7···]
P
```

```
                                                        SECURITY.DOC
SEARCH text:
        direction: Up(Down) case: Yes(No) whole word: Yes(No)
Enter text
Pg1 Co1              {}              ?                   Microsoft Word
```

Tip **To help Word pinpoint the text you're after, type several words exactly as they appear in the printed copy.**

Assume that you're looking for a paragraph that begins, *It was a dark and stormy night*. If you search just for *dark*, Word may find several places where that word is used. Searching for *It was a dark and stormy night* is preferable; chances are that this phrase is unique in your document. You can enter up to 255 characters. Normally, four or five words should suffice to make sure that you have entered a unique phrase.

Tip **If you see the message** Search text not found**, check to make sure that you typed the search text correctly.**

Use the **S**earch command again. The last search text you used is now the proposed response, the one Word uses unless you type new text. If you find that you made a typographical error in typing the search text, press F9 or F10 to move the highlight to the end of the text field without canceling the response. Use the Backspace and Del keys to make your correction and then press Enter to perform the search again.

Tip   **You can search for text that has exactly the same pattern of capitalization as the search text.**

Use the `case` command field to tell Word to ignore capitalization (the No option) or to consider it (the Yes option) when searching. If you choose No, the default, Word locates *ALLIGATOR*, *alligator*, and *Alligator* even if you type *alliGator* as your search text. If you choose the Yes option, however, a search retrieves only those instances of the word that precisely match the search text's pattern of capital letters.

Tip   **Eliminate unwanted matches by choosing the** Yes **option in the** whole word **command field.**

The `whole word` field tells Word whether to match the search text to entire words (the Yes option) or to text embedded in other text (the No option). If you search for *cake* after choosing No in the `whole word` field, for instance, Word finds *cupcake* and *cheesecake* as well as *cake*. If you're just interested in *cake* (and not in *cupcake* or *cheesecake*), choose Yes.

Trick   **Broaden a search by using truncation.**

So far, this section has discussed ways of narrowing or focusing the search to pinpoint its destination. Sometimes, however, you may want to broaden the search so that any conceivable variant of a word is retrieved. One method you can use to perform a search in this way is to type a truncated or shortened version of a word and leave the `whole word` command field set to the default setting of No.

Instead of typing *sociology*, for example, you can type *soc* as your search text, and Word matches all the following:

    pseudosociological
    social
    societal
    society
    sociological
    sociologist's

Such a search may, however, retrieve unwanted items, such as the following:

    sock
    Socrates
    soccer

The more you truncate the word, the greater the chance that you retrieve unwanted items. A search for *soci*, for example, retrieves all the words in the first list but none of the words in the second one.

Tip   **Repeat the search without retyping the search text.**

Because Word inserts the previously used search text as the proposed response in the `text` field of the **S**earch command, you needn't retype the search text to continue searching for the same text. Just use the **S**earch command again and press Enter. Or better yet, use the Shift-F4 key. Shift-F4 repeats the last search command you gave, using the same settings in the command menu.

Trick   **Use the ? wild card in the Search command.**

You can use the ? wild-card character in the `text` field to look for similar pieces of text that may vary by one character. The wild card tells Word that any character can appear in the position of the ?. Entering *th?n*, for example, tells Word to find *than*, *then*, and *thin*.

Note: To search for a question mark, precede it with a caret (ˆ) when you type the question mark in the `text` command field.

Trick   **Search for division marks, forced page breaks, and other special characters.**

You can search for Word's special characters, such as the division mark. Enter formatting characters in the `text` command field by typing a caret (ˆ) followed by a code. The codes for common formatting characters are listed in table 9.2.

Table 9.2
Codes for Special Characters

Code	Character
ˆD	Division mark or forced page break
ˆN	Newline character
ˆP	Paragraph mark
ˆS	Nonbreaking space
ˆT	Tab character
ˆW	Any white space, including spaces, tabs, newline characters, paragraph marks, division marks, and forced page breaks
ˆ-	Optional hyphen

The program finds these characters even if they're not displayed on the screen. (Word displays the special characters only when you chose `Partial` or `All` in the Options command's `show non-printing symbols` field.)

Trick **Write a macro that searches for specific text and allows you to move the text back to the cursor's original location.**

Searching is used frequently in editing situations. Suppose, for example, that you're working on page 17, where you describe the soil and climatic conditions favorable to artichokes. Suddenly, you realize that you had discussed the same subject somewhere else, and you decide to bring together on page 17 all the text on that subject. You want to search for *artichoke*, cut the relevant text, and move it to page 17.

The following macro is designed for precisely this editing task. This macro creates a bookmark, performs the search, permits the user to perform an editing operation if the search is successful, and returns to the bookmark. Finally, the macro deletes the bookmark.

```
«ASK query = ?Type the search text and press Enter when done.»
«SET response = "N"»
«WHILE response = "N"»
     «ASK direction = ?Search (U)p or (D)own?»
     «IF direction = "U" or "D"»
          «SET response = "Y"»
          <f8><ctrl esc>fkjump2<enter>
          <ctrl esc>s«query»<tab>«direction»<enter>
     «ENDIF»
«ENDWHILE»
«IF notfound»
     <ctrl esc>fk<enter>y«QUIT»
«ENDIF»
«SET response2 = "N"»
«WHILE response2 = "N"»
     «ASK continue = ?Continue the search (Y/N)?»
     «IF continue = "Y"»
          <shift f4>
     «ENDIF»
     «IF continue = "N"»
          «SET response2 = "Y"»
          «PAUSE Alt-F3 to copy to Scrap or Del to move; Enter
               to return.»
```

```
<ctrl esc>jkjump2<enter>
  «ENDIF»
«ENDWHILE»
<ctrl esc>fk<enter>y
```

To create and use this macro, follow the instructions in Chapter 13, "Macros." Save the macro, using the macro name quick_retriever.macˆ<ctrl q>r.

Replacing Text

The Replace command goes through your document, substituting specified replacement text for the search text. You can choose to confirm each replacement or have Word perform all the substitutions automatically. Unlike the Search command, the Replace command continues until all matches have been found.

Tip **To replace text throughout a document, type the search text in the** text **field of the Replace command and the replacement text in the** with text **field.**

Figure 9.11 shows the Replace command menu. If you type the search text in the text field and the replacement text in the with text field, Word replaces the search text with the replacement text but asks for your confirmation each time.

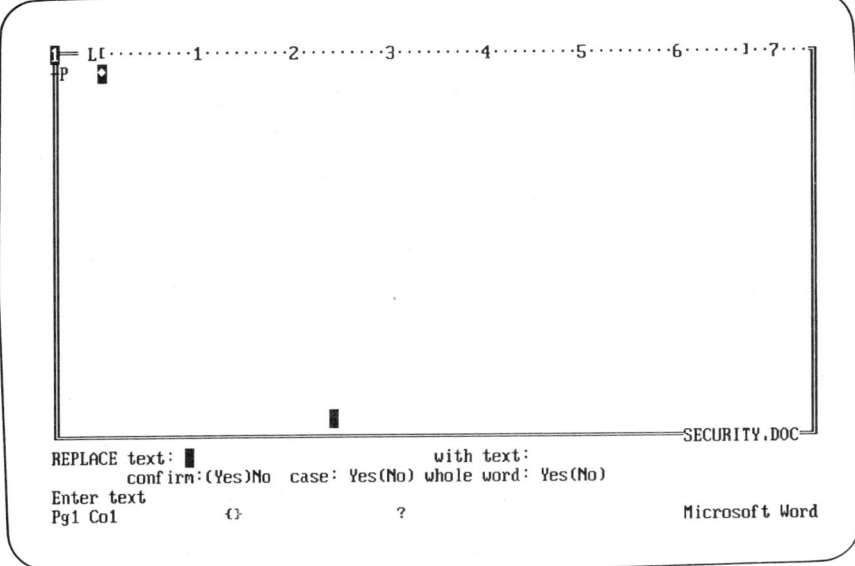

Fig. 9.11.

The Replace command menu.

Tip **To replace text throughout your document without confirmation, choose** No **in the** confirm **field.**

Choosing No in the confirm field sets in motion a global replacement operation, one that replaces text throughout your document automatically. But be careful. As you will see, this command is powerful enough to make a mess out of your work.

Tip **Cancel a Replace operation by pressing Esc.**

If you have turned off the confirmation option, you can cancel a Replace operation by pressing the Esc key. All the changes made up to the point you press Esc are retained; you have just prevented Replace from going any farther.

Tip **Use the** case **and** whole word **fields to specify precisely the text to be replaced.**

If you're planning to replace *Nation* with *State*, for instance, choose the Yes options in the case and whole word fields to make sure that only occurrences of *Nation* (and not *nation* or *national*) are targeted for substitution.

Trap **The Replace command can sprinkle your document with errors.**

One frequent problem with Replace operations is that Word substitutes text even where inappropriate. Suppose, for instance, that you decide to replace *land* with the fancier *territory*. You forget to choose the Yes option in the whole word field, but you turn off confirmation so that Word does all the substitutions automatically. On inspecting your document, you find that the sentence *The aircraft landed safely* has been changed to *The aircraft territoryed safely*. And what was formerly *outlandish* is now *outterritoryish*. To avoid this problem, choose Yes in the confirm field unless you're absolute sure that you know what you're doing. And if you do choose No in the confirm field, be sure to choose Yes in the whole word field.

Trick **If you don't like the results of a Replace operation, use the Undo command.**

Suppose that you have just performed a Replace operation without confirmation. If you haven't done any additional editing, using Undo restores your text to its state before the Replace operation.

Tip **Choose** Yes **in the** confirm **field until you're sure that Replace is functioning correctly.**

Once you gain confidence that you're using the correct search text, press Esc to cancel the search. You can then restart the search and select or click the No option in the confirm field to automate the rest of the search.

Tip **You can have Word replace text in only part of a document rather than in the entire document.**

If you want to change a piece of text in only part of a document, having Word work its way through the whole document is pointless. Because Word makes replacements from the cursor to the end of the document, the area of the document the program searches is determined by the position of the cursor when you invoke the Replace command. You can also have Word replace text in only part of the document by selecting that part before you use Replace.

Trick **Use the Replace command to remove or replace unwanted special characters.**

Suppose that you typed a document with Word before you understood paragraph formatting, and in the document you pressed Enter twice instead of formatting each paragraph with a blank line after it. Now you want to double-space the document, but you find that the extra paragraph mark is causing problems. You can use the **R**eplace command to remove special characters. Use the symbols listed in table 9.2 for the search text. You enter a paragraph mark as the search text, for instance, by entering ^p. To solve the extra paragraph mark problem, enter ^p^p in the text command field and ^p in the with text field.

Trick **You can replace characters from the extended character set.**

Word can search for and replace the characters of the extended character set. Use the Alt key and a number from the numeric keypad, such as Alt-141, to enter the extended character in the text command field. You can also enter extended characters in the with text field.

Use this technique to remove extended characters from a document if you find that your printer cannot handle them. To replace the accented foreign language character Alt-141 with *i*, for instance, type *Alt-141* in the text command field and type *i* in the with text command field.

Collaborative Writing with Word 5

About one out of every five documents produced in professional and business writing settings is collaborative—for good reasons. For many writing ventures that count big, such as contract proposals, two—or three—heads are better than one. Everyone has different strengths, and it makes sense to dovetail strengths in a team.

But coordinating collaborative writing isn't always easy when you're using an ordinary word processing program. For one thing, who in the team has the right to make permanent changes to the file? Everyone? No one? The problem is built into the very nature of word processing technology. Word processing programs were initially devised, not to track the path of revisions, but rather to maintain a single, authoritative version of a file. If one author sits down and changes things, the preceding version is lost, and no record of what's changed exists—and other authors cannot see what's been changed.

Here's where Word 5 comes in. Word 5 offers two superb features for collaborative writing:

❑ *Revision-marks*. This feature, also called *redlining*, shows all editing operations clearly and allows collaborators to approve them (or reject them) before making changes to the document's text.

❑ *Annotations*. A new feature in Word 5, annotations are like footnotes, except that you use your name or initials as the reference mark. With annotations, you can place notes or comments in the file for your collaborators to read. When you're finished collaborating, you can remove all the annotations quickly with a macro supplied with Word.

The next sections explain these two features in more detail.

Using Format revision-Marks

Like the overtype mode, the revision-Marks command can be toggled on and off by choosing Yes or No in the Format revision-Marks Options command add revision marks field (see fig. 9.12). Unlike overtype mode, however, revision-Marks applies to just one document at a time. (For this reason, you can display one document with revision marks and another without them at the same time.) If you turn on revision-

Marks for a document and save the document, moreover, the revision marks are visible the next time you load the document.

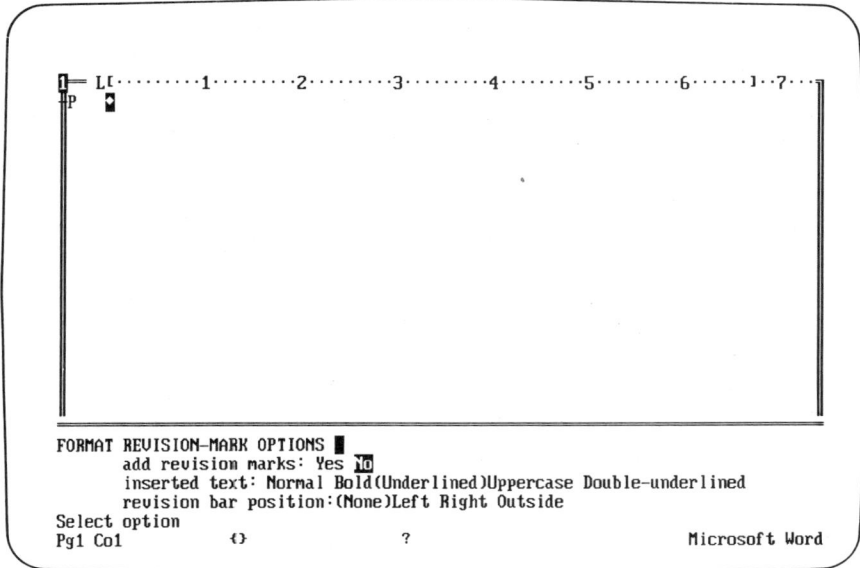

```
┌─ L[·······1·······2·······3·······4·······5·······6·····]··7···]
┤P   ░

 │
 │
 │
 │
 │
 │
 │
 │
 │
 │
 │
 │
 │
 │
════════════════════════════════════════════════════════════════
FORMAT REVISION-MARK OPTIONS ▌
     add revision marks: Yes ▐No▌
     inserted text: Normal Bold(Underlined)Uppercase Double-underlined
     revision bar position:(None)Left Right Outside
Select option
Pg1 Co1            {}              ?                    Microsoft Word
```

Fig. 9.12.

The Format revision-Marks Options command menu.

When you turn on revision marks, the following conditions are true:

❑ All new text is shown with the special character formatting you choose (by default, underlining).

❑ The text you delete is retained in the document but printed with strike-through characters.

❑ If you prefer, lines that have been modified can be marked with revision bars in the margin. These small vertical bars clearly mark the lines in which changes have been made.

After you edit a document with revision marks, your collaborators can do the following:

❑ Search the document for changes. The Format revision-Marks Search command automatically combs the document for all lines on which changes have been made. When the program finds a revision, Word stops and displays the Format revision-Marks menu.

❑ Accept the change. If your collaborator accepts the change found by the search, the strike-through text disappears, and the new text is inserted and stripped of special-character formatting. To accept a change, choose the accept-**R**evisions option in the Format revision-**M**arks menu.

❑ Reject the change. If your collaborator rejects the change found by the search, the strike-through text is retained and stripped of the strike-through formatting. The new text is deleted.

Tip **If you have a monochrome monitor, switch to graphics mode when using redlining.**

In text mode, strike-through formatting appears as underlining; distinguishing strike-through from ordinary underlining is impossible. On color systems, however, you can choose distinctive colors for the two formats by using the colors field in the Options menu.

Tip **Use revision bars to help reviewers quickly spot sections for which you are suggesting changes.**

Revision bars may seem somewhat gratuitous. After all, character-formatting changes should make spotting suggested edits easy enough. In a document that already includes character formatting, such as bold and italic words and phrases, however, distinguishing between a suggested change and a piece of text formatted for other reasons can be time consuming. Use revision bars to indicate clearly the parts of the text you think should be changed.

To turn on revision bars, choose an option other than None in the revision bar position field of the Format revision-**M**arks Options menu. You can position the marker on the left margin, the right margin, or the outside margins of pages printed on both sides of the paper (left margin on odd pages, right margin on even pages).

Trick **Accept or undo all revisions with a few keystrokes.**

If you trust your collaborator's judgment and want to accept all the proposed revisions without going through the whole document, here's how: press Shift-F10 and choose the **F**ormat revision-**M**arks accept-**R**evisions command. Word deletes the strike-through text and removes any special formatting from the inserted text. To undo revisions throughout the whole document, press Shift-F10 and then use the **F**ormat revision-**M**arks **U**ndo-changes command. Word removes the strike-through formatting, erases the revision bars, and deletes the suggested insertions. The text is restored to its original state.

Trap   Overtype mode doesn't work when you turn on redlining.

When you choose the Yes option in the add revision marks field of the **F**ormat revision-**M**arks **O**ptions command, Word automatically switches to insert mode. Overtype mode is disabled; pressing F5 has no effect.

Using Annotations

In collaborative writing, authors circulate drafts among one another and write extensive comments. Before the computer, such comments were written on hard copy. After the computer (but before Word 5), they were still written on hard copy, because computers offered no way to enter the annotations without disturbing the document's text. With Word 5's annotation feature, collaborators can mark up the document to their heart's content—and all the comments can be removed later with a macro supplied with Word.

Creating annotations is a simple matter—it's almost exactly the same procedure used to create a footnote (discussed in Chapter 5). Like a footnote, an annotation has a mark, which is placed in the text, and annotation text, which is placed in a special annotation area beyond the end mark. Here's how to create an annotation:

1. Position the cursor where you want the annotation mark to appear and choose the **F**ormat **A**nnotation command.

2. When the Format Annotation menu appears (see fig. 9.13), type your name or initials in the mark field and choose Yes in the date and time fields if you want to include this information in the annotation text automatically. Press Enter to carry out the command.

   Word scrolls automatically to the annotation area beyond the end mark.

3. Type the annotation text in the special area beyond the end mark.

4. Choose the **J**ump **A**nnotation command to return to the annotation mark in the text.

Fig. 9.13.

The Format
Annotation
command menu.

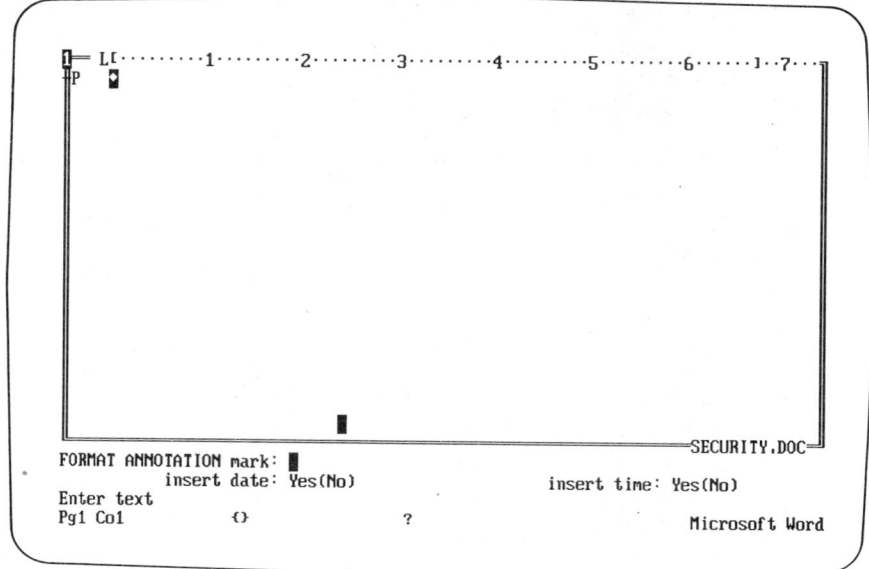

```
 L[·········1·········2·········3·········4·········5·········6·····]·?···
P      ▌




                                ▌

                                                    ═══════SECURITY.DOC═
FORMAT ANNOTATION mark: ▌
            insert date: Yes(No)              insert time: Yes(No)
Enter text
Pg1 Co1            {}              ?                    Microsoft Word
```

Tip **Merge annotations from several copies of a document by using a macro supplied with Word.**

Suppose that you give several copies of a document on disk to your collaborators and they take them off to their desks to review your work. When they bring them back, you're in for a headache—if you're not using Word, that is. With other programs, you would have to review each file separately. But with Word, you can use a macro supplied with Word to extract all the annotations from separate disks and put them all in a single file. The macro is called annot_merge.mac, and is found in the MACRO.GLY file on Word Utilities Disk # 2.

To use the macros supplied with Word, follow the instructions in Chapter 13, "Macros."

Trap **If you want to merge annotations from several copies of a file, ask your collaborators not to alter them in any way besides entering annotations.**

The annot_merge.mac macro, which merges annotations from several copies of a document, works well only if your collaborators have refrained from changing the files in ways other than annotation. If other changes have been made, Word cannot compile the merged annotation list without help from you—and the help must be extensive and time consuming.

Trick **Review annotations by using the footnote window.**

To review annotations, choose the **W**indow **S**plit **F**ootnote command to open the footnote window. This window is "smart": as you scroll the document window, it displays the footnotes or annotations whose reference marks appear in the text currently displayed. (You can distinguish between footnotes and annotation by looking at the reference mark. Footnotes are numbered, and annotations have the mark you specify.)

Trick **Remove all the annotations from a file with a macro supplied with Word.**

When you are finished reviewing annotations, you can remove all of them from the document with a macro called annot_remove.mac. You can find this macro in the MACRO.GLY file on Word Utilities Disk # 2.

To use the macros supplied with Word, follow the instructions in Chapter 13, "Macros."

Chapter Summary

Always work with the No option chosen in the save between sessions field of the Transfer Options command. Start Word from a document directory to make that directory the default. To load an existing document, use the Transfer Load command or the Ctrl-F7 shortcut. Make full use of the F1 file, directory, and drive displays.

Library Document-retrieval provides excellent tools for searching a huge hard disk for files, but Version 5 changes also make this command an equally good file-management utility. Version 5's Document-retrieval command doesn't save the choices you make in the Query command's path field; the default setting is automatically the default directory shown in the setup field of the Transfer Options menu. To get good results from Document-retrieval, you must fill in summary sheets fully. Learn how to broaden and narrow Document-retrieval searches. Make full use of Version 5's new Copy command for backing up and archiving documents.

To move around in a large document, use the Jump Page command. To move quickly to a heading, switch to the outline view, select the heading, and move back to the document view. If you need to come back to an area later for further editing, define it as a bookmark and jump to the area with the Jump bookmarK command. Make full use of multiple windows while editing. To move text safely, cut it to a glossary instead of the scrap. To restructure a big document with a few keystrokes, rearrange the headings in outline organize mode. Use the Undo command to cancel the effects of a misconceived command.

Search for text you need to edit using the Search command; write a macro to search for text, retrieve it, and return to the cursor's location. Replace text throughout your document automatically with the Replace command.

If you write collaboratively, make full use of revision-Marks and Version 5's new Annotation commands.

10

Using the Thesaurus and Checking Spelling

Business and professional writing standards demand precision in word choice. Often, finding just the right word is the key to communicating effectively—and vividly. Instead of saying, "His business in the outdoor footwear area is prospering," you can say, "His mail-order moccasin business took in $2.5 million in 1981." What's more, these same standards require accuracy in spelling. Make no mistake: a misspelling is in the same league with a big greasy spot on your business suit. A misspelling sends the wrong message about you and your commitment to professional standards.

Word 5 comes with two excellent utilities to assist you in your quest for word-choice precision and spelling accuracy: Thesaurus and Spell. With its 220,000-word synonym list, Thesaurus, based on Microlytic's Word Finder™, may well be the best electronic thesaurus available for personal computers. Thanks to Version 5 improvements, Spell, which was formerly one of the weakest features of Word, is finally in the same league with the rest of this powerful program.

Both features are easy enough to use, but more than a few hidden perils—and possibilities—lurk beneath the surface. In this chapter, you learn how to make the most of these features in the context of high-productivity business and professional writing. The following topics are covered in this chapter:

❑ Using the Thesaurus

❑ Checking spelling

❑ Creating User dictionaries

Using the Thesaurus

Containing more than 220,000 words in its huge, disk-based dictionary, Thesaurus is accessible through 15,000 root words—4,000 more than the printed *Random House Thesaurus College Edition*. Even if you normally don't use a printed thesaurus, be sure to explore Word's electronic version. You can see that the program is not only a good electronic thesaurus but also one of the most interesting and useful thesauruses available anywhere.

The number of root words is critical to an electronic thesaurus program's performance. Every such program begins with a selected word in the document and then hunts through the list of root words to find synonyms. If a thesaurus program has only 5,000 root words, many searches turn up nothing. With Word's Thesaurus and its 15,000-word root dictionary, you're much more likely to hit pay dirt when you search for a synonym. The program also automatically searches for the synonyms of a word's root. If you type *procrastination*, for instance, Thesaurus automatically displays the list of synonyms for the word *procrastinate*.

Even a casual browse through a Thesaurus word list tells you that this electronic thesaurus is, by any definition, a good one. The word lists, created specifically for Thesaurus, are extensive, and are based on contemporary business usage. A good printed thesaurus still is useful, however, because such books frequently contain mini-essays on important but subtle shades of meaning. Many writers, however, may find that Word's Thesaurus fulfills their quest for just the right word.

When you use Thesaurus, you begin with a word for which you want to see a list of synonyms. Thesaurus looks for a root word that matches the word in your document. If Thesaurus finds a root word, Thesaurus displays a windowful of synonyms. If you like one of the synonyms, select it and press Enter. Word erases the original word and puts the replacement word in your document. The link requires a good deal of disk-drive activity, but the speed is satisfactory.

Tip **You can use Thesaurus with a dual-floppy system, but Thesaurus is most useful with a hard disk.**

When using a dual-floppy system with Thesaurus, you are instructed to remove the Word disk and insert the Thesaurus disk. After you return to your document, you must swap disks again. This disk-swapping process is tedious.

Tip **If you're using a hard disk, install Thesaurus in the same directory as the Word program.**

If you install Thesaurus in a directory other than the one Word is in, you are prompted to place the Thesaurus disk into the floppy disk drive. Because of this delay, Thesaurus should be installed in the same directory that holds Word. That directory is where SETUP, Word's installation program, places Thesaurus if you choose to install Thesaurus when you run SETUP (see Chapter 1).

Trick **If the cursor is positioned between two words or at the end of a word, Thesaurus looks up the word to the left.**

Normally, you select a word by pressing F7, F8, or the right mouse button before using Thesaurus. If the cursor is positioned after a word, however, Word looks up the word to the left when you use the thEsaurus command. In such cases, Word ignores all spaces and punctuation.

Note: If more than one word is selected, Word looks up the first word.

Trick **Use the Ctrl-F6 shortcut to start Thesaurus.**

You can start Thesaurus using the Library thEsaurus command (press Esc and type *le*). Because this command is not mnemonic, however, you probably will find that pressing Ctrl-F6, the keyboard shortcut, is faster and easier. The same shortcut works in Thesaurus, as you will see, to look up synonyms of synonyms.

The Thesaurus window, always a half-screen window, appears on the top or the bottom of the screen depending on where the original word is located. You always can see your original word in its context.

Tip **The Thesaurus list is divided by parts of speech.**

If you are looking up a word that can be either a noun or verb, depending on its context, you may appreciate knowing that the program divides word lists into parts of speech categories (see fig. 10.1). If you know that you're looking only for synonyms of *favor* (the noun), for example, you can examine only the list that contains synonymous nouns (and ignore the unrelated list of verbal synonyms).

Tip **If Thesaurus cannot find the highlighted word or its root, you're shown a list of similarly spelled words.**

If Thesaurus cannot find the word you highlighted to look up, Word displays the 30 words nearest in spelling to the word for which the program was searching (see fig. 10.2). Highlight one of these words and press Enter to look up the new word, or press Esc to exit.

Fig. 10.1.

Thesaurus word
list divided by
parts of speech.

Root word

Document window

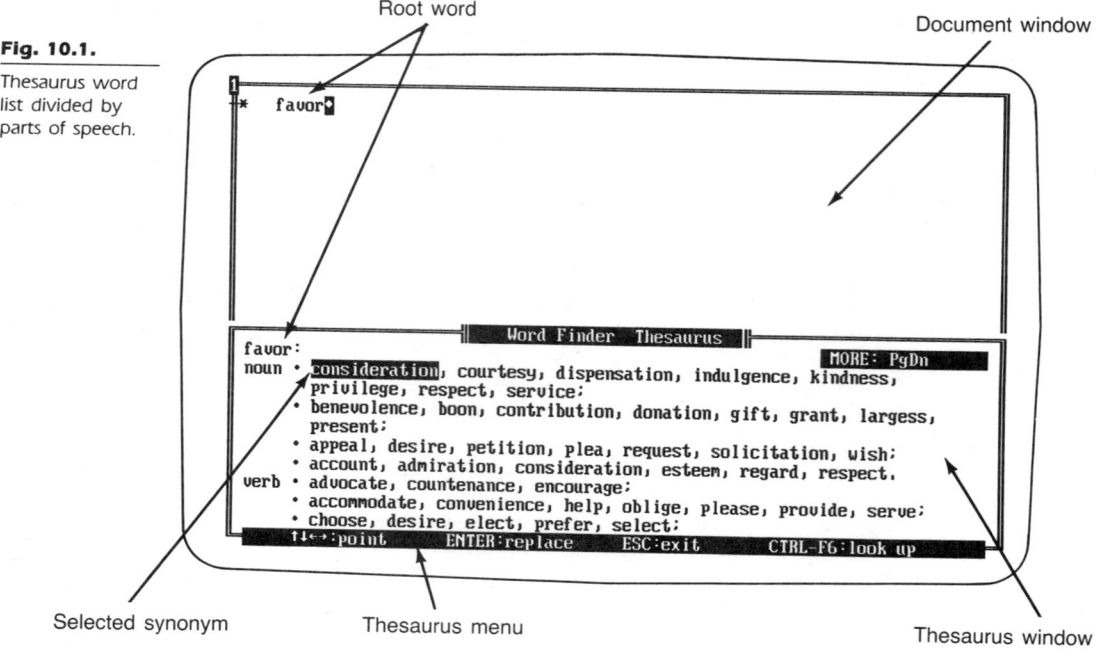

Selected synonym

Thesaurus menu

Thesaurus window

Fig. 10.2.

List of similarly
spelled words
that appears
when Word
cannot find your
chosen word or
its root.

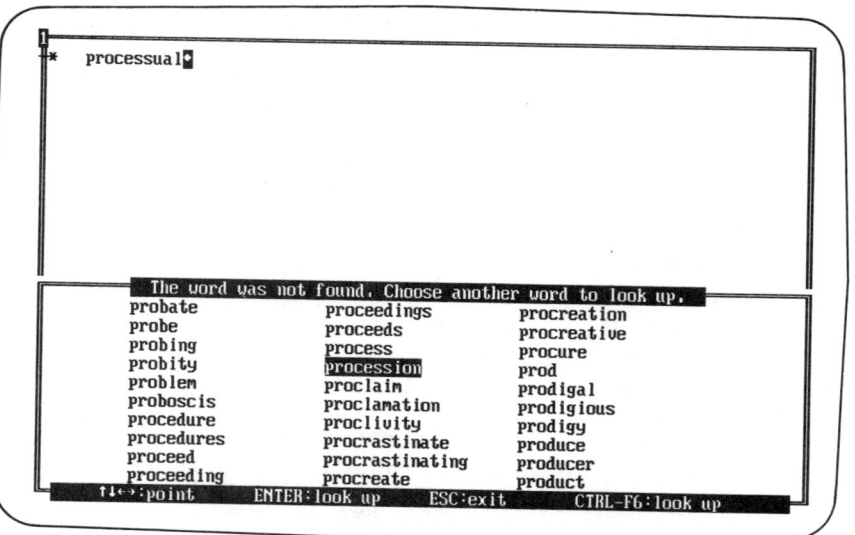

Tip **Press PgUp or PgDn to scroll through the lists of synonyms, or click the left or right mouse buttons on the left window border.**

If a search retrieves more words than Word can display in a single half-screen window, you see the message MORE: PgDn in the window's upper right corner (see fig. 10.3). Press PgDn to scroll down one windowful at a time. Press PgUp to go back up again.

You also can use the mouse to scroll in Thesaurus. Move the pointer to the left window border. Click the right button to scroll up one windowful; click the left mouse button to scroll down one windowful.

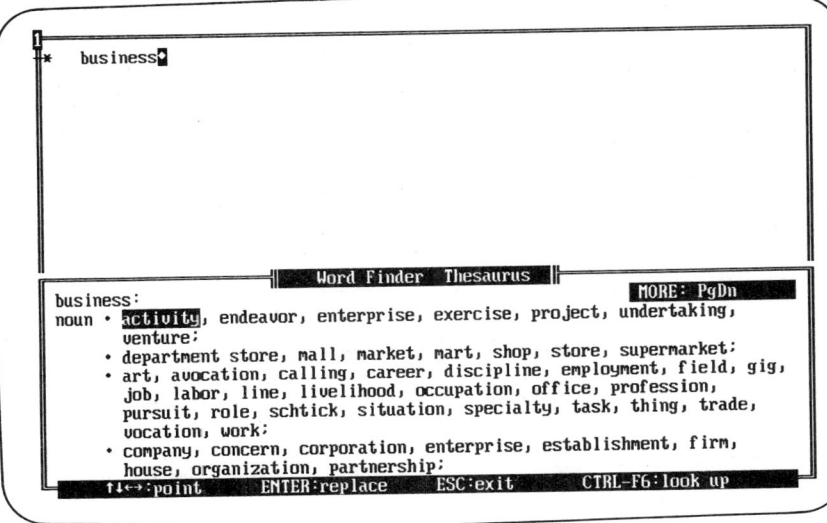

Fig. 10.3.

Message in upper right corner indicating that more synonyms can be viewed by scrolling.

Tip **Use Thesaurus to find simpler and more vivid words.**

Word's Thesaurus provides excellent tools for improving your writing. As effective business writers know, documents using simple, vivid words get their message across. You can use Thesaurus to choose simpler, more vivid words. When you use a polysyllabic word (especially one ending in -tion), such as *utilization*, press Ctrl-F6. You see many simpler, vivid ones, such as *form*, *method*, *technique*, and *use*. Similarly, you can use Thesaurus to help you replace vague words or phrases with more vivid, concrete ones. Instead of referring to a *place of business*, for instance, pick an option from Thesaurus' list of synonyms for *business*, such as *shop*, *office*, *mall*, *department store*.

Trap **The left window border in the Thesaurus window isn't like the document window's left border.**

The left window border in the Thesaurus window isn't like the document window's left border because you cannot scroll line by line or scroll a portion of the Thesaurus window. No matter where you position the pointer on the Thesaurus window border, clicking the left or right mouse button scrolls up or down one windowful at a time.

Tip **Use the arrow keys or the mouse to select a word from the list.**

Use the arrow keys to move word by word or line by line in the Thesaurus window. If you have a mouse, however, the fastest way to select a word is to move the pointer to the word and click the left mouse button.

Trap **The Tab and space bar keys do not work in the Thesaurus window.**

Pressing Tab or the space bar in the Thesaurus window has no effect. Even if you set the `mute` command field from the Options menu to No, Word does not beep to tell you that you pressed the wrong key.

Tip **Press Enter to select the word you want.**

When you have selected the word you want from the list of synonyms presented, press Enter. Alternatively, click the left mouse button on the word ENTER in the Thesaurus window menu. Word erases the original word in your document and puts the replacement word in its place.

Trick **Choose a word and replace it in your document with one click.**

You can select a word, quit Thesaurus, and replace the word in your document just by clicking the right mouse button.

Tip **A replacement word retains the capitalization and formatting of the original word.**

This feature saves you the trouble of capitalizing and formatting the word again.

Trap **If you choose a synonym of the word's root, you may need to add a suffix after Word makes the replacement.**

If you look up *undulation*, for example, Thesaurus automatically shows you synonyms of the word's root (*undulate*), which is a verb rather than a noun. If you choose a synonym of this verb (such as *flutter* or *oscillate*), you must modify the synonym after the replacement so that the new word fits the grammatical structure of your sentence.

Trick **Use Undo to restore the original word after Thesaurus has replaced it.**

If you don't like the replacement after Thesaurus has done its job, use the **Undo** command. The original word appears.

After you use Undo to restore the original word, you can use the command again to bring back the replacement word. In this way, you can switch between the original word and its replacement, noting the shift in the sentence's meaning as each one appears.

Trick **If you don't see the word you want, select a word in Thesaurus and press Ctrl-F6.**

In this way, you can look up synonym after synonym in an adventure trip through the English language. No limit exists to how far you can go.

Trick **Press Ctrl-PgUp to return to the preceding synonym list.**

If you are looking at synonyms of synonyms and decide that you like a previous list better, press Ctrl-PgUp to see the preceding list. Alternatively, click the left mouse button on the words CTRL-PgUp in the Thesaurus window menu. (CTRL-PgUp doesn't appear on the Thesaurus menu until you look up more than one word in an editing session.) You can repeat this command up to 10 times, assuming that you have browsed through at least that many synonym lists.

Tip **Press Esc to quit Thesaurus without changing your document.**

Alternatively, click both mouse buttons or click ESC in the Thesaurus window menu. You are returned to your document, and the Thesaurus window disappears.

Tip **Learn the mouse commands for Thesaurus.**

If you plan to make regular use of Thesaurus, learn the mouse commands that work in the Thesaurus window (see table 10.1). You may find that some of the mouse commands are faster or more convenient than their keyboard equivalents.

Table 10.1
Mouse Commands in the Thesaurus Window

Click	Effect
Left button in window	Select word
Right button in window	Select word and replace in document
Both buttons	Quit Thesaurus without making change in document
Left button in menu	Select command
Left button on left border	Scroll down one windowful
Right button on left border	Scroll up one windowful

Checking Spelling: The Basics

Once one of Word's weakest features, Spell has been much improved for Version 5: your document doesn't disappear when you use the Spell command, and several irritating features of the preceding version have been changed in response to user suggestions. Spell is now much easier to use, and its good qualities are easier to appreciate.

One of these good qualities is the size of Spell's dictionary: 130,000 words. The more words the dictionary contains, the less likely the program is to flag as unknown a word spelled correctly. If an 80,000-word dictionary is good, a 130,000-word dictionary, like Spell's, is excellent. Even with Spell, however, not every correctly spelled word you use is in Spell's dictionary. As you will see, however, you can expand Spell's dictionary to include new words.

Another good feature of Spell is its capability to catch several kinds of errors in addition to misspellings. Spell can detect certain capitalization and punctuation errors as well as doubled words (for example, *the the*) and some invalid compound words. These features are far from complete, however, so be sure to give your document a final proofreading of your own for these and other errors.

Trap **If you install Spell in a directory other than the one that contains Word, you must update the** speller path **field of the Options menu.**

If you installed Word on your hard disk with SETUP, Spell is in Word's directory and the speller path field of the Options menu contains the correct information. If you move Spell out of this directory, however, you must place the dictionary's new path name in the `speller path` field.

Trap **Word doesn't detect misspellings; rather the program detects words that do not match entries in the program's dictionaries.**

Understanding this distinction is important. If you don't, you may overestimate what Spell—or any other computer-based spell checker—can do. Besides misspellings and typographical errors, Word questions the following correctly spelled words:

❏ Plural forms of a word that appears in the dictionary in singular form only

❏ Possessives formed with an apostrophe

❏ Proper nouns such as names of places and people

❏ Technical terms not widely used outside a specialty area

In addition, Spell cannot detect certain other kinds of spelling errors. Such errors include the following:

❏ Homonyms. If you type *their* when you should have typed *there* or you type *auger* when you should have typed *augur*, Spell cannot help you. To Spell, both words are spelled correctly. Spell cannot judge whether a word is used in the correct context.

❏ Incorrectly divided words. Words such as *can not*, *for mat*, or *alter natives* cannot be detected if each half is correctly spelled.

In short, no substitute is available for your own final proofreading of a document.

Correcting Spelling with Spell

Professional and business writing requires letter-perfect spelling. Don't let a document go out the door without running Spell first.

Trick **To check your whole document, don't bother pressing Ctrl-Up first.**

By default, Spell begins at the cursor's location and moves down. You may be tempted to press Ctrl-Up to check your whole document, but this step really is not necessary. When Spell comes to the end of your document, you see the message, Enter Y to continue checking from the beginning of your document. If you press Y, Word continues checking and brings you back to the cursor's location.

Trick   **Check the spelling of a word, a sentence, or a paragraph.**

If you select a block of text, from a single word to many paragraphs, Spell checks only the text you highlight. You can use any of the fixed-unit text selection techniques discussed in Chapter 7 before using Spell.

Trick   **Use the Alt-F6 keyboard shortcut to start Spell.**

If you prefer, you can start Spell by using the **Library S**pell command. After you use this command, the screen splits; you still see your document in the top window, and Spell appears in the bottom one (see fig. 10.4). This split screen is a new Version 5 feature; in previous versions, your document went bye-bye, and it was frequently hard to judge the context of an unknown word from the text Spell displayed for you. After you invoke the **S**pell command, Spell begins checking your document immediately, starting from the cursor's location or the beginning of the selection.

Fig. 10.4.

Spell's display screen and menu.

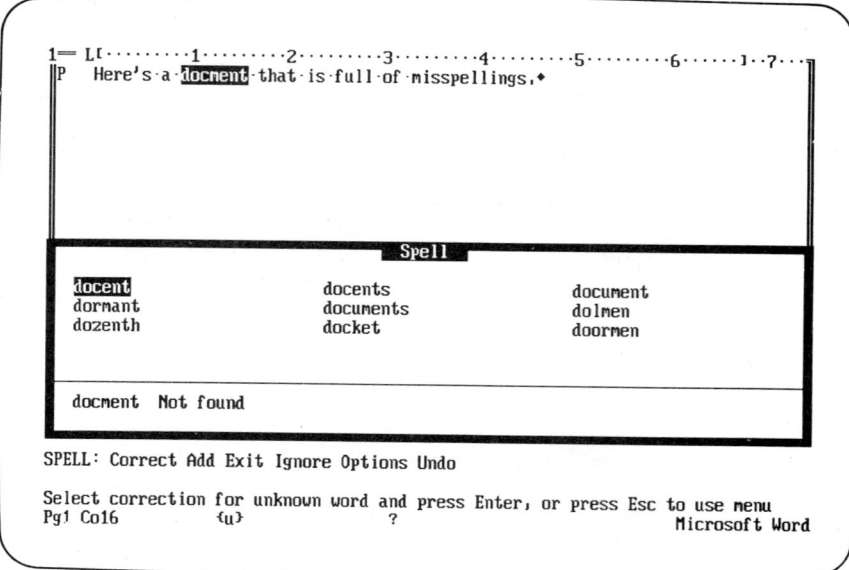

Trick **The first time you use Spell, save time by disabling the automatic lookup option.**

As already noted, Spell flags as unknown many proper nouns, such as your name and those of the important people and places in your life (the names of your boss, spouse, and correspondents, for example, as well as street and city names). In addition, Spell flags as unknown many words peculiar to your business or professional speciality. You can add these words to Word's Standard dictionary so that they're not flagged as unknown. (You learn how to add words to the Standard and other dictionaries elsewhere in this chapter.) The first few times you use Spell, you are in for tedious sessions as Spell, by default, tries to guess the correct spelling of all the unknown words, using a pattern-matching search technique.

You can speed Spell considerably the first few times you use it by disabling the automatic lookup procedure. To do so, follow these instructions:

1. Misspell a word deliberately and select it.

2. Press Alt-F6 to start Spell.

3. When Spell echoes the word with the message Not found, choose the **O**ptions command on the Spell menu (see fig. 10.5).

4. Choose the Manual option in the alternatives field.

5. Press Enter to carry out the command; press Exit to exit Spell.

Once you add most of the proper nouns and special words you use to Word's Standard dictionary, you can turn automatic lookup on again, if you want, by following this procedure again and choosing the Auto option in the alternatives field. The procedure for adding words to the Standard dictionary is explained in the section "Creating User Dictionaries," in this chapter.

Note: If you work in a highly specialized field that uses many unusual terms, create your own User dictionary before using Spell. For information on creating a User dictionary, see "Creating User Dictionaries" in this chapter.

Tip **To speed the lookup procedure, choose the** Quick **option from the** lookup **field of the Spell Options menu.**

Once you add proper nouns and place names to the Standard dictionary, the automatic lookup option is convenient. Most of the time,

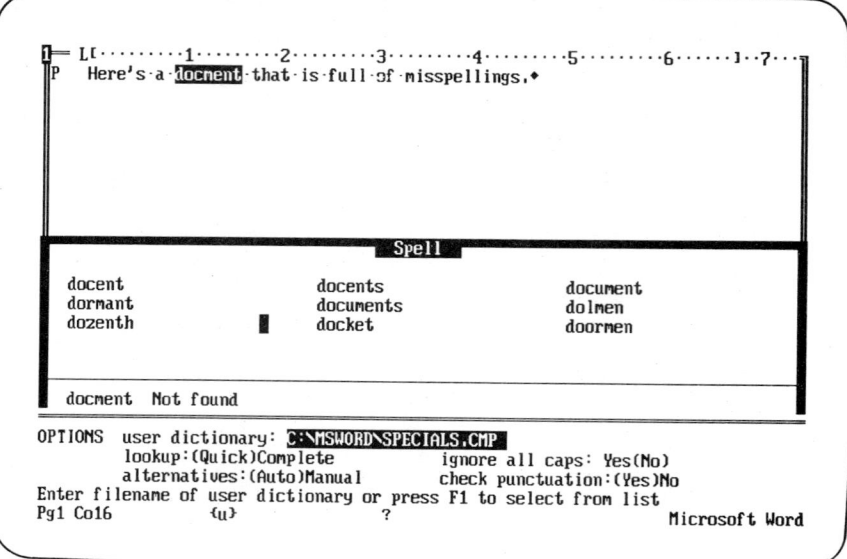

the automatic lookup option finds the word you want; choosing the correct spelling from a list is much easier than typing the correction manually. Automatic lookup is still rather slow, however, unless you have a super-fast 80386 system with a fast hard disk. You can speed automatic lookup considerably by choosing the Quick option in the lookup field of the Spell Options menu. This option restricts the lookup search by assuming that the first two letters of any misspelled word are correct. (The default option, Complete, investigates all potentially correct spelling, including ones with different first letters.)

Tip **If you're spell-checking a technical document that contains program listings or other highly technical material, turn off punctuation checking.**

By default, Spell flags all instances of inappropriate punctuation in text strings, such as *?valleys* or *moun*tains*. In highly technical material such as program listings, however, "misplaced" punctuation marks such as these may actually be correct. You can turn off punctuation checking easily: just use the **L**ibrary **S**pell **O**ptions command, and choose No in the check punctuation field.

Tip **Spell remembers the choices made in the Spell Options menu.**

Here's another welcome change in Version 5's spelling checker. In previous versions, Spell lost all the choices you made in the Spell

Options menu when the Spell program finished; you had to make all the changes again manually the next time you used the program.

Trap **You cannot get into Spell from Word if a new, blank document is on the screen.**

Don't try to access the Spell Options menu from a blank document. If you try to get into Spell when a new, blank document is on-screen, nothing happens—no error message, no beep. Type a misspelling or two and try again: Spell comes to life.

Tip **When Spell finds a misspelling, you can correct it, add it to a dictionary, or ignore it.**

When Spell encounters a word it cannot find in its dictionary, the program echoes the word to the screen with the message Not found.

If you use Spell's default automatic lookup option, the program searches its dictionaries to try to find the correct spelling. One or more spellings likely to be correct appear on the screen, although sometimes Spell cannot find any potential matches. In such cases, you see the message No alternative words found. (If you used the **S**pell **O**ptions command to choose Manual lookup, you can still use the lookup feature. Choose the **C**orrect command and press F1 to generate the list of potentially correct spellings.)

When Word flags a word as "not found," you have three options: you can add the word to one of Spell's dictionaries, correct the word, or ignore it.

- ❑ If you know that the word is correct, choose the **A**dd command. You can add the word to one of three dictionaries. For Words you use frequently, choose the **S**tandard option. You learn more about the other dictionary options elsewhere in this chapter.

- ❑ If the word is not spelled correctly, choose the **C**orrect command and use the arrow keys to highlight the correct spelling in the list. Alternatively, type the correct spelling in the Correct command menu, and carry out the command.

- ❑ If the word is spelled correctly but you don't believe you will use it in another document, choose the **I**gnore command. Word skips all other instances of this word in the document.

Trick   **Correct a word immediately by choosing the correct spelling from the list.**

If you use the automatic lookup option, you don't need to use the Correct command if the correct spelling appears in the list of potentially correct words. Just use the arrow keys to highlight the word and press Enter. If you use the mouse, just right-click the word. Spell chooses the Correct command for you and makes the correction.

Trick   **If you think that you may make the same mistake again, use the Correct command and choose the Yes option in the remember correction field.**

If you choose the Yes option in the remember correction field of the Correct command (see fig. 10.6), Spell automatically makes the same correction if it encounters the misspelling in the future.

Fig. 10.6.

The Spell Correct command menu.

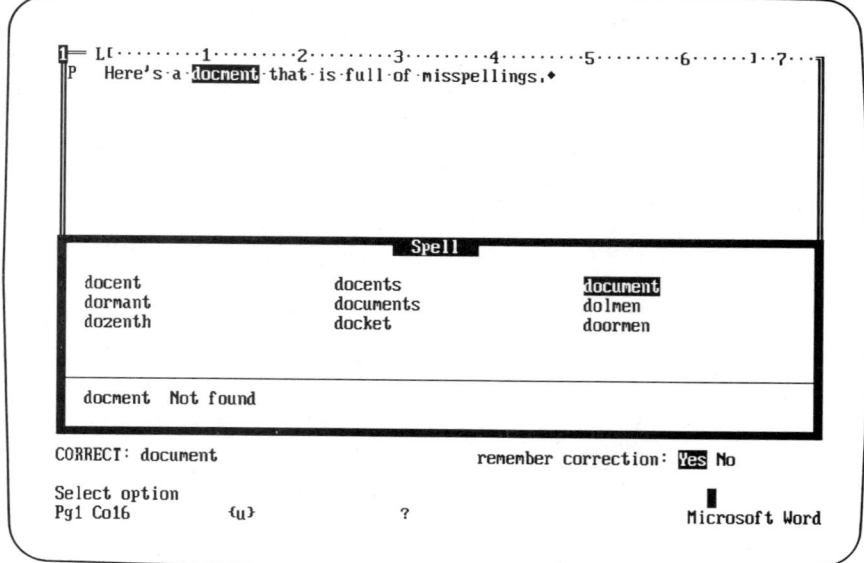

This very important and useful feature deserves some emphasis. Normally, a spelling checker's dictionary contains only correctly spelled words. If you tend to make the same mistake again and again, such as leaving an *r* out of *occurrence* or confusing suffixes (*precedance* and *appearence*, for example), you make the same correction again and again—and that's tedious. If you tell Spell to remember the correction, the program performs the correction automatically the next time it detects the error. In other words, besides containing a list of correct words, Spell's dictionary also contains a list of incorrectly spelled words, together with instructions that tell Spell how to make the correction automatically. In other words, Spell adapts to the pattern of spelling errors you tend to make and automatically corrects them. Neat! Use this option if you think that there's any chance you might make the same error again.

Tip   **Spell detects errors you make in typing the correction.**

If you make a typographical error while typing a correction in the Correct command menu, Word detects the error and beeps. The message `Not in dictionary. Retype? Y/N` appears. Press Y to retype the word or N to accept the word as typed.

Trap   **If the correction requires you to type two or more words, Word beeps even if you spell the words correctly.**

Sometimes you forget to press the space bar between words, creating a typo like this one: *launchwindow*. Spell finds the error. When you correct the error by typing *launch window*, however, Word displays the message `Not in dictionary. Retype? (Y/N)`. This message doesn't necessarily mean that you misspelled one or both words in the correction, although you should check the words to make sure. After checking the words, press N, and Word makes the correction.

Trap   **If you accidentally insert a space within a word and a misspelling results, you cannot fix it with Spell.**

Suppose that you typed *catas trophe*. When you check spelling, Spell flags *catas* and *trophe* as separate, unknown words. You cannot fix the error with Spell. If you correct *catas*, Spell leaves *trophe* in your document. To cope with errors of this sort, don't make a correction—just quit Spell and use Word to fix the problem. Then start Spell again. Because Spell always starts at the cursor's location, the program will pick up where it left off.

Tip   **If you change your mind about the choice you made for a word, use the Undo command to change the choice.**

The Spell Undo command really ought to be called "Undo_previous," because that's what it does: returns Spell to the preceding correction and permits you to correct it again, ignore it, or add it to the dictionary. If you want to redo a correction made preceding the last one, you're out of luck. Search for the correction and redo it manually after quitting Spell. To undo all the corrections in a session, choose **U**ndo from the edit command menu immediately after quitting Spell.

Note: Earlier versions of Spell had a Previous command, which you could use to go back in your list of corrections. Spell works differently now—it actually makes the corrections as it goes through your document. You only can redo your last correction, just as you can undo only your last editing change in normal editing mode.

Tip **You can exit Spell at any time without losing your corrections.**

To stop spell checking, choose Exit. Word saves all the corrections made so far.

Note: In previous versions of Spell, you had the option of abandoning your changes when you quit Spell. Not so in Version 5. Spell actually makes the corrections one by one as it goes through your document.

Creating User Dictionaries

As you check the spelling of a document, you can use the Add command to add words to three different dictionaries:

❑ *Standard*. If you add words to the Standard dictionary by using the Add command from the Spell menu, Spell puts the words in a file called UPDAT-AM.CMP. These words are used to check all documents.

❑ *Document*. This dictionary is created and saved for use with a single Word document. You create the dictionary by adding words to it, using the Spell Proof Add Document command. The first time you use this command, Spell creates a Document dictionary for the document currently being checked. The dictionary has the same file name as your document with the extension CMP. Spell automatically consults this dictionary if you check this document's spelling again. These words aren't used to check any other documents.

❑ *User*. Unlike the Document dictionary, which Spell uses only when you proof the document to which Spell is attached, the User dictionary can be used to proofread more than one document. Spell does not use this dictionary, however, unless you specifically instruct the program to, using the Dictionary command at the start of a Spell session. When you add a word to a User dictionary for the first time, Word proposes a default name (SPECIALS.CMP) for the dictionary. You can change that name as long as the extension CMP is still used.

Why not just add all the words to the Standard dictionary? Remember, even though the Standard dictionary is limited only by disk size, adding words to it slows Spell down. Keep the Standard dictionary as small as possible by adding words to it only when you're sure that they may pop up in virtually any document you write. If the words are likely to appear in only some of your documents, put them in a User dictionary.

Trap   **When you choose the Add option, Spell does not stop you from adding a misspelling to its dictionaries.**

Make sure that any word you add to the dictionaries is correctly spelled. If you're not sure, check your spelling against a printed dictionary.

Remember that Spell doesn't really check spelling. Spell only matches the words in your document with the words in its dictionaries. If a match isn't found, the word is reported as a problem word. If you put a misspelling in a dictionary, the misspelling becomes the standard against which your document is compared.

Tip   **If you add a word to the Standard dictionary and discover that the word isn't spelled properly, you can fix the error.**

When you add a word to the Standard dictionary, the word doesn't go into the disk version of the dictionary (the American disk version is called SPELL-AM.EXE). This file is in binary format and cannot be edited or displayed on the screen. Instead, the words you add to the Standard dictionary go to a Word file called UPDAT-AM.CMP.

You can edit this file as if it were a Word document. After quitting Spell and returning to the document, open a new window and load UPDAT-AM.CMP. Edit the error and save the file.

Trap   **UPDAT-AM.CMP doesn't store words in compressed format, so a limit exists to the number of words the file can store.**

Unlike the Standard dictionary, UPDAT-AM.CMP doesn't store words in compressed format. A limit therefore exists to the number of words the file can store. The limit is set by disk size, but adding too many words to this file slows Spell considerably. You may add several dozen words to this file safely, but after you add more than several hundred, processing time degrades.

If you sometimes write in specialized fields that use technical terms, try creating a series of special User dictionaries, each of which contains just those words that pertain to a given specialty. That way, you can keep the dictionaries' sizes to a minimum. An attorney, for example, can create one such dictionary for tax law and another for real estate law. For more information on User dictionaries, see the section called "Creating User Dictionaries," in this chapter.

Tip **Plan your User dictionaries carefully.**

Take some time to think about how to create and use User dictionaries. Think about the fields in which you write. Suppose that you write on two subjects: the politics of the New South and the legal implications of hazardous waste disposal. The terms used in documents pertaining to the first subject more than likely do not appear in documents pertaining to the second subject. It makes good sense to create two User dictionaries, one for New South terms and the other for hazardous waste. You are wise to create two User dictionaries: one called SOUTH and the other called WASTE.

Tip **To create a new User dictionary, name it when you add a word to it the first time.**

To create a User dictionary, do the following steps:

1. Start Spell. When the program finds an error, choose the **O**ptions command.

2. Type the User dictionary's name in the `user dictionary` field. If the dictionary doesn't exist, Spell creates it.

3. Press Enter to carry out the command.

4. To add words to the User dictionary, use the **A**dd command and choose the **U**ser option.

Trap **Spell saves the choice you make in the** `user dictionary` **field as the program's new default.**

Bear this point in mind the next time you use Spell. Begin each Spell session by choosing a User dictionary.

Trick **If you use User dictionaries, start Spell with this macro.**

Here's a macro that reminds you to specify the user dictionary at the start of a Spell session. The macro starts Spell and takes you directly to the Spell Options menu when the program encounters the first error.

```
<alt f6>
<esc>o«PAUSE Type User dictionary name or select from list;
    Enter to continue.»
```

To create and use this macro, follow the instructions in Chapter 13, "Macros." Save the macro using the macro name options_userdict.mac^<ctrl 0>u.

Trick **Create a User dictionary quickly by listing the words in a Word document.**

Here's a quick way to add words to a User dictionary. Start a new Word document and type all the words you want to add to the User dictionary. Then call the **S**pell command. Use the **O**ptions command to name the User dictionary, and then use the **A**dd **U**ser command repeatedly to add all the words in the list.

Tip **Add words to a Document dictionary when you're sure that the words appear only in that document.**

If you're creating a highly specialized document with many unusual terms not used elsewhere, add correctly spelled words to the Document dictionary. The next time you check the spelling of this document, Spell consults this dictionary as well as the Standard dictionary.

Trap **You cannot add words to a Document dictionary if you haven't named your document.**

Spell lets you check a document's spelling even if you haven't saved the document using the **T**ransfer **S**ave command. In such cases, the word untitled appears on the lower right border instead of the file name. You can check the spelling of an untitled document, but Spell does not create a Document dictionary if you have not named the original document.

Trap **You cannot use User dictionaries created with versions of Spell earlier than Version 4 unless you convert them first.**

Spell has changed so much that it cannot use the User dictionaries created with Versions 3 and earlier. A program on Utilities Disk #1 called SPELCONV.EXE can be used to convert your User dictionaries to Spell 5's format.

Chapter Summary

Use Word's excellent Thesaurus to make sure that you're using the correct word. Take advantage of the features that enable you to browse through many related screens of synonyms. Use Thesaurus to choose simpler and more vivid words.

Version 5's much-improved Spell not only detects misspellings, it remembers the corrections you make and repeats the corrections automatically the next time you use Spell. To make use of this feature, choose the Yes option in the remember corrections field of the Spell Options menu. To speed Spell's operation, choose the Manual option in the alternatives field of the Spell Options menu, or choose Quick in the same menu's lookup field.

11

Printing Your Work

O nce you install Word with SETUP, printing your document is as simple as making sure that your printer is properly connected and choosing the Print Printer command. If you want to get the maximum from your system, however, it pays to understand how Word controls printers, what's in the PRD files that Word uses, and how to make sure that your document prints properly before you waste paper and ink. These and other subjects are covered in this chapter, which also includes an extensive discussion of laser printers and downloadable fonts.

This chapter covers the following topics:

❏ Understanding your printer's capabilities

❏ Using laser printers and downloadable fonts

❏ Choosing printing options

❏ Ink-saving and paper-saving strategies

❏ Printing your document

❏ Troubleshooting printing problems

Understanding Your Printer's Capabilities

When you install Word with SETUP, you choose a printer from the list. SETUP automatically does the following:

❏ Copies the printer's printer description file (a file with the extension PRD) to your Word program disk

313

❑ Updates the Print Options command menu with the printer description file name in the `printer` field, your printer's model name in the `model` field, and the output port selected in the `setup` field

The printer description file (a special file with the PRD extension) contains the information Word needs to operate your printer. Here's a brief overview of information contained in this file:

❑ *Model name.* Many PRD files contain information for more than one model of printer. The HPDWNACP.PRD file, for instance, contains information for six Hewlett-Packard LaserJet models. SETUP modifies the `model` field in the Print Options menu correctly, but in some cases you can change the model name to take advantage of additional features, such as different combinations of font cartridges. For example, the Hewlett-Packard LaserJet printer option has many other choices—each a unique combination of font cartridges. After installing your printer, you can use the Print Options command to change the model name. In this way, you can take full advantage of a wide range of font cartridges.

❑ *Line-drawing font.* If your printer has two or more internal fonts, Word chooses one to use for its line-drawing mode. If the printer supports the IBM extended character set, the font containing these characters is the one Word uses for line drawing.

❑ *IBM graphics characters.* Not all printers support the IBM extended character set. If your printer does not contain these characters, you cannot use the extended characters accessed by pressing Alt and typing a two-number or three-number code.

❑ *Graphics resolution.* If your printer can print graphics, you can choose from two or three different levels of graphics resolution. Resolution, measured in dots per inch (dpi), refers to the density of the printed image. You choose resolution using the `graphics resolution` field of the Print Options menu.

❑ *Fonts and font sizes.* If your printer can print more than one font and font size, Word automatically updates the Format Character command menu. When you press F1 in the `font name` or `font size` field, you see the list of fonts and sizes available for that printer.

❑ *Bin support.* Some printers include sheet or envelope feeders. If Word supports these options, you see a choice in the `paper feed` field of the Print Options menu.

❑ *Unprintable regions.* Laser printers cannot print on the whole page. In previous versions of Word, you had to compensate for this problem by entering a reduced page size in the Format Division Margins command menu. Word 5's PRD files include this information, so you do not need to enter a reduced page size in the Format Division Margins menu.

❑ *Downloadable fonts.* If you use downloadable fonts for Hewlett-Packard or PostScript-compatible laser printers, here's some good news: Word 5 may be able to download the fonts automatically. This feature is discussed in a subsequent tip.

Trap **You may need more than one PRD file to make full use of your printer.**

When you install Word using SETUP, you choose your printer name and model from a list. If your printer can use multiple fonts and font cartridges, you see another list, and you can choose the fonts or cartridges you have from the second list. You may possibly have several font cartridges, however, and not all the fonts you have are contained in the PRD file chosen.

Tip **You can copy more than one PRD file to your Word disk or directory.**

If you need more than one PRD file to make use of all your font cartridges, there's nothing to stop you from copying two or more PRD files to your Word program disk. Use SETUP to copy the required files. (As mentioned, SETUP explains on-screen the features and cartridges a selected printer file supports, so you're not in the dark about which file you need if you don't have Microsoft's manual handy. (See table 11.1 for a list of the PRD files that support Hewlett-Packard LaserJet font cartridges.) To change PRD files after you have installed them with SETUP, type the name of the PRD file you want to use in the `printer` field of the Print Options menu. After Word loads the file, the program automatically updates all the command fields affected by your printer choice.

Table 11.1
PRD Files for LaserJet Font Cartridges

PRD File Name	Orientation	Cartridges
HPLASER.PRD	Portrait	Internal fonts only
HPLASER1.PRD	Portrait	A, B, C, D, E, G, H, J, L, Q, W, X
HPLASER2.PRD	Portrait	F, K, P, R, U
HPLASER3.PRD	Portrait	J, R, Z
HPLASPS.PRD	Portrait	B
HPLASRMN.PRD	Portrait	F
HPLAS2S1.PRD	Portrait	S2
HPLASTAX.PRD	Portrait	T
HPPCCOVR.PRD	Portrait	Y
HPLASMS.PRD	Portrait	Z (ECMA symbols)
HPLASMS2.PRD	Portrait	Z (Roman 8 symbols)
HPLASMSA.PRD	Portrait	Z (ASCII symbols)
HPLASLAN.PRD	Landscape	A, B, C, G, H, L, M, N, P, Q, R, U, V
HPLASMSL.PRD	Landscape	Z

Tip **Use MERGEPRD.EXE to combine fonts from two or more PRD files into one PRD file.**

If you find yourself switching frequently from one PRD file to another, use a utility program called MERGEPRD.EXE to combine fonts and font sizes from two or more PRD files into one new PRD file. You will find MERGEPRD.EXE on one of the Word Utilities disks.

Note: You cannot use the MERGEPRD.EXE program to combine PRD files for different printer brands.

To use MERGEPRD.EXE, do the following steps:

1. Write down the names of all the PRD files you want to use. You must know their names once you start MERGEPRD.EXE. Consult Word's *Printer Information* manual to determine their names—or if you don't have the manual handy, browse through the printer installation menu in SETUP and select the files you need.

2. Use DOS to copy all the PRD files you want to merge to a single disk or directory. Copy MERGEPRD.EXE to the same disk or directory.

3. Type *MERGEPRD* on a DOS command line and press Enter.

4. Choose your printer type from the list.

5. When the Main menu appears, type *1* to enter the PRD file names you want.

   Type the PRD file names, one after the other. To return to the Main menu, leave the Enter selection field blank and press Enter.

6. At the Main menu, type *4* to select fonts and font sizes.

   Word displays a list of all the fonts and font sizes in all the PRD files named.

   To choose a font to merge into the new file, type its number. Then type the sizes of the font you want to merge into the new file, or type *ALL* to use all available sizes in that font.

7. When you have finished selecting the fonts you want, type *6* to return to the Main menu.

   You can display the fonts chosen by selecting option 5 at the Main menu. To add more fonts or delete fonts you added, choose option 4 to return to the Select Fonts and Font Sizes menu.

8. Type *7* from the Main menu to name and create the new PRD file.

9. Type *8* to leave MERGEPRD.

To use the new PRD file you have created, name it, using the printer field of the Print Options menu.

Trick **If your printer supports the IBM extended character set, you can enter an em dash by pressing Ctrl-Alt-hyphen.**

In professional typesetting, dashes are constructed from a single, unbroken character called an *em dash*. When writing with word processors, most people simulate an em dash by typing two hyphens. For a professional appearance, however, use the em character in the IBM extended character set. The extended character, Alt-196, is used by Word for internal purposes, but Version 5 includes a useful command, Ctrl-Alt-hyphen, to bypass this problem.

Note: Your printer must be capable of printing the IBM extended character set in order to print this character.

Using Word with Laser Printers and Downloadable Fonts

As you already know, Word's font-printing capabilities are determined by the printer you use. If you use one of today's high-quality laser printers, you can create attractive documents using several different fonts and font sizes. In general, laser printers conform to two standards: the one set by the Hewlett-Packard LaserJet, and another set by the Apple LaserWriter®. LaserWriters and compatibles use the PostScript printer description language, which Word 5 fully supports.

Laser printers make fonts available in three different ways:

❑ *Internal fonts* are the ones available in the printer without your having to purchase additional cartridges or software. Hewlett-Packard LaserJet and compatible printers come equipped only with the Courier font, a typewriter-style, fixed-width font. LaserWriter and compatible printers usually include several internal fonts.

❑ *Font cartridges* equip LaserJet and compatible printers with additional fonts and font sizes. Font cartridges are relatively expensive and have a limited life, usually measured in the number of times you can insert them. They do not require additional memory, however, and you do not need to spend time downloading them from disk.

❑ *Downloadable fonts* provided on disk can be used with LaserJet and LaserWriter printers, as well as all compatible printers. Downloadable fonts tend to be much less expensive than cartridges, but with most programs, you must use a utility program to copy the fonts from the disk to the printer (a procedure called *downloading*) at the beginning of every operating session. Moreover, your printer must have enough memory to hold the fonts you download. (Most laser printers come with some memory, but you may need to add more.)

Tip **Version 5 automatically downloads fonts for some printers.**

With Word 5, you needn't worry about downloading disk-based fonts with some printers. Word takes care of the job automatically, downloading just the fonts and font sizes you need to print a given document. You simply format your document with the fonts and font sizes you want.

You can download fonts, however, only when Word's PRD files contain specific support for each font. In general, the support is good for PostScript-compatible laser printers; you can use any Adobe PostScript downloadable font. The support is also good for Hewlett-Packard laser printers; you can download any soft font sold by Hewlett-Packard.

The following PRD files offer downloading support:

❏ *PSDOWN.PRD.* This PRD file supports downloadable fonts that require a PostScript-compatible printer, such as an Apple LaserWriter. (PostScript is a font-generation programming language that stores fonts by means of mathematical formulas.) PSDOWN.PRD supports 10 standard PostScript fonts.

❏ Files beginning with *HPDWN.* These files support the downloadable fonts available from Hewlett-Packard for that company's LaserJet printers. See table 11.2 for a list of these files and the font sets they support.

Table 11.2
PRD Files for Downloadable Font Support (LaserJets)

PRD File Name	Orientation	Font Set
HPDWNACP.PRD	Portrait	AC
HPDWNACL.PRD	Landscape	AC
HPDWNADP.PRD	Portrait	AD
HPDWNADL.PRD	Landscape	AD

Tip **You can add additional Adobe PostScript fonts to the PSDOWN.PRD file.**

The PRD file called PSDOWN.PRD supports all the PostScript-compatible laser printers supported by Word, including the Apple LaserWriter. PSDOWN.PRD supports the 10 fonts; you can expand this file by modifying it with MERGEPRD.EXE, discussed in a previous tip. More than 200 Adobe PostScript fonts are available. After the modification, additional fonts appear when you press F1 in the Format Character command menu font name and font size fields, and Word downloads the fonts automatically.

Trap **Adding downloadable fonts to PRD files is difficult unless the fonts are Adobe PostScript fonts.**

Unfortunately, you have no easy way to add additional downloadable fonts to PRD files unless they are Adobe PostScript files. If you purchase non-Hewlett-Packard fonts for your Hewlett-Packard LaserJet, for instance, you cannot use MERGEPRD.EXE to add the names of the fonts to the list of downloadable fonts. You can add fonts to a PRD file using the program called MAKEPRD.EXE, supplied on one of the Word Utilities disks, but the process is extremely difficult and time consuming.

Happily, this limitation may not be a problem for you. Many companies that make downloadable fonts provide Word PRD files with their fonts. If you want to purchase additional downloadable fonts for your laser printer, ask the company that makes the font whether they distribute a PRD file that Word 5 can use. The PRD file must contain full support for all the fonts, or you cannot download them with Word.

Note: The PRD file must be compatible with Word 5. Version 5 cannot use Word 4's PRD files.

Tip **If you have a Hewlett-Packard DeskJet™ or LaserJet, get the Supplemental Printers Disk.**

The Supplemental Printers Disk, available on request from Microsoft, supports downloadable fonts for the DeskJet. In addition, you will find support for Hewlett-Packard soft fonts AE, AF, AG, DA, EA, RA, RB, SA, SB, TA, TB, VA, and VB.

Tip **To use downloadable fonts, place the PRD and other necessary files, together with all the fonts, in their own directory.**

Make the separate directory using the DOS MKDIR command. Name the directory \MSWORD\FONTS. Copy the following files to this directory:

- ❏ All the files containing the fonts you want to download

- ❏ The Word PRD file that supports your printer and downloading. For Hewlett-Packard LaserJet printers, choose from the PRD files that begin with *HPDWN*. For PostScript-compatible printers, choose PSDOWN.PRD.

- ❏ The DAT file with the same file name as the PRD file. If you are using HPDWNACP.PRD, for instance, copy HPDWNACP.DAT to your directory.

❏ PSDWN.INI if you are using a PostScript-compatible laser printer

When you start Word, choose the **P**rint **O**ptions command, highlight the `printer` field, use the F1 key to list all the available PRD files, and highlight the PRD file you want to use. After you press Enter, Word automatically enters all the path information the program needs to find the PRD, DAT, INI, and soft-font files.

Tip **If you use a PRD file with downloading capabilities, understand your options when you print your document.**

If you have chosen a printer description file with downloading capabilities, using soft fonts is a simple matter.

When it's time to print, Word displays the message, `Enter Y to download new fonts, A to download all fonts, N to skip`. Following is a brief review of what these options mean:

❏ Press Y to download any fonts that have not already been downloaded in the current Word session, adding to the fonts already downloaded. If you have already downloaded many fonts, you may run out of printer memory if you choose this option.

❏ Press A to download all the fonts used in this document. Choosing this option erases from the printer's memory the fonts that were previously downloaded in this Word session. Choose this option if your printer's memory is limited.

❏ Press N to skip downloading. Your printer substitutes built-in fonts for the fonts you chose.

Trap **You see the message** ... `.DAT was not found` **when you try to use a downloadable font in Word.**

All PRD files supporting downloadable fonts have a companion file containing data Word needs to download the fonts correctly. This file has the same file name as the PRD file, with a DAT extension. Copy this file to the directory that contains the PRD file and try again.

Trap **You see the message** `Font download unsuccessful`.

If you see this message, your printer may not be connected properly or turned on. Check your printer to make sure that this is not the case. If you have already printed successfully in this operating session, however, your printer probably has insufficient memory to contain all the fonts you tried to download.

To minimize the amount of memory your printer needs to print downloadable fonts, choose fonts that contain only the ASCII characters, not the full extended character set. Also, minimize the number of large fonts you choose. Large fonts take up much more memory than small ones.

If you run into this problem frequently, you can solve it by purchasing additional memory for your printer.

Trap **The PRD file you use may list fonts and font sizes your printer cannot print.**

When you use a PRD file that supports cartridges, the PRD file may list fonts and font sizes for cartridges you don't own. You can choose these fonts and sizes when you use the **Format Character** command, but they don't print.

You can eliminate fonts and font sizes of cartridges you don't own by using MERGEPRD.EXE to create a new PRD file. To use MERGEPRD.EXE, follow the instructions in a preceding tip.

Choosing Printing Options

The Print Options command controls the printing of documents (see fig. 11.1). The fields in this command provide many alternatives for printing your document. The Print Options menu fields are described in the following list.

Field	Comment
printer	Use this field to name the PRD file you are using. If you used SETUP to install Word, SETUP added the file name automatically. If you want to choose a new printer, press F1 to choose from a list.
model	Use this field to choose the printer model you are using. The list of models comes from the PRD file you selected. If you used SETUP to install Word, SETUP added the model name automatically. If you want to name a new printer, choose its PRD file by pressing F1before looking for the model in this field.

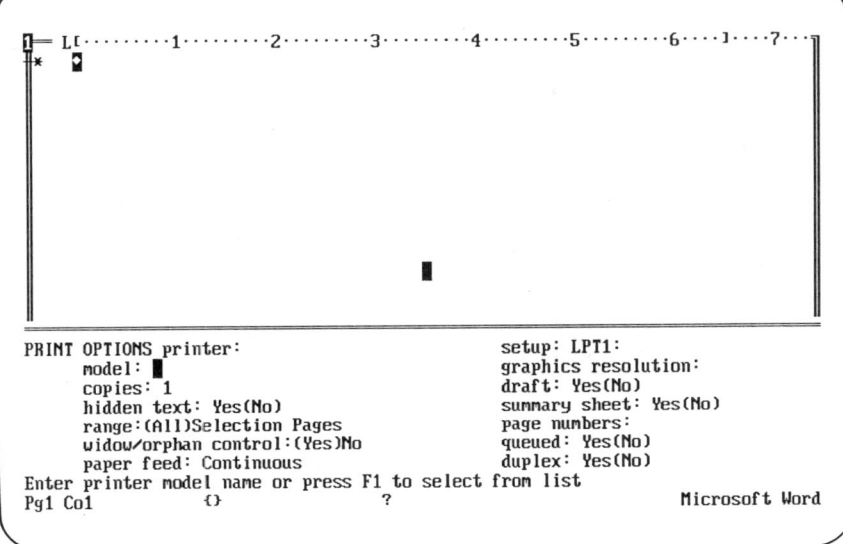

Fig. 11.1.

The Print Options command menu.

Field	Comment
setup	Use this field to enter the port through which your computer sends signals to the printer. Press F1 to choose from a list. If you used SETUP to install Word, SETUP added the port automatically.
graphics resolution	(Default varies by PRD file.) If your laser printer supports graphics, it may be capable of printing in different resolutions, measured in dots per inch (dpi). Press F1 to see a list of available resolution levels for your printer. Choose low resolution levels (such as 75 dpi) for quick printings of drafts; choose high-resolution (such as 300 dpi) for the much slower, but higher-quality, printing of final copy.
copies	(Default is 1.) You can print as many copies of a document as you want.
draft	(Default is No.) Choose draft mode (the Yes option) to print without microspace justification,

Field	Comment
	font changes, graphics, or formatting. Word prints your document much more rapidly. If you are not using microspace justification, graphics, or font changes, however, the speed gain is insignificant.
hidden text	(Default is No.) You can choose to print hidden text if you want. If you select the Yes option, the hidden text prints whether or not it is visible on the screen.
summary sheet	(Default is No.) If you choose the Yes option, Word prints the summary sheet on a separate page.
range	(Default is All.) You can print specific pages in your document (the Pages option) or just selected text (the Selection option).
page numbers	This field works with the Pages option in the range field to determine the pages to be printed.
widow/orphan control	(Default is Yes.) Word suppresses widow lines and orphan lines by default; choose No if you do not want this feature. A *widow* is the last line of a paragraph left alone at the top of a page. An *orphan* is the first line of a paragraph left alone at the bottom of a page. Note that if you choose Yes, some pages may have more printed lines than others.
queued	(Default is No.) Use this field to print one or more files in the background while you work on another document.
paper feed	(Default is Continuous.) The options in this field depend on the PRD file you are using.
duplex	If your printer can print on both sides of the page, choose Yes in this field to enable this feature. The default setting is No.

The following suggestions help you use the print options correctly. If you're not careful, you may be in for some frustrating surprises when you check your printout.

Trap **Typing page numbers in the** page numbers **field does not turn on range printing.**

You also must choose Pages in the range field. Microsoft, how about fixing this for Version 6 so that a page range entered in the page numbers field automatically selects the Pages option?

Trick **Use a hyphen or colon in the** page numbers **field to select a range of pages. Use a comma to separate individual pages.**

To print pages 12 through 16, for instance, type *12-16* or *12:16* in the page numbers field. To print pages 12, 14, 18, and 91, type *12,14,18,91* in the page numbers field. Don't forget to select the Pages option in the range field.

Tip **If your document is broken into divisions, include division numbers with page numbers when you select pages to be printed.**

To print page 12 in Division 2 through page 16 in Division 3, for instance, type *12D2-16D3* in the page numbers field. If you fail to indicate divisions, Word may not print the pages you want.

Trick **You can combine ranges, individual pages, and divisions when selecting pages to be printed.**

To print pages 1 through 12 of Division 1, and pages 19 and 63 of Division 4, for example, type *1D1-12D1,19D4,63D4* in the page numbers field.

Tip **Word saves some of the choices you make in the Print Options menu, but not all the choices.**

As you have already learned, Word saves the choices you make in the Options menu when you choose the **Q**uit command. Word also saves some of your choices in the Print Options menu. Not saved are the choices you make in the copies, summary sheet, range, and queued fields. Following is a list of the Print Options menu fields whose option choices are saved when you Quit Word:

    printer
    setup
    model
    graphics resolution
    hidden text
    widow/orphan control

draft
paper feed
duplex
draft
paper feed

Ink-Saving and Paper-Saving Strategies

Word 5 shows many more formats on-screen than previous versions of the program. You are wise to check for several common mistakes, listed in this section, and to preview print output before printing.

Tip   **Check your page-number options before printing.**

Remember, Word does not put page numbers on your printout unless you tell Word to do so using the **F**ormat **D**ivision **P**age-numbers command or a running head (see Chapter 6 for more information on formatting pages). To turn on automatic page numbers, choose the Yes option in the Format Division Page-numbers command.

Tip   **Check page breaks before printing.**

A common cause of wasted time (and paper) in printing is a bad page break, causing such problems as a heading positioned at the bottom of a page. Version 5 inserts page breaks automatically as you write, but that capability doesn't automatically rule out bad page breaks. As you add more text on page 3, for instance, you may push the page break on page 6 down so that it breaks up a table—and because you cannot see what's happening, you won't see the problem until you print.

To check page breaks and adjust them as necessary, choose the **P**rint **R**epaginate command and choose the Yes option in the confirm page breaks field. Be sure that the document is in the form it is to take when printed, with hidden text not visible (if you don't want to print it).

When you choose the **P**rintr **R**epaginate command with the Yes option in the confirm page breaks field, Word displays each page break by moving to the first character of the first line of the new page. Word waits for you to confirm the position of the page break. Enter Yes or use the up-arrow key to select a new page break. The page break can be moved above, but not below, the position Word chooses. When the page break is acceptable, enter Yes. Word places a page break at that position and moves on to the next page break for confirmation.

Remember that problems with page breaks can be reduced through
the proper use of Format Paragraph command's keep together and
keep follow fields.

Trick **Avoid orphaned headings by creating heading key codes in a
style sheet.**

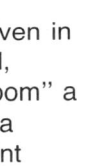

A common printing flaw is a heading or a subheading left all alone at
the bottom of a page. You can avoid this problem by checking your
document with Print Repaginate, but letting Word prevent these
isolated headings is much faster. For instructions, see "Modifying
NORMAL.STY" in Chapter 12, "Style Sheets."

Tip **Preview all document formats by using Print preView.**

Word 5's new Print preView command displays all the formats given in
the following list. Print preView does *not* display font choices and,
unlike a similar feature in WordPerfect, does not allow you to "zoom" a
portion of a page to view font choices. All fonts are displayed in a
special "preview" font, scaled to show your font-size choices. Print
preView shows the following aspects of your document:

All character formats, except fonts
All paragraph formats
Footnotes
Frames anchored with Format pOsition
Graphics
Line numbers
Lines and borders
Margins
Multiple columns of text
Page numbers
Proportionally spaced text
Revision marks
Running heads
Side-by-side paragraphs

You can use Print preView to check for common formatting errors,
such as lack of page numbers, misplaced running heads, improperly
formatted graphics (such as inadequate white space between the
graphic and the text), and problems in "floating" text around graphics.

Trick **Position the cursor on the page you want Print preView to
display first.**

Print preView always begins by displaying the page on which the
cursor is located. You can see other pages by pressing PgUp or PgDn
and other page-control keys in Print preView.

Trick **Press Ctrl-PgUp to view your whole document, page by page, in Print preView.**

If you place the cursor at the beginning of the file, and then select Print preView, you can preview each page of your document beginning with page 1.

Trick **Press Ctrl-F9 to preview your document.**

This new function-key assignment replaces the old Version 4 key that started the Print Repaginate command.

Trick **Press Ctrl-PgUp and Ctrl-PgDn to scroll immediately to the beginning or end of a document in Print preView.**

You can also drag the scroll boxes if you have a mouse.

Trick **Jump to a page or bookmark you specify.**

Choose the Jump command from the Print preView menu to scroll immediately to a page or bookmark you specify.

Trick **If all formats look OK, print directly from Print preView.**

Just choose the Print command from the Print preView menu.

Printing Your Document

Once you are sure that your document is properly formatted (using the techniques presented in "Ink-Saving and Paper-Saving Strategies"), you are ready to print your document. This section provides helpful information for the printing process.

Tip **To start printing, choose the Print Printer command or use the Ctrl-F8 shortcut.**

The Print Printer command sends print output directly to the printer. If you see the not-very-informative message, Enter Y to continue and Esc to cancel, it means that Word cannot get the printer to respond. Check your printer to make sure that it's plugged in, on-line, and stocked with paper.

Tip **Automatically print several files one after the other with queued printing.**

You can edit documents while printing goes on in the background. To print in the background, you put the files to be printed in a *queue*.

To start queued printing, do the following:

1. Load the document you want to print.

2. Choose the Yes option in the queued field of the Print Options menu.

3. Start printing by choosing the **P**rinter option in the Print menu.

4. To print additional documents one after the other, repeat steps 1 through 3 for each document you want to print.

At this point you can load another document and continue to edit. To interrupt queued printing, choose the **P**rint **Q**ueue **P**ause command. To continue queued printing after a pause, choose the **P**rint **Q**ueue **C**ontinue command.

Queued printing slows Word's screen response slightly, but the feature has been improved so much that it's usable even on slower systems.

Note: Because Word needs ample disk space to store the print files temporarily, this feature requires a hard disk or high-density floppy disks.

Trick **Print several documents at once by Using the Library Document Retrieval command.**

Queued printing gives you a way of printing as you work. If you want to print several documents while your system is unattended, however, use new features of the Library Document-retrieval command. Before you start, make sure that your printer has plenty of paper. The following procedure explains how to use the Library Document-retrieval command to queue printing:

1. Choose the **L**ibrary **D**ocument-retrieval command. Word retrieves the documents in the default directory. Use the **Q**uery command, if necessary, to expand the scope of the search. For information on using Query, see Chapter 9.

2. Highlight the first document you want to print and press Enter to mark it.

3. Continue marking documents this way—in the order in which you want them to print—until you have marked all the documents you want to print.

4. Choose the **P**rint command in the Document-retrieval menu. When the submenu appears, choose the Document or Both option to start printing. The Both option prints the summary sheet and the document.

Trick **You can chain many documents together to get continuous pagination through all the documents.**

This useful technique tells Word to continue printing with another document. You can use this feature, for instance, to chain 15 chapters together into a book, with continuous pagination throughout.

Chain printing with Word requires the INCLUDE statement, inserted into the first document you print. You then print the documents by using the **M**erge command in the Print menu. To use the INCLUDE instruction, follow these steps:

1. Move the cursor to the end of the first file in the series of files you want to print.

2. Press Ctrl-[(left bracket) to enter the left chevron.

3. Type *INCLUDE* (in uppercase or lowercase letters) and the file name of the next document in the series to be printed. Include path information if necessary.

4. Press Ctrl-] (right bracket) to enter the right chevron.

Your entry should look something like this:

«INCLUDE c:\MSWORD\DOCS\CHAPTER2.DOC»

To print a file with an INCLUDE statement, use the **P**rint **M**erge command. When Word encounters this instruction in your document, the program looks for the file named CHAPTER2.DOC and begins printing it at the INCLUDE statement's location. (You can embed an INCLUDE instruction in the middle of a document so that Word will insert at the INCLUDE instruction's location the file you name—with no page break.)

You can chain together several documents in this way by giving several INCLUDE instructions. The following instructions print four chapters of a book-length manuscript, plus the appendix and bibliography. You can place all the instructions at the end of Chapter 1.

«INCLUDE c:\MSWORD\DOCS\CHAPTER2.DOC»
«INCLUDE c:\MSWORD\DOCS\CHAPTER3.DOC»
«INCLUDE c:\MSWORD\DOCS\CHAPTER4.DOC»
«INCLUDE c:\MSWORD\DOCS\APPENDIX.DOC»
«INCLUDE c:\MSWORD\DOCS\BIBLIOGR.DOC»

The printout will have continuous pagination through all five documents.

Note: Insert forced page breaks between the INCLUDE instructions if you want Word to start a new page where each new file begins.

Troubleshooting Printer Problems

This section provides information about problems you may encounter when using Word with your printer.

Trap **Your document prints without fonts or graphics.**

You probably selected the Yes option in the Print Options menu draft field to print a draft, and then quit Word. As you have seen, Word saves the choice you make in this field.

Trick **If you cannot get your printer to work with Word, quit Word and make sure that your printer works with DOS.**

Check to make sure that your printer is plugged in, turned on, and on-line. Check all the connections and tighten them if necessary. At a DOS prompt, press Ctrl-P. Then type *dir* and press Enter. Your printer should print the disk directory. If the printer doesn't print the directory, consult your printer and computer manuals to make sure that you have installed your printer properly. Don't hesitate to ask for your dealer's help; many people encounter difficulty setting up printers, especially serial printers. If you are using a serial printer, you may have to boot your computer every time with a MODE instruction in an AUTOEXEC.BAT file. For more information, see your DOS and printer manuals—and get help.

Trick **If your printer works with DOS but not with Word, check that you have chosen the correct port in Print Options** setup **field.**

Many computers have more than one serial or parallel port. You may have entered the wrong port assignment in the setup field of the Print Options command. If you did, Word displays the message Printer is not ready, even though your printer is turned on, hooked up, and on-line. Try changing the port assignment.

Trap **The printer output may be garbled if you choose the wrong printer description file or set the DOS MODE command incorrectly.**

Make sure that you are using the correct printer description PRD file. If you use a serial printer, double-check the MODE instruction you use to boot your computer.

Trap   **Your printer may not print the ASCII extended character set.**

Not all printers can handle the extended character set, the one you use to enter foreign-language characters, symbols, and mathematical characters—even though you see the symbols on the screen. Before wasting time creating documents with these symbols, make sure that your printer can print them.

Trap   **The printer switches fonts in inappropriate places.**

Because you cannot see your font choices on the screen, you're almost certain to run into this problem if you like to use more than one font. Suppose that you choose Helvetica and start typing. Next, you type a word in boldface. To continue typing without boldface, you press Alt-space bar to cancel the character emphasis. But you have also canceled Helvetica without realizing that fact, so the printer's default font (perhaps Courier) reappears at this point.

The only way to solve this problem once and for all is to wait until Word can display your font choices on-screen. For now, however, try these strategies:

❏ Define a new default font (see Chapter 12, "Style Sheets"). Then when you press Alt-space bar, Word reverts to Helvetica, Times Roman, or any other font you specify.

❏ If you have a color monitor, choose distinctive colors for different font sizes.

❏ Enter all formats with style-sheet key codes. If you create style sheets, you can combine font, paragraph, and other formatting choices so that you enter them all simultaneously with just once command (see Chapter 12, "Style Sheets," for instructions).

If you follow these instructions, you will find that this problem surfaces very infrequently.

Chapter Summary

Word's printing capabilities are constrained by your printer. When you choose a printer description file in the `printer` field of the Print Options menu, Word reads information from this file, such as the fonts and font sizes your printer supports and whether it can print graphics.

Word provides excellent support for laser printers. With Hewlett-Packard LaserJet printers and compatibles, you can use all the font cartridges Hewlett-Packard offers. What is more, you can use the downloadable, disk-based fonts sold by Hewlett-Packard. You can also use other downloadable disk fonts, as long as they come with a Word 5-compatible PRD file. Many font manufacturers provide this support. Word downloads disk fonts automatically; you simply format your document, and when it's time to print, Word automatically downloads the fonts you need.

If you have a PostScript-compatible printer, such as the Apple LaserWriter, you can use all the internal fonts your printer has. What is more, you can choose from more than 200 downloadable disk fonts sold by Adobe Corporation. Downloading of PostScript fonts is automatic.

If you use downloadable fonts, put all the fonts and other necessary files (including the PRD, DAT, and INI files for your printer) in their own separate directory. Use the Print Options command to name your PRD file so that Word knows the full path name.

The Print Options menu gives you many ways to print. Remember, though, that most options are saved, including your choices in the `graphics resolution` and `draft` fields. You may not want to use these options the next time you print, and you may forget you have chosen them. To avoid such problems, use a printing macro (see Chapter 13 for instructions for creating macros).

Before printing, choose the Print Repaginate command and select the Yes option in the `confirm page breaks` field. Check for bad page breaks and fix them. Preview all other document formats, using the Print preView command. Look for misplaced running heads, lack of page numbers, and other common formatting errors. If everything looks fine, print directly from Print preView.

To print while you work on other documents, use queued printing. To print many documents at once while your system is unattended, use the Library Document-retrieval Print command.

12

Style Sheets

Relatively few Word users use style sheets regularly. That's a pity, because probably no single Word feature can increase productivity—and quality—more rapidly than style-sheet formatting. Using style sheets, you can do the following:

❑ Modify existing speed keys so that they enter precisely the formats you want. If you want the Alt-T (hanging indent) key to enter a 0.3-inch hanging indent, you can easily modify this key to enter precisely the format you want. You can add additional formats to existing keys, as well. You can modify Alt-T so that it prints text right-justified, for instance.

❑ Create new speed keys to handle your own unique formatting tasks. You can create a speed key to enter a list format, which prints a product name flush to the left margin, sets a tab at 3.0 inches, and prints a product description with a 3.0-inch hanging indent.

❑ Customize formatting defaults with automatic styles. Perhaps the most powerful technique of all, this style-sheet feature gives you a way to correct some of Word's most irritating default formatting settings, such as printing page numbers in the default font and failing to superscript footnote reference marks.

Style sheets truly open the pathway to high-productivity formatting with Word. You learn how to get off the country roads and on to the expressway by reading this chapter. It covers the following:

❑ Introducing style sheets

❑ Understanding style-sheet entries

❑ Modifying NORMAL.STY

❑ Creating copies of NORMAL.STY for other directories

335

❏ Editing and managing style sheets

❏ Formatting documents with style sheets

❏ Handling problems

Introducing Style Sheets

Style sheets provide an easy way to customize Word's formatting capabilities. Using style sheets, you can modify existing speed keys (the Alt-key formatting commands), create entirely new speed keys, and customize many of Word's default formatting settings.

To create, edit, and save style sheets, you use the Gallery command. The Gallery command menu includes all the commands you need to do these tasks.

Once you create and save a style sheet, you attach it to documents using the Format Stylesheet Attach command. When you attach a style sheet to a document, the style sheet's key codes become available for use while you write and edit. When you save the document using the Transfer Save command, Word saves hidden information that tells the program which style sheet to use. The next time you load the document, Word automatically uses the style sheet you attached to that document.

If you name no style sheet in the Format Stylesheet Attach command, Word uses a default style sheet called NORMAL.STY.

You should understand how Word looks for NORMAL.STY. When you start the program, Word looks for NORMAL.STY in the default directory—the directory from which you start Word (or the directory named in the Transfer Options command menu setup field). If Word finds a file called NORMAL.STY in that directory, Word uses that file automatically for all new documents, as well as any document stored in the default directory to which no style sheet has been attached.

This information is very important if you are to take full advantage of the default style sheet. Because Word always uses the default directory's NORMAL.STY file, you can create several copies of NORMAL.STY, modify them, and store each in its own document directory. That way, every time you make that directory the default and open a document in that directory, that directory's NORMAL.STY is automatically applied to the document. This technique is extremely powerful, yet almost totally automatic, and you learn how to take full advantage of it in this chapter.

If you have used previous versions of Word, you should know that modifying NORMAL.STY is no longer so costly. In previous versions of Word, the NORMAL.STY speed keys were disabled when you modified NORMAL.STY. Although you could still use the NORMAL.STY speed keys if you pressed Alt-X before pressing the speed key's code, the number of keystrokes used in formatting a document was substantially raised. If you wanted to use the default speed keys without pressing Alt-X, however, you had to recreate all the speed keys manually in your new style sheet. In other words, creating a style sheet penalized users by increasing the keystrokes needed for formatting tasks or by forcing them through the tedium of re-creating all the default key codes.

In Version 5, modifying NORMAL.STY no longer disables the default speed keys. If you modify NORMAL.STY, you no longer have to press Alt-X to use the default speed keys. Nor do you have to add the default speed keys to the edited version of NORMAL.STY. You can make just a few quick modifications to NORMAL.STY, and you're in business.

Because modifying NORMAL.STY is so easy now, and because the payoff is enormous, this chapter concentrates on modifying NORMAL.STY. Occasions may still arise when you want to create much larger and more complex style sheets, but almost all users will find the techniques in this chapter sufficient.

Understanding Style-Sheet Entries

Style sheets consist of style-sheet entries, each of which is numbered. To create and use style sheets successfully, it pays to understand what these entries are and what they contain.

When you create a style-sheet entry in the Gallery, you define a style that Word can use. In this context, a style is a character, paragraph, division, or tab format, or a collection of these formats. You can set up the entry so that it can be used by pressing a speed key. Some styles can be applied automatically—in other words, they apply to any document to which the style sheet is attached.

Every style-sheet entry contains the following components:

❑ *Key code.* For styles you apply with speed keys, you choose a key code. The key code is a one-letter or two-letter command entered by holding the Alt key and pressing the appropriate keys. If you create automatic styles, you do not enter a key code in most cases.

❑ *Usage.* When you choose a usage, you tell Word what kind of format you are creating (character, paragraph, or division). For clarity, this component ought to be called "format type." If you think of usage that way, it shouldn't give you trouble.

❑ *Variant.* Every style-sheet entry must have a unique number, called the variant. The variant number is needed to distinguish one entry from others. Some variants are named; these variants are Word's automatic styles. If you choose one of these named variants (such as `footnote ref` or `running head`), Word automatically applies the formats you choose to the document.

❑ *Remark.* This component of the entry is optional. Use the remark to describe the key code so that its function is obvious.

❑ *Formatting information.* This component consists of the character, paragraph, division, or tab formats you attach to the entry by using the Format command in the Gallery menu.

Now that you have surveyed the basics, you can get to the details, starting with the mysterious Gallery itself. In the following section, you learn to modify NORMAL.STY so that Word formats precisely the way you want with a minimum of keyboard fussing.

Modifying NORMAL.STY

To modify NORMAL.STY, you use the Gallery. Think of the Gallery as a workshop for creating, editing, loading, and saving style sheets. The Gallery's tools provide everything you need to define character, paragraph, and division styles precisely the way you want them. You can assign each style you create to a different Alt-key code so that the style is readily available as you work in your document.

Tip **Use the Gallery command to enter the style-sheet creation mode.**

After you use the **G**allery command, a new window and command menu appear (see fig. 12.1). The commands in the Gallery command menu resemble their counterparts in the edit menu, with one major exception: the Gallery commands affect style-sheet entries, not text.

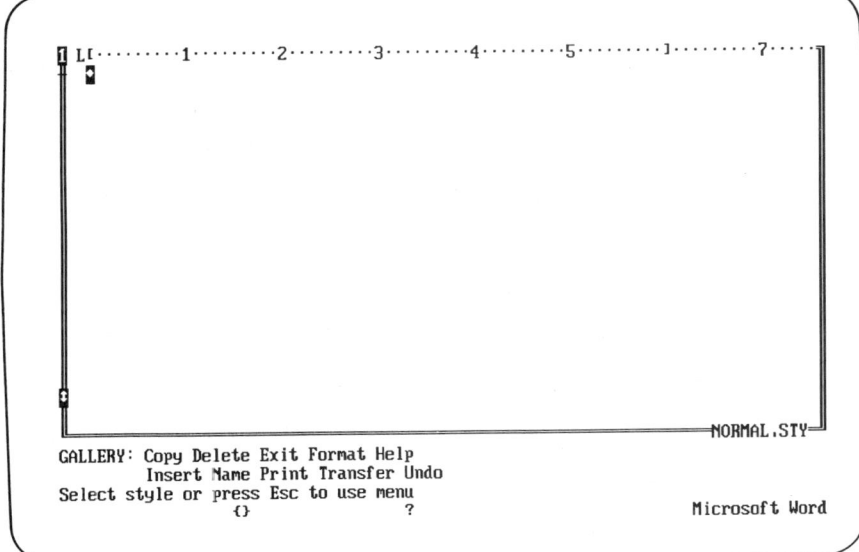

Fig. 12.1.

The Gallery command menu and window.

Working with the Gallery may be somewhat disconcerting at first; you cannot enter or edit text directly in the style-sheet display window. You must use command menus to create key codes, to name usages and variants, to add remarks, and to choose formatting information for the entries. In general, you use the Insert command to name a new entry, choose a usage and variant, and enter a remark. Then you use the **F**ormat command or commands to attach formats to the style you have created.

Trick **Modify the standard paragraph and character formats.**

As you have already learned, using Word without style sheets means putting up with two frustrations:

❑ If you like to format standard paragraphs as you write, you lose all the standard formatting when you shift formats to type a heading, table, quotation, or list. You must enter the standard formats all over again or copy them from earlier paragraphs.

❏ If you like to use a nondefault character font, you lose the font whenever you press Alt-space bar to cancel character formatting.

You can cure both of these problems simply by creating a new standard paragraph with Word. When you define an entry that employs the standard paragraph usage, Word automatically applies the character format you choose to all the NORMAL.STY speed keys. When you press Alt-space bar to cancel character emphasis, Word reverts to the font you chose for this entry.

The following tutorial is basic to the other tricks in this chapter. Follow the steps carefully the first time through; subsequent tricks assume that you know the procedure.

To modify the standard paragraph and character style, do the following:

1. In DOS, create a new directory called \MSWORD\TEST. You will use this directory to modify NORMAL.STY in a way that does not disturb existing documents.

2. Start Word from the new directory you created. Choose the **T**ransfer **O**ptions command and make sure that the directory name appears in the setup field.

3. Type two or three paragraphs of text to use as a "guinea pig."

4. Choose the **G**allery command.

5. When the Gallery appears, choose the **I**nsert command (see fig. 12.2).

Fig. 12.2.

The Gallery Insert command menu.

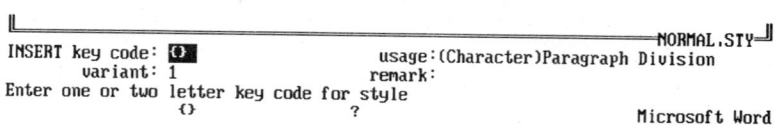

```
INSERT key code: ▯             usage:(Character)Paragraph Division
          variant: 1            remark:
Enter one or two letter key code for style
             {}                     ?
                                                    Microsoft Word
```

6. Press P in the key code field.

7. Choose Paragraph from the usage field.

8. Highlight the `variant` field and press F1. Choose `standard` from the list (see fig. 12.3).

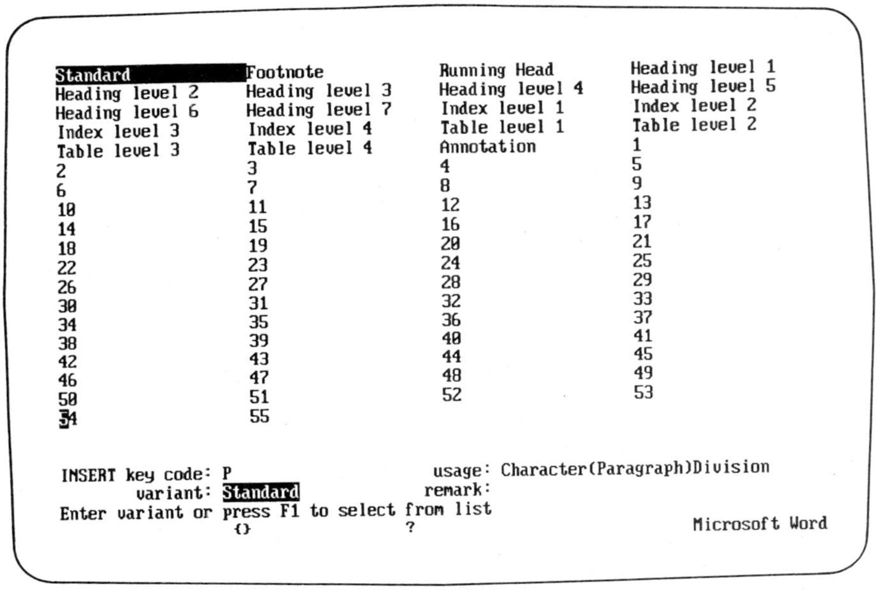

Fig. 12.3.

Choosing a paragraph variant from the F1 list.

```
Standard               Footnote           Running Head      Heading level 1
Heading level 2        Heading level 3    Heading level 4   Heading level 5
Heading level 6        Heading level 7    Index level 1     Index level 2
Index level 3          Index level 4      Table level 1     Table level 2
Table level 3          Table level 4      Annotation        1
2                      3                  4                 5
6                      7                  8                 9
10                     11                 12                13
14                     15                 16                17
18                     19                 20                21
22                     23                 24                25
26                     27                 28                29
30                     31                 32                33
34                     35                 36                37
38                     39                 40                41
42                     43                 44                45
46                     47                 48                49
50                     51                 52                53
54                     55

INSERT key code: P              usage: Character(Paragraph)Division
      variant: Standard         remark:
Enter variant or press F1 to select from list
                 {}             ?                    Microsoft Word
```

When you press F1 in the `variant` field after choosing the paragraph usage, you see the paragraph variants. (If you choose `Character` or `Division`, you see a different list.)

9. Type *standard paragraph format* in the `remarks` field, and press Enter to carry out the command.

Word enters a new style-sheet entry in the Gallery window (see fig. 12.4). Note, however, that the entry still has the default formats. You must now use the **Format** command to attach new formats to this entry.

10. Choose the Gallery menu's **Format Paragraph** command. Choose `Justified` in the `alignment` field, type *0.5"* in the `first line` field, and type *2* in the `line spacing` field (see fig. 12.5). Press Enter to carry out the command.

Word creates the new style-sheet entry (see fig. 12.6). Note that line spacing is shown in points; the default is a 12-point font printed with 24-point line spacing.

Fig. 12.4.

Style-sheet entry
without
formatting.

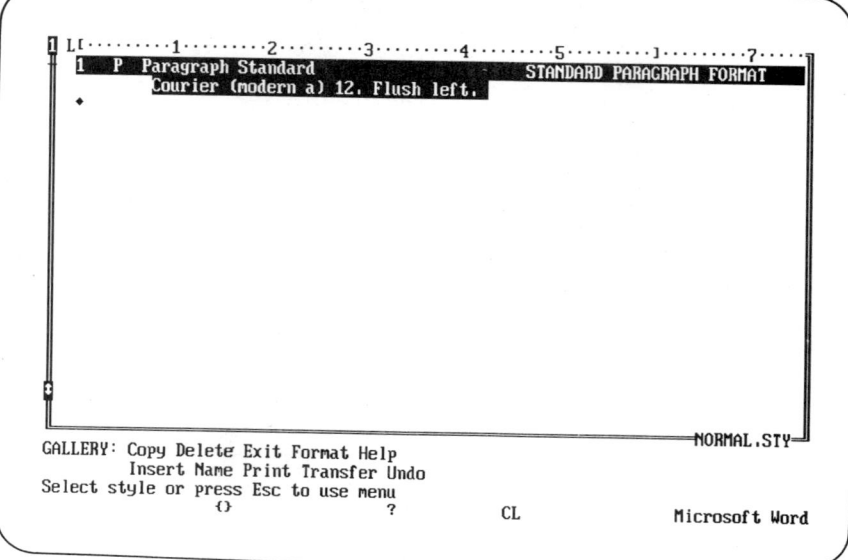

Fig. 12.4.

Style-sheet entry
without
formatting.

```
L[········1·····2·····3·····4·····5····]·····7····
1  P  Paragraph Standard                    STANDARD PARAGRAPH FORMAT
            Courier (modern a) 12, Flush left,
  ◆




                                                              NORMAL.STY
GALLERY: Copy Delete Exit Format Help
         Insert Name Print Transfer Undo
Select style or press Esc to use menu
              {}                    ?          CL        Microsoft Word
```

Fig. 12.5.

Using the Gallery
menu's Format
Paragraph
command.

```
L[········1·····2·····3·····4·····5····]·····7····
1  P  Paragraph Standard                    STANDARD PARAGRAPH FORMAT
            Courier (modern a) 12, Flush left,
  ◆




FORMAT PARAGRAPH alignment: Left Centered Right(Justified)
      left indent: 0"        first line: 0.5      right indent: 0"
      line spacing: 2        space before: 0 li   space after: 0 li
      keep together: Yes(No) keep follow: Yes(No) side by side: Yes(No)
Enter measurement in lines or type Auto
              {}                    ?          CL        Microsoft Word
```

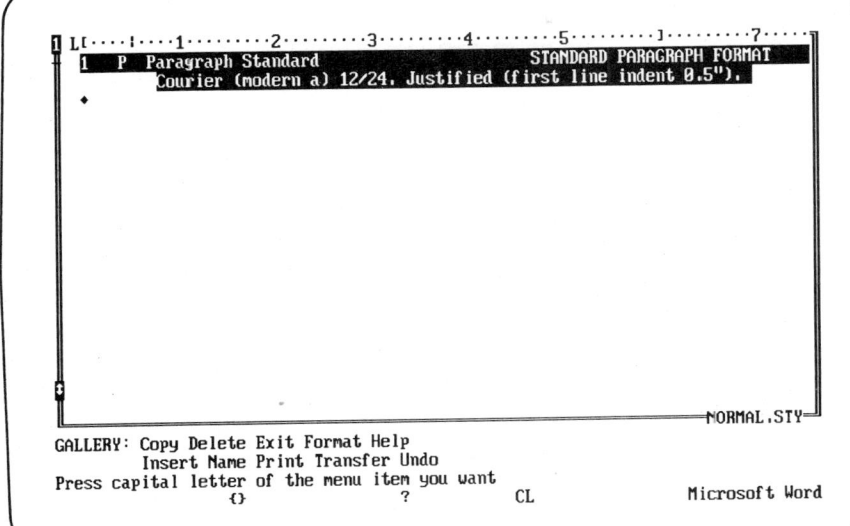

Fig. 12.6.

Formatted style-
sheet entry.

11. Press Alt-F8 to display the font name field of the Format Character menu. Press F1 to see a list of available fonts and choose the font you want for your new default paragraph. Then carry out the command.

Word adds the chosen formats to the style-sheet entry (see fig. 12.7).

12. Press **E**xit to leave the Gallery. Examine your "guinea pig" paragraphs.

The paragraphs should show the chosen formats. Word applies these formats automatically to all standard text paragraphs in your document.

Trick **Modify the Alt-L format so that it enters the old default paragraph formats.**

After you create the new Alt-P standard paragraph format for typing standard text paragraphs, you may find occasions when you need the old "plain vanilla" format (single-space, flush-left, no automatic indent). This format is useful, for instance, when typing free-form text, tables, and lists. To modify Alt-L to hold the old paragraph formats, choose the **G**allery **I**nsert command. Press L in the key code field, choose Paragraph from the usage field, and tab over the variant field so that Word automatically chooses a number. Type *old standard paragraph*

Fig. 12.7.

Entry after adding
new character
formats.

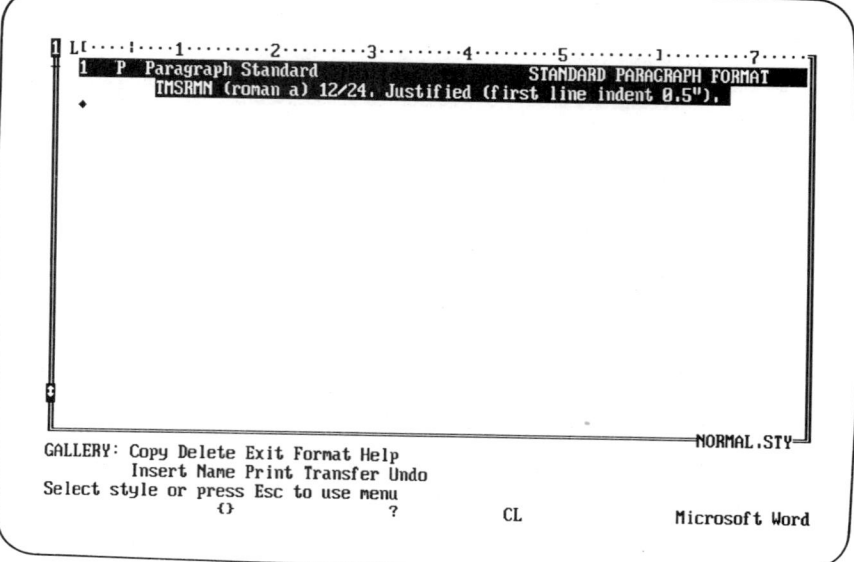

```
L[····!····1·········2·········3········4·········5·········]·······7····
 1   P   Paragraph Standard                    STANDARD PARAGRAPH FORMAT
         TMSRMN (roman a) 12/24, Justified (first line indent 0.5"),
     ◆

                                                            NORMAL.STY
GALLERY: Copy Delete Exit Format Help
         Insert Name Print Transfer Undo
Select style or press Esc to use menu
              {}              ?          CL          Microsoft Word
```

in the remarks field, and press Enter to carry out the command. Next,
choose the **F**ormat **P**aragraph command from the Gallery menu.
Choose Left alignment, and type *0* in the first line and *1 li* in the
line spacing fields. Carry out the command.

After you return to your document, position the cursor on one of your
"guinea pig" paragraphs. Press Alt-L to cancel the new standard
paragraph format. Then press Alt-P to restore it. As you can see, style-
sheet formatting is very easy—and very powerful.

Trick   **Modify the default character format for page numbers.**

As noted in Chapter 8, when you use the Format Division Page-
numbers command, you're stuck with the default font for your printer.
Even if your text is formatted in Helvetica, you see Courier in the page
numbers!

The way out of this trap is to define an automatic style for page
numbers using the character formatting you want. To do so, choose
the **G**allery **I**nsert command. Leave the key code field blank. Choose
the Character usage. Highlight the variant field and press F1.
Choose page number from the list. Press Tab, type *page number
format* in the remarks field, and press Enter. Now press Alt-F8 to bring
up the Format Character menu's font name field. Press F1 to see a list
of available fonts and choose the one you want for page numbers.

Press Tab to choose a font size, if you want. Then carry out the command. Save the modified style sheet using the **G**allery **T**ransfer **S**ave command, using the NORMAL.STY file name.

After you define the character format this way, Word uses it automatically for every document to which this style sheet is attached.

Trick **Create a new default style for footnote reference marks.**

As noted in Chapter 5, Word doesn't superscript footnote reference marks—you must do so manually. You can use an automatic style to redefine the footnote reference mark format.

To do so, choose the **G**allery **I**nsert command. Leave the key code field blank. Choose the Character usage. Highlight the variant field and press F1. Choose footnote ref from the list. Press Tab, type *footnote ref mark* in the remarks field, and press Enter. Now use the **G**allery **F**ormat **C**haracter command and choose the Superscript option in the position field. Then carry out the command. Save the modified style sheet using the **G**allery **T**ransfer **S**ave command, using the NORMAL.STY file name.

After you define the character format this way, Word uses it automatically for every document to which this style sheet is attached.

Trick **Create a new default style for footnote text.**

By default, Word uses the standard paragraph format for footnote text. If you have created a new standard paragraph format for text paragraphs, the footnote text format changes too. If the format is satisfactory for footnotes, you need do nothing to change it. If the format is not satisfactory, however, you can modify the footnote text format, using an automatic style.

To create a new default format for footnote text, choose the **G**allery **I**nsert command. Leave the key code field blank. Choose the Paragraph usage. Highlight the variant field and press F1. Choose footnote from the list. Press Tab, type *footnote text* in the remarks field, and press Enter. Now use the **G**allery **F**ormat **P**aragraph command and choose the paragraph formats you want for footnote text. If you want a new default character format, use the **F**ormat **C**haracter command. If you want, you can specify a different character format, such as a smaller font size.

After you define the footnote text format this way, Word uses it automatically for every document to which this style sheet is attached.

Trick **Define a new default format for headings.**

As you learned in Chapter 6, linking document headings and outline headings opens up powerful techniques for tracking your document's organization and restructuring large text domains. This link is far from automatic, however. When you enter headings in document mode, you must deliberately format them as outline headings by shifting to outline edit mode and pressing Alt-0 and Alt-9.

To take full advantage of the dynamic link between documents and outlines, create speed keys for headings. Speed keys can automatically choose fonts, enter blank lines, keep the heading with following text to prevent unwanted page breaks, and create dynamic links with outlines. The key to this trick is using a `Heading level` variant that automatically defines the format as an outline heading. If you choose the `Heading level 1` variant, for instance, the entry is automatically formatted as a Level 1 entry in outline edit mode.

Before you start, plan your headings. Table 12.1 lists one pattern of headings from which you can draw ideas. Use this table to enter a series of three headings that automatically format text as headings in outline edit mode.

Note: After you create speed keys using Alt-H, you still can get Help by pressing Alt-XH.

Table 12.1.
Speed Keys for Headings

Key code:	*H1*
Usage:	Paragraph
Variant:	Heading level 1
Remark:	First-level heading
Format Character menu:	
bold:	Yes
font name:	Helvetica
font size:	14
Format Paragraph menu:	
alignment:	Centered
space before:	2 li
space after:	2 li
keep follow:	Yes

Table 12.1—Continued

Key code:	H2
Usage:	Paragraph
Variant:	Heading level 2
Remark:	Second-level heading
Format Character menu:	
bold:	Yes
font name:	Helvetica
font size:	12
Format Paragraph menu:	
alignment:	Left
space after:	1 li
keep follow:	Yes
Key code:	H3
Usage:	Paragraph
Variant:	Heading level 3
Remark:	Third-level heading
Format Character menu:	
italic:	Yes
font name:	Helvetica
font size:	12
Format Paragraph menu:	
alignment:	Left
space after:	1 li
keep follow:	Yes

Trick **Enter running head formats automatically.**

As you have learned, choosing the Format Running-head command doesn't actually format the running-head text; this command just defines the text as a running head. To format the text, you must use the **F**ormat **C**haracter and **F**ormat **P**aragraph commands. If you find yourself doing so frequently, define a running-head style-sheet entry using an automatic style.

To do so, choose the **G**allery **I**nsert command and leave the key code field blank. Choose Paragraph usage. Highlight the variant field, press F1, and choose the Running Head variant from the list. Carry out the command. After Word inserts the style-sheet entry, try formatting it with flush-right paragraph alignment. Be sure to use the **F**ormat **C**haracter command to choose the character format you want.

Trick   **Create a new standard division format.**

You can modify the standard division format with another useful automatic style, the standard division usage. To use it, select the Gallery Insert command. Leave the key code field blank. Choose Division usage, press F1 in the variant field, choose standard from the list, and carry out the command. Use the Format command to bring up the Format Division menu. (If you choose Division, you can use only division formats, so Word immediately displays the Format Division menu.) Choose division formats to your heart's content—change the margins, redefine the page size, alter the vertical placement of running heads, choose a new location for page numbers, place footnotes at the end of the document, and so on. All these formats become the defaults for any document to which this style sheet is attached!

Trick   **Add new styles to your style sheet with the Format Stylesheet Record command.**

You have learned, so far, how to modify existing key codes and how to create some new ones. As you create your documents, you will doubtless think of additional modifications for existing key codes, and you will probably think of some new ones to add to your style sheet. In general, if you have just entered a format in your document by using the Format commands, and you think that you may use that format again, it is a likely candidate for a style-sheet entry. Thanks to the Format Stylesheet Record command, you needn't duplicate your efforts to create the entry: you can record the formats already chosen so that they automatically appear in your style sheet.

To record a style, do the following steps:

1. Select the format you have created.

   If you have created a character format, select just the characters you formatted that way. If you have created a paragraph or division format, just place the cursor in the paragraph or division. If you have combined character and paragraph formatting, use the extend-selection mode to select all the text that has the formats you have chosen.

2. Choose the Format Stylesheet Record command or use the Alt-F10 keyboard shortcut.

   When the Format Stylesheet Record menu appears, you see a version of the Gallery Insert command menu (see fig. 12.8).

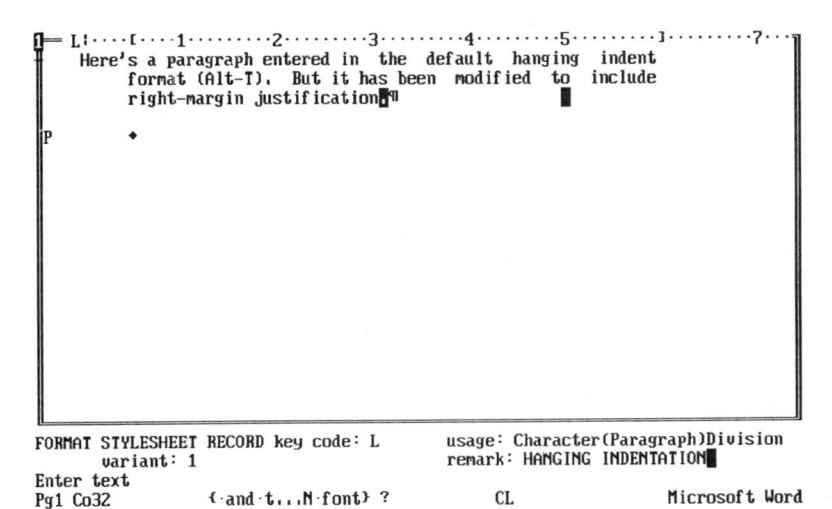

Fig. 12.8.

The Format
Stylesheet Record
command menu.

3. Enter the key code in the key code field.

   If you are modifying an existing key code, enter the key
   code's letter. (To modify the Alt-Q key, for instance, type *Q*.) If
   you are creating a new key code, choose a letter or number
   that's not already used by NORMAL.STY, such as A, G, H, V,
   W, Y, or Z. (If you create a code using a NORMAL.STY key
   code's letters, you cancel the default key code for any
   document to which this style sheet is attached.) You can
   create two-letter key codes, but they shouldn't start with one
   of the NORMAL.STY key code's letters.

4. Choose the Character usage if the format contains character
   formatting exclusively; choose the Paragraph usage if the
   format contains both character and paragraph formats. The
   Paragraph usage format can include tabs too.

5. Tab over the variant field so that Word chooses a number
   automatically.

6. Type in the remarks field a remark about the format you are
   recording.

7. Press Enter to carry out the command.

That's all it takes to record a format. Word automatically enters the
format in your style sheet, together with all the chosen formats.

Trick   Use the recording technique to modify existing speed keys.

If you have chosen justified alignment for standard paragraphs, you may want to modify other paragraph speed keys, such as Alt-N (indent), Alt-Q (quotation), and Alt-T (hanging indent), so that they include justification too. It's easy to do so. Just type some text, and format it using one of the speed keys that you want to modify. Then use the **F**ormat commands in the edit command menu to modify the format as you wish. Finally, choose the **F**ormat **S**tylesheet **R**ecord command. Use the same key code, and complete the entry as explained in the preceding trick.

Creating Copies of NORMAL.STY for Other Directories

Now that you have created a NORMAL.STY style sheet with modified default formats, modified default speed keys, and a few new speed keys, here's some excellent news:

❏   You can copy this style sheet to other directories where it becomes the default for documents in those directories.

❏   You can modify the copies of NORMAL.STY with a few keystrokes so that they have fonts, line-spacing formats, and other formats appropriate for the documents in these directories.

Trick   Copy the modified version of NORMAL.STY to another directory.

To copy NORMAL.STY to another directory, use the **G**allery command to view the style sheet. Then use the **G**allery **T**ransfer **S**ave command. Type the full path name of the directory to which you want the copy of the style sheet to be saved, including the file name NORMAL.STY, in the filename field. If you want to save a copy of NORMAL.STY to the directory called \MSWORD\LETTERS, for instance, type *msword**letters**normal* in the filename field. (You can omit the extension, STY, which Word supplies.)

Continue in this way, putting a copy of the modified NORMAL.STY file into every document directory.

Trick **Customize the modified NORMAL.STY with a few keystrokes.**

When you created the first modified version of NORMAL.STY, you chose double-line spacing, right-margin justification, and an attractive font such as Helvetica. These formats are not necessarily appropriate for writing letters. For letters, you may prefer the Letter Gothic font, flush-left paragraph formatting, and single-line spacing. You can modify the NORMAL.STY file you copied to the directory in which you write letters to accommodate these more appropriate formats.

Now hold on to your seat—the following technique is extremely powerful.

1. Use the **G**allery command's **T**ransfer **L**oad command to load the modified version of NORMAL.STY.

2. Press Shift-F10 to select all the entries in the Gallery.

3. Press Alt-F8 to bring up the Format Character command font name field (see fig. 12.9).

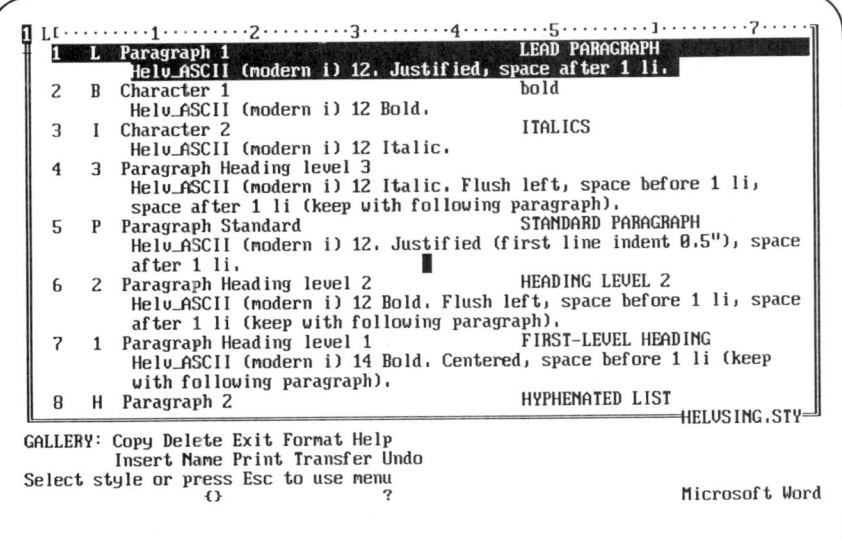

Fig. 12.9.

Changing the entire style sheet's character format.

4. Press F1 to see a list of available fonts. Choose the font you want for all formats and press Enter. After you carry out the command, Word changes the font assignment in each entry (see fig. 12.10).

Fig. 12.10.

The effect of
changing the
entire style
sheet's character
format.

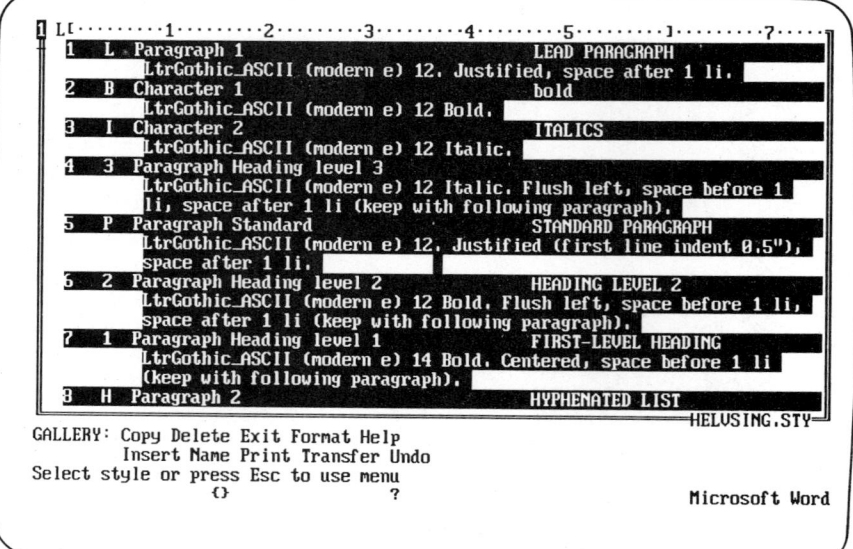

5. Choose the **F**ormat **P**aragraph command and choose the
   paragraph formats you want to apply to all entries.

   For instance, you can choose flush-left alignment and single-
   line spacing.

6. Save the new version of the style sheet to a different directory
   (so that you don't overwrite the first version). To save the new
   version to \MSWORD\LETTERS, for instance, type
   \MSWORD\LETTERS\NORMAL (in uppercase or lowercase
   letters) in the filename field of the Gallery Transfer Save
   menu and carry out the command.

As you can see, this technique is very powerful indeed. Using it, you
can create versions of NORMAL.STY appropriate for each type of
document you create. The first version, the one with the Helvetica font
and double-line spacing, is appropriate for reports. The new one, the
one with flush-left alignment, Letter Gothic fonts, and single-line
spacing, is more appropriate for letters. Use your imagination—and
take full advantage of your printer's multiple-font capabilities—to create
default style sheets appropriate for each type of document you create.

Editing Style Sheets

As you work with your style sheets, you find room for changes—and additional entries. Happily, editing existing entries and adding new ones are easy to do.

Tip **You don't need to attach a style sheet to the current document to be able to view and change the style sheet.**

If you want to work with a style sheet other than the one attached to the current document, choose **G**allery **T**ransfer **L**oad, specify the name of the style sheet you want to work with (or select it from a list), and then press Enter. Word displays the specified style sheet in the Gallery window, replacing the style sheet attached to the current document.

Tip **Use the cursor-movement keys to highlight styles in a style sheet.**

When you choose the **G**allery command, the first style in the style sheet is highlighted. You can move forward through the style sheet, highlighting one style at a time, by pressing the down-arrow or right-arrow key. You can move backward through the entries by pressing the up-arrow or left-arrow key. If the style sheet contains more styles than fit on one screen, you can press PgDn and PgUp to move forward and backward one screen at a time.

Tip **You can delete, copy, and move style-sheet entries.**

Although you cannot directly edit the text in a style sheet, you can delete entries or rearrange them, using standard techniques. Here's a brief overview:

- ❏ To delete an entry, select it and press Del or use the **G**allery **D**elete command.

- ❏ To copy an entry to the scrap, use the **G**allery **C**opy command.

- ❏ To move an entry, use the Del key or **G**allery **D**elete command, and move the cursor to the place you want the entry to appear. Then press Ins.

Trick **Rearrange style-sheet entries quickly with the mouse (Ctrl-left-click).**

As you create style-sheet entries, Word inserts them above the currently selected entry. Unless you pay attention to what you're doing, you probably will wind up with a style sheet of entries in helter-skelter order. This lack of order is no problem for Word but could pose problems for you as you set out to edit or modify a lengthy style sheet.

You can use standard keyboard techniques to move entries around in a style sheet, but an even better way is available to mouse users. To move an entry with the mouse, select the entry by clicking. Point to where you want the entry to appear, hold the Ctrl key, and click the left button.

Tip **Extend the selection just as you do when working with a document.**

You can press F6 to turn on extend mode and then use the direction keys to extend the selection either backward or forward, selecting as many styles as you want. You can select all the styles in a style sheet and change the font in all of them at once, for example, instead of changing the font of each entry individually.

When more than one style is highlighted, the Format command fields are blank. You should enter options in only the fields you want to apply to all the highlighted styles. Otherwise, you may inadvertently change a format that you intended to retain in one of the highlighted styles.

When you use F6, you extend the selection to include entire styles. You cannot select only part of a style definition.

Trick **Use Shift-F10 to attach a character style to every entry in the style sheet.**

Here's a trick for those who wish to use a nondefault character style consistently throughout a document. The default style for a laser printer, for instance, is the Courier font. To use the Palatino font throughout your document, create a style sheet. When you have inserted all the entries you want, press F10 to select all the entries and use the **G**allery **F**ormat **C**haracter command. Type the desired font name in the font command field and press Enter.

Tip **You can change a style's key code or remark.**

You can use the Gallery menu's **N**ame command to change a style's key code or remark. You may not have much occasion to use this command, especially if you have taken the time to plan a style sheet in advance. Sometimes, however, you may need to change an obscure or hard-to-remember key code, or you may want to change a remark you typed in lowercase to uppercase.

Trick **Use the NORMAL.STY Alt-key formatting commands to add formats to style-sheet entries.**

Here's an undocumented, super-nifty trick unknown even to most Word cognoscenti. Select a style-sheet entry in the Gallery and use one of the NORMAL.STY Alt-key formatting commands. Presto! The formats you entered with the Alt key are added instantly to the entry's formatting definition.

Note: You can add character formats to entries created with the character usage, but you cannot add paragraph or division formats to such entries. Likewise, you cannot add character or paragraph formats to division usages. Paragraph usages, on the other hand, can receive character *and* paragraph commands.

Managing Style Sheets

Like all other work you do with Word, you have to save style sheets deliberately if you want to keep the work for the next Word session. You may encounter a number of pitfalls, however, in naming style-sheet files. You will find it helpful to devote some thought to this subject before creating many style sheets.

Trick **Store a NORMAL.STY file in all your document directories.**

When you start Word, the program looks in the current directory for the default NORMAL.STY style sheet. If NORMAL.STY is not in the directory, the program then looks in the Word program directory. If you created subdirectories for your Word documents and divided them by document type (letters, memos, reports, etc.), you can put this Word feature to work for you. By placing a NORMAL.STY file in each document directory, Word automatically uses the style file specific to the types of documents in that directory.

Trick **Make more than one style sheet for your documents.**

You can print the same document in different forms for different purposes by attaching alternative style sheets to it. Producing a variety of style sheets eliminates the necessity of modifying a particular style sheet every time you want a document to have a slightly different look. To change the style sheet attached to a document, choose the **F**ormat **S**tylesheet **A**ttach command from the edit command menu.

The author of a newsletter, for example, may want to work with a normal page layout and double-spaced lines while writing articles. This format makes editing easier. When the final version is ready to be printed, however, attaching a different style sheet may be all that's needed to print articles in 3-inch columns.

Switching style sheets can make Word even more adaptable to your needs. If you use two printers with different capabilities, for example, design a style sheet for each one. Perhaps you print final documents using double-strike characters on a dot-matrix printer: You may want to format one style sheet with single-strike characters for drafts and another style sheet with double-strike characters for the final copy.

Trap   When you switch from one style sheet to another, you see asterisks in the style bar and some formats are incorrect.

When you switch to a new style sheet, all the styles with the same variants in both the old and new style sheets are switched and the paragraphs to which you have applied those styles are reformatted. When the new style sheet has a corresponding style for every style in the old style sheet, Word transforms the entire document.

When the corresponding style is missing from the new style sheet, however, the old style is discarded. As a result, the text to which you applied the old style reverts to Word's default formats, and the conversion process seems incomplete. You see an asterisk in the style bar informing you that the format isn't described in the style sheet currently attached.

To solve this problem, use the **G**allery command and add the entries you need. Then format the document, using the new entries.

Trick   Use a macro to "freeze" style-sheet formatting so that all formats are expressed as direct formats.

If you're sharing a document with a colleague who doesn't grasp style sheets or if you're planning to convert your Word document by using a file-conversion utility, use Word's supplied macro freeze_style.mac to convert all style sheet formatting to direct formatting. For information on the supplied macros, see Chapter 13, "Macros."

Trap   Watch out for older versions of style sheets.

You will find that your style sheets evolve over time—you make refinements and additions as you become increasingly aware of this feature's usefulness. Be careful, however, of inadvertently loading an older version of a style sheet, one that contains older versions of entries (or lacks some entries altogether). If you're working on a dual-floppy system, you can quite easily find yourself with several different versions of the same style sheet floating around on various disks. If you unknowingly load an older (incorrect) version of a style sheet, you could make a formatting mistake that is not obvious until you waste time and paper, printing your document.

Formatting Documents with Style Sheets

Once you have created your own style sheets, the key codes and automatic styles you formatted are available for your use. Here are some tips and tricks to help you use these formats effectively.

Tip **Turn on the style bar so that you can see the key codes of the styles you apply to a document.**

When working with style sheets, turn on the style bar so that you can see which paragraph styles have been applied to the current document. (Character- and division-style key codes are not displayed in the style bar.) Choose the Yes option in the Options command's `style bar` field.

The *style bar* is a vertical area, two characters wide, located between the text in the document area and the left border. When you turn on the style bar, the text moves two characters to the right to make room. If you have attached a style sheet to the current document and applied styles to each paragraph, the key codes for the styles are displayed in the style bar, next to the first line of each paragraph.

Tip **Select key codes from a list.**

When you cannot remember a key code, Word can help jog your memory. Select one of the **F**ormat **S**tylesheet commands (choose from the `Character`, `Paragraph`, or `Division` options on the menu), and press F1. A list of the styles and key codes you created appears on the screen.

Trick **Combine style-sheet formatting with direct formatting.**

Just because you use a style sheet doesn't mean you cannot use direct formatting. After attaching a style sheet to a document, you still can use any default key code that you didn't modify, and you even can use the codes you have modified—just by pressing Alt-X first. You also can use the Format commands in the edit menu.

Note: In versions before Version 5, you had to press Alt-X to access *any* default speed key after you attached a style sheet. Now you press

Alt-X only if you want to use a speed key whose key code you have used in a style-sheet entry. If you create a style sheet that modifies Alt-C but not Alt-N, you have to press Alt-XC to use the default Alt-C format, but you *don't* have to press Alt-XN to use the Alt-N format; you press just Alt-N.

Tip **If you apply direct formatting on top of text already formatted with a style sheet, the direct formats are added to the ones already in place.**

If you combine style sheet and direct formatting, direct formatting *adds* to the formats already assigned by the style sheet. Suppose that you define a paragraph style with a 0.5-inch hanging indent, and you add double-line spacing to the style by pressing Alt-X2. Word adds the double-line-spacing format to the paragraph without canceling the 0.5-inch hanging indent.

Trap **In some cases, adding direct formatting cancels the link between the altered text and the style sheet.**

One of the chief advantages of style-sheet formatting is that any text you format with a style-sheet key code is linked to the style sheet. That link means that you can change all the text formatted in your entire document with just one keystroke simply by making changes to the style-sheet entry. If you use direct formatting on top of style-sheet formatting, however, you may sever this link inadvertently.

Here's the rule: If the type of formatting command you use parallels the style-sheet key code's usage (character, paragraph, or division), you sever the link. In other words, if you add direct character formats to text formatted with a key code employing the character usage, the text's format is no longer controlled by the style sheet; so if you change the style-sheet entry, the change won't affect this text.

Should you take care to preserve the link between a style sheet and the text you have formatted with it? Yes, and here's why. Suppose that you use a style-sheet entry to format all your footnotes in 8-point Times Roman. You print the document, only to find that the 8-point type is too small. To change all the notes to 10-point Times Roman, all you have to do is change one style-sheet entry. As long as you haven't broken the link between the entry and the footnotes, all of them will reformat automatically after you edit your style sheet. Remember: style sheets are of value not only because they make attaching complex formats to text easy; style sheets also let you change a format throughout a document just by making a small change to the style-sheet entry. For this reason, preserving the link between the text and style-sheet entries is important.

If you add direct character formats to paragraphs formatted with a style sheet, however, the direct formatting doesn't sever the link. The same is true if you add direct paragraph formats to divisions formatted with a style sheet.

Tip **An asterisk in the style bar means that the paragraph has received direct paragraph formatting and is no longer linked with the style sheet.**

You can restore the link to the style sheet if you're willing to lose the direct formats. Just use the style-sheet key code to reformat that paragraph.

Trap **If you use a style-sheet key code on text formatted with direct formatting techniques, Word may replace the direct formats completely.**

The same rule of identity applies to text reformatted with style-sheet key codes. If you add a character style-sheet format on top of a direct character format, the style-sheet format replaces the direct format completely. The same is true of paragraph style-sheet formats applied to direct paragraph formats, and of division style-sheet formats applied to direct division formats.

If you add a character style-sheet format to a direct paragraph format, however, Word doesn't cancel the direct paragraph format. The same is true of paragraph style-sheet formats added to direct division formats.

If Something Goes Wrong

You will certainly see error messages as you're getting used to using style sheets. This section provides a brief overview of the most common problems that arise—and how to cope with them.

Trap **When you load a document, the message** Style sheet not available **is displayed at the bottom of the screen.**

When you load a document for editing, Word automatically attempts to load the style sheet attached to the document. (Remember that Word stores the name of the style sheet attached to the document in a hidden area of the document file.) If Word cannot find the style sheet in the directory it was in the last time you worked, however, you see the message Style sheet not available. To remedy this problem, use the **F**ormat **S**tylesheet **A**ttach command and type the correct path name for the style sheet that was previously attached to the document.

Trap   **When you try to leave the style sheet after adding new entries, you see the message** Key codes conflict.

When you see this message, you have created two entries that use the same first letter in their key codes. Use the **G**allery **N**ame command to change one of the key codes and try again.

Trap   **When you try to leave the style sheet after adding new entries, you see the message** Style already defined.

When you see this message, you have created two entries that use the same variant. Select one of the entries and use the **G**allery **N**ame command to change the variant.

Chapter Summary

You can use style sheets to bring about major gains in your writing productivity. With style sheets, you can modify existing speed keys, create new speed keys, and customize default formats with automatic styles.

When you start Word, the program automatically looks for a NORMAL.STY file in the default directory. If Word finds a NORMAL.STY file, Word uses the file as the default style sheet for all the documents in that directory. For this reason, you can put modified versions of NORMAL.STY into each document directory. Each type of document you create then has its own appropriate formats—and the process is completely automatic.

To modify NORMAL.STY, use the Gallery command and insert entries by using the Insert command. Begin by modifying the standard paragraph and standard character formats. Then modify the default formats for page numbers, footnote reference marks, and footnote text. If you write reports or proposals, create new key codes for headings that automatically create dynamic links between outlines and document headings. Create a new standard division format.

After you have created a modified version of NORMAL.STY, use it for a while to explore its possibilities. Use the Format Stylesheet Record command to modify existing speed keys.

Once you have created a workable version of your modified NORMAL.STY file, copy it to other directories by typing new path names in the Gallery Transfer Save menu. Access these style sheets by changing the default directory with Transfer Options. Select the whole style sheet, using Shift-F10, and reformat it quickly using the Format Character and Format Division commands.

13

Macros

You have already seen many examples of macros in this book, and they all testify to the same conclusion: If you find yourself giving the same series of commands over and over again, you should learn how to create a macro to automate these commands. What's more, you can use macros to overcome some of Word's most serious shortcomings and pitfalls. Creating macros, in short, is one of the best ways to raise your writing productivity with Word.

You can approach macros on several levels. The simplest technique is to create macros by recording them using the record macro mode. In this mode, Word records your keystrokes, which can include text as well as virtually all commands (you cannot, however, include mouse actions in any macro, recorded or otherwise). Later, you can "play back" the recording, and Word enters the keystrokes you recorded, just as if you were pressing them at the keyboard—but at super-fast speed.

The second approach is to create macros by typing the macro keystrokes in a Word document instead of recording the keystrokes. When you use this approach, you must exercise caution to make sure that you follow rules—called *syntax rules*—to type these keystrokes correctly. Often, you find that the macro doesn't work the first time, and you must test and edit the macro (a process called *debugging*).

Writing macros is more difficult than recording them but has a big payoff. When you record macros, you cannot make Word pause for user input, often desirable when you need to select text or type a file name. If you create macros by writing them, you can include pauses. What's more, you also can include macro instructions: instructions that tell Word how to carry out the macro. Using macro instructions, you can create macros that branch depending on test conditions or keep on executing until a condition has been fulfilled. In short, you truly can program Microsoft Word to do your bidding. In this book, you have seen many examples of macros that use control structures.

Although writing macros is more difficult and prone to error than recording them, anyone can understand the simple concepts that underlie macro programming with Microsoft Word. Do as programmers do: learn these concepts by copying the macros in this book and modifying them until they work the way you want. Before long, you can create your own, completely original macros. The big, complex Word program then becomes your obedient servant!

This chapter includes discussions and information about the following topics:

❏ Understanding macros

❏ Planning macros

❏ Recording macros

❏ Managing glossary files

❏ Using the macros supplied with Word

❏ Using the macros in this book

❏ Testing and editing macros

❏ Writing macros

Understanding Macros

A *macro* is a miniature computer program that automates a Word operation. When a macro is in operation, Word follows preset instructions. A macro can contain text (which is entered directly into the document as if someone were pressing the keys), command keys (which initiate and control Word commands), and instructions (which tell Word how to carry out more advanced operations, such as repeating a command until a condition is fulfilled).

You can create macros in two ways. The easiest way is to *record* macros using the record macro mode (toggled on and off with Shift-F3). When the record macro mode is on, Word "records" all the keys you press. When you toggle the mode off, Word stops recording. You can "play back" macros you record this way and save them for future sessions. You can even assign them to control keys so that you can enter them at a keystroke.

The second way to create macros is to type them in a Word document. If you create macros this way, you must use special symbols to refer to Word keystrokes. Using these symbols is more tedious than recording macros but has a big payoff. When you type macros instead of recording them, you can use the instructions included in Word's macro programming language, such as «PAUSE» and «WHILE». These are the same instructions programmers use to create sophisticated application programs for your personal computer.

Almost all the macro examples you have seen in this book were written using the second technique. Even if you don't understand everything in the macros, you can still put them to work. You find instructions in this chapter for using these macros.

One other point about macros: When you create a macro, you store it as a glossary entry by using the Copy command. To use macros, you recall the macro you want from a glossary by using the Insert command. If you want, you can assign macros to Ctrl-key codes. To use the macro, however, you must make sure that you have loaded the glossary file which contains them. Part of using macros, then, involves learning how to manage glossary files.

Glossary files are described in more detail elsewhere in this chapter. For now, learn how to plan and record simple macros.

Trap   **If you created macros with Word 4, convert them before using them with Word 5.**

Most macros navigate command menus, and as you know, many Version 5 command menus include minor or major changes; one Version 4 menu, Window Options, no longer exists. You must edit your Word 4 macros to make sure that they will run with Word 5. For information on editing macros, see "Testing and Editing Macros," in this chapter.

Planning Macros

Creating a macro that works takes planning; the task takes a great deal of planning and a wary eye on the potential for disaster in order to create one that works well.

Tip   **Experiment with the commands you want to use in order to learn how to give them unambiguously. Consider what can go wrong.**

To create a macro that works, you must plan in advance precisely which keys to press, which commands to give, and what can go wrong. Suppose, for example, that you record a macro which presses the Esc key, chooses the Print Options command, presses Tab 10 times and, in the feed field, moves the highlight one item left from the Continuous option. In this way, the macro selects the Manual option. After you record the command, it looks like this:

    \<esc\>po\<tab 10\>\<backspace\>\<enter\>\<esc\>

Unfortunately, two mishaps can occur when the macro is written this way and used:

❑ If Word is already in command mode when you start the macro, the first keystroke—Esc—puts the program in the edit mode; the rest of the macro then affects the document text.

❑ If some option other than Continuous is chosen in the feed field, moving the highlight one option left creates the wrong result. If the highlight is positioned on the Manual option when the Print Options command is selected, for instance, this macro selects the Mixed option.

Many of this chapter's tricks and traps concern such pitfalls. In this example, you can avoid unwanted outcomes by observing two rules:

❑ Always use the Ctrl-Esc command to enter the command mode. If you do, Word stays in the command mode even if it's already in that mode.

❑ If possible, choose options in command menus by typing the first letter rather than using the space bar or Backspace key.

Here's a correct version of the faulty macro:

    \<ctrl esc\>po\<tab 10\>m\<enter\>\<esc\>

Note that the macro begins with Ctrl-Esc, not Esc, and chooses the option in the feed field by using the letter *M*, not the Backspace key. (In this menu, *m* selects Manual, not Mixed. You must press the space bar to select Mixed. You can discover such facts only through testing and exploration.)

Tip   **Use style sheets if you're automating formatting commands only.**

Nifty as Word's macros are, they're significantly slower than the Alt-key formatting commands you can create with style sheets. The Alt-key codes are stored in memory; macros, sad to say, are stored on disk. If you want to give a series of formatting commands, and these commands do not include any other commands, create a style sheet instead of a macro.

For more information on creating new key codes for formatting commands, see Chapter 12.

Tip   **Use macros if you want to combine formatting commands with other Word commands or if you want to use nonformatting commands exclusively.**

Although macros run slower than Alt-key formatting commands created with style sheets, you can include formatting commands in macros. Do so when it makes sense to combine the macro's capabilities with formatting. Here's part of a macro, for instance, that creates a table of contents heading after Word has finished compiling a table by using the Library Table command:

```
<enter><alt c><alt b>
TABLE OF CONTENTS<alt space><enter><enter>
```

This macro not only formats the heading by boldfacing it and centering it, the macro actually types the heading for you—and that task is something you cannot do with a style sheet.

Recording Macros

The easiest way to create a macro is to use the record macro mode.

Trick   **As you learn to use macros, test them on a junk document.**

In the first flush of excitement, many new macro users become so enchanted with their creations that they unleash them on valuable documents. But be careful. Word doesn't stop you from creating macros containing extremely dangerous commands. Here's an example:

```
<esc>wc1n
```

This command closes window 1 and, when Word asks whether it should save the document, answers No. The outcome? Lost work. Test your macros on documents you can live without.

Trick **You cannot include mouse actions in macros.**

As this book has stressed repeatedly, just about anything you can do with the mouse also can be done with the keyboard. That's fortunate because otherwise Word's macros—which cannot include mouse actions—would have severe limitations.

Even if you're a fanatic mouse user, you will find it helpful in writing macros to explore the peculiarities of Word's keyboard functions.

Tip **Press Shift-F3 to start recording a macro.**

When you press this key, you turn on Word's macro "tape recorder." Every key you press on the keyboard is recorded—until you press Shift-F3 again to exit the record macro mode. When you're in this mode, every key you press—and virtually any command you use—can be captured in a Word macro. You can tell whether you're in record macro mode by looking at the key indicator, which displays the message RM when the mode is toggled on.

Tip **You cannot include the Transfer Glossary Clear or Transfer Clear All commands in a macro.**

Such a macro would wipe itself out, and a Word macro's first imperative is to protect itself at all costs. (If Microsoft's programmers ever create robots, maybe they will rethink this point.) A macro containing the Transfer Glossary Clear or Transfer Clear All command simply beeps and continues to the next instruction, with unpredictable results thereafter.

Tip **To create efficient macros, choose commands by typing the command's capitalized letter.**

This technique is much faster than using the Tab, space bar, or arrow keys to select commands.

Following are some of the additional command-selecting rules that seem to have guided Word's programmers:

❏ You can choose Yes/No options in command menus by pressing Y or N. Why? They're capitalized!

❏ The most frequently used option is, in many cases, the first field in a command menu; you can usually choose from the field's options by typing a letter.

❑ In most submenus (as opposed to command menus), the selections are capitalized.

❑ If two items in a menu are capitalized with the same first letter, typing that letter selects the first of them. The second must be selected with the space bar or Backspace key.

Tip   **Press Shift-F3 to stop recording a macro.**

When you press Shift-F3 a second time to toggle off the record macro mode, the Copy command menu automatically appears. You use the Copy command menu to name your macro and copy it to a glossary.

Tip   **If you make a mistake, cancel recording by pressing Shift-F3 and when the Copy command menu appears, press Esc.**

Word won't save your keystrokes if you follow this procedure.

Tip   **A macro name can include up to 31 alphanumeric characters, and can employ periods, underline characters, and hyphens.**

When the Copy command menu appears, name your macro by typing a name in the to field. When you press Enter, Word inserts the macro you created into the glossary currently in Word's memory.

Trick   **Use the MAC extension to distinguish macros from other glossary entries.**

Because you can use periods when naming macros, you can use an extension (as if you were naming a DOS file) to remind you that the glossary you're saving is a macro. The extension differentiates the macro from other glossary entries and comes in handy when you run macros by choosing one from a list. Such a list appears after you use the Insert command and press F1.

Tip   **A macro name cannot include spaces.**

Like any glossary name, macro names cannot include spaces. You can use underline characters, however, to link separate words. Use this feature to name macros descriptively, as suggested in these three examples:

    copy_to_bibliography.mac
    mark_table_entry.mac
    capture_address.mac

Tip   **Run a macro directly from the keyboard by using the Ctrl key and a keyboard character.**

When you name your macro, you can define a Ctrl-key code with which you can run the macro from the keyboard. To name a macro so that it starts when you press Ctrl-B, for example, add to the name of the macro a caret (^) and the key code enclosed within angle brackets:

^<ctrl b>

Here's how a complete macro name appears in the to field of the Copy command when you add a Ctrl-key code:

copy_to_bibliography.mac^<ctrl b>

Tip **Make your Ctrl-key codes mnemonic.**

Try to use Ctrl-key codes that suggest the macro's function. Ctrl-B is a logical choice for a macro that cuts a bibliographic citation to a glossary where the citation can be retrieved later to compile a reference list.

Tip **You can use a two-character Ctrl-key code to name macros.**

If you plan to create many macros, and you probably will, you quickly run out of key codes if you use just one letter. Happily, you can use a two-letter key code. To name the bibliography macro so that it runs when you press Ctrl-CB, for instance, type the following in the to field of the Copy command:

copy_to_bibliography.mac^<ctrl c>b

Note that the second letter of the key code must be placed outside the closing angle bracket.

A major advantage of two-letter key codes is that you can create even more mnemonic codes. Ctrl-CB, for instance, is a good code to use for a macro that copies a bibliographic reference. With a little forethought, you can organize your macros so that the first code expresses the action performed (such as Copy, Mark, Move, Capture, etc.), and the second code expresses the object of the action (such as table entry, index entry, bibliographic reference, etc.). Ctrl-MT, for instance, could be the key code for a macro that marks a table of contents entry.

Trap **You see the message** Duplicate macro code.

If you see this message, you have tried to name a macro with a key code already in use. Try a different key code.

Trick **Avoid using the function keys to run macros unless you specifically intend to reassign Word's function-key layout.**

You can name macros so that they run with a function-key code, such as Shift-F7. Doing so is not recommended, however, because you then have to give up the ordinary Word function keys. Name a macro with a function key only when you have decided that you don't like one of Word's function-key assignments.

Here's an example: Some users don't like the Word 5 Shift-F1 function-key assignment, which chooses the Undo command. You can easily press Shift-F1 by accident when you're aiming for Ctrl-F1 (zoom window) or Shift-F3 (record macro). Pressing Shift-F1 by accident leads to disconcerting (and sometimes unrecoverable) changes in a document.

To reassign the Shift-F1 key, create a macro that doesn't do anything. For example, press Shift-F3 to begin recording the macro. Then press the space bar to enter a space and the Backspace key to delete the space. Finally, press Shift-F3 again to stop recording the macro and save it with the following name:

    does_nothing.mac^<shift f1>

As long as this glossary entry is in memory when you press Shift-F1, you have effectively disabled the function-key route to the Undo command. (You can still use Undo by choosing the command from the edit command menu.)

One reason Microsoft included this feature is so that people used to other word processing programs using function keys instead of command menus can reconfigure the function-key layout to resemble their old program. Think twice, however, before engaging in an extensive enterprise to reconfigure the function keys to make their actions the same as another program's. Some Word function keys perform actions not accessible, or not easily accessible, from Word's command menus—and this limitation is particularly true if you don't use a mouse. These keys include F1 (next window), Shift-F1 (zoom window), F2 (calculate), Shift-F2 (outline view), F3 (insert from glossary), Shift-F3 (record macro), Ctrl-F3 (step macro), F4 (repeat edit), Shift-F4 (repeat search), Ctrl-F4 (update list), F5 (toggle overtype mode), Shift-F5 (outline organize), Ctrl-F5 (line draw), F6 (extend select), Shift-F6 (column select), Shift-F7 (preceding sentence), and Shift-F8 (next sentence).

If you reassign a function-key code,you can still use the original function-key assignment, but the method is cumbersome. Suppose that you reassign the Ctrl-F10 assignment. To use the old assignment, press Ctrl-X-F10.

Tip **Run your macro by choosing its name with the Insert command, using the F3 key or a key code.**

You can run macros in three ways:

❏ *Use the Insert command*. Choose the Insert command, press F1, and select the desired macro's name from the list. Press Enter.

❏ *Use the F3 key*. Type the name of the desired macro and press F3.

❏ *Use a key code*. If you named your macro with a Ctrl-key code, just use the key code to start the macro.

Trap **Copying a macro to a glossary is not the same thing as saving the macro.**

Make a special note of this point. To save the macros you create, you must save the glossary to which you copy them. Save glossaries using the **T**ransfer **G**lossary **S**ave command. For more information on saving glossaries (and managing glossary files in general), see the following section, "Managing Glossary Files."

Trap **You cannot allow for user input if you record your macro.**

A major disadvantage to recording macros is that you cannot allow for user input. As you quickly will discover, the most useful macros are the ones that stop running temporarily so that the user can perform an action (such as selecting text) or choose an option. For this reason, you may want to learn how to write macros. The macros in this book provide many examples of the extraordinary power and graceful style of Word's macro programming language.

Managing Glossary Files

As you have learned, you store the macros you create as glossary entries. These glossary entries are stored as a glossary file, which isn't an ordinary Word document. Like the NORMAL.STY style file, the glossary file is a special file. It contains one or more glossary entries. (The maximum number of entries is limited only by disk size, but if you put more than 50 entries in a glossary, choosing their names from an F1 list becomes tedious.)

By default, Word uses the glossary file called NORMAL.GLY to store macros. NORMAL.GLY is Word's standard glossary, the one Word loads automatically at the beginning of every Word session. You can add macros to this file, but you should do so only when you are sure that you will use them frequently. At the end of the session, you must save the file, using the Transfer Glossary Save command. Like the changes you make to documents, macros aren't saved unless you use this disk-saving command. If you try to exit Word without saving new macros, you are prompted to save or abandon the changes made to the glossary.

Managing glossary files is much easier with Word 5 than with previous versions of the program. In previous versions, you could not load a distinct glossary file: you had to merge the file you loaded with the one already in memory. The result was uncontrollable growth in the size of the glossary file, as well as other glossary-management problems. Version 5's new Transfer Glossary Load command, however, makes it possible to load distinct glossary files just as you can load a specific document. With this command, you can keep glossary files separate. You can create glossary files containing macros for letters, for instance, and keep them separate from a file containing macros for reports.

For the macros discussed in this book, however, you needn't worry about keeping them separate. All are suitable for inclusion in NORMAL.GLY, Word's default glossary file.

Using the Macros Supplied with Word

Word Utilities Disk 2 contains a file called MACRO.GLY. If you load this file with the Transfer Glossary Load command, you can take advantage of 30 macros (see table 13.1). Most macros have been saved with Ctrl-key codes. To view a list of these key codes, load MACRO.GLY, choose the Insert command, and press F1.

Table 13.1
Macros Supplied with Word 5

Macro	Description
annot_collect.mac	Complies a formatted list of annotations
annot_merge.mac	Merges annotations from several copies of a document into one copy
annot_remove.mac	Removes all annotations from a document
authority_entry.mac	Marks a legal citation for entry into a table of authorities
bulleted_list mac	Creates a list with each item preceded by a hyphen
chainprint_mac	Links two or more documents for chain printing with continuous pagination
character_text.mac	Prints all the characters in a font, including the extended character set
copy_text.mac	Copies text
dca_load.mac	Converts a DCA-RFT document into Word format
dca_save.mac	Saves a Word file to DCA-RFT format
freeze_style.mac	Converts all style-sheet formatting to direct formatting
index_mac	Marks text with index codes, based on a list you compile (The words must be stored in a Word document, one word per line.)
index_entry.mac	Codes a word for inclusion in an index
mailing_label.mac	Merges mailing list data into a mailing label template
memo_header.mac	Enters a memo header with *From*, *To*, and *Subject*
move_text.mac	Moves block of text
next_page.mac	Scrolls to top of next page
prev_page.mac	Scrolls to top of preceding page

Table 13.1—Continued

Macro	Description
repl_w_gloss.mac	Replaces search text with contents of a glossary
repl_w_scrap.mac	Replaces search text with contents of scrap
save_selection.mac	Saves selected text to a file
sidebyside.mac	Creates format for side-by-side paragraphs
stop_last_footer.mac	Cancels the footer on the last page of a document
table.mac	Sets tabs for a table
tabs.mac	Sets tabs and allows you to specify type of tab
tabs2.mac	Prompts for number of columns in a table and calculates equidistant tab settings
toc_entry.mac	Codes headings for entry into a table of contents
3_delete.mac	Cuts text to glossaries (not scrap)
3_undelete.mac	Recovers up to three most recent deletions made with 3_delete.mac

Note: Do not use Transfer Glossary Merge to load MACRO.GLY—if you do, you will merge all these macros with the entries in NORMAL.GLY, your standard (default) glossary file. That idea is bad for two reasons. First, you won't use most of the supplied macros, so you won't want them cluttering up your screen. Second, their key codes conflict with the ones assigned to this book's macros, which you may very well find more useful. Microsoft's macros seem to be designed to remedy certain marketing shortcomings of Word when compared to its chief competition (WordPerfect). The macros recommended in this book, however, are specifically intended to realize the program's potential for high-productivity word processing.

Using the Macros in This Book

You can use any of the macros in this book by typing them into a Word document, selecting them, and copying them to the standard glossary file, NORMAL.GLY.

Tip　**Use the suggested Ctrl-key codes.**

Key codes can conflict if you're not careful. The macros presented in this book have been named to avoid conflicts. See table 13.2 for a list of the key codes used by macros in this book. As you can see, to rationalize and organize these macros, they have been divided into two categories: Options macros, which select Word operating options, and Quick macros, which automate tedious or highly specialized procedures.

Table 13.2
Key Codes Assigned to This Book's Macros

Key Code	Macro Name	Chapter
Ctrl-OD	options_display	4
Ctrl-OS	options_symbols	4
Ctrl-OH	options_hidden	4
Ctrl-OR	options_ruler	4
Ctrl-QA	quick_archive	2
Ctrl-QB	quick_backup	2
Ctrl-QL	quick_loadchange	9
Ctrl-QM	quick_move	5
Ctrl-QO	quick_outline	6
Ctrl-QQ	quick_quit	1
Ctrl-QS	quick_side by side	7
Ctrl-QT	quick_tabs	5
Ctrl-QU	quick_user archive	2
Ctrl-QW	quick_window	6
Ctrl-QZ	quick_zoomload	9

Tip **Before copying the macros in this book, understand the components of a written macro.**

When you write a macro, you can use up to six components. You need not use all of them. Following is a list of the components that comprise a macro:

❏ *Keynames*. The names of the keys on the keyboard, enclosed in greater-than and less-than brackets, such as <esc> or <shift>. You must type these keynames in exact conformity to Word's expectations. Details about naming keys are presented in "Writing Macros," later in this chapter.

❏ *Text*. If you include in a macro letters, numbers, or punctuation not enclosed by brackets or chevrons, Word "types" them just as if you were pressing keys on the keyboard. In the edit mode, such characters appear as if someone were actually typing them. In the command mode, such characters start commands, just as if you typed the command's first letter.

❏ *Macro instructions*. Macro instructions are commands, enclosed in chevrons, that tell Word to undertake complex actions. A major benefit of writing your own macros is the availability of these instructions. You cannot use them when you record macros. You may choose from nine macro instructions (ASK, COMMENT, IF...ELSE...ENDIF, MESSAGE, PAUSE, QUIT, REPEAT...ENDREPEAT, SET, and WHILE...ENDWHILE). Take care to use these instructions in precise accord with syntax rules, which state the order in which the elements of the instruction are written. You must enter the chevrons that surround these macro instructions by pressing Alt-[(left bracket) for the opening chevron and Alt-] (right bracket) for the closing chevron.

❏ *User Variables*. Variables are special named areas of memory that Word sets up to store text, numbers, or dates as a macro is running. You, the user, can create variables with the SET and ASK instructions (hence the term *user variables*). The contents of a variable may change as the macro executes.

❏ *Reserved variables*. Word's macro programming language includes 10 reserved variables—variables whose names are reserved for special functions. These variables are listed and described in "Writing Macros," later in this chapter.

❑ *Constants*. A constant is a fixed set of characters, a number, or a date entered in a Word macro. A constant doesn't change.

❑ *Operators*. You may include math or logical expressions using operators in Word macros. An operator is a symbol that tells Word what kind of mathematical or logical operation to perform. Word uses five arithmetic operators (addition, subtraction, multiplication, division, and percentage) and six logical operators. Logical operators tell Word how to compare one variable or constant to another (equal to, greater than, less than, greater than or equal to, less than or equal to, and not equal to).

Don't worry if this information seems overwhelming. The concepts are simple enough once you have seen some specific examples. To use the macros in this book, you simply reproduce them by typing them verbatim.

To illustrate these macro components and many common macro techniques, here's a line-by-line explanation of one of this book's macros, the one that lets you choose display options.

«SET response = ″N″»

This statement creates a variable called *response* and sets its value to the text string N. The variable *response* is a user-defined variable, and the quotation marks around *n* are necessary so that Word will treat the character as a text string.

«WHILE response = ″N″»

This instruction tells Word to keep executing a list of instructions as long as the value of *response* is N. The list of instructions begins right after the WHILE instruction and ends at the ENDWHILE instruction.

«ASK symbols = ?Press (N)one, (P)artial, or (A)ll»

This statement is the first instruction in the WHILE clause. It instructs Word to ask the user to enter a value for a new variable, called *symbols*. A message appears on the screen asking the user to press the N, P, or A key.

«IF symbols = ″N″»

This instruction begins an IF structure, which includes all the instructions up to the next ENDIF. The instruction is carried out only if the user presses N.

<esc>o<right><down>«symbols»<enter>

Here's how a macro navigates a command menu: Esc-O brings up the Options menu, and the right- and down-arrow keys highlight the show non-printing symbols field. The expression *«symbols»* types the current value of the variable *symbols*, just as if someone were pressing keys at the keyboard. The value is currently N. Entering N selects the None option in the show non-printing symbols field, and <enter> carries out the command.

«SET response = "Y"»

This statement is the second instruction in the IF structure. It sets the value of the variable called *response* to Y. This instruction is very important because it turns off the menu that asks the user to press A, P, or N. The menu stays on the screen as long as *response* is N. When this instruction sets *response* to Y, Word can go on to the next step and clear the menu from the screen.

This technique is useful for keeping a menu on the screen until the user types the appropriate answer. If you press X, L, or M in response to the menu, the menu just stays on the screen. The menu stays, in fact, until you press A, P, or N (in either uppercase or lowercase).

«ENDIF»

Every IF instruction must end with an ENDIF statement. This ENDIF instruction signals the end of the IF structure telling Word what to do if the user presses N.

```
«IF symbols="P"»
    <esc>o<right><down>«symbols»<enter>
    «SET response = "Y"»
«ENDIF»
```

Here's the second IF structure, the one that tells Word what to do if the user presses P. This IF structure selects the Partial option in the show non-printing symbols field of the Options command menu.

```
«IF symbols="A"»
    <esc>o<right><down>«symbols»<enter>
    «SET response = "Y"»
«ENDIF»
```

This statement is the third IF structure, which comes into play if the user presses A. The instruction selects the All option in the show non-printing symbols field of the Options command menu.

«ENDWHILE»

This final statement shows the end of the WHILE..ENDWHILE structure. Without it, the macro would not run.

As you can see from this example, every WHILE must be followed by an ENDWHILE; every IF must be followed by an ENDIF. Many common macro errors occur when you forget to put in the ENDWHILE or ENDIF.

Tip **Word ignores tab strokes, newline characters, paragraph marks, division breaks, and page breaks when running macros.**

You can create your macro using any of the available techniques for starting a new line. You also can use tab indentations to make the structure of your macro clear.

Tip **Word does not ignore spaces when running macros.**

Extraneous blank spaces are treated as if you ask the macro to enter a space into your document. The exception to this rule is that blank spaces in macro instructions or keynames are ignored.

Trick **Create a written macro, using one of the macros in this book.**

To enter one of the macros in this book into your computer, do the following:

1. Use the **T**ransfer **C**lear **W**indow command to clear the window.

2. Type the macro's text very carefully. Be sure to enter the opening and closing chevrons by pressing Alt-[and Alt-], respectively.

3. When you are finished, check your work. Be sure that you have spelled all the variable names and instructions correctly and consistently. Make sure that every left angle bracket and chevron is followed, respectively, by a right angle bracket or chevron.

4. When you have proofread your work, select the entire macro. Then choose the **C**opy command. Type the macro name, the period, and the extension (MAC). Then press the caret (^) key. To enter the control code, hold the Ctrl key and type the one-letter code; Word enters the brackets automatically. Finally, type the second letter of the code, if it has one, and carry out the command.

5. Test the command. If you find problems, check the command, using the suggestions in the following section.

6. Be sure to save your work by using the **T**ransfer **G**lossary **S**ave command before you quit Word.

Testing and Editing Macros

If your macro doesn't work the first time, don't despair—you're doing fine. Word's macro programming language, like all programming languages, is very persnickety about syntax (getting all the right components in just the right order). Fortunately, most errors fall into a few categories, and dealing with most problems is easy. To help you do so, Word includes a step mode, which lets you go through the macro one action at a time.

Tip   **Many macro errors stem from choosing the wrong option in a command menu.**

You cannot select most command menu options by typing the first letter, because few of the options are listed with capital letters. In the Options menu, for instance, the display option cannot be accessed with the macro command <esc>od; instead, you must type <esc>o<tab 5> to reach this option. If you get the number of tab strokes wrong, you wind up in a different command option, and you don't get the results you want.

Trick   **Use the step mode to watch what your macro is doing.**

If your macro doesn't seem to work correctly, press Ctrl-F3 to turn on the step mode. (The message SM appears on the key indicator.) Now run your macro. Press Enter to move your macro forward one instruction at a time. You see what the macro does as it navigates command menus, carries out instructions, and enters text. Chances are good that you can find the error. When you do, press Esc to stop the macro, and press Ctrl-F3 again to turn off the step mode.

Trick   **Edit your macro by entering it into a document as text.**

After you copy a macro to a glossary, the macro executes if you load it using the Insert command. You also can retrieve the macro as text: just type a caret (^) after the macro name in the from field of the Insert command menu. Here's what you type to retrieve the macro copy_to_bibliography.mac as text:

    copy_to_bibliography.mac^

If the macro has a Ctrl-key code, you have to type the code too, following everything with the caret:

copy_to_bibliography.mac^<ctrl c>b^

Because typing the whole macro name can be tedious in such cases, save time by pressing F1 after using the Insert command. When you highlight your macro's name, Word echoes the name in the `from` field of the Insert command menu. Just type the caret and press Enter to retrieve the macro as text.

Once you retrieve the macro as text, you can edit the macro just as you would any other Word document. When you're finished making changes, use the **C**opy or **D**elete command to copy or cut the macro back to the glossary. When you save the macro with the same name, however, you see the message `Enter Y to overwrite glossary, N to retype name, or Esc to cancel`. Press Y, because there's no reason to leave a macro that doesn't work in your glossary. Overwrite the macro with the edited version.

Writing Macros

If you choose to write macros rather than record them, you can create a macro that pauses and waits for user input. You also can use macro instructions that perform loops and branches.

To write a macro, you create the instructions in any Word document, select them, and use the **C**opy or **D**elete commands to create a glossary entry. As you do, you name the macro as indicated in "Recording Macros" earlier in this chapter. You may name the macro, for example, so that it starts running when you use a Ctrl-key code.

If you're unfamiliar with computer programming, the concepts of looping and branching may be unfamiliar to you. They are fundamental, however, to almost all programming languages, including Word's macro language. Here's a brief overview:

❑ *Loops.* In a macro containing a loop, the instructions tell Word to perform an action over and over again. You can tell Word to perform an action a fixed number of times, or to keep doing the action until a condition is met. Using loops, you can create macros that perform an action automatically throughout an entire document.

❏ *Branches.* In a macro containing a branch, the macro may accomplish two or more different tasks. Branches figure prominently in macros for menus, from which the user selects one option. In a menu for loading template documents, for example, Option 1 loads a memo template, Option 2 loads a letter template, and Option 3 loads a report template.

Loops and branches provide tools for high-productivity macro applications. If you think that all these terms sound too much like computer programming, you're right in one sense—the use of such instructions figures prominently in programming the computer. Programmers, however, must also worry about data structures, input/output problems, and other problems, and with most languages these elements are the biggest challenge. You don't have to worry about such things when you write Word macros. You can concentrate on the fun part, and it's easy. To be sure, writing macros is more difficult than recording them, but anyone can learn how.

Trick **Begin writing your macro by recording what you can and inserting additional commands later.**

Rather than writing a macro from scratch, try recording as much of the macro as you can. Then enter the result in your document, and build on the recorded version. Here's how:

1. Press Shift-F3 to begin recording your macro.

2. Go through as much of the macro as possible with manual keystrokes. When you get to a place where you want to accept user input later, enter one of the responses that the user can make at this point in the macro.

3. Save the macro using the **C**opy command.

4. Use the **I**nsert command and type the macro's name. Before pressing Enter, however, type a caret (ˆ). Word does not run the macro; instead, Word inserts the text of the macro into the current document.

5. Add to the macro instructions and other components that you cannot record.

Here's an example: Suppose that you want to create a macro which lets you choose between continuous- and manual-feed paper before you print. Record the macro, and select the Manual option in the feed field in the Print Options menu. Save the macro and retrieve it by using the Insert command (don't forget to type the caret after the macro name). After Word inserts the text into your document, the macro text should look like this:

<esc>po<tab 10>m<enter><esc>

Now use this text to build a more complex macro that includes macro instructions:

«ASK feed = ?(M)anual or (C)ontinuous feed?»
<esc>po<tab 10>«feed»<enter><esc>

You will find more information on the ASK instruction elsewhere in this chapter. For now, the point is that the record mode is useful for building an accurate skeleton of a macro's keynames.

Tip **Learn how to refer to all keystrokes when writing macros.**

When you write a macro, you must refer to keys by using the exact spelling shown in table 13.3. In addition, you must surround the keyname with less-than (<) and greater-than (>) brackets. If you spell the keyname incorrectly or leave off one or both brackets, Word treats what you have written as text or a variable name.

Table 13.3
Keynames for Macros

Keyname	Keyboard Equivalent
<alt>	Alt key
<backspace>	Backspace key
<capslock>	Caps Lock key
<ctrl>	Ctrl key
<del>	Del key
<down>	Down-arrow key on numeric keypad
<end>	End key on numeric keypad
<enter>	Enter key
<esc>	Esc key
<f1>	F1 key on function keypad
<f2>	F2 key on function keypad
<f3>	F3 key on function keypad
<f4>	F4 key on function keypad
<f5>	F5 key on function keypad

Table 13.3—Continued

Keyname	Keyboard Equivalent
<f6>	F6 key on function keypad
<f7>	F7 key on function keypad
<f8>	F8 key on function keypad
<f9>	F9 key on function keypad
<f10>	F10 key on function keypad
<home>	Home key on numeric keypad
<ins>	Ins key
<keypad*>	Asterisk on numeric keypad
<keypad + >	Plus key on numeric keypad
<keypad->	Minus key on numeric keypad
<left>	Left-arrow key on numeric keypad
<numlock>	NumLock key
<pgdn>	PgDn key on numeric keypad
<pgup>	PgUp key on numeric keypad
<right>	Right-arrow key on numeric keypad
<scrollock>	Scroll Lock key
<shift>	Shift key
<space>	Space bar
<tab>	Tab key
<up>	Up-arrow key on numeric keypad

Tip **Include the second letter in brackets when writing Ctrl-key, Alt-key, or Shift-key codes.**

Here's a point inadequately treated in Word's documentation: when you use in a macro a key code that requires you to hold one key as you press another, you must include both keys in the brackets. That fact is true of the Ctrl, Alt, and Shift keys—but not of the Esc key. Some examples:

```
<alt b>
<ctrl x>
<shift enter>
<shift f1>
<shift tab>
<ctrl f10>
<shift ctrl enter>
```

Note that these key codes should not include punctuation. Don't be waylaid by the conventions used in this book, which writes these codes as Alt-B. Omit the hyphen.

Trick **You can make certain keys repeat a specified number of times.**

Enclose within the keyname brackets a number telling Word how many times to "press" the key. Typing the following, for example, tells Word to enter 20 tab keystrokes:

```
<tab 20>
```

You can use this technique only with the keys listed in table 13.4.

Table 13.4
Macro Repeat Keys

Keyname	Example (to enter two times)
<tab>	<tab 2>
<shift tab>	<shift tab 2>
<enter>	<enter 2>
<esc>	<esc 2>
<ins>	<ins 2>
<del>	<del 2>
<backspace>	<backspace 2>

Tip **To use an Alt-key or Ctrl-key code, enclose both keynames—the Alt or Ctrl key and the other keyname—in brackets.**

To use the formatting key code Alt-B (boldface) in your macro, write the key code this way:

```
<alt b>
```

This point isn't clear from Word's manual, but if you think about this fact, it's clear why it's true. If you press Alt or Ctrl and let go, and then press a second key, Word enters the second key as text. To make these keys work as commands with key codes, you must hold the Alt or Ctrl key and, while the key is held, touch the second one. Enclosing both keystrokes in the brackets is the same thing as holding the first key while pressing the second.

Trick **In macros that move through text, use F7 and F8, respectively, to move to the word left or right, and use F9 and F10, respectively, to move to the preceding or next paragraph.**

To move three words past the currently selected word, enter the following commands:

    <f8><f8><f8><f8>

To move down two paragraphs from the currently selected paragraph, enter the following commands:

    <f10><f10><f10>

Tip **Text entered by a macro takes the format currently assigned to the cursor.**

The text entered by a macro is like any other text; it takes the character and paragraph formats currently assigned to the cursor. If the cursor is "programmed" with centered paragraphing and boldface character style, that's the way the inserted text appears.

Trick **Make sure that text has the formatting you want by including formatting instructions in the macro.**

Suppose that you create a macro to enter today's date automatically. The macro may look like this:

    date<f3>

You plan to use this macro in letters. You type your name and address with centered paragraphs and press Enter. Now you use your macro. Word centers the date instead of typing it flush left.

Following is a revised version of the macro. It clears any extraneous character-style formatting by using the Alt-space bar command and resets the paragraph alignment left flush.

    <alt space><alt l>date<f3>

Tip **Surround macro instructions with chevrons.**

Every macro instruction must be surrounded with chevrons. To enter the left chevron, press Ctrl-[. To enter the right chevron, press Ctrl-].

Tip **Understand the data types you can use in macro instructions.**

When you write a macro instruction, you often include text, numbers, dates, and variable names. Word needs help to tell the differences among the components of a macro instruction. Following is a list of the data types and how to make sure that Word recognizes them properly:

❑ *Text.* If you want Word to interpret what you type as text, enclose it in quotation marks. Here's an instruction that creates a variable called *name* and stores the text *Agatha*:

«SET name = "Agatha"»

A common cause of error messages is forgetting to enclose the text in quotation marks. If you forget the marks, Word interprets what you type as a variable name. Because Word cannot find any definition for the variable, you get the message, Unknown field name. If you see this message, check your macro instructions to make sure that you have surrounded all text with quotation marks.

Note: You need to place text in quotation marks only when the text is between the chevrons in a macro instruction. Text outside the chevrons doesn't need to be put in quotation marks, as shown in the following example:

«IF status = "overdue"»
    Please pay up immediately.
«ENDIF»

Also, you don't have to put quotation marks around text added to SET and ASK instructions, as shown by the following example:

«ASK response = ?Please type your name.»

❑ *Numbers.* If you include numbers with no letters, spaces, or quotation marks, Word defines what you type as a number. You can use a minus sign to indicate a negative number, and you also can use dollar signs and decimals, if you wish. Here's an example:

«SET assets = $208.91»

If you include operators, Word solves the expression as it evaluates it. If you type the following, Word defines the variable *assets* as $240.25:

«SET assets = $208.91 * 1.15»

❏ *Dates.* Type a date using the mm/dd/yy or mm/dd/yyyy format. You also can use hyphens or periods (mm.dd.yy or mm-dd-yy).

❏ *Variables.* Anything you type that doesn't conform to the three rules just explained is interpreted as a variable name.

Tip **Some variable names are reserved and have special functions.**

Version 5 of Word features an expanded list of *reserved variables*, or variables whose names you cannot use for other purposes. Reserved variables perform vital functions. You will find it useful to familiarize yourself with these functions; every one of them is needed because you have no other way of solving particular macro-writing problems (see table 13.5 for a full list with examples).

Table 13.5
Reserved Variables

Name	Function and Example
echo	Controls screen updating «SET echo = "on"» «SET echo = "off"»
field	Sets variable to content of highlighted field «SET filename = field»
found, notfound	Tests result of search «IF found»<alt b>«ENDIF»
promptmode	Determines whether responses to prompts are to come from the macro or the user (or be ignored entirely) «SET promptmode = "macro"» «SET promptmode = "ignore"»
save	Tests whether SAVE indicator is displayed «IF SAVE»<ctrl f10>«ENDIF»

Table 13.5—Continued

Name	Function and Example
scrap	Refers to current contents of scrap
	«SET response = scrap» «IF scrap = "junk"»
selection	Refers to contents of current selection
	«IF selection = "text"»
window	Refers to value of active window
	«SET window = 3»
wordversion	Tests Word's version number
	«IF wordversion =< 5» «QUIT»«ENDIF»

If you try to use one of these variable names for a purpose other than the intended ones, your macro may behave erratically or generate an error message. Choose names other than these for your variables.

Here's a brief overview of some of the reserved variables:

❑ *selection*. This variable automatically contains whatever is selected on the screen, whether the selection is in the document window or the command menu. The following instruction, for example, creates a variable called *text* and defines it so that it includes the current selection:

«SET text = selection»

❑ *scrap*. This variable automatically contains whatever is in the scrap. The following instruction, for example, creates a variable called *text* and defines it so that it includes whatever is in the scrap at the time the macro is executed:

«SET text = scrap»

❑ *field*. This variable automatically contains the option chosen in the currently selected command field. If the macro positions the highlight in the show menu field of the Options command, for instance, and if that field is currently set to Yes, then the variable *field* automatically contains Yes. The same applies to text fields in command menus. The following instruction sets the variable *filename* to contain the text in the current field:

«SET filename = field»

❑ *found* and *notfound*. These two variables are useful in search and replace operations. The following instruction, for instance, boldfaces the text found by a search and repeats the search using the same search text:

«IF found»
   <alt b>
   <shift f4>
«ENDIF»

The *notfound* variable works the same way, but comes into play only if the Search command doesn't find a match.

❑ *save*. This variable tests to see whether the SAVE indicator appears on the status line. This variable is useful when your macro performs search, replace, indexing, or sorting operations on a system with limited memory. These operations may exhaust Word's free memory. To free up memory, you save your work. The following macro performs this task automatically when the SAVE indicator appears:

«IF save»<ctrl esc>ta«ENDIF»

If you write lengthy macros with many operations, include this line here and there.

❑ *window*. This variable contains the number of the active window, the one in which the cursor is positioned. As the active window changes, so do the variable's contents.

The following macro creates a variable called *window_to_size* and defines it as the active window. If the active window is #2, then the variable contains 2. Then the macro chooses the Window Move command and inserts the number 2 in the # command field.

«SET window_to_size = window»
<ctrl esc>wm«window»

❑ *echo*. This highly useful variable provides a way to turn off screen updating while a macro is running. Normally, Word shows all the changes a macro makes to your document as the macro executes. But showing these changes slows the macro. If you begin a macro with the following instruction,

Word does not display the changes until the macro finishes running:

«SET echo = "off"»

If during the macro, you want to show a change, you can turn on the display again by using this instruction:

«SET echo = "on"»

❏ *promptmode.* Another important and useful variable, this one lets you control how the macro handles the prompts Word displays. Suppose that you write a macro which creates a glossary entry for temporary purposes. You can save the glossary entry with instructions that cause Word to erase the glossary automatically, but you don't want to do that. To give the user control over the destruction of the glossary, you should include a Transfer Glossary Clear command in your macro. However, this command displays the confirmation prompt, Enter Y to clear glossary names.

When such prompts appear, you can handle them in three different ways. First, you can make sure that the user has a chance to make the response. The macro can stop and wait until the user presses a key. Here's an instruction that makes sure that the user, not the macro, responds to the prompt:

«SET promptmode = "user"»

Second, you can make sure that the macro makes the response. The macro does not wait for the user to respond to the prompt; indeed, the prompt doesn't even appear. Here's the instruction:

«SET promptmode = "macro"»

If you choose this approach, you must include the response in the macro.

Third, you can tell Word to ignore all prompts. Here's the instruction to do this:

«SET promptmode = "ignore"»

This instruction can be dangerous because it tells Word, in effect, "Go ahead and do whatever you're told, no matter how drastic, and ignore all confirmation messages." Using this instruction, you can write a macro that erases all the files on a disk without asking for confirmation.

❑ *wordversion*. This macro automatically contains the correct version number of the Word program you are using. As noted earlier, it's essential that macros be used with the correct version—almost all macros navigate command menus, and if the menu changes in a new version, the macro can go astray. If you want to create macros that don't run unless they're used with Version 5, here's the instruction you need:

«If wordversion <>5»«QUIT»«ENDIF»

Tip **Type macro instruction names in capital letters.**

By typing macro instruction names in capital letters, you easily can distinguish macro instruction names (such as SET or ASK) from other components of the macro.

Tip **Use the ASK instruction to define a user variable.**

The ASK instruction prompts you to define a variable. The following instruction creates a variable called *yourname* and causes Word to display the RESPONSE prompt in the command area. (The command menu disappears, and in its place you see RESPONSE:) If you include a message after the question mark, Word displays the message at the bottom of the command area.

«ASK yourname = ?Please type your name»

Tip **The message displayed with an ASK instruction cannot exceed 80 characters.**

You may be surprised at how quickly you can use 80 characters. If you use the ASK instruction extensively, you will start looking for ways to make your messages more concise.

Caution: You cannot use the ASK instruction if the macro is inside a command menu.

Suppose that you want to write a macro which selects the Print Options command, prompts you to name the printer, and types the printer name in the printer field. You may be tempted to write the macro as follows:

<esc>po
«PAUSE Type the printer's name»
<enter>

When you run this macro, however, you see the message Nested command not allowed, macro aborted. For the solution to this problem, see the following trick.

Trick **When you surround a variable name with chevrons, Word types the variable's contents.**

You can use this feature to get around the preceding trap. Use the ASK instruction to define a variable before choosing the command. Then include the variable name, enclosed by chevrons, in the macro so that Word types the text just as you did. The following instructions ask for a printer description file name before choosing the Print Options command:

«ASK printer = ?Which printer do you want to use?»
<esc>po«printer»
<enter>

Tip **Use the SET instruction to let the macro define the variable for you.**

The ASK instruction sets up a variable and asks you to define its contents. The SET instruction also creates a variable, but SET defines the new variable's contents without your intervention. The following macro, for example, asks you to type the amount of sales (a numeric variable). The SET instruction creates a new variable called *commission* and defines it as *sales* multiplied by 0.175. Finally, the macro prints the text *The commission is* and inserts the value of the new variable.

«ASK sales = ?What were the first quarter sales?»
«SET commission = sales *.175»
The commission is $«commission».

Tip **You can use constants in a macro.**

A *constant*, unlike a variable, doesn't change. A constant is a fixed number, date, or text. In the following expression, for example, the number *.25* is a numeric constant:

«SET leftmargin = leftmargin - .25»

Here's a date constant:

«SET date = 11/30/89»

Caution: If you don't enclose a text constant in quotation marks, Word cannot distinguish the text constant from a variable name.

Numeric and date constants don't require any special formatting, but text constants do require special formatting because, otherwise, Word cannot distinguish them from variable names. Here's a properly formatted text constant (the variable called *name* is defined with the constant *John*):

«SET name = "John"»

Suppose that you write the expression like this:

«SET name = John»

Word starts hunting for a variable named *John*. When the program does not find this variable, the message `Unknown field name, macro aborted` appears.

Tip **You may use arithmetic and logical operators in Word macros.**

Table 13.6 lists the operators you can use in macro expressions. Arithmetic operators are used in SET instructions. Logical operators are used most frequently in IF...ELSE...ENDIF instructions, where they are used to compare one variable or constant with another.

Table 13.6
Arithmetic and Logical Operators for Use in Word Macros

Operator	Function
+	Addition
−	Subtraction
*	Multiplication
/	Division
=	Equal
<>	Not equal
<	Less than
<=	Less than or equal
>	Greater than
>=	Greater than or equal

Tip **Use the PAUSE instruction to accept user input.**

The PAUSE instruction is useful when the macro requires human intervention. The following instruction halts the macro's execution and displays at the bottom of the screen the message `Select the text and press Enter`:

«PAUSE Select the text and press Enter»

You may press any key except Enter while PAUSE is in effect. When you press Enter, control is returned to the macro.

Tip   **Use the IF...ENDIF instruction to set up a branching macro.**

An IF...ENDIF instruction is a conditional instruction, which means that it works by testing to see whether a condition is true. If a condition is true, the macro takes one course. If a condition isn't true, the macro takes no action.

The macro that follows shows a conditional instruction. The macro asks, Are you using Word for the first time? and requests a Yes or No response. If the response is Yes, the macro uses the Options command and makes sure that the command menus are left on. If the response is anything other than Yes, however, nothing happens.

```
«ASK newuser = ?Are you using Word for the first time (Y/N)?»
«IF newuser = "Y"»
<esc>o<tab 2>y<enter>
«ENDIF»
```

Trick   **If you use IF instructions to create a menu structure, the macro may not work correctly.**

Because IF instructions create program branches, you may be tempted to use them to create a menu macro. Here's an example:

```
«ASK document = ?Type a (M)emo, (L)etter, or (R)eport today?»
«IF document = "M"»
     <esc>tlMEMO.DOC<enter>
«ENDIF»
«IF document = "L"»
     <esc>tlLETTER.DOC<enter>
«ENDIF»
«IF document = "R"»
     <esc>tlREPORT.DOC<enter>
«ENDIF»
```

This macro works just fine as long as the user enters *M, L,* or *R.* But what happens if the user accidentally presses a different key? Nothing stops Word from defining the variable *document* with whatever the user types.

For this reason, it's best to create menus by nesting these IF statements in a WHILE...ENDWHILE instruction, as shown by the following example:

```
«SET response = "N"»
«WHILE response = "N"»
        «ASK document = ?Type a (M)emo, (L)etter, or
              (R)eport today?»
          «IF document = "M"»
             «SET response = "Y"»
             <esc>tlMEMO.DOC<enter>
          «ENDIF»
          «IF document = "L"»
             «SET response = "Y"»
             <esc>tlLETTER.DOC<enter>
          «ENDIF»
          «IF document = "R"»
             «SET response = "Y"»
             <esc>tlREPORT.DOC<enter>
          «ENDIF»
 «ENDWHILE»
```

This macro structure is echoed in many macros you have seen in this book. The macro sets up a variable called *response* and defines it as N. The WHILE...ENDWHILE instruction says, in effect, "As long as *response* = N, display the message, Type a (M)emo, (L)etter, or (R)eport today?" When the user types *M, L,* or *R,* the variable *response* is set to Y, so Word stops displaying the message. With this instruction, the user can enter anything—but the response is ignored unless it's M, L, or R.

Trap   **If you write an expression using comparisons, the two variables or constants being compared must have the same kind of contents.**

Comparisons are commonly used in IF...ELSE...ENDIF instructions. Consider these lines from a macro:

```
«SET name = "Smith"»
«IF name = "Smith"»
```

This macro works because the *name* variable and the constant *Smith* both have the same kind of contents—text. The following example does not work, however, because the *date* variable was already defined with date contents:

```
«SET date = 11/30/89»
«IF date = "today"»hi«ENDIF»
```

If you try to write an expression that compares two different types of variables or constants, you see the message Conflicting types in IF statement, macro aborted.

Trap **Every IF instruction must conclude with an ENDIF.**

Watch out for this trap, which is a common error in macros. If you fail to include the ENDIF instruction, you see the message, Missing ENDIF, macro aborted. Edit the macro and add the missing instruction.

Tip **Use the REPEAT...ENDREPEAT instruction to repeat a command or commands a fixed number of times.**

This instruction sets up a loop that repeats a fixed number of times. The following macro formats the next 30 paragraphs with justified text alignment:

```
«REPEAT 30»
<esc>fpj<enter>
<f10>
«ENDREPEAT»
```

Trap **Every REPEAT instruction must conclude with an ENDREPEAT.**

Just as every IF instruction must conclude with an ENDIF, every REPEAT instruction requires an ENDREPEAT. If you neglect to include the ENDREPEAT instruction, you see the message, Missing ENDREPEAT, macro aborted. Edit the macro and add the ENDREPEAT instruction.

Tip **Use the WHILE...ENDWHILE instruction to repeat a command or commands until a condition is met.**

This instruction sets up a loop that continues operating until a condition is met. In the following macro, the WHILE loop keeps operating as long as the search has not found a match for the search text:

```
«ASK searchtext = ?What's the search text?»
<esc>s«searchtext»<enter>
«WHILE notfound»
<esc>s
«PAUSE Try a different spelling of the search text»
<enter>
«ENDWHILE»
```

Trap **Every WHILE instruction must end with an ENDWHILE.**

WHILE...ENDWHILE instructions, like IF...ENDIF and REPEAT...ENDREPEAT instructions, must close with an ending statement. If you neglect to include the ENDWHILE statement, you see the message, `Missing ENDWHILE, macro aborted`. Edit the macro and add the missing instruction.

Tip **Use the COMMENT instruction to document a complex macro.**

For lengthy or complex macros, you may want to add COMMENT instructions that clarify what the macro does. Word ignores any text included with the COMMENT instruction. You can include such text in two ways.

One way is to enter the COMMENT instruction, follow the instruction with text, and close the expression with an ENDCOMMENT instruction. Here's an example:

«COMMENT»
This macro presents the user with a list of options for loading template documents.
«ENDCOMMENT»

If you choose this approach and fail to include the ENDCOMMENT instruction, Word displays the message `Missing ENDCOMMENT, macro aborted`.

The second way to include comments is to enclose the comment text in the chevrons used to enclose the COMMENT instruction. Here's an example:

«COMMENT The text within the chevrons is ignored.»

Tip **You can nest macros.**

One macro can call another. In fact, you can nest up to 16 macros in this way. In the following example, the IF statement tests to see whether the variable *response* contains the text *true*. If the variable does contain *true*, the IF statement uses the Insert command to load the macro LOADDOCS.MAC.

«IF response = "true"»
<esc>i LOADDOCS.MAC<enter>
«ENDIF»

Tip   Create an autoexec macro.

Every glossary file can contain one autoexec macro, a macro that runs automatically as soon as you load the glossary file with Transfer Glossary Load. If you copy the macro to the default glossary, NORMAL.GLY, the macro executes every time you load Word.

Tip   Study the macros in this book for further tips and tricks.

You can find plenty of practical solutions to macro-programming challenges in this book's many macros. Use them, modify them, play with them, explore them—that's the way to learn.

Chapter Summary

Macros automate Word operations. You can create macros by recording them or by writing them. Written macros can contain macro instructions, which enable Word to carry out advanced operations. Recording macros is easy, but you cannot make the macro pause to accept user input, and you cannot use other advanced operations.

Writing macros (as opposed to recording them) is more challenging, but written macros are more powerful. You must enter keynames, instructions, and other macro components carefully. Keynames must be surrounded with angle brackets, and instructions must be surrounded by chevrons, entered with Alt-[and Alt-]. If you leave out an angle bracket or chevron by mistake, the macro does not run correctly.

Whether you record macros or write them, you store them in glossary files. If you use the macro in almost every writing session, store the macro in NORMAL.GLY, Word's default glossary file. That way, you need do nothing special to use your macros. You can start macros in three ways: by choosing the Insert command, pressing F1, and choosing the macro from the list; by typing the macro's name and pressing F3; and by assigning the macro to a Ctrl-key code.

To use one of the macros in this book, type the macro in a Word document. When you have checked the macro carefully, select it and use the Copy command. Name the macro with the MAC extension, and then press the caret (ˆ) key. Hold the Ctrl key and press the first letter of the code. Then press the second letter of the code. Press Enter to carry out the command.

To test macros, use the step mode to see what your macro is doing. When you find an error, edit your macro by copying it back to your document. To do so, highlight the macro's name and press the caret key before carrying out the Insert command.

14

Creating and Printing Form Documents

Everyone is familiar with one particularly egregious impact of the computer on modern life: the quasi-personalized form letter. "Dear Ms. Smith, you have DEFINITELY won one of the following prizes—at the minimum, a cheap transistor radio! All you have to do is drive 600 miles and subject yourself to a grueling, high-pressure ordeal at the hands of our unscrupulous salespersons!" Yet personalized form letters have many legitimate uses. If you find yourself frequently sending the same message to dozens or hundreds of people, you will want to explore Word's form letter capabilities.

You easily can create personalized form letters and other form documents with Word. Begin by creating a *master document*, which contains the text you want everyone to receive. Then create a *data document*, which contains names, addresses, and other information for each person who is to receive the letter. Finally, use the **P**rint **M**erge command.

With no further action from you, Word takes the information from the data document and prints personalized versions of the letter. In other words, the program merges the data document information with the form letter—hence the name of the command that sets the operation into motion: Print Merge. Because the operation is entirely automatic, you can let your computer crank out dozens, hundreds, or even thousands of letters while you sit back sipping coffee, practicing your golf putting, or catching up on back issues of the *New Yorker*.

You can use Word's form letter capabilities for these purposes with relative ease; and you can go much further. In your master document, you can use conditional instructions to tell Word whether to include certain information in a letter. You can include instructions that prompt

403

the user to add specific information at the time of printing. With these capabilities, you can create a sophisticated document-generating system to help you achieve higher productivity in your daily correspondence.

The merge applications discussed in this chapter involve two documents:

❑ *Main document.* This document contains the text you want to send to every recipient. The main document also contains commands that tell Word where to find the data document and how and where to insert the information from the data document. The latter commands, called *field names*, indicate the type of information you want Word to insert when the document is printed (see fig. 14.1). As each letter is printed, the field names are replaced with specific information from the data document.

Fig. 14.1.

The main document for a Print Merge application.

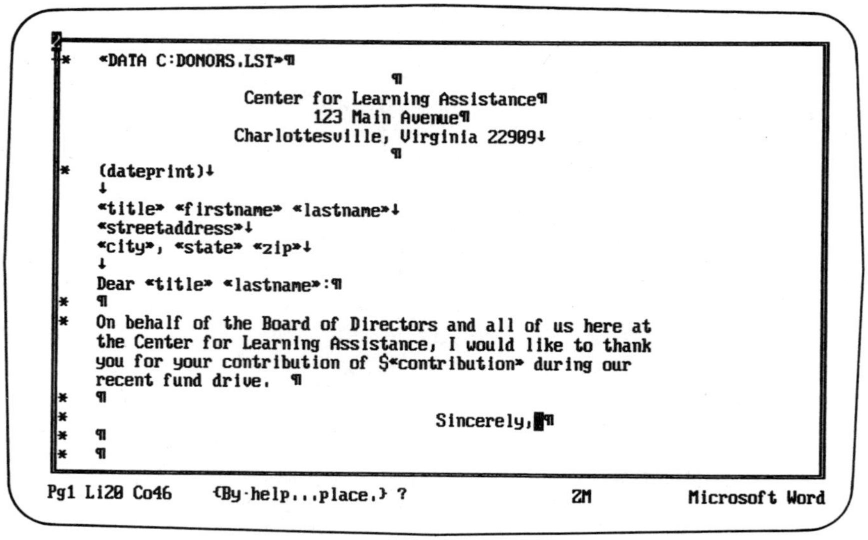

```
«DATA C:DONORS.LST»¶
                             ¶
             Center for Learning Assistance¶
                   123 Main Avenue¶
             Charlottesville, Virginia 22989↓
                             ¶
(dateprint)↓
↓
«title» «firstname» «lastname»↓
«streetaddress»↓
«city», «state» «zip»↓
↓
Dear «title» «lastname»:¶
¶
On behalf of the Board of Directors and all of us here at
the Center for Learning Assistance, I would like to thank
you for your contribution of $«contribution» during our
recent fund drive.  ¶
¶
                             Sincerely,█¶
¶
¶
```

```
Pg1 Li28 Co46    {By·help...place.} ?            2M        Microsoft Word
```

❑ *Data document.* This document is a database containing the information you want inserted into the main document. The data document contains information organized into data records, each of which contains a fixed number of special areas for specific information (called data *fields*). The first record, called the *header record*, names the fields and defines the order in which the information is stored in each data record (see fig. 14.2).

Header record

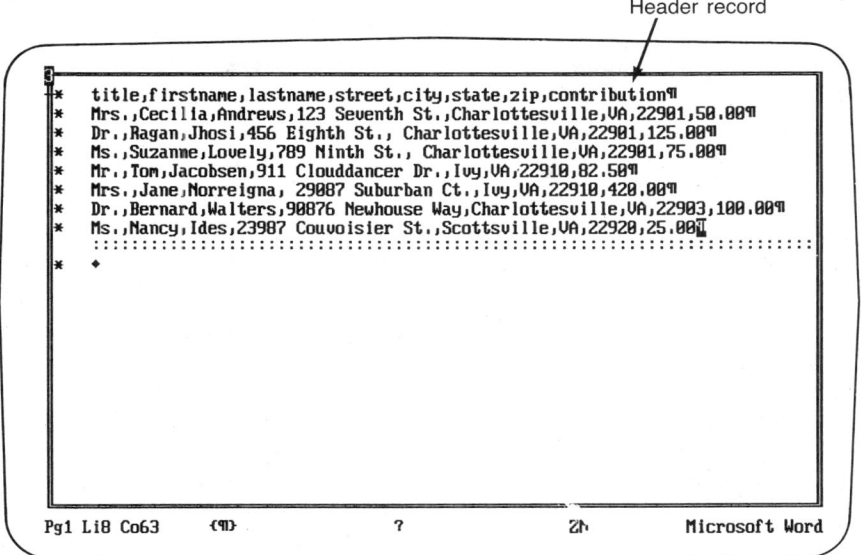

```
title,firstname,lastname,street,city,state,zip,contribution¶
Mrs.,Cecilia,Andrews,123 Seventh St.,Charlottesville,VA,22901,50.00¶
Dr.,Ragan,Jhosi,456 Eighth St., Charlottesville,VA,22901,125.00¶
Ms.,Suzanne,Lovely,789 Ninth St., Charlottesville,VA,22901,75.00¶
Mr.,Tom,Jacobsen,911 Clouddancer Dr.,Ivy,VA,22910,82.50¶
Mrs.,Jane,Norreigna, 29087 Suburban Ct.,Ivy,VA,22910,420.00¶
Dr.,Bernard,Walters,90876 Newhouse Way,Charlottesville,VA,22903,100.00¶
Ms.,Nancy,Ides,23987 Couvoisier St.,Scottsville,VA,22920,25.00
```

Pg1 Li8 Co63   {¶}   ?   2⟩   Microsoft Word

Fig. 14.2.

The data document for a Print Merge application.

The result of a Print Merge application, shown in figure 14.3, is a personalized form letter. When you print the main document by using Print Merge, Word goes to the data document, extracts the information you have named, and inserts it in the appropriate places. The whole operation is entirely automatic. If done correctly, the letter looks as though it had been typed personally.

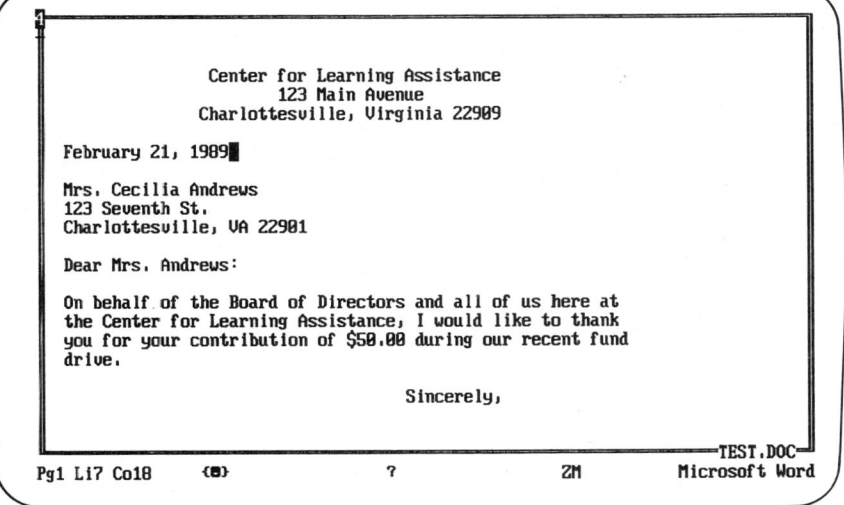

```
                    Center for Learning Assistance
                            123 Main Avenue
                    Charlottesville, Virginia 22909

February 21, 1989

Mrs. Cecilia Andrews
123 Seventh St.
Charlottesville, VA 22901

Dear Mrs. Andrews:

On behalf of the Board of Directors and all of us here at
the Center for Learning Assistance, I would like to thank
you for your contribution of $50.00 during our recent fund
drive.

                            Sincerely,
```

TEST.DOC

Pg1 Li7 Co18   {8}   ?   2M   Microsoft Word

Fig. 14.3.

Personalized form letter produced by Print Merge.

Planning the Print Merge Application

If you have a specific Print Merge application in mind, consider the many ways you can use this command's powerful features. Print Merge, for example, can include automatically special text in only the letters that meet a condition you specify—"Because your account is overdue, won't you send us a check today"—or can print mailing labels. You learn more about how to take advantage of such features later in this chapter. For now, however, consider the type of information you want to include in form letters to be sure that all the information you need gets into your data document.

Tip **Plan your Print Merge application by first deciding what types of information you want Word to insert.**

In a form letter, obviously, you want to include basics: title, name, address, city, state, and ZIP code. But you also often have reason to include additional information in the data document.

In the application shown in figure 14.3, for instance, a nice touch is to indicate the amount of the contribution. The donors appreciate the personal touch all the more because including the amount gives them a receipt for income tax purposes. An additional—and good—reason exists for including this information. You can include conditional instructions that add extra text when a contribution is above a certain amount.

Creating the Main Document

Your first step in creating a main document is to type the text you want to include in every letter. Next, add commands that tell Word how to insert the information from the data document.

Tip **In the main document, you don't need to use all the field names in the data document.**

You can create your data document for future applications. The data document can contain more information than you actually use in any one application. In fact, having more than the essential information is desirable. In the sample application, you don't need the recipients' phone numbers, but having them would be nice. Because you are going to the trouble to create a database, why not include the telephone numbers? You may need this information for a future application.

You can create up to 256 field names for each Print Merge application. For this reason, there's nothing to stop you from creating a complex data document with many kinds of facts about each person on your mailing list.

Tip **Word cannot generate form letters correctly unless you tell it precisely where to find the data document.**

The main document begins with a DATA instruction, which tells Word where to find the data document. To create this instruction, press Ctrl-[to enter the left chevron and type *DATA*. Press the space bar and type the data document's file name. Then press Ctrl-] to enter the right chevron. The instruction should look like this:

«DATA DONORS.LST»

If the data document's file name ends in DOC, you needn't include the extension.

Trick **Include the full path name in the DATA instruction if the data document is not in the default drive or directory.**

If Word cannot find the data document, you see the message File not available when you use the Print Merge command. To avoid this error message, include the drive designator and directory names in the DATA instruction:

«DATA C:\WORD\DATADOCS\DONORS.LST»

Trap **The field names in the main document and in the data document must match exactly.**

Although the main document needn't use all the field names in the data document, the ones that are used must be spelled precisely the same way in both places. You cannot have a field called «name» in the main document unless you have a field called «name» in the data document.

Tip **When you enter field names in the main document, be sure to include spaces before and after the field names.**

Type the field names where you want Word to insert information automatically. Enclose the field names in chevrons (entered by pressing Ctrl-[and Ctrl-]).

Word inserts the information beginning precisely where the field name is located. Remember to add spaces before and after the field name; the information stored in the data document doesn't contain these spaces. If you don't include spaces in the main document, Word prints the inserted text jammed up against surrounding words.

Trap   **Field names cannot contain spaces, periods, underline characters, or hyphens.**

If you are accustomed to creating macro and glossary names using punctuation, you are in for trouble with Print Merge. Every field name must be a single word consisting only of letters or numbers. You may not create a two-word or three-word field name linked with underline characters, hyphens, or periods. If you do, you get the message Unknown field name when you try to print.

Tip   **Use field names that are as short as is practical.**

Field names may be 64 characters long, but you should keep them shorter in practice. The longer the field name, the greater the chance that you will type the name incorrectly somewhere. As you discover quickly, inconsistencies in typing field names are a major cause of Print Merge problems.

Tip   **Field names in the main document need not be entered in the same order as in the data document.**

You must enter the information in the data document in a definite order. In the data document shown in figure 14.2, for instance, each data record stores information in this precise sequence:

title,firstname,lastname,street,city,state,zip,contribution

When you are inserting field names in your main document, however, you don't need to keep to this sequence. You can enter the field names in the main document in any order you choose.

Tip   **You can use the same field name more than once in the main document.**

In figure 14.1, the field names «title» and «lastname» are used twice. You can use any field name as many times as you wish.

Trick   **You can format field names so that the inserted text has the same format.**

When Word inserts information from the data document, the inserted information takes on the formatting given to the field name. If you format the field name in boldface, for instance, Word boldfaces the information inserted in place of the field name. Use the usual techniques (the Format menu or Alt-key command) to format field names.

Trick **You can use math in field name expressions.**

You can include arithmetic operators and constants in field name expressions in your main document. In the following example, the field name «contribution» is used with the division operator (/) and the number of weeks per year (52) to show what the contribution amounts to per week.

> Thanks to your contribution, $«contribution/52» is available every week to help the Center's disabled children. That's helpful, but just consider that it costs us $48 per hour of instruction.

If the amount of the contribution is $100, this paragraph prints as follows:

> Thanks to your contribution, $1.92 is available every week to help the Center's disabled children. That's helpful, but just consider that it costs us $48 per hour of instruction.

Creating the Data Document

When you have finished your main document, you are ready to create your data document. Although you can create the data document first, the best practice is to create the main document first. That way, you know exactly what kinds of information your data document should contain. As you discover, however, creating the data document so that errors do not occur can be tricky.

Be sure that you understand how Word stores information in the data document. After the header record, Word stores data in distinct units called *data records*. Each data record contains *fields*, which contain certain types of information. Each field has *entries*, the information you supply when you create the data record. The following list summarizes these terms:

❑ *Data record*. Information in the data document is stored in distinct units called records. Word prints one copy of the main document for each record the program encounters. A record is defined as a paragraph.

❑ *Data field*. A space within the data record, each data field holds a specific type of information. Each data field is set off from the others by commas or tab keystrokes. The number of data fields in the data record must be precisely equal to the number of data fields in the header record.

❏ *Field entry*. The information you type in the data field, such as a name or street address, is the field entry.

Tip **Begin the data document with a header record that states the precise order in which you are to store information.**

Word needs the header record so that the program can tell what kind of information is stored where. Suppose that you begin your data document with the following header record:

title,firstname,lastname,street,city,state,zip,contribution

When Word encounters a data record below the header, the program knows that *Mr.* is a title, *Tom* is a first name, *Jacobsen* is a last name, and so on. Note that all the items in the header record are separated by commas and that no extra spaces are inserted.

You can define up to 256 data fields in a header record. As mentioned previously, you may want to enter more information in your data document than you plan to use in a specific application. You need not use in your main document all the field names in a data document. If you think that you may have a future use for some information, such as a phone number, include that information in your data records.

Tip **Enter the information in each data record in the pricise order set up by the header record.**

The information in each data record must parallel the information in the header record. In the following example, note how the field names in the header record parallel the field entries in the data record:

title,firstname,lastname,street,city,state,zip,contribution
Mr.,Tom,Jacobsen,911 Clouddancer Dr.,Ivy,VA,22910,82.50

Remember that computers cannot understand the meanings of words. If an item is out of sequence, Word has no way of knowing that it has made an error. Suppose that you write the data record as follows:

Tom,Jacobsen,Mr.,911 Clouddancer Dr.,Ivy,VA,22910,82.50

If you do, Word prints a letter that says this:

Dear Tom Mr.:

To avoid these problems, make sure that you always create data records with all the information in precisely the right sequence.

Trap **Every data record must contain precisely the same number of data fields.**

Here's a very common error: you create a data record with fewer than or more than the required number of data fields. If you include fewer data fields, Word prints the letter without the missing information, creating a particularly insidious error—you can catch it only by careful proofreading. If you include more data fields than the header record has, you see the message, `Too many fields in data or header record`.

Trick **If you lack information for a particular field entry, leave the field blank—but don't omit the commas or tabs.**

Word counts the number of data fields by counting the number of commas. The application discussed in this chapter has eight data fields—and seven commas (or tabs, if you choose to delimit your fields with tabs).

You can leave a field entry blank, but be sure to include the commas so that Word won't lose track of the order of data fields. If you don't know the ZIP code, for instance, the «zip» field can be left blank as follows:

Mr.,Tom,Jacobsen,911 Clouddancer Dr.,Ivy,VA,,82.50

If you omit the comma that normally comes after the «zip» field, however, Word "thinks" that the ZIP code is 82.50—and that's what the program prints in the main document!

Tip **If a field entry includes commas, enclose the entry in quotation marks.**

Suppose that you are creating a data document in which one of the entries is *Acme Ceramics, Ltd*. So that Word won't mistake the comma in this record for a data field delimiter, enclose the field entry in quotation marks as follows:

"Acme Ceramics,Ltd."

Trap **You may not leave manually inserted blank lines in the data document.**

As far as Word is concerned, every paragraph is a data record. If you include blank lines, therefore, Word interprets these lines as records, and finding an error, Word stops printing the data records. Don't include any extra blank lines or paragraph marks in your data document.

Trick **To make data documents easier to read, use borders and format paragraphs followed by blank lines.**

Figure 14.4 shows a data document in which the header record has been formatted with a border. Each data record has been formatted with the Format Paragraph command so that one blank line appears after each record. Because this formatting method does not increase the number of paragraph marks in the data document, the format doesn't cause any problems with Print Merge.

Fig. 14.4.

A data document with paragraph formatting.

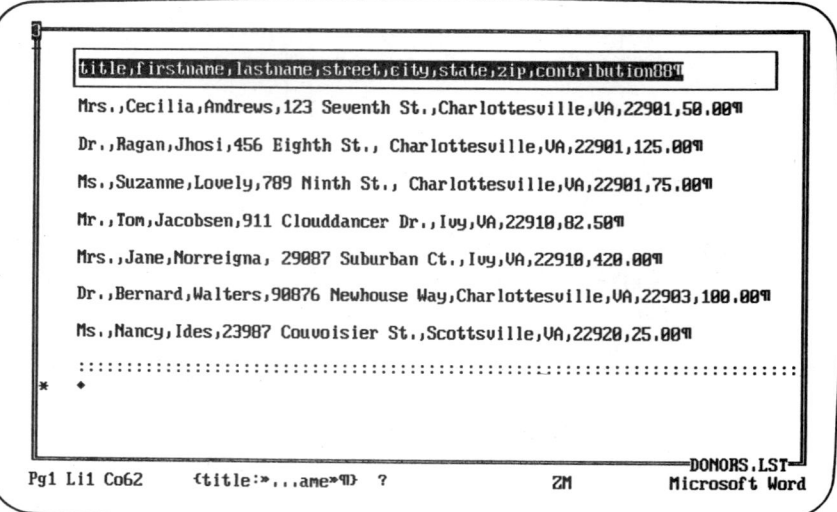

Trap **If you enter a newline character in a data record, the main document is printed with an extra line break.**

If the data record is wider than the screen, Word wraps the record down to the next line. A long data record prints properly if Word wraps the record automatically down to the next line: Do not enter the newline character to force the line break. If you press Shift-Enter to enter a newline character, Word does not print your main document properly. Word sends the newline character to the printer with the field entry with which the newline character occurs, giving you an extra and unsightly line break.

Trick **Use tabs to separate the field entries.**

You can use tabs instead of commas to separate field entries and make the data records easier to read (see fig. 14.5). Using tabs also allows you to sort the data records on any field. Use the **F**ormat **T**ab **S**et command to set up the tab stops the way you want them.

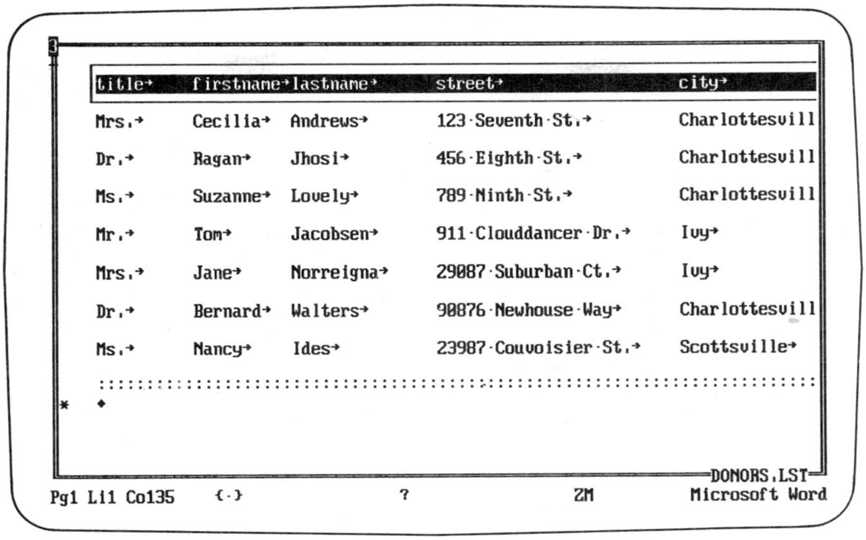

Fig. 14.5.

Data document field entries separated by tabs.

title→	firstname→	lastname→	street→	city→
Mrs.→	Cecilia→	Andrews→	123·Seventh·St.→	Charlottesvill
Dr.→	Ragan→	Jhosi→	456·Eighth·St.→	Charlottesvill
Ms.→	Suzanne→	Lovely→	789·Ninth·St.→	Charlottesvill
Mr.→	Tom→	Jacobsen→	911·Clouddancer·Dr.→	Ivy→
Mrs.→	Jane→	Norreigna→	29087·Suburban·Ct.→	Ivy→
Dr.→	Bernard→	Walters→	90876·Newhouse·Way→	Charlottesvill
Ms.→	Nancy→	Ides→	23987·Couvoisier·St.→	Scottsville→

=DONORS.LST=

Pg1 L11 Co135   {·}   ?   2M   Microsoft Word

Trick **Use the Format Division Margins command to widen the page so that a record fits on one line.**

Choose the width field in the Format Division Margins menu and specify a number larger than the default 8.5 inches. You can type a number as large as 22 in the width field. After widening the margin for the data document, scroll right and left to see all the information stored.

Sorting the Data Records

You can use the Library Autosort command to organize records the way you want them. If you used commas to delimit your fields, you can sort the records by the first field (such as «lastname»). If you used tabs to delimit your fields, you can do much more interesting sorts, such as sorting all your records by ZIP code or by area code. Word merges the data records with the main document in the order in which the records are entered in the data document. Word prints the data records in the order it finds them. If you are sending out form letters, however, printing them in alphabetical order sorted by ZIP code is convenient. Sorting also helps you find records for updating.

Trick   Use the column select mode to determine the sort key.

Suppose that you want to organize your data document by the last names of the individuals listed in the document. To do so, use the column select mode (press Shift-F6) to select the column under the «lastname» field (see fig. 14.6). Be sure that you do *not* include the header record in the selection.

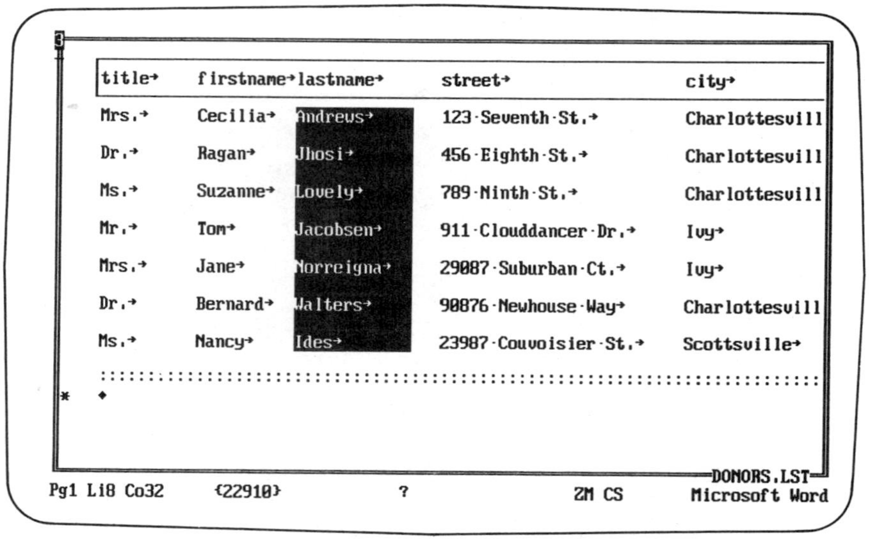

Fig. 14.6.

Selecting a column to determine the sort key.

title→	firstname→	lastname→	street→	city→
Mrs.→	Cecilia→	Andrews→	123·Seventh·St.→	Charlottesvill
Dr.→	Ragan→	Jhosi→	456·Eighth·St.→	Charlottesvill
Ms.→	Suzanne→	Lovely→	789·Ninth·St.→	Charlottesvill
Mr.→	Tom→	Jacobsen→	911·Clouddancer·Dr.→	Ivy→
Mrs.→	Jane→	Norreigna→	29087·Suburban·Ct.→	Ivy→
Dr.→	Bernard→	Walters→	90876·Newhouse·Way→	Charlottesvill
Ms.→	Nancy→	Ides→	23987·Couvoisier·St.→	Scottsville→

Pg1 Li8 Co32   {22910}   ?   2M CS   Microsoft Word
DONORS.LST

Select the column of field entries on which you want to base your sort. You can sort the data document in different ways—by amount of donation, for instance, in descending numerical order.

Once you have selected the column, use the **L**ibrary **A**utosort command to sort the records (see figs. 14.7 and 14.8).

Printing the Form Document

Once you have created your data document and saved it to disk, you are ready to print form letters, using Print Merge. This command prints one copy of the main document for every record encountered in the data document.

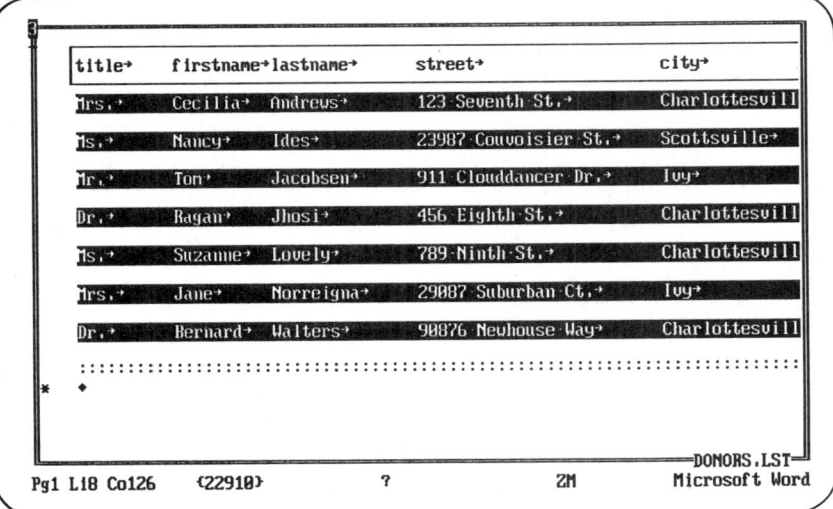

Fig. 14.7.

The data document before sorting.

Fig. 14.8.

The data document after sorting.

Trick **The first time you print a document, split the screen. Put the main document in one window and the data document in the other.**

You doubtless will find yourself fixing errors the first time you print. Perhaps you have misspelled field names in the main document or the data document; perhaps a data record has too many entries; perhaps the entries are out of order. In any case, you will find it helpful to have both documents on the screen as you try your first printing. Then you can quickly locate and correct errors in both documents.

Tip **To print a Print Merge application, put the main document in the active window and choose Print Merge.**

You are merging data into the main document, so the main document is the one you want to print. Choose the **P**rint **M**erge command for the main document. When the Print Merge menu appears, choose to print to the printer or to a file. Choose the **P**rinter option in the Print Merge menu to print the documents directly.

Trap **You get the message** Not a valid file.

This error message means that Word cannot find the data document. Check the DATA instruction in the main document. Is the file name correct? Is the path name correct?

Trap **You get the message** Unknown field name.

Common causes of this error message include a misspelled field name (in either the main or data document), blank lines, extra paragraph marks, or a comma after the last field in a data record. Check your main and data documents carefully.

If the problem is in the data document, you can locate the problem by noting which record Word is working on when the error message appears. Watch the status line as Word prints the documents in order to keep track of the record number being printed. When Word encounters an error, printing stops.

Trick **Print to a document if you want to add additional personalized information to some of the letters.**

Cranking out form letters saves time, but in business the best letters are those that show some personal attention and awareness of special situations. You may want to add to Cecilia Andrews' letter, for instance, a note that says "I would like to thank you, too, for your kindness in introducing me to Dr. Williams the other day. His interest in the Center is good news for all of us!"

To customize your letters with additional personal information, print to a document instead of the printer. Word sends all the letters to a single file, with the letters separated by page breaks. You can load the file into Word and add additional information to any or all of the letters, and then print the document as usual with Print Printer.

Printing Mailing Labels

Printing mailing labels is easy once you have set up a mailing list data document with Word.

Trick   **To print mailing labels, set up a main document that prints just the name and address.**

Include the DATA instruction in the first line of the main document's field names. This way, Word doesn't skip a line on the first label:

«DATA filename»«title» «firstname»
«lastname» «street» «city», «state»
«zip»

Tip   **Use the Format Division Margins command to define the page length for the label size.**

If you are using continuous-feed, single-column labels, the kind you are most likely to use in a dot-matrix or letter-quality printer, type the label height (for instance, *1"*) in the page length field of the Format Division Margins menu. Be sure to type *0* in the top and bottom fields. You may have to experiment to get the settings just right.

Trick   **If you are printing labels on cut sheets, use the NEXT command.**

Printing labels on continuous-feed label stock is easy because the printer feeds the labels one at a time into the printer. You can define each label, therefore, as a page—although a very little one. As Word comes to each new address, the program skips to the next "page" (actually, the next label).

If you are printing labels on a cut sheet with 10 or more labels on it, however, you have a problem. When Word finishes printing a label, the program moves to the next page and therefore skips all the rest of the labels on that sheet. To get Word to stop inserting a page break after printing a record, use the NEXT command. The NEXT command tells Word to print the next record and leave out the page break that the program normally sends to the printer.

To create a main document using the NEXT command, include the same number of groups of field names as you have labels on the sheet. If the sheets you are using have 11 labels per sheet, for instance, you need 11 copies of the field names for the address labels. Create the first group as you do normally. Precede the second and subsequent ones with the NEXT command, as follows:

«DATA filename»«title» «firstname» «lastname» «street» «city», «state» «zip»

«NEXT»«title» «firstname» «lastname» «street» «city», «state» «zip»

«NEXT»«title» «firstname» «lastname» «street» «city», «state» «zip»

Keep adding records until the number of records equals the number of labels on the sheet. You may have to experiment with the spacing between these instructions to get the labels to print correctly.

Using Conditional Instructions

Now that the basics of creating form documents have been covered, you are ready to survey advanced Print Merge applications. You may use additional commands—IF...ENDIF and IF...ELSE...ENDIF—to add text to a document when certain conditions are met.

Trick **Use the IF...ENDIF instruction to add text only if a condition is met.**

When you insert the IF...ENDIF command into your main document, Word tests to see whether the condition is met. If the condition is met, Word prints the text between the IF and ENDIF instructions. If the condition isn't met, Word skips the text. In figure 14.9, for instance, the IF...ENDIF instruction tests the entry in the contributions field to see whether the amount exceeds $100. If so, Word prints the text between IF and ENDIF.

If the amount is not greater than $100, the text is not printed. Tom Jacobsen's contribution was under $100, so he gets the short form of the letter (see fig. 14.10). Dr. Jhosi, however, contributed more than $100, so he gets the expanded version of the letter (see fig. 14.11).

Trap **Without the ENDIF instruction, Word does not print the letter.**

Every IF instruction must be followed by an ENDIF. If you forget the ENDIF, you get the message, `Missing ENDIF`. If this message displays, load your main document and add the missing instruction.

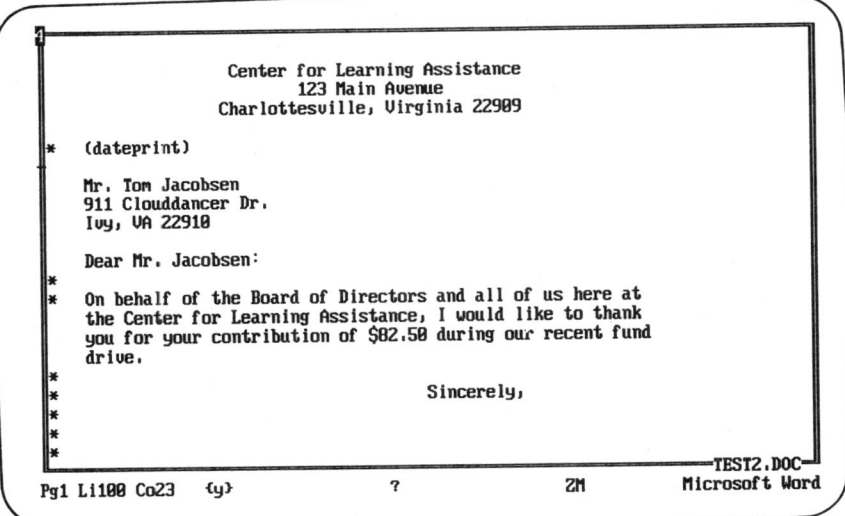

Fig. 14.9.

Conditional merging with the IF...ENDIF instruction.

Fig. 14.10.

Letter sent when condition is not met.

Trick Use the IF...THEN...ELSE instruction to print two different messages depending on a condition you specify.

The IF...THEN...ELSE instruction prints the text following the IF clause if the condition is met. If the condition isn't met, Word prints the text following the ELSE clause. In figure 14.12, the ELSE clause includes text used only if the contribution does not exceed $100. Mrs. Andrews' contribution didn't, so she gets the text in the ELSE clause (see fig. 14.13).

Fig. 14.11.

Letter sent when condition is met.

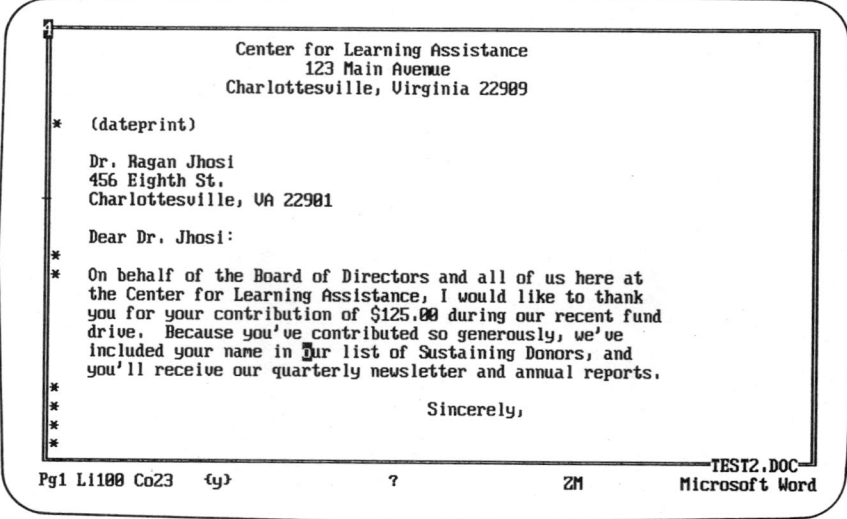

Fig. 14.12.

Conditional merging with the IF...ELSE...ENDIF instruction.

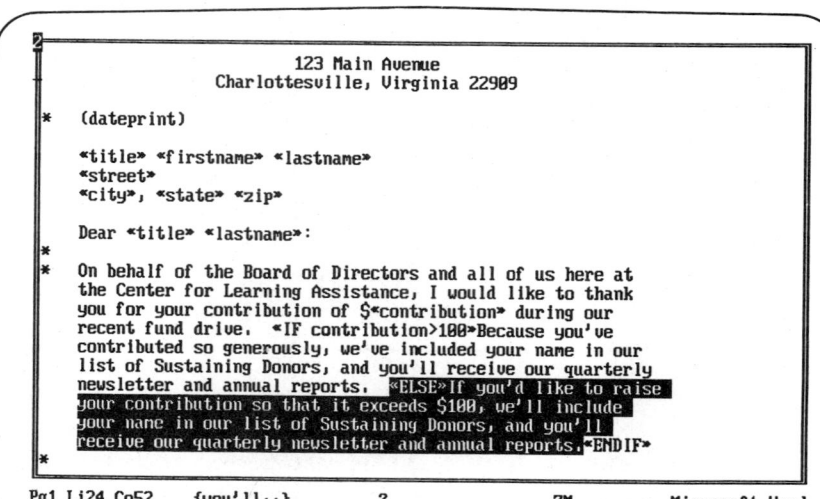

```
┌─────────────────────────────────────────────────────────────┐
│                  Center for Learning Assistance              │
│                       123 Main Avenue                        │
│                Charlottesville, Virginia 22909               │
│ *  (dateprint)                                               │
│                                                              │
│    Mrs. Cecilia Andrews                                      │
│    123 Seventh St.                                           │
│    Charlottesville, VA 22901                                 │
│                                                              │
│    Dear Mrs. Andrews:                                        │
│ *                                                            │
│ *  On behalf of the Board of Directors and all of us here at │
│    the Center for Learning Assistance, I would like to thank │
│    you for your contribution of $50.00 during our recent fund│
│    drive. If you'd like to raise your contribution so that it│
│    exceeds $100, we'll include your name in our list of      │
│    Sustaining Donors, and you'll receive our quarterly       │
│    newsletter and annual reports.                            │
│ *                                                            │
│ *                          Sincerely,                        │
│ *                                                            │
│                                          ══════TEST2.DOC═════ │
│ Pg1 Li1 Co1      {you'll··}        ?           ZM   Microsoft Word │
└─────────────────────────────────────────────────────────────┘
```

Fig. 14.13.

Letter including text following the ELSE clause.

Tip **If the condition to be met involves matching text rather than calculating numbers, enclose the text to be matched in quotation marks.**

You can create an IF...ENDIF or IF...ELSE...ENDIF instruction so that Word tries to match text in the record. In the following instruction, Word examines each data record to see whether the entry in the city field contains the text *Charlottesville*. If the record does contain the entry, the message following the instruction is printed. When referring to text in such instructions, you must enclose the text to be matched in quotation marks.

«IF city="Charlottesville"»Because you are in town, why don't you stop by to see our new computer-assisted diagnostic facility? Your contributions helped make it possible!«ENDIF»

Trick **Skip a data record that meets a condition you specify.**

Sometimes you may want to exclude some people from a mailing. Suppose, for instance, that you are sending out a letter asking people to increase their donations, but you don't want to bother the people who have given $1,000 or more. You can include an instruction like this one in your main document:

«IF contribution>=1000»«SKIP»«ENDIF»

This instruction says, in English, "If the amount stored in the data record's contribution field is greater than or equal to 1,000, skip this record and go on to the next one."

Using User-Supplied Information

Another way you can create more flexible merge applications is to use the SET and ASK instructions. The SET instruction defines a field entry for all the documents to be printed during a session. The ASK instruction defines a field entry for individual documents. You can set up both instructions to prompt the user to supply the needed information.

Trick **Use SET to prompt the user to define a field entry to be inserted into every document to be printed.**

Place the SET instruction at the beginning of the main document, just below the DATA instruction. Here's an example of a valid SET instruction:

«SET eventname = ?Type the name of the next public event.»

This instruction tells Word to look in the main document for a field named «eventname» and to prompt the user to supply a value for that field name. In figure 14.14, note that the eventname field occurs in the letter's main body. When this main document is printed using Print Merge, a RESPONSE: prompt appears with the message, Type the name of the next public event. (see fig. 14.15).

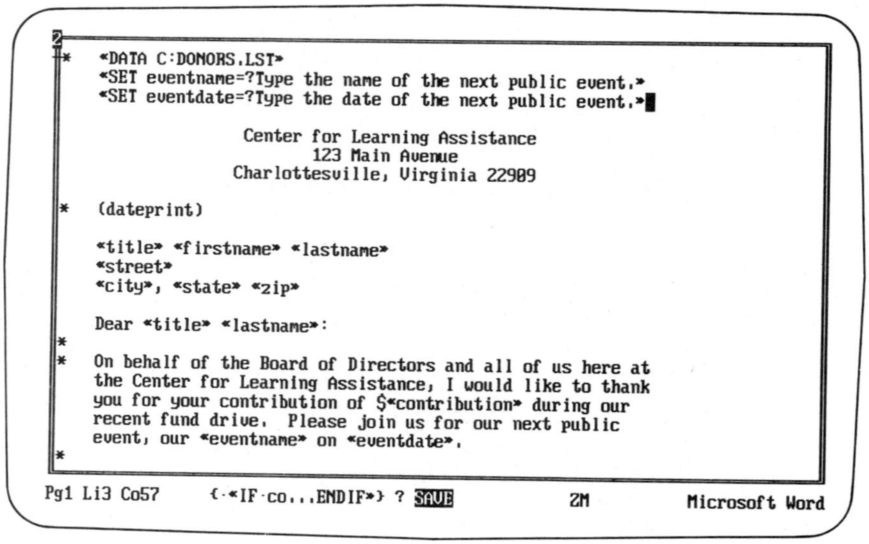

Fig. 14.14.

Using the SET command to define a field at the time of printing.

```
2
│* «DATA C:DONORS.LST»
│  «SET eventname=?Type the name of the next public event.»
│  «SET eventdate=?Type the date of the next public event.»█
│
│              Center for Learning Assistance
│                     123 Main Avenue
│              Charlottesville, Virginia 22909
│
│* (dateprint)
│
│  «title» «firstname» «lastname»
│  «street»
│  «city», «state» «zip»
│
│  Dear «title» «lastname»:
│*
│* On behalf of the Board of Directors and all of us here at
│  the Center for Learning Assistance, I would like to thank
│  you for your contribution of $«contribution» during our
│  recent fund drive.  Please join us for our next public
│  event, our «eventname» on «eventdate».
│*

 Pg1 Li3 Co57     {·«IF·co...ENDIF»} ?  SAVE            2M      Microsoft Word
```

```
*   «DATA C:DONORS.LST»
    «SET eventname=?Type the name of the next public event.»
    «SET eventdate=?Type the date of the next public event.»▮

                     Center for Learning Assistance
                            123 Main Avenue
                     Charlottesville, Virginia 22909

*   (dateprint)

    «title» «firstname» «lastname»
    «street»
    «city», «state» «zip»

    Dear «title» «lastname»:
*
*   On behalf of the Board of Directors and all of us here at
    the Center for Learning Assistance, I would like to thank
    you for your contribution of $«contribution» during our

RESPONSE: ▮

Type the name of the next public event.
Pg1 L13 Co57     {·«IF·co...ENDIF»} ? SAVE          2M        Microsoft Word
```

Fig. 14.15.

The RESPONSE
prompt for the
SET instruction.

If the user types *Open House* in response to this query, Word inserts
this response in place of the «eventname» field in every letter.

**Trick Use the ASK instruction to supply information for individual
letters.**

In contrast to the SET instruction, which defines a field for all
documents to be printed, the ASK instruction permits the user to define
fields one document at a time. In figure 14.16, the ASK instruction
prompts the user to identify a specific contact person for each letter to
be printed:

«ASK contactperson = ?Type the contact person's name»

Note that the «contactperson» field appears in the text of the main
document. When the Print Merge command is used, Word presents a
RESPONSE: prompt, which asks the user to type the name of the
contact person (see fig. 14.17).

Note that the ASK instruction displays the RESPONSE: query for each
document to be printed. The user can specify different contact people
for different donors.

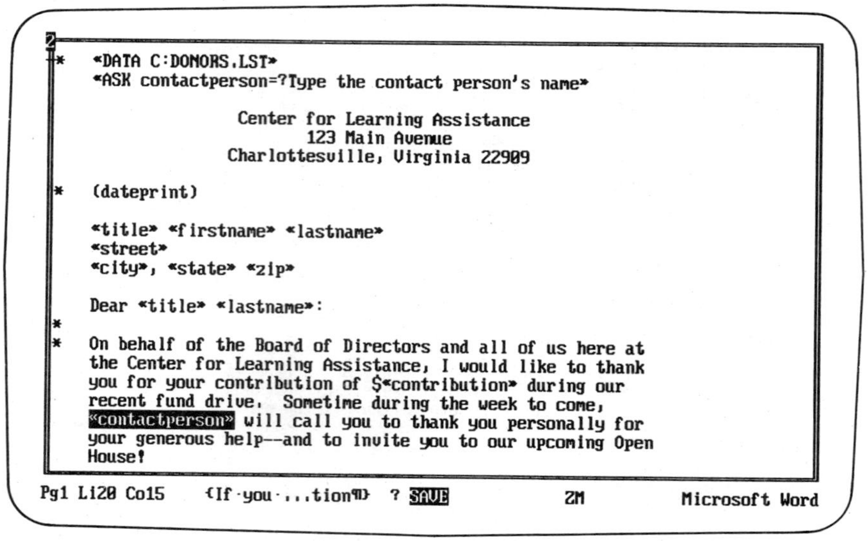

Fig. 14.16.

Using the ASK command to define a field at the time of printing.

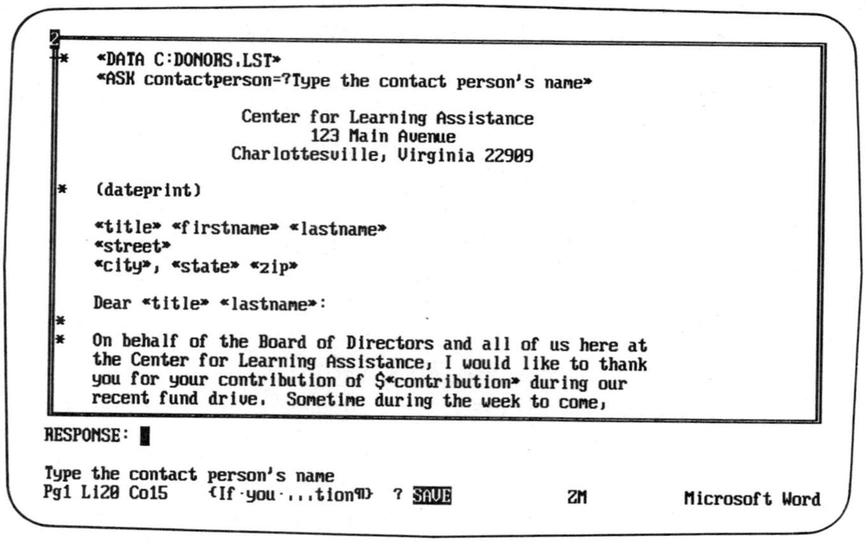

```
2
* «DATA C:DONORS.LST»
  «ASK contactperson=?Type the contact person's name»

                Center for Learning Assistance
                        123 Main Avenue
                  Charlottesville, Virginia 22909

* (dateprint)

  «title» «firstname» «lastname»
  «street»
  «city», «state» «zip»

  Dear «title» «lastname»:
*
* On behalf of the Board of Directors and all of us here at
  the Center for Learning Assistance, I would like to thank
  you for your contribution of $«contribution» during our
  recent fund drive.  Sometime during the week to come,
  «contactperson» will call you to thank you personally for
  your generous help--and to invite you to our upcoming Open
  House!

Pg1 L120 Co15     {If·you·...tion¶}  ? SAVE              2M       Microsoft Word
```

Fig. 14.17.

The RESPONSE prompt for the ASK instruction.

```
2
* «DATA C:DONORS.LST»
  «ASK contactperson=?Type the contact person's name»

                Center for Learning Assistance
                        123 Main Avenue
                  Charlottesville, Virginia 22909

* (dateprint)

  «title» «firstname» «lastname»
  «street»
  «city», «state» «zip»

  Dear «title» «lastname»:
*
* On behalf of the Board of Directors and all of us here at
  the Center for Learning Assistance, I would like to thank
  you for your contribution of $«contribution» during our
  recent fund drive.  Sometime during the week to come,

RESPONSE: █

Type the contact person's name
Pg1 L120 Co15     {If·you·...tion¶}  ? SAVE              2M       Microsoft Word
```

Chapter Summary

Although Word's Print Merge capabilities are most obviously illustrated by form letter applications, you can apply these features in many different ways. Think of Print Merge generally as a way of getting information out of a database and into documents automatically. If you do, you can see that Print Merge can be used to handle the printing of monthly time sheets, quarterly reports, invoices, and many other printed documents.

With this chapter, we come to the end of *Microsoft Word 5 Tips, Tricks, and Traps*. I have enjoyed sharing these high-productivity techniques with you, and I hope that I have warned you away from some of Word's pitfalls.

Like many proficient Word users, you will surely find that many of these complex techniques aren't all that easy to remember after you have learned them—especially if you don't use them for a while. So I would like to suggest Que Corporation's *Microsoft Word Quick Reference Guide*, a handy, pocket-size summary of many of the commands and techniques discussed in this book.

INDEX

G–H

More Computer Knowledge from Que

SELECT QUE BOOKS TO INCREASE
YOUR PERSONAL COMPUTER PRODUCTIVITY

Using Microsoft Word 5: IBM Version

by Bryan Pfaffenberger

This is the definitive guide to new Microsoft Word 5 for IBM and compabitle personal computers. Using a series of examples and applications, word processing expert Bryan Pfaffenberger takes you step-by-step from Word basics to the advanced features of new Word 5. If you want to get the most from Microsoft Word, this is the book for you!

Using Microsoft Windows

by Ron Person

Using Microsoft Windows is an easy-to-follow guide to Windows 2.0 and Windows/386. Incorporating a series of hands-on practice sessions, this well-written text helps you get up and running with Windows and Windows applications. Both an in-depth tutorial and a lasting reference, this book shows you how to manage the Windows interface; control the MS-DOS Executive; customize Windows; and use Windows Write, Windows Paint, and the desktop applications. Open the world of Windows with Que's *Using Microsoft Windows*!

Using PageMaker on the IBM, 2nd Edition

by Diane Burns and S. Venit

Updated for the IBM-compatible version of PageMaker 3.0, this popular text now covers the cover separations capabilities of the program. An ideal introductory text, *Using PageMaker* presents both program basics and basic design concepts. Soon you'll be producing professional publications—just like the dozens of detailed examples presented in this book!

Using Excel: IBM Version

by Ron Person and Mary Campbell

Excel is one of the most advanced spreadsheets available for IBM and compatible personal computers. Que's *Using Excel: IBM Version* helps you master this powerful program. If you are a spreadsheet novice, the Quick Start tutorials will help you get up and running with the program. More experienced users will appreciate the tips and tricks that help you improve your efficiency and troubleshoot Excel problems. This well-written text also includes a special section for 1-2-3 users making the switch to Excel. *Using Excel* will help you excel with Excel!

ORDER FROM QUE TODAY

Item	Title	Price	Quantity	Extension
943	Using Microsoft Word 5: IBM Version	$21.95		
804	Using Microsoft Windows	19.95		
953	Using PageMaker: IBM Version, 2nd Edition	24.95		
87	Using Excel: IBM Version	24.95		

Book Subtotal

Shipping & Handling ($2.50 per item)

Indiana Residents Add 5% Sales Tax

GRAND TOTAL

Method of Payment

☐ Check ☐ VISA ☐ MasterCard ☐ American Express

Card Number _____ Exp. Date _____

Cardholder's Name _____

Ship to _____

Address _____

City _____ State _____ ZIP _____

If you can't wait, call **1-800-428-5331** and order TODAY.

All prices subject to change without notice.

FOLD HERE

Place
Stamp
Here

Que Corporation
P.O. Box 90
Carmel, IN 46032

REGISTRATION CARD

Register your copy of *Microsoft Word 5 Tips, Tricks, and Traps: IBM Version*, and receive information about Que's newest products. Complete this registration card and return it to Que Corporation, P.O. Box 90, Carmel, IN 46032.

Name _____ Phone _____

Company _____ Title _____

Address _____

City _____ State _____ ZIP _____

Please check the appropriate answers:

Where did you buy *Microsoft Word 5 Tips, Tricks, and Traps: IBM Version*?
- ☐ Bookstore (name: _____)
- ☐ Computer store (name: _____)
- ☐ Catalog (name: _____)
- ☐ Direct from Que _____
- ☐ Other: _____

How many computer books do you buy a year?
- ☐ 1 or less
- ☐ 2–5
- ☐ 6–10
- ☐ More than 10

How many Que books do you own?
- ☐ 1
- ☐ 2–5
- ☐ 6–10
- ☐ More than 10

How long have you been using Microsoft Word?
- ☐ Less than 6 months
- ☐ 6 months to 1 year
- ☐ 1–3 years
- ☐ More than 3 years

What influenced your purchase of *Microsoft Word 5 Tips, Tricks, and Traps: IBM Version*?
- ☐ Personal recommendation
- ☐ Advertisement
- ☐ In-store display
- ☐ Price
- ☐ Other: _____
- ☐ Que catalog
- ☐ Que mailing
- ☐ Que's reputation

How would you rate the overall content of *Microsoft Word 5 Tips, Tricks, and Traps: IBM Version*?
- ☐ Very good
- ☐ Good
- ☐ Satisfactory
- ☐ Poor

How would you rate *Appendix A: Style Sheets for Business and Professional Writing*?
- ☐ Very good
- ☐ Good
- ☐ Satisfactory
- ☐ Poor

How would you rate *Appendix B: Word 5 Macros for Business and Professional Writing*?
- ☐ Very good
- ☐ Good
- ☐ Satisfactory
- ☐ Poor

How would you rate *Chapters 5 and 6, on writing strategies*?
- ☐ Very good
- ☐ Good
- ☐ Satisfactory
- ☐ Poor

What do you like *best* about *Microsoft Word 5 Tips, Tricks, and Traps: IBM Version*?

What do you like *least* about *Microsoft Word 5 Tips, Tricks, and Traps: IBM Version*?

How do you use *Microsoft Word 5 Tips, Tricks, and Traps: IBM Version*?

What other Que products do you own?

For what other programs would a Que book be helpful?

Please feel free to list any other comments you may have about *Microsoft Word 5 Tips, Tricks, and Traps: IBM Version*.

_____

_____

_____

_____

_____

_____

FOLD HERE

_____

_____

_____

_____

Que Corporation
P.O. Box 90
Carmel, IN 46032